The Risks of Knowing

Developmental Impediments to
School Learning

Perspectives in
Developmental Psychology

Series Editor: Michael Lewis
                 Robert Wood Johnson Medical School
                 New Brunswick, New Jersey

ACTION IN SOCIAL CONTEXT
Perspectives on Early Development
Edited by Jeffrey J. Lockman and Nancy L. Hazen

ASSESSMENT OF YOUNG DEVELOPMENTALLY
DISABLED CHILDREN
Edited by Theodore D. Wachs and Robert Sheehan

COGNITIVE DEVELOPMENT AND CHILD
PSYCHOTHERAPY
Edited by Stephen R. Shirk

THE DIFFERENT FACES OF MOTHERHOOD
Edited by Beverly Birns and Dale F. Hay

FATHERING BEHAVIORS
The Dynamics of the Man–Child Bond
Wade C. Mackey

PSYCHOLOGY OF DEVELOPMENT AND HISTORY
Edited by Klaus F. Riegel

THE RISKS OF KNOWING
Developmental Impediments to School Learning
Karen Zelan

SOCIAL AND PERSONALITY DEVELOPMENT
An Evolutionary Synthesis
Kevin B. MacDonald

The Risks of Knowing

Developmental Impediments to School Learning

Karen Zelan

Berkeley, California

With a Foreword by
Bruno Bettelheim

PLENUM PRESS • NEW YORK AND LONDON

Library of Congress Cataloging-in-Publication Data

Zelan, Karen.
    The risks of knowing : developmental impediments to school
learning / Karen Zelan ; with a foreword by Bruno Bettelheim.
        p.   cm. -- (Perspectives in developmental psychology)
    Includes bibliographical references and index.
    ISBN 0-306-43759-7
    1. Learning disabilities--United States--Case studies.
2. Cognition in children--United States. 3. School phobia.
4. Cognitive therapy--United States.   I. Title. II. Series.
LC4705.Z45 1991
371.9--dc20   90-29300
                                                         CIP

ISBN 0-306-43759-7

© 1991 Plenum Press, New York
A Division of Plenum Publishing Corporation
233 Spring Street, New York, N.Y. 10013

Printed in the United States of America

Foreword

It gives me great pleasure to introduce this important and fascinating book on the internal dilemmas youngsters face in school, which often cause them to stop learning. We are all too ready to ascribe learning problems to an inability to learn and leave it at that. This book should go a long way toward convincing us that using such simpleminded explanations and remedial efforts based on them do not work. Unlike other books that identify the causes of learning disabilities in children or that detail society's impact on the so-called helpless child, *The Risks of Knowing* is an in-depth study of young people who for reasons of intrapsychic conflicts and of intellectual development make a negative decision about the learning process. This book is unique in its thorough analysis of the conflicts young people have with learning and in its treatment prescriptions. In case after case, Karen Zelan demonstrates that if young people declare themselves unable to learn it is because for some valid reasons they believe learning is dangerous. The reasons that cause a decision to fail often remain unconscious until they are brought to the child's awareness. When the child is helped to understand the source of any inner dilemmas, both child and parents are able to find better solutions to immediate learning difficulties.

Karen Zelan brings a rare expertise to the problems young people find in academic learning. Her clinical work as a psychotherapist to seriously disturbed youngsters at the University of Chicago's Orthogenic School taught her the ways in which inner conflicts can and do interfere with learning. Attending to their battles with learning in which many of these young people either forcibly refused all learning or suffered from particular inhibitions, such as alexia or acalculia, prepared her to understand the motivation underlying a seriously psychopathological decision to fail. By treating severe learning inhibitions, she became sensitized to the particular factors in any psychological impediment to learning.

To understand a young person's decision to fight learning, we must also be acquainted with the normal learning process as it unfolds for the child or the adolescent. Karen Zelan's clinical expertise as she observed normal children react to today's curriculum prepared her to understand the ways in which young people choose to deviate from the requirements of this curriculum. The

5

observations she made, which inform the book *On Learning to Read* (Bettelheim & Zelan, 1981), taught her how normal children in modern classrooms learn and how they often approach learning eagerly. Thus, she discusses the young person's decision to fail from two observational perspectives: the one that enlightens the reasons for an extreme aversion to learning and the other that illuminates not just the developmental impediments to learning but also the child's normal and earnest quest for knowledge. So her approach to a youngster's conflicts regarding learning emphasizes pathology *and* normality. The lucid narrative style she uses to describe the thoughts and feelings of these young people in psychotherapy who, in spite of themselves, *do* learn identifies the many sources of their learning conflicts. Her portraits are remarkable for their clarity in presenting the struggles young people have with their families, their teachers, the school setting, and the school's curriculum. Through her descriptions of their learning commitments, we perceive young people as observing, evaluating, achieving, caring, discerning—and not as disabled persons.

Today's clinician diagnoses and treats many youngsters who have school troubles. Although similarly concerned with those symptoms associated with school learning, the parents and teachers of nonlearning young people are often swamped by the notion that *any* learning problem signifies a learning deficit. How, then, can parents and teachers overcome by themselves the biased attitudes of professionals who perceive deficits in the child's functioning to the detriment of perceiving strengths? This book, then, is a must for psychotherapists who diagnose and treat learning problems. It will also appeal to parents and teachers who are seriously interested in young people and in their attitudes toward learning. We can understand a great deal about the learning of all young people and how we may better teach them from the struggles of those who refuse to learn. Although they are expressed in different ways, the risks of knowing involved for children who renounce learning apply to all young scholars.

Bruno Bettelheim

Santa Monica, California

Preface

During the medieval period, children were not consistently perceived as developing individuals but often viewed as small adults (Aries, 1965). For example, they were invited to preside over traditional family practices, such as saying grace and serving food and drink. Although it is plausible that children might have felt burdened by adult expectations, they surely recognized the social importance of their family role. Performing adequately must have added to their self-esteem. When children failed to behave in expected ways, just as plausibly their behavior could have been seen as evidence of moral or characterological deviation.

Now in the late twentieth century, we perceive the differences between childhood and adulthood and indeed embrace childhood — even honor it — but we make yet another error. Instead of realizing that children are capable persons who can make their own decisions, including decisions about learning, we view them as incapable of self-determination until they reach full maturity. Because we do not perceive the learning child as fulfilling an important social need, we neglect to estimate the cost to the child and to society when a youngster deliberately rejects the role of "learner." We deprive him or her of the potential pleasures in enacting an important social role.

Sometimes we go even further with those who choose not to learn in school. We label these young people "incapable" of learning or "dis-abled." Children who do not learn are no longer morally flawed; now they are physiologically deficient. By labeling these children *disabled*, we not only protect them by implying they are not to blame for the fact that they do not learn, but we also deny them the responsibility for their decisions. True, this wrongheaded attitude may rescue them from a punitive evaluation of their nonlearning but, most important, it overlooks their autonomy. We have reversed the medieval attitude which sometimes gave children more responsibility than they could handle. In effect, we have helped the youngsters abdicate their learning responsibilities.

How many children are identified as having learning problems? In 1989, epidemiological data indicate that of the 63 million children in the United States, 15% (9.5 million) to 19% suffer from emotional disturbance or other

7

symptoms (Tuma, 1989). It is well known that emotional disturbance often causes a child's learning problems or is itself the result of a child's problems with learning or some aspect of the school environment. So it is not surprising that a second 1989 study notes that 4% of American children (well over 2 million) were classified in 1984 as learning disabled (Chalfant, 1989). What is surprising is that the number of students so classified has doubled in the past 10 years. One reason cited for the remarkable increase is the fact that the learning disabilities diagnosis was listed as a category in the definition "handicapped" under Public Law 94-142. Moreover, the *Diagnostic and Statistical Manual of Mental Disorders* (DSM-III-R) reported in 1987 that from 2% to 8% of the child population (over a million children) suffer from "developmental reading disorders."

How many of these diagnosed young people are actually receiving services? In 1984, schools were mandated to become more active in the mental health care of schoolchildren, so 4 million students received mental health services under Public Law 94-142, although it is unclear how many of these children were actually handicapped—educationally or otherwise (Tuma, 1989). According to the author, "mental health professionals serve as consultants to teachers and other school personnel" (p. 197). A 1983 study found that of the over 18,000 health service providers who responded, 44% reported treating individuals with school-related problems "regularly or often" or "most frequently or exclusively." This same study found that of the over 9,000 educational service providers responding, 38% reported treating learning disabilities "regularly or often" or "most frequently or exclusively." Another 50% of those responding reported treating individuals for "attitude problems" related to school attendance "regularly or often" or "most frequently or exclusively" (VandenBos & Stapp, 1983). Similarly, since 1968, over half the some 200 children and adolescents referred to me while I practiced psychotherapy in four regions of the country had learning problems as their primary symptom. Thus, a significant proportion of those youngsters with learning problems—whether actually disabled or not—are referred for psychotherapeutic or educational services as an adjunct to their regular school programs. The hope may be that psychotherapy or educational counseling will improve the child's self-esteem, allowing both educational and rehabilitative services to operate effectively.

Yet a close look at these young people who do not learn reveals there are two types of nonlearners. Children either *cannot* learn because of a real physical deficit or children *choose* not to learn because learning activates something in them they wish to avoid. The fact that experts rarely identify a child's complicity in not learning implies to the youngster—and to the general public as well— that he is incapable of making this decision. Perhaps we ignore this decision-making process because it would appear to make rehabilitation more difficult. Attending to individual reasons for nonlearning could lead professionals to conclude that just as many remedial methods are required as there are children. I declare in this book first that when we ignore the reasons young people have for behaving certain ways we deprive them of their personal identity. Second, concentrating on the *one* salient fact that a child who will not learn has made a decision regarding learning centers the professional on a *limited* number of nonlearning variations. Third, and most important, when we give genuine learning little or no intellectual or social value, we reduce the learning context to a series of empty and tedious rituals.

To change the young person's act of simulated stupidity to one of deliberate intelligence requires us to understand why a charade of stupidity serves the child. We often think that since learning is good for the youngster, he could not possibly have any good or valid reasons for not learning. But we must keep in mind that though refusing to learn does not benefit the young person, his reasons for engaging in nonlearning behavior are good and valid to him. Sometimes we even assert that the youngster has "no reason" for not learning. However, if we assume that children and adolescents are incapable of having reasons, then why should we expect them to apply their intelligence to the reasoning required to learn in school? Recognizing that childhood is different from adulthood does *not* mean children do not have reasons.

My intent in talking with the nonlearning children and adolescents who have surfaced in my psychotherapy practice for the last 20 years has been to get at the reasons each child or adolescent has with resisting learning. Often I have conversations with these young people about what knowing means to them and what the imagined consequences are should they possess a large store of knowledge or some specific fact. These conversations help me understand the ways in which learning both attracts and repels them. Then, as they begin to understand how and why they turn off their minds to school learning, I gain many valuable insights about how these growing individuals get caught up in the risks of knowing.

Two Traditions

I contend that accepted assumptions about the etiology and treatment of disabilities in youngsters are inapplicable to those who refuse to learn. A truly disabled young person should receive assistance with each specific disability; that is, professionals ought not to ignore or misdiagnose learning incapacities just as they ought not to misperceive learning rejections or evasions. Thus, it is important for clinicians and teachers to realize that children who will not learn, unlike children who cannot learn, have no specific cognitive deficits and therefore cannot be helped by practice sessions in skill-learning. Furthermore, I believe deliberate nonlearners cannot be helped by psychotherapy which is predicated on the assumption that low self-esteem is the result of a cognitive deficit. Instead, I investigate how the nonlearning child or adolescent *thinks* since learning depends so often on thinking. Piaget's cognitive-developmental psychology is useful because he credits childhood with a certain rationality. Since he sees their reasoning as a precursor to mature rationality, Piaget's view is that the knowing attitude is familiar to children—not alien. By tracking the development of thought processes from childhood to adulthood, he offers answers to certain epistemological questions about knowledge acquisition and the structure of intelligence.

Similar to cognitive-developmental psychology, the psychoanalytic tradition is helpful in forming some hypotheses about the behavior of these intriguing, inquiring children who nonetheless fight learning. Sigmund Freud and Piaget were consummate naturalists as well as brilliant "system-makers" (Anthony, 1957). Although for different reasons, they both believed that children are people who possess a capability for knowing. Both scholars searched the children's development for the answer to why we as adults are the way we are and how we came to be that way. For Freud, the growing child provided "the key to the specificity of human emotions" and for Piaget "the key...to the universality of logical reason" (Furth, 1987, p. 13).

Thus, one tradition in modern psychology perceives the child as knowing in his progressive accumulation and transmutation of knowledge (Piaget), and the other perceives the child as uninnocent and as capable of human emotions and thus in that sense knowing (Freud). If anything, Freud (1959b) may have attributed too advanced a capability for understanding as he perceived, for example, that uninnocent children had formed ideas about such events as procreation which they then tried to repress for intrapsychic reasons. Indeed, Freud thought that the origins of scientific curiosity lay in the child's quest for knowledge about sexual differences and the act by which children are conceived and born. Thus, Freud gave the child the benefit of the doubt in believing he was eager to understand and capable of perceiving especially sexual facets of his and other's experiences. What Freud passed over, which Piaget attended to, was the child's curiosity about a multitude of happenings that cannot be called "sexual" without grossly distorting the child's manifest behavior. For example, the infant at certain ages likes to make objects disappear only to retrieve them so that while he may not be able to control his mother's absences, he can assuredly control the reappearance of the object. The infant's ability to make the object reappear is, to him, satisfying in itself. We, not the infant, resort to fanciful hypotheses regarding the underlying reasons for his investigations. Because it consists from its infant beginnings of repeated inquiry into many aspects of the physical environment—not just the interpersonal or the sexual—scientific curiosity cannot be a derivative solely of early sexual curiosity.

A BACKWARD GLANCE

Ideas for this book began to germinate during my tenure at the University of Chicago's Orthogenic School, where I treated severely emotionally disturbed children for 8 years. There I learned that a child's nonlearning could stem from an active rejection of knowledge. But at the same time that knowledge threatened these extremely symptomatic youngsters, it also held out great promise and hope. An 8-year-old girl who was afraid of growing up and also of the changes in her body that it would entail rejected the distinction between animate and inanimate objects by believing that she herself was inanimate. She eventually understood that this belief, which could be reassuring momentarily, would in the long run cause more problems than it would solve. But even more important, this girl became fascinated with what knowledge could tell her about the differences between things and people. As she struggled with this all-important distinction, she experienced the risks that accompany knowing. As she survived each risk she derived comfort and pride from building her store of knowledge. Knowledge, for example, told this girl that in being animate she was more like an orange than like a chair. The risk in knowing this fact was that chairs do not "spoil" while unrefrigerated oranges do. What rescued her from the dangers of thought was the idea that while she was in some respects like an orange, in others she was quite unlike a piece of fruit. When she lay in her bed frightened and unable to go to sleep for fear of "spoiling," she was helped when she heard me say that although she was very much alive like the orange on the table beside her (and not "dead" like the chair), she would not spoil or "change overnight" in her sleep just because she was alive. These distinctions and others like them impressed upon her the power of knowing to help with her problems. As therapist to this girl and many others like her, I fashioned some of Piaget's problem-asking techniques and problem-answering interpretations for these severely disturbed children. This enabled me to understand their astonishing ignorance of the world, and the incredible clumsiness of their efforts to explore it. At the Orthogenic School we found it was not enough to restore a fuller emotional life to these children (Bettelheim, 1967). Their abilities to investigate and make constructive use of knowledge needed our attention as well.

Since 1968, I have treated nonlearning children and adolescents in outpatient psychotherapy. My primary interest in working with these young people is not to educate them directly but to help resolve the conflicts they have with knowledge acquisition. Although unconscious and preconscious conflicts with learning require my attention in the therapeutic hour, the conscious rejection of learning has been my principle focus in working with these young people. I began to crystallize the main ideas contained in this book about 1984. There is a hazard—Erikson (1964) called it a "mixed blessing" (p. 64)—in writing about a particular clinical problem at the same time we try to remedy it:

> Clinical work is always research in progress, and I would not be giving a full account of the clinician's pitfalls if I did not discuss in passing the fact that this [one of Erikson's] patient's dream happened to fit especially well into my research at the time.... A research-minded clinician—and one with literary ambitions at that—must always take care lest his patients become footnotes to his favorite thesis or topic. (p. 64)

To minimize the hazards in simultaneously writing about and working with patients, I chose to write about the 60 nonlearning children and adolescents whom I saw in psychotherapy before 1985 which, of course, does not mean that my understanding of their symptoms and their progress was uninformed by the ideas I was refining at the time. The children and adolescents (over 40 at this writing) who rejected learning and whom I treated since 1985 have responded well to psychotherapeutic intervention of the sort described in this book. While I was simultaneously treating these children and adolescents and writing the book, I decided not to use their clinical progress for case narratives because I wished to avoid soliciting or appearing to solicit clinical support for my thesis. I hoped to preserve the therapeutic atmosphere which would encourage them to bring their own concerns. Follow-up data, when available, on the progress in school of the learning-disordered children and adolescents I treated both before and after 1985 is given in the Appendix (see pp. 323–324).

A FORWARD GLIMPSE

The subject of the 10 chapters that follow is the process whereby the young person's affectivity cooperates with his intelligence when he decides not to learn. Although they seem *unable* to learn, nonlearning young people who lack cognitive deficits are *unwilling* to learn. For this reason, my primary audience is those professionals who diagnose and treat youngsters who do not learn. Teachers and parents often do not have the expertise to discriminate between the youngster's incapacities and his decisions regarding learning and, equally often, they have little interest in doing so. Their main concern is that young people actually learn and, if possible, enjoy learning. Although my hope is that this book will be useful to teachers and parents, it is mainly directed to those experts who are expected to remedy a youngster's "educational handicap": most importantly, psychotherapists of all persuasions and remedial learning specialists; but also school psychologists, school counselors, school administrators, and other educators; psychometricians, neurologists, pediatricians, and developmental psychologists.

All too often we professionals attempt to respond to the questions of teachers and parents about nonlearning by labeling the causes for it. Putting a label on the child's nonlearning behavior often masks our wish to find an automatic solution. We hope that labeling a child's problem will suggest an appropriate treatment plan. Sometimes our labeling attempts represent our wish to be rid of the child's learning problem especially when there is no obvious remedy; then, we feel we have at least located the "problem" even if we cannot identify the solution. Automatic or dead-end resolutions do not help young people who deliberately reject learning and, for this reason, I have concentrated herein on the psychological processes which lie *behind* the labels applied to them, and on how psychotherapy which focuses on their personal learning experiences reactivates their learning in school.

Chapter 1 discusses thinking, learning, and knowing from the youngster's perspective since it is his ideas about these activities the psychotherapist or the learning specialist ought to investigate.

Chapter 2 describes the young person's learning problems first from the teacher's perspective, then from the parent's, and finally from the child's own perspective.

The clinical importance of normal intellectual development in young people who reject or evade learning is the subject of Chapter 3. I show in which ways Piaget's theory is compatible with certain aspects of psychoanalytic theory and enhances psychotherapeutic efforts.

Chapter 4 presents the case narratives of Timothy, an apparently "dyslexic" child, and Annie, a child who was believed to be "math disabled." Their learning problems highlight the many important puzzles nonlearning youngsters present to adults and to themselves. Both Tim and Annie tried simultaneously to approach and avoid learning, and their stories bring into sharp relief the ambivalence felt by the nonlearning young people who are the subjects of this book. Tim's rejection of reading and Annie's evasion of math are thus paradigmatic because their behavior revealed they had acquired knowledge despite appearances to the contrary.

Chapter 5 presents two erroneously diagnosed children whose learning was compromised by past and present events which told them that learning is identical to the growing-up process. Like Tim and Annie, these two children sought to distort or transform what they had accurately apprehended in order to make their reality safe.

Chapter 6 presents clinical data in fine detail to set forth what can be done with nonlearning children and adolescents if clinicians are to understand not only the depth of the problems these young people bring to learning but also how to reach them effectively. Verbal interventions, the most important of which is the clinical interpretation, must be formed by the therapist in line with the child's understanding and mode of thinking. The child will be reactivated to learning in school only as he comes to feel the positive benefits of knowing which, in part, he must comprehend by listening to and processing his psychotherapist's intelligible statements.

Chapter 7 describes the ways in which the young person's cognition feeds his desire to escape school—that very situation in which he is expected to learn. I explore the ways in which the attitudes of these "school phobic" young people are significantly different from the attitudes of other nonlearners.

Chapter 8 shows how the child or adolescent often confuses two different forms of inhibition. Nonlearning young people often confuse not having learned a fact or thought or an idea with having warded off what was once keenly felt or fully apprehended. Throughout this chapter and Chapter 9, I investigate from the youngster's perspective the two very different forms of not knowing—immature thinking and inhibition—with the aim of differentiating clinical methods to convert each not knowing process into a knowing one.

A youngster's determination to learn is the subject of Chapter 10. His willingness (often eagerness) to learn once again results from his and his parents' understanding the reasons for his previous nonlearning behavior and from their new and different understanding of his learning behaviors.

DATA COLLECTION

A few words are in order about the observations used to produce the clinical narratives in this book. Piagetian psychology is vital to understanding the child's changing view of the world, modulations which the child reveals in exploration of his natural habitat. As a youngster's therapist, I find out how his or her natural efforts to investigate have become compromised. I make special efforts to observe the unfolding of his or her perspective in what he or she says or does. This kind of therapeutic work requires getting to know the child in a most profound way. It is the contrast in the youngster's and my perspectives, and not the overlap, that is therapeutically useful. Viewing the child's orientation as legitimate in its own right saves me from loading my observations of the children in favor of their failures and from forgetting their successes.

A child's activity is important because it can be straightforward, unambiguous, and therefore revealing. A child who refuses to come into the office makes his meaning pretty clear. However, at other times, the child's intent can be unclear—his activity can often be clumsy, easily distracted, or interrupted before he reaches his goal. Careful observation helps the adult understand what is sometimes mistakenly called "misdirected" behavior or behavior "without apparent reason." (Often the phrase "without apparent reason" is a euphemism for the adult's intention to stop the search for the child's reasons.)

The child's words even more than his or her overt actions are likely to be misunderstood by the adult because of the immature conceptual level the words are linked to. Although ambiguous, the words the child chooses to form a phrase or sentence are important because they are often a clue to his thought level. There is a vast difference between a child who says on one occasion "I can't know" and on another "I don't know." In my clinical work, I pay special attention to the child's vocabulary as well as to his or her syntax in order to understand what conceptual level might underlie verbal behavior. The child's conceptual level determines the ways he or she will interpret a therapeutic intervention as well as the ways he or she will try to solve a problem. Just as important as the words the child chooses are the gestures, postures, or facial expressions accompanying the words which often provide clues about his intent and *his* understanding of that particular intent. These behaviors also reveal much about the ways he understands me and my meaning. Attention to such detail represents the naturalist present in any sensitive clinician. Both Freud and Piaget understood the importance of the naturalist tradition in the work they did; and it is just as important to modern psychology today.

To capture these many nuances in my encounters with young people, I write down immediately after the therapeutic hour what the child or adolescent does or says during his visit. Any behavior that I consider important is included in my notes as well as what the special significance might be. Two or three days later, I go over the material and add my interpretations in terms of its meaning to me in the larger context of what I know about the child's or adolescent's core problem. Speculations and hypotheses thus become part of the notes but separate from observations. (When I was in training this method of record-keeping was standard practice at the University of Chicago's Orthogenic School. To understand the meaning of a psychotic child's behavior is more difficult than is usually the case in 50-minute therapy sessions when it can hardly be called easy.)

Ordinarily, what the youngster says or does is not recorded during the therapy appointment, with three important exceptions: (1) when twice I interview him or her (Piagetian interview techniques are described in the Appendix, on pp. 317–322); (2) when I make some attempts to obtain a speech sample from a child believed to have language disorders; (3) or when I write down sentences or words verbatim because I wish to record the precise vocabulary or syntax chosen by the child, especially when he or she is struggling with an advanced concept. For example, when a 4½-year-old girl explained her understanding of the concept "infinity," I wrote down what she said because it was so startling and revealing of precocious thought. When a youngster is quoted in the text, it means that his or her statements have been memorized during the hour and written down immediately after, or the statements were written down verbatim as he or she talked.

I do not audio- or videotape therapeutic interviews. When the patient is informed that what he says or does is being recorded, he reacts to this—and probably less to his own agenda. This reaction impedes my goal of attending to his agenda and renewing his learning. It may be true that a child or adolescent will become accustomed to recording equipment, but such equipment, I believe, never loses its meaning as that part of the office which is present for the therapist's purposes. By contrast, the dollhouse or even a typewriter, if the child is permitted to use it, says to him that the office and its equipment are to be used for his purposes.

The care with which I keep records should not be confused with a veridical account of events as they occur in all their detail but is rather a serious attempt to approximate those events. Memorization, for example, is not free of distortion but, as a clinical tool, it does reflect a serious attempt to be as true as possible to what happens. Each youngster's record, then, can be considered a narrative account (Spence, 1982) of his or her progress in therapy, an account which may be seen as an approximation of the whole truth.[1] The whole truth continues to be elusive and is probably best approximated by combining the renditions of many observers. In the case of a therapeutic exchange, these "many" consist of therapist and patient—the two who were present when a therapeutic event occurred. Even if the exchange was taped, it contains only a portion of the "truth" if the patient is not present to make known to others his own interpretations of what appears on the tape.

[1]A "narrative" truth surely means more than making something up. Reading Spence (1982) convinced me that it was precisely his understanding that one rarely arrives at *the* (historical) truth in remembering that prompted him to refine what a plausible "narrative" truth consists of. While Holt's (1989) attempt to apply scientific criteria to psychoanalytic thinking and practice is well argued, nonetheless I believe that the truth as reported by the patient is subject to the impact of development—particularly child and adolescent development. When an event happens, to a child it simply isn't the same as what is remembered. The discrepancy in experiencing and remembering should *not* be taken as simply distortion or as patient malingering. Rather, it reflects the individual's changing intellectual lens through which he perceives "real" events. Still, all of us who try to help people should heed Holt's warning that psychoanalysis—and probably all of psychotherapy—is at risk if more rigorous methods are not applied to the collecting and reporting of clinical events.

The data for this book also consist of my notes on parent conferences, including an account of the child's early history given by his parents; school reports and teacher evaluations; psychometric or other examination reports (when available); notes on my conversations with teachers; observations or reports of other psychotherapists (if any) who had worked with a child or family; polaroid photographs (taken only with the child's permission) of drawings, building constructions, dollhouse setups, or other attempts to create something in my office; and finally, any products the child chose to give me, such as original stories, drawings and paintings, clippings from the newspaper or magazines, and homework papers.

CONFIDENTIALITY

During my psychotherapeutic work with nonlearning young people and their parents, I make every effort to maintain the privacy of their communications to me. I do not divulge to parents what the youngster tells me in confidence. I always inform the younger child of a meeting between his parents and me and ask him what he wants me to keep private. I also inquire what he might want me to tell his parents. It does not always occur to the younger child that I might tell his parents something positive about him. I always ask the older child or adolescent for permission to meet with his parents and inquire what he or she might want me to keep private. Although I also ask them what they might want me to tell their parents, it should be noted that older children and adolescents usually tell their parents what they want them to know. If a child or adolescent informs me that he does not want me to talk to his parents, I respect this decision and do not schedule a parent meeting. I should add, though, that this is a rare occurrence. Younger children often enjoy the idea that I wish to talk to their parents about them. Older children and adolescents often appreciate my concern about confidentiality and relish the opportunity to instruct me as to what topics I may pursue with their parents and what topics I must keep private. Apart from the willingness of young people to be the center of attention in these discussions, in my opinion the psychotherapist must carefully consider what to divulge in parent conferences.

Similarly, I inquire of parents what they wish me to keep private about their conversations with me regarding their children. Sometimes parents confide personal problems which they wish to keep from their offspring, believing their own problems would exacerbate those of their youngsters. Quite frequently, parents ask that I not divulge family problems to individuals outside the family, such as teachers. So if I report a conversation in the text between me and a parent about the young person's progress, this means that I secured permission from the youngster to talk to his parents about him. Similarly, if I describe a conversation between me and a youngster's teacher it means that I had permission from both the young person and his parents to talk to his teacher about his academic and/or therapeutic progress.

DATA PRESENTATION

The clinical data that form the basis of the case narratives are used in two ways. Some children are described at length, but even then, only those events that I thought were relevant to a child's decision to fail and to his decision to renew attempts at learning are included. These children are introduced by a brief account of the child's early history, which includes those significant events that led to his or her decision to reject learning. Although not distorting actual events as they occurred or were reported to me, in order to ensure the privacy of the individuals I describe, in the case narratives I have made every effort to minimize the inclusion of identifying data. At other times, a child or a child's behavior is used to illustrate a point, where my intent is not to present a full case history or narrative.

I have not used clinical data to prove a theory. In my opinion, the kind of clinical evidence I report is not appropriate for proving or disproving a theory because, without adequate controls, we tend to see what we wish to see, most especially when we are attempting to help a patient or trying to find reliable methods for helping a group of patients with similar symptoms. Clinical data *can* suggest hypotheses. Eagle (1984), who writes of recent trends in psychoanalysis, urges us to draw upon research outside the therapeutic hour to support hypotheses that may have been formed within the hour. This is one reason, among many others, why I have referred to Piaget's work. But, even though I cite Piaget often and apply some aspects of his theory to my group of nonlearning children and adolescents, it should be said that his method is different from mine in at least two respects. He interviewed presumably *normal* children across age and developmental stage groups in order to investigate some hypotheses he advances to explain the acquisition of knowledge and the structure of intelligence. I observe *learning-inhibited* children and adolescents, some of whom I have known and talked to for 2 or 3 years (and often longer, when I have been able to follow the individual's progress after therapy was terminated). Thus, this book is *not* an attempt to replicate Piaget's findings, but it is an attempt to tease out what in Piaget's work helped me as a clinician of nonlearning children and adolescents, and how what helped me might help other clinicians. I intend my clinical data to support hypotheses and to suggest avenues for investigation. Because I refer to Piaget's theory to enlighten clinical narratives, I define in Chapter 3 the cognitive-developmental terms relevant to psychotherapeutic work with nonlearning youngsters. All other terms I use in this book are consistent with dictionary definition.

ACKNOWLEDGMENTS

Many people gave their wisdom and enthusiasm to my writing efforts. Bruno Bettelheim taught me much of what I know about children and adolescents, and I thank him for his perceptive reading of this book. The idea that Piagetian psychology could help with clinical dilemmas was encouraged by three more of my graduate school professors, although their fields of substantive interest are quite different from my own. I thank Jacob W. Getzels at the University of Chicago and Paul R. Ammon and William D. Rohwer, Jr., both at the University of California, Berkeley, for their support in my graduate student days.

For their efforts to improve portions of an early draft, I would like to thank the poet Joan Houlihan and the historian Jean Quataert. I thank Joseph P. Lord for his support in helping me begin this book and for his ongoing interest in the manuscript. To Gerald P. Koocher I am grateful for his concise commentary on the book's purpose which he deciphered from an early prospectus. I am indebted to Katherine Trow who many years ago helped spark my interest in children who do not learn. And I thank Indira Talwani for doing the blind analyses of the children's interviewing responses.

A number of colleagues, some of whom are educators and some psychotherapists, read and commented on portions of later drafts. Kristin Field and Margot Griffin Kenney read large portions with a sharp sensitivity to the perspectives of teacher and learner. The time they took from their own work to review mine is gratefully acknowledged. I thank Kathryn Carlson, Gail Donovan, Gloria Kaplan, Gail Lundholm, and Randy Sorkin for their sensitive reading of some portions of this book.

My psychotherapist colleagues provided precious and incisive interpretations of the book's major themes and deepened my understanding of the clinical narratives. I thank Stanley Berman, Elizabeth Colt, Miriam Elson, Suzanne Gassner, Diana Grossman Kahn, Kathy Lubin, Marc Lubin, Andrea Farkas Patenaude, and Covie Silverthorne for the intuitions they shared with me. I am particularly indebted to Elizabeth Colt, Marc Lubin, Andrea Farkas Patenaude, and Covie Silverthorne whose clinical insights often challenged my views and improved my exposition as the book developed. Miriam Elson's wise counsel during the last stages of this enterprise is greatly appreciated.

I gratefully acknowledge the helpful conversations, also during the last stages of the manuscript, clarifying the book's major theme I had with social psychologist Robert S. Weiss. His sensitive reactions as well as those of psychotherapist Joan Weiss were immensely helpful.

I thank my husband, Joseph Zelan, a sociologist and an educator, for reading the book twice as it evolved over 5 years. I am grateful for the ideas he generated during our late-night discussions and for his care and support of our children while I sat at the typewriter. I thank our son, Saul, and our daughter, Jeana, who set me straight about the perspectives of adolescents and children, and who continuously reminded me of the ways in which young people are intelligent and aware. They not only patiently tolerated my many hours of writing, but they actually helped the book. I am grateful to Saul for suggesting the book's subtitle and to Jeana for thoughtfully answering my many questions about children's early learning, and to both of them for their spontaneous reactions to the book's major themes.

I want to acknowledge the efforts of Theron Raines who throughout my writing of this book encouraged me to stay with it. I am grateful to my editor,

Elenore Souza, who turned a garbled manuscript into a readable one. And I would like to thank Mackie Korrell for not only typing many early drafts but also for responding to the book's message.

Finally, I am especially grateful to all the children and adolescents who have helped me learn what this book chronicles. Their patience is stunning as I attempt to grasp their perspectives and brings strength to both my efforts to assist them and to my task of narrating their stories.

Note to the Reader

The names of the children and adolescents whom I describe in this book are fictitious. Sometimes I use the conventional pronoun *he* to indicate that I am talking about children and adolescents in general. This practice by no means acknowledges the fact that just as many young people who are female as young people who are male are the subjects of this book. At other times I refer to young people generally as "he" or "she." However, this construction can become awkward if used throughout the book. So for this reason, I have sometimes chosen to use the personal pronoun appropriate to the clinical material I am discussing. Hence, if the ideas I advance were suggested by the therapeutic progress of a female, I use the pronoun *she* even if I am not always describing a particular female. I appreciate the reader's patience with my choice of a personal pronoun depending on the context.

Contents

CHAPTER 1

An Introduction to the Young Person's View of Learning

I want to know if I can live with what I know, and only that.
Albert Camus

The unknown attracts the youngster from his very first learning attempts whether he is walking, talking, learning the alphabet, or endeavoring to understand literature and the sciences. Exploring his world in bits and pieces, he is much like the scholar who seeks knowledge on a larger scale and in a more organized fashion. Whatever is not immediately comprehensible to the child and the scholar holds compelling fascination. For the scholar, repeated attempts to explore the unknown result in increasingly comprehensive versions of what is true and real. Children, too, must learn to replace earlier, immature "theories" with more accurate thought constructions, accounting for additional, sometimes unexpected reality features.

Although glimpses of the true and the real beckon the youngster to learn once more, the limits of his childhood knowledge do threaten his learning. Because he is often unaware of what *he* actually knows, he is uncertain how valid his learning attempts *are*. At a young age, he does not think to question what he knows, and when he begins to question it he sometimes doubts that knowing could have productive outcomes. On the one hand, he declines to question what he knows because he is unaware of his capability to understand. On the other hand, when he becomes aware that it is *he* who understands, he nonetheless retreats from evaluating what he knows because he often cannot imagine doubting "the known" or is uncertain about the outcomes of his personal inquiries. Validity can be questioned and resolved only by those individuals who are either aware of themselves as cognizing persons or who are confident that the outcomes of the inquiry will be productive.

More than the youngster, the scientist knows how to live with what he knows because he is aware of what he does not understand and is precise in forming hypotheses. Because the new is apprehended by the same systematic process as the familiar, the new is often integrated with the familiar rather readily. Even when the new challenges the scientist to reconsider the familiar, the reconsidering process remains systematic. The young person's thought has not yet developed this facility. By using inductive and deductive processes, it takes the child many years to understand the true cause of an event. As he progresses toward understanding scientific inquiry, he often engages in magical thinking and is unaware that logical thinking is more reliable. Furthermore, disorganized aspects of his experience threaten his equilibrium. If a child could integrate his observations easily, his equilibrium might not be threatened so often. Thus, when the child apprehends the new and realizes that it requires a more systematic integration with the familiar, he must change the very process by which he perceived the familiar.

Adults and youngsters differ dramatically in understanding the connotations that they attach to acquiring knowledge. Meanings attached to knowing by adults are more likely to be associated with acquiring knowledge per se, whereas the meanings perceived by children often extend beyond what adults consider knowing. Adults are likely to perceive an act of knowing as achieving or succeeding. Children are apt to expand "knowing" beyond discovering and to blur knowing with actions other than achieving or succeeding. Adults then misperceive the child on two counts. First, they are often uncertain which aspects of child development naturally limit childhood knowledge. We overlook the fact that young people confuse academic learning with other phenomena, such as magical thinking, or intuitions about themselves or other people. Second, adults often fail to grasp the full range of connotations the child gives to gaining understanding. For example, we no longer believe acquiring knowledge makes us more "grown up" while children do believe understanding creates this effect.

Moreover, when the young person correctly understands that learning leads to knowledge acquisition and thus begins to approach our understanding, we adults underestimate his formative epistemological efforts and believe that he only "learns" but does not really "know." We minimize the youngster's genuine interest in epistemological questions because they seem rudimentary. So we participate in the youngster's misappraisal of what he does know and, therefore, fail to appreciate the power of his accurate understanding. An antidote to this complex situation would be to recognize that there is *no* definite age which predicts mature inquiry. It is simply untrue that childhood and adulthood are divided by ignorance in the child and sagacity in the adult. The main thesis in this book is that the maturing child, whether eager for learning or not, has a long history of transforming learned material into a personal "theory" of himself in a physical and interpersonal world and into a general theory. He does not suddenly become a mature, cognizing adult.

It is essential that clinicians of youngsters who *will not* learn adopt a receptive attitude to what they *do* know in an epistemological sense since they, too, are becoming acquainted with the ways learning leads to knowledge acquisition. In my attempts to help young people who reject or resist learning, I begin by attending to the ways in which they abort discovery attempts by refusing to accept what they consider to be "the known." I also investigate the special meanings they attach to the *activity* of acquiring knowledge.

To stress the meanings knowledge acquisition has for young people who zealously approach and avoid learning, I cite many case narratives and verbatim statements. These special meanings connected to thinking, learning, and knowing should be central in any therapeutic work that aims to revitalize the youngster's inquiring attitude. Young children especially blur the meanings they associate with thinking, learning, and knowing. Adolescents and adults differentiate these activities and even consider how they are related to other activities, such as willing and judging (Arendt, 1978). Although young people are continuously progressing toward the mature rational stance, as Piaget and Inhelder (1969) have shown, they often equate thinking and knowing with such other processes as doubt or certainty and then are more likely than adults to doubt or be certain of isolated aspects of their experience. If a child could express his reactions to knowing in the sophisticated manner that Albert Camus does, he might tell us that what he can afford to know about reality and himself equals only what he can accept. By their behavior, children often do assert it is the implications that acquiring knowledge have for their individual experiences which lead them to learn and to avoid learning. When learning and knowing enhance their experience, children eagerly continue their inquiries and thus implicitly question, as Camus does, whether it is enough to know only that which can be lived with.

In my opinion, it is only in late childhood and adolescence that the inquiring individual coordinates thinking, learning, and knowing and conceptualizes these three activities as an ongoing process leading to humanistic or scientific knowledge. For this reason, I discuss separately what thinking, learning, and knowing are likely to mean to young people before they have reflected on these activities in combination as central to knowledge acquisition.

THINKING

According to Piaget (1976, 1978), children begin to become aware of the thinking process that leads to an intended result at about the age of eight. At earlier ages, when they use the word *think*, they generally mean something other than the standard definition of thinking: "thought, cogitation, meditation, mental action or activity" (*Oxford English Dictionary [OED]*, 1971). When given a task in school, they may use the verb to think when they mean they are not sure how to complete a task, or when they would rather not complete it. They may answer the teacher's question by saying, "I think I know," and mean to express they doubt their understanding. Or, they might intend to voice an opinion or judgment about their understanding and, if so, touch upon the *OED*'s second meaning of thinking: "the holding of an opinion...judgement or belief."

Like a younger child, an older child expresses uncertainty by using the word *think*. When presented with a difficult learning task, rather than say "I think I know" an older child might say, "I'll have to think more about it." This would indicate that he understands the relationship between learning and thinking when he says about a task to be learned that he must think. Just as important, many older children make this statement when they wish to delay thinking. They have correctly surmised that more thought is required and that concentrated thought is likely to lead to an unknown result, or if they have some inkling about that result, they may express ambivalence about it as they postpone thinking.

Furthermore, children often associate the verb *think* with other imagined actions. I treated two children who connected thinking with hoping, an action which has no obvious relationship to the actions of learning and knowing. One 8-year-old girl eventually differentiated thinking from hoping when she told me about the games in my office: "There are 'hope' games and 'think' games." Pointing to Candyland she said, "That's a hope game, you don't think about it." Then she pointed to the chess game and said, "That's a thinking game, hoping doesn't help." In differentiating the actions of hoping and thinking, she stressed the value of thought as a reliable antecedent to winning in games of skill in contrast to hoping for "good luck" in games of chance.

Contrarily, a 7-year-old boy who associated thinking with hoping became confused when quoting a passage from the story of Snow White. Unlike the girl quoted above, his confusion was not easily resolved. He said that people don't think something if they also don't hope it. Because he understood the story told that the dwarfs *thought* Snow White was dead, he deduced that they *hoped* she was dead. The association he made between thinking and hoping is more complex than the connection between fearing and hoping ordinarily noticed by clinicians. This boy tried to express that he *feared thinking* because his thoughts might tell him what he hoped for in regard to a story character—who stood for a real person. He avoided understanding that in an angry moment, he would hope Snow White were dead.

LEARNING

Learning is an easier concept for children to grasp than the concept of thinking. It refers to a specific and concrete activity or product whereas thinking is an abstract concept. Children often conceive of learning as "being taught" as expressed by a capable 9 and a-half-year-old girl—or as "the action of receiving instruction or acquiring knowledge" (*OED*, 1971). Or, they might connect learning to a specific skill or piece of information as revealed by an underachieving 8-year-old girl who told me learning is the same as spelling when she said, "Learning in school is t-h-e."

A 7-year-old boy, afraid to go to school, who was in psychotherapy with me for 16 months felt better about himself because of what he "learned" during his appointments. So when he tried to express his appreciation for the help he had received, he thanked me for "the things I *learned* in therapy." The ideas that he had solved internal problems or changed his self-image were too abstract for him to grasp and articulate. Rather, he remembered what he had learned about playing table games as he explained what helped him feel better about himself in his home and school environments.

After a year of therapy, a low-achieving 12-year-old boy attributed very interesting meanings to acquiring knowledge when he reluctantly understood the connection between learning and thinking. He saw that the results of learning embody no inherent controls and could be used destructively. The link between what one learned and what one could think as a result of learning frightened him when he realized that what he learned in chemistry class could be put to ill use: "Kids can think about science in different ways once they've learned it. I don't think schools should teach kids about science because that gives them the idea to build bombs. They might blow up the world!" His statement helped him understand his fear of learning chemistry, which derived from his intuition about himself. Because he knew *he* often exploded with feeling, he became afraid that his inner explosions might contaminate the world. Knowing about chemistry would lead automatically to a proliferation of outbursts. When I told him that the social sciences often focus on those very problems that concerned him and that technology creates, he began to question his earlier assumption that knowledge acquisition inevitably leads to destruction. He could differentiate the knowledge which to him was potentially dangerous (chemistry) from the knowledge which he understood might mitigate these dangers (sociology). Eventually he realized that even chemists could and did decide how to use their knowledge. Then, learning chemistry did not seem so threatening to this boy because he recognized that he, too, could make decisions about his "explosions" —both his personal explosions and the ones he imagined in chemistry class.

KNOWING

Compared to thinking and learning the concept of knowing as "understanding, discovery, or rediscovery" (*OED*, 1971) is even more elusive to children. Perhaps because scholars understand that children often impute naive or personal meanings to knowing, they resist calling what children know *knowledge* and instead deny the continuity across the various developmental knowing levels. About scholars, Furth (1987) wrote

> They would readily agree that at a young age children's knowledge is inextricably mixed up with personal desires. For this reason they are unsympathetic to the use of the word *knowledge* for children...and would prefer to limit it to the objective knowledge recognized in the adult world. (p. 166)

And since before the ages of 7 or 8, children do not even begin to define what the term *objective knowledge* refers to, they, too, restrict what they mean by *knowing* to (1) the concrete here-and-now and, sometimes simultaneously, to (2) personal, often idiosyncratic associations. About the former, most children do understand the meaning of knowing as an acknowledgment or recognition (*OED*, 1971). This fact is observed in statements like "Oh, I *know* her!" or "Do you know that guy? He's a friend of mine." About the latter, sometimes when a child says he knows something, he refers to feeling certain. He means to stress that he possesses a skill or information which he thinks the other person believes he lacks. The boy who felt he had "learned" in therapy often asserted that he *did know* facts or feelings when he suspected that his parents, teachers, friends, or I didn't believe him.

One 4-year-old girl who had not yet learned to read or spell thought the verb *know* had the same meaning as the word *no*. Because of the auditory equivalence of these two words, she concluded that a negation was implicit in the act of knowing—a conclusion she was predisposed to reach for intrapsychic reasons. Because often she was afraid of knowing, every time she used the verb *to know* she felt she was saying "no" rather than "know." When, for example, she said "I know the alphabet," she became confused because she thought she was asserting and denying simultaneously. Although she wished to assert that she knew, she also felt as though she said, "I no the alphabet [say no to or do not know the alphabet]."

Some children's desire to say "no" to "knowing" occurs when they realize their magical thinking distorts reality. Because they continue to want to avoid certain aspects of reality, they reject logical thinking and cling to magical thinking. The underachieving girl who perceived learning as the same as its product ("learning in school is t-h-e") resisted differentiating logic and magic because blurring this distinction enabled her to avoid understanding the circumstances leading to her father's death. Because she was sure she would suffer her father's fate, knowing the reasons for his death threatened her whereas not knowing them was infinitely more attractive because it appeared to ensure her survival.

Similarly, children often resist knowing what thinking processes lie behind "magic tricks." In this case, knowing deprives them of an absorbing experience rather than enhancing it. Magic fascinates especially young children because it appears to produce results through an *un*knowable force. Two children, a 4-year-old boy and a 5-year-old girl, told me they did not want to understand a trick in which a coin appears to disappear because that meant the trick was not really magic. They were referring to a rectangular piece of wood into which a thinner piece of wood could be inserted which contains two circles large enough for coins. The inner piece can be removed, rotated 180°, and then reinserted so that the coin in one of the circles slides out of sight. As he was about to understand where the coin went, the boy said, "It's not magic! But I *want* it to be magic!" The girl was more direct: "I *know* where the penny went so it's *not* magic! I *don't want to know* that magic trick because then it's not magic anymore." Knowing how this trick worked for both of these children meant having to give up a playful fantasy which suggested they, like adults, could triumph over an audience. If it is a matter of magic, children take their "turn" prevailing over adults. If it is a matter of knowing, children understand that adults have the advantage. Knowing then becomes a risk they do not want to take because it deprives them of magic rather than allowing them to achieve.

THE INTEGRATION OF THINKING, LEARNING, AND KNOWING

In my view, children younger than 10 or 11 discover only slowly the many ways thinking, learning, and knowing can be compared, contrasted, and integrated into a comprehensive thought system. The first step toward integration is the child's recognition that these cognitive processes are different. Then he or she is more likely to realize that it is possible to think about school learning in other life situations. That is, when learning and thinking are combined to consolidate an individual's knowledge base and/or to achieve a higher level of functioning, he or she recognizes the relationship the two have to knowledge acquisition—including *self*-knowledge acquisition. The connections the child makes between thinking about learning and knowing both about the world and about the self are the very reasons he avoids learning.

A beginning attempt at integrating the three activities of thinking, learning, and knowing can be seen in this example. The 9½-year-old girl quoted before was asked: "Would you tell me the ways in which thinking, learning, and knowing are different?" Initially, she was taken aback by the question but then responded humorously, "Well, okay, but let me *think*!" As she continued to ponder the question, she came forth with:

> Learning is when you are taught something. After you've learned something, you *know* it. And when you know it you can think about it, but when you know it you don't always think about it, but you *can* think about it.

I asked her to apply what she said about the three activities to her homework assignment for the next day:

> I have to make sure that I've learned about animals and people so I will know it when I'm tested and I have to think about it during the test so I can answer the questions. Then I'll *know* I know it!

As she considered my questions within the homework assignment context, she put thinking, learning, and knowing together in a way that made sense in terms of her immediate experience and that, moreover, enabled her to consider the advanced idea that one can reflect on what one knows ("I'll *know* I know it").

Contrarily, an 8½-year-old boy resisted a mature integration of the thinking, learning, and knowing processes. Although he had been asked by his teacher at age 5 to repeat kindergarten, he nonetheless resolutely attended school. After he had been in psychotherapy with me for 3 years, he struggled to understand just as he was about to leave therapy why he had refused to learn in kindergarten (and often thereafter). He was motivated to understand the origins of his learning problem when he realized that his past attitude toward learning was in conflict with his present attitude. His disappointment at having to repeat kindergarten was at odds with his recent relentless need to achieve in the second grade.

One day he told me he still could not concentrate in school when he missed his mother "who is always off working at the University." When I asked, "Maybe you don't want to do the very thing—schoolwork—which takes your mother away?" he answered emphatically, "Yes! Why should I?" Several weeks later, he asserted adamantly, "Thinking and knowing are the opposite." He explained further: "Either you know something or you don't. If you know it, you don't have to think about it anymore, you just know it!" I asked him whether he meant "think" in the sense of "I'm not quite certain I know this so I must mull it over." He nodded yes and said, "If you just *think* something, you don't really know it." I answered, "But you can always think about what you really know." To this he replied, "No. You never *think* what you *know*." I thought he tried to express that knowing was safer than thinking because it was his mother's "thinking in school," which was required to get an advanced degree, that separated him from her. So every time he thought about learning and what he knew he felt uncertain about his mother's whereabouts because he was reminded she was "off working at the University." Since what he genuinely knew seemed stable and did not, therefore, create doubt leading to a change in the status quo, he could accept knowledge—even welcome it—but only if it did not lead to further thought which implied uncertainty to him. But this does not mean he did not value knowledge; like one of Piaget's (1964) subjects who said, "Once you know, you know for always" (p. 17), he attributed a substantial significance to knowing but not to thinking. Unlike knowing which to him embodied permanence, thinking continued to be dangerous because it was identified with a transmuting process which meant his mother's absence. Most importantly, a child does not have to identify thinking with his mother's absence to conclude that thinking often is less sound than knowledge.

Many children of 7 years or younger react even less maturely than the 8½-year-old quoted above. They often react with a blank look during a conversation about the differences between learning, thinking, and knowing. They usually focus on only one of the three activities and endow it with personal meaning, as illustrated by the girl who concentrated on the "no" in "knowing." Especially young children wander easily into personal meaning and forget what little they might have discovered about deduction.

Equally as often, children and some adolescents identify investigating with other activities, especially the young person who has problems with knowledge acquisition and who must learn to separate the act of knowing from other acts equally salient to him. Knowing is frequently confused with perceiving or "seeing." A child attempting to solve a difficult problem might exclaim, "Oh! I see! [I understand]." Quite common is the tendency of young people to believe that knowing is the same as growing or "growing up." This is because they observe accurately that "grown-ups" understand more than children do. For the same reason, some children equate knowing with dying. They observe that older, educated individuals are more likely to die than younger, less educated individuals and then come to the surprising deduction that learning or acquiring knowledge causes death.

Likewise, knowing is often identified with stealing, cheating, tricking, entrapping, deceiving, winning, threatening, and concealing. The confusion of the knowing act with these other activities often arises in the child's mind as he plays table games or perfects his sports' skills. Then, he often thinks of "knowing" as "knowing how" to participate in organized games. To the child, knowing how to play games is identical to some or all of the aforementioned activities.

Equally confusing to young people is their tendency to associate knowing with a myriad of other activities, such as placating, confounding, remembering, feeling, and even denying. The insightful youngster in psychotherapy often believes that learning in school and/or understanding his own symptomatic behavior will placate his parents or his therapist. Or, he believes he might confound his parents and his therapist when he understands something all too well which he would like to keep secret from them. Knowing is often associated with remembering when the young person suddenly or gradually becomes attuned to his past. Especially when he comes in touch with past or present affects does he feel a powerful connection between knowing and feeling. Most important is the link the youngster in psychotherapy makes between knowing and introspecting. Introspecting about intrapsychic events, including defensive reactions wherein he wishes to deny what he knows, seems like "knowing" to the young person in therapy because he has either eagerly or reluctantly acquired knowledge about himself.

What is worth noting in the 9½-year-old's statement quoted before is her spontaneous understanding that one's self is capable of knowing—that is, of applying what has been learned. Then, knowing seems related to learning and less united with some other activities, such as stealing, cheating, threatening, denying, concealing, etc. The realization that knowing is different from these other activities awards acquiring knowledge a central position in her experience as she considers its own intrinsic rewards. Each child, then, might discover anew what Piaget (1971) and Dewey (1956, 1963) stressed when they said that children can be led to the unfamiliar by way of the familiar; so what is taught ought to begin with the child's experience. Then, the child who learns and who "knows she knows it" has a double experience of the world and the self. This experience affirms her attempts to learn while establishing the inner connection between scholarship and selfhood.

ACTIVE LEARNING

Academic learning must be put in the broader context of the youngster's acquired competencies in order for the clinician to understand more fully what it means to young people. When a child is younger and learning to walk and talk, he is a conspicuously active learner. His own excitement and our adult approval are components of the pleasure he feels in discovering. Because the developing child's mastery of both the activities of walking and learning give him more autonomy than he had before, learning to walk to a child could serve as an analogy to learning in school. Both have great symbolic salience. But the school child, even if drawn to knowledge for its own sake, is still often seen as a passive recipient of what the world dishes out—although he behaves in a noticeably active fashion as he learns, and despite Piaget's impact on modern psychology. Our inattention to the child's own impulse to learn explains why we ignore the inherent pleasures he gains from knowing and why we continue to view social approval of routine tasks as the only stimulus to learning.

A child's spontaneous learning often begins with her merging wondrous playing with learning. A child might pretend that letters or words have personal meanings. To a child the letters of the alphabet can stand for interesting people engaged in activity, as they did for a 7-year-old who saw the capital letter K as "me running," and a small t as "mommy waiting" with outstretched arms. The letters K and t suggested a little story to this girl, named Katy, who told me she liked words with these letters because that meant she was running into her mother's arms. Another child made words out of letters, such as "be" (b) and "why?" (y). Playful and symbolic activities like these occur while children participate in the school curriculum. They represent thoughtful activity and help the child learn the teacher's assignments. Their spontaneous behavior stands in contrast to the rote memorization of the alphabet, which has little symbolism beyond that of gaining their parents' or teachers' approval.

Moreover, as the child admits to thinking about school learning, his thoughts extend what he has learned in school to include aspects of his home environment. For example, a child in the early grades often comes home from school announcing what he learned that day knowing he possesses information his younger siblings do not. As he becomes increasingly self-conscious about his learning, the child also "learns" of his dawning capability to comprehend. Most important, he becomes aware of the meanings he attributes to the acts of learning and acquiring knowledge.

But the child's march toward autonomy is not a simple matter. A collapse in adaptation can occur while learning to walk or while learning in school. The walking child can either walk toward or away from his parents, depending on how he feels about them at any moment. As Mahler, Pine, and Bergman (1975) have shown, the child might feel inhibited in locomotor activity if his parents wish to keep him with them longer than is beneficial for him. Likewise, the knowing child can restrict what he knows to that which his parents know, or he can move beyond it. The child can become an inhibited knower or learner if his parents wish to keep him from knowledge which threatens them. The child who thereupon tries to protect his parents by avoiding the meanings inherent in the learning task, or the meaning of learning itself, must forego the pleasures of learning. He gains only that which has the approval of his teacher or parents who view rote learning as safe.

ACTIVE NONLEARNING

The decision to fail is more complex than the decision to succeed. The simple view is that the child who does not learn does not think. Yet doubt about the automatic connection between a learner and a thinker lurks in our minds. Although we label a child like this a *nonlearner*, we still see an occasional flash of insight. Moreover, we sometimes even question whether thought is part of a learner's activity: What does learning the ABC's have to do with serious thought? The minimum of thought required by rote learning may make it difficult to understand the deliberation involved in any school learning. If we fail to perceive the determination involved in thoughtless alphabet learning, we are blinded to the determination involved in the act of not learning it.

Clinicians and teachers who deal with nonlearning children and adolescents are especially prone to perceive them as passive, not autonomous, because professionals believe nonlearning originates in a youngster's deficits. A deficit is something the child "can't help" and not something he chooses. Far more accurate is the view that the intelligent youngster who fails in school intends to do so; he refuses to see what is put before him or hear what is being said. If he does see it or hear it, he refuses to process it in a fashion that is meaningful to or expected by the teacher or his parents. A child's determination to fail is obvious to any careful observer who considers his observations from the child's perspective. Years ago, as Holt (1964) watched the children he taught, he asked questions of central importance about one nonlearning girl in particular:

> I can't get Nell out of my mind. When she talked with me about fractions today, it was as if her mind rejected understanding. . . . Several times she would make a real effort to follow my words, and did follow them, through a number of steps. Then, just as it seemed she was on the point of getting the idea, she would shake her head and say, "I don't get it." Can a child have a vested interest in failure? What on earth could it be? (p. 3)

What Holt suggests is that both learning *and* nonlearning require a decision. A child who learns behaves in ways we expect and a child who refuses to learn understands what the teacher wants her to learn and rejects it.

There can be many individual reasons and motives for a child's decision to fight learning. A most compelling reason is the child's perception that "the essential principles underlying a learning task would throw him into inner turmoil *when applied to himself*" [italics added] or when he "understands some subject matter all too well" but resists its implications (Bettelheim, 1980, p. 156). In answer to Holt's questions, "Can a child have a vested interest in failure?" and "What on earth could it be?" we might speculate that "Nell" shook her head no on the point of getting the idea about fractions because whatever was required of her to learn about them held implications she could not accept. Children like this resist assimilating school learning to other life experiences. For example, "Nell" might have imagined that breaking up a mathematical whole was similar to breaking up another entity. She might have compared a divided pie to a fractionated family. That is, while she may have accepted a rote learning of fractions, she, like many children I treat, could have rejected the "idea" of fractions because rejecting it enabled her to escape the implications of this particular learning activity. And, since the choice of fighting knowledge acquisition goes against the child's natural tendency to find out about the world and other people, "it often takes a good deal more determination on the part of the nonlearner to fail than for the good learner to do well" (Bettelheim, 1980, p. 154). What a battle with learning represents is the child's inner conflict between two affinities—a much more complex fight than the manifest combat with the school, teacher, or parents. But the manifest battle does reveal the child's ambivalence about learning and brings his school troubles to our attention.

LEARNING DISORDERS DEFINED AND DESCRIBED

A learning disorder is distinct from a learning disability and is best viewed as the result of the child's use of cognition to avoid understanding or to fight it. Children with disabilities may use cognition for the same purposes, particularly the understanding that they are disabled, but children with learning disorders avoid or fight understanding they are *competent*. Just as important, many deliberate nonlearners ignore the *intrinsic* value of learning. The learning disordered child's past and present attitudes toward learning are often compressed into an almost automatic rejection of thinking and learning the moment the child suspects the expectation of either. Knowledge, which is the result of thinking and learning, is either passively ignored, avoided, or actively fought. Therefore, it is not integrated in a meaningful way into the child's perspective. Because he often confuses knowing with antisocial processes, such as cheating, stealing or trapping—or unwelcome processes such as growing or dying—he tends to reject the associated act of knowing. Thus, children with learning disorders are quite different from normal children who experience temporary difficulties with certain school subjects or assignments because the normal child does not overload learning and knowledge acquisition with peripheral meaning and seeks instead to overcome learning difficulties and uses his cognition to that end. Although the learning disabled child might fight the realization that he is disabled, he often uses intact cognitive abilities to master or compensate for his disabilities.

In my psychotherapy practice, I treat three distinct types of learning disorders. Sixty nonlearning children and adolescents are the subjects of this book. Many deliberate nonlearners (37 of those I treated) seem to blanket their minds with feigned boredom or stupidity in an attempt to convince their teachers or parents that they are incapable of learning. The utmost exemplars of these *underachievers* are those children who fake the personality of the mentally retarded (7 of the 37 *underachievers*). These youngsters not only act bored or stupid but also sometimes take on other characteristics of the mentally retarded, such as a blank stare or clumsy gross-motor movements.

A second group (11 of those I treated) consists of youngsters who reach for academic competence beyond what they are comfortably capable of achieving. Because their need to know is launched by an urgency apart from the learning task, a pressure epiphenomenal to the assigned material prevents them from integrating school learning into their thinking. Because these children are only interested in proving that they are grown-up, they fragment their learning process and often miss that, whether spontaneous or assigned, it has intrinsic meaning. For want of a better word to describe how their striving for academic competence creates the paradoxical effect of nonlearning, I have thought of these children as *overachievers*.

A third group of children (twelve of those I treated) express their rejection of learning by refusing to attend school. Their manifest symptoms of panic and anxiety lead professionals to label them *school phobic*. Often these youngsters comprehend what learning is all about compared to their classmates who either under- or overachieve. They understand the power of knowing more vividly and comprehend that both school and teacher are implicated in the knowing process. Their panic reactions expose just how important academic learning is to them. By way of contrast, the underachiever blocks out massive amounts of what is taught in school, and the overachiever often distorts the overall meaning of what he is taught. But child who is labeled school phobic often correctly understands what is taught and therefore avoids knowledge by avoiding the very place where it is transmitted.

All learning disordered children and adolescents intuit a relationship between what they know about academic subjects and what they know about themselves or their parents. When they are expected to learn academic subjects in school, they often feel instantly that they are then expected to learn about themselves or their families—a process they do not want to undergo. For example, when they learn in school, they also "learn" that they have gained information their parents do not possess. Then they might conclude that they are "smarter" than their parents, a thought which threatens both child and parent.

Moreover, these children often see as isomorphic that process by which we recollect something once known but later forgotten as the apprehension of something unfamiliar or misunderstood (such as new mathematical concepts). Again, identities are constructed out of the two very different processes of remembrance and initial understanding. One 11-year-old underachieving boy expressed his confusion and his conception of these two different apprehending processes: "Sometimes you don't know what you know; you could have known it and forgotten it, or you could have misunderstood the teacher and the homework." Past events or knowledge which are suddenly recalled as the "old stuff" are confused with the sometimes sudden and initial understanding of "new stuff"—such as those new math facts communicated by the teacher or by homework assignments.

Even though much of the clinical material that follows asks for diagnoses of the youngsters in question, I have chosen not to subsume "learning disorders" under other more familiar diagnostic categories. That is, I have not shaped my discussion of nonlearning symptoms by concentrating primarily on the ways in which they reflect "neurotic," "borderline," or "psychotic" disturbance. My principal reason for not doing so is the emphasis I place in this book on the young person's own perspective regarding learning and knowledge acquisition. When the focus is diagnostic, a discussion, for example, of a "neurotic" child's problems with learning is likely to center on ways in which the child's behavior reveals one or many facets of a "neurotic conflict." Since it is the individual's *own* renewed learning professionals ought to be concerned with, it is his attitudes toward knowledge acquisition which have shaped my discussion of his symptoms and his treatment progress. Unlike the adult, the child does not perceive himself as "neurotic."

There are two other reasons for proceeding by describing experience-near phenomena: (1) diagnostic categories have permanence connotations not just to young people but also to professionals which is problematic precisely because (2) symptomatic youngsters are *also* continuously developing. Nonetheless, the reader would doubtless like to know that by far the greatest proportion of nonlearners I treat can be classified as "developmentally deviant" or as "psychoneurotic" (*Psychopathological Disorders in Childhood: Theoretical Considerations and A Proposed Classification* [GAP], 1966, pp. 225–237; *Diagnostic and Statistical Manual of Mental Disorders — Revised* [DSM-III-R], 1987, pp. 39–64, 241–243, and 245–246; Pine, 1985, pp. 207–209). A few interesting youngsters I treat for nonlearning symptoms can be classified as *borderline* or as having a *personality disorder* (GAP, pp. 237–250; DSM-III-R, pp. 346–347; Pine, p. 209).

LEARNING DEFICITS AND LEARNING DECISIONS: CAN'T VERSUS WON'T

What a child with a learning problem is actually capable of is the subject of much of the literature on the identification and remediation of such children. Pine (1985) has cautioned clinicians not to overestimate a child's intellectual potential and offers advice on ways to communicate to parents and children about their genuine capabilities. Two recent works aimed at parents, teachers, and educators discuss the child's potential intellectual strengths as one component in the larger diagnostic portrayal of the child's deficiencies or disabilities (McGuinness, 1985; Vail, 1987). Perceiving cognitive potential in children who have problems with learning is a step in the right direction. But the focus in neither book is on what a child *decides* to do with his intellectual potential. For example, McGuiness described what a child lacks when she discussed gender differences in predisposition for certain skills. She hypothesized that the difficulties girls have with math may result from their relative lack of visual acuity compared to boys. But her perspective begins to approach mine when she commented about learning problems: "Last but not least, it does matter what you're [boys and girls are] interested in" (p. 165). Vail asserted that many disabled children are also gifted and called them "conundrum kids." Pairing gifts with disabilities in a discussion of learning problems often obscures what a child *decides* to do with his intelligence and leads clinicians to attempt remediation of the weakness or "disability" rather than to recognize and validate the child's strengths. For the child to learn, he must feel that his strengths are genuine.

Coles (1987) shattered the "learning-disability" myth and asserted that there is a sociopolitical reason for our perceiving children as incompetent and labeling them *LD*. In line with my hypotheses, he purported that learning incompetence results from the interaction of many factors, such as how the child feels about his teacher in combination with how his teacher (and other experts) perceive him. Berger, Prentice, Hollenberg, Korstvedt, and Sperry (1969) delved deeper into the learning inhibited children's actual competencies by interviewing these children using Piagetian tasks. They found that children with psychogenic learning problems are significantly behind their peers who are not learning inhibited. Further, they noted that after a period of 18 months, the learning-inhibited children improved in understanding reasoning tasks.

The authors then cautiously link this improvement with the facts that the children were receiving individual psychotherapy, supplemental tutoring, and were attending remedial schools. Presumably, the psychotherapeutic and educational therapies these children received helped them get in touch with what they actually knew and with how they wished to use their knowledge.

In a paper directed to clinicians, the authors asserted that a group of verbal and allegedly gifted "underachievers" were in reality only normally intelligent. These "neurotic" youngsters whose average—not gifted—abilities were interfered with by their individual family dynamics sought to camouflage their inner conflicts by verbal precocity (Newman, Dember, & Krug, 1973). A developmental perspective informs the authors that the child's abilities change over the life span and that children with learning problems are at risk for structural deficits by virtue of selective disuse of particular cognitive abilities. Because the child does not develop and use these abilities, he becomes unable to perform certain tasks. The child thereupon seeks to mask the atrophy of these abilities by asserting "I won't" when he "can't." The authors' view is that the highly verbal child who nonetheless has some cognitive deficits is capable of a defensive self-presentation as someone who "can't, but I'll say I won't" (Newman *et al.*, p. 85). We must ask what it requires of a child to conceptualize the distinction between "can't" and "won't" not to speak of what is required to convince others that a real deficit could be masked by stubbornness.

My view is that children often assert they "can't" when in reality they "won't." This book documents the cognitive processes by which young people can and do mask one psychological process by another. One 7-year-old girl, whom I will call Sonja, was referred to me for an evaluation because neither her teacher nor her mother felt she was ready for third grade. The important adults in her life thought she could neither read nor spell because of a "developmental disability," a term which remained vague throughout Sonja's evaluation. It was not clear in which ways her teacher or parents thought she was disabled, or whether they thought she had an "attention deficit," or whether they thought simply that she was immature. In spite of the diagnostic ambiguity, the connotations of "developmental disability" exerted conspicuous pressure on Sonja to act in a certain way.

At the first appointment her mother explained that she believed Sonja was "just incapable of third-grade work." As soon as her mother left, Sonja wrote on the blackboard the words *couldn't, don't,* and *doesn't.* I praised her for her correct spelling of these contractions (many second-grade children have difficulty spelling them). When she heard her teacher and her mother repeatedly say, "She's not ready," Sonja assumed that *don't* (her decision not to learn) was equivalent to *couldn't.* But as she thought about it, she knew better—it was more like she *does not* do schoolwork. As she later told me, "not ready means you can't." Why else would she at the beginning of her initial appointment with me juxtapose just these three words? Moreover, by spelling the words correctly, she demonstrated it was not a case of *couldn't,* but a case of *don't* and *doesn't* since she could when she wanted to. Not wishing to contradict her mother's opinion, nor to reveal it was her choice when she did not spell in school, Sonja erased the words just before her mother returned to pick her up.

Sonja became puzzled when during her next appointment I reminded her that she has correctly spelled the words it *couldn't, don't,* and *doesn't* the previous week. But she smiled broadly when I again remarked that contractions are often difficult for children her age to remember and to spell. Then I asked her why she had hurriedly erased the words just as her mother entered the office. She answered, "Because I thought I didn't spell them right and then Mom would be mad. I guess I *could* [spell the words] because I *did!*"

Sonja's behavior reveals that her uneven spelling performance did not reflect a structural deficit or even reduced motivation or interest in spelling. She revealed that she believed she could not spell which led her to anticipate her mother's anger. Thus, a clinician's statement that absence of motivation can lead to mind atrophies or "structural deficits" needs further examination. Cognitive disparities often occur when a child does not understand all the applications of a certain concept. When cognitive disparities persist they can lead to structural deficits if the child reacts negatively or phobically to concept generalization per se because she resists applying new conceptual processes to herself and to her life experience. In this context, Cowan's (1970) observation is pertinent; he writes that some children are "involved in a life-and-death struggle not to learn academic material or not to let anyone know that they have learned" (p. 60). When Sonja began to believe she could spell, she talked with me about her mother's dropping out of college and her anxiety that she would suffer the same fate. Then she exclaimed, "But if I *do* learn in school, Mom will feel bad about dropping out." Sonja's resolution was to learn to spell while simultaneously preventing her mother from knowing what she had learned.

Another case in point is an adopted 11-year-old boy, Dillon, who avoided studying history because it suggested to him not just the past of civilizations but also of individuals. He perceived that the word *story* is contained in the word in *history* and he even sometimes interpreted history as "his story." Thus, his attempts to avoid learning history suggested that he was avoiding his own story, which included his adoption. If he were to continue shunning history, he could have suffered cognitive deficits if his attempt to escape his own history included increased attempts to stop thinking about assigned materials.

Nonetheless, it is erroneous to assume that the problem in such a child's behavior is simply one of "won'ts" masking "can'ts." Implicit in "can" is his clever, if defensive, attempt to escape the underlying problem aroused by the study of history. A closer look at this child's behavior reveals that there are structures and concepts embedded in his defense. Dillon made a cognitive link between civilizations' history and one's own history—indeed he *must* have made this connection to discern his escape. He understood that both civilizations and individuals have a past. Resisting the study of history because he wished to avoid "studying" his own past history rested on Dillon's correct understanding. More important, he invented "his-story" to understand himself better.

Doubtless scholars would be skeptical of or would reject entirely the idea that Dillon's attitude toward learning history was based on a previous "knowing"—that is, an epistemological attitude. When thinking about such a child's behavior, clinicians might feel torn between recognizing that psychotherapy ought to begin with the patient's perspective and being unwittingly influenced by the prevailing social view that children are not intellectually sophisticated enough to choose when and what not to know. The essence of Dillon's conflict, and of many other children like him, is the puzzle surrounding the similarities and differences between reluctant, ambivalent knowing and genuine knowing. Concepts and structures are common to resistance and to knowing. But if a child resists sundry ambiguous situations just because a history lesson seems to implicate his own history, we clinicians might say he is at risk for "structural deficits" in his present and therefore future development. Even though Dillon did not possess a truly knowing attitude regarding the history of civilizations, he used concepts and structures to discern what history was about and how it might apply to him, whereupon he directed his intellect to understand other people sufficiently to cleverly resist his history teacher because he was ambivalent about his story. Sonja, who refused to apply what she had learned about contractions because others thought she "couldn't," but who *did* apply her knowledge about them with me because she knew I believed she *could*, showed selective use of concepts when their application seemed safe. The adult's interest in and respect for the child's reactions to learning often makes it safe because this interest and respect communicate to the *insecure* child that she is thinking about learning, which implies she is capable of learning. Learning begins to appear safe to a *stubborn* child because he realizes that he has used reasoning effectively to avoid learning. Again, he is reassured by his thinking capability.

Newman *et al.* (1973) correctly stated that nonlearning serves some purpose, such as to "carry out [the children's] rebellion against family and society by neglecting academic tasks rather than by active social transgressions" (p. 117). But these authors failed to consider the latent meaning behind statements like "I was messing around" or "goofing off" in regard to learning and take them at face value. In other words, what did learning itself mean to these children when they asserted that they were "messing around" and "goofing off?" The authors concluded, mistakenly in my opinion, that the child's highly developed verbal abilities primarily reflect parental attributes—not the child's attributes. The authors discounted what the children they observed *decided* to learn with whatever intellectual potential they *did* possess. Instead, they concentrated on the parental narcissism evident in a mother's bragging about her child's academic achievements which blocks her perception that her child is probably "neurotic" and not gifted. It may be true that the children described by Newman *et al.* were not gifted, but this fact does not in itself mean they were neurotic—even if their mothers did brag about them.

Furthermore, Newman *et al.* stated that the professional who deals with the structurally deficient child is easily subject to "countertransference pitfalls," such as a professional's believing, like a parent, that the child is gifted when he is only "normally" intelligent (p. 121). The argument runs that adult fascination with the gifted child is counterproductive and only repeats but does not correct attitudes leading to the child's symptoms. My view on this is that taking an overt strength for a genuine weakness depreciates the child's intelligence and autonomy in that what he considers his strength in verbal ability is seen as mere fakery. Such an attitude can hardly help the therapeutic plan if the aim is to help the child trust thinking, learning, and decision-making. And since fakery would show up in an evaluation of the child's thought level—which in effect would distinguish between the latent and the manifest in his ability to know and in his attitude toward knowing—it is especially ironic that Newman *et al.* referred to Piaget to support their thesis. What a child actually knows—not what he fakes—and how he knows it forms the basis for Piaget's genetic epistemology.

REDEFINING DEFICIENCIES

When intelligent children and adolescents lack skills or knowledge, they are not permanently deficient. All youngsters pass through temporary, though sometimes painful, phases in development when they lack capacities (Inhelder & Sinclair, 1969; Inhelder, Sinclair, & Bovet, 1974; Langer, 1969). A child lacks capacities because he has yet to consolidate all that he has learned. At more mature stages, capacities are not only more fully developed but integrated with one another. What a child lacks can be most clearly seen as he struggles with disequilibrium in development—a comfortable perspective fades with the emergence of a new, but yet unstable view. Normal children develop transitional phases through spontaneous inquiries and move most efficiently through these phases a result of their own "perturbations" (Langer, 1969). They actively participate in settling inner disputes between that which both appeals to them and confuses them. The difference between the nonlearning and the normal youngster is the manner in which they approach and resolve transition phases. Unlike normal young people, nonlearning youngsters approach these phases fearfully and often retreat from them rather than resolve them.

The importance of transitory phases of the child's learning something new and for his overall intellectual and social development cannot be overestimated. Distinguishing between extrinsic and intrinsic motives for learning, Elkind (1987) identified a "structural imperative" that motivates children to realize an intellectual potential or mental structure. Furthermore, he stated that the "structural imperative" is

> most in evidence when a structure is in the process of formation. Once the structure is formed, the intrinsic structural imperative diminishes and other intrinsic or extrinsic motives serve to activate the utilization of the fully formed structure. (p. 148)

Especially in intellectually gifted or talented children the structural imperative needs a forum for practice and development. According to Elkind, when opportunities for intellectual development are curtailed in these children, it is not only the children's loss but also society's (p. 151). Important too, is that these gifted children blossom when they find encouragement from their families, their teachers, or their therapists to practice not just what they know but the very *act* of knowing—a point to be illustrated by the stories of Timothy and Annie in Chapter 4.

But before therapeutic intervention, the intelligent or gifted child who fights learning has often sensed that "something is not quite right" with his understanding of or solutions to problems. With successful therapy, he again becomes motivated to search and to prove, but not just by underlying "unconscious" motives—hidden impulses he seeks to sublimate—but also by the "need to function" intellectually or, during transitory phases, by the need to bring more thorough closure to an intellectual problem. Furth (1987) called these transitory phases "knowledge disturbances" and perceptively described their potential for knowledge disruption or inhibition *and* for knowledge acquisition. Speaking of the child's development from infancy through early adolescence, Furth stressed the *activity* of the child in overcoming natural knowledge disturbances and in favoring further development.

> But this is no passive imposition from outside. Only their own active structuring of their schemes—Piaget's equilibration—can lead infants out of the magic of their action world, as in subsequent years it will lead the symbolizing children out of the magic of their symbol world. (p. 27)

Like Elkind, Furth recognizes the value of disequilibrium for knowledge development. In fact, he goes so far as to say that individuals become "reflectively aware" during transitory phases because then they experience a gap in understanding. Gaps in understanding motivate an individual to ask himself, "Why did I think that?" or to conclude about a problem, "That can't be right" and to go on from there. Although a knowledge disturbance may be experienced preconsciously in that the individual is only partially aware of the many facets of his misunderstanding—including his reasons for having misunderstood—nonetheless it is *the* necessary prerequisite for intentional knowledge development. Without knowledge disturbances, we would never reconsider and seek to alter our views.

But what happens when transitory phases in development are not welcomed and resolved—when a knowledge disturbance is suppressed so that it does not lead to new structuring or to insight? Furth noted that Piaget's theory assumes circumstances favorable to the child's inquiring mind. But, Furth asked, what of family or school environments that do not encourage inquiry but overtly or covertly discourage it?

> What if the child had not been motivated to expand the energy of compensating for a gap in understanding and simply suppressed the vaguely experienced insufficiency? What if society discouraged such questions as idle speculations and expected useful work or some other activity as the customary role for children? [What if] the specific subject matter—for psychological or physiological reasons—was highly unpleasurable to the child? (p. 77)

These questions highlight the double-edged quality of transition phases. Typically, children welcome disequilibrium as "an intentional challenge that drives them to compensate for felt knowledge deficiencies" (Furth, 1987, p. 136). In atypical cases, children do not feel supported in exercising their "structural imperatives" and relinquish further inquiry for a safe, but immature developmental perspective. Or they may develop unevenly, excelling in some subject areas where support from a teacher or a parent is experienced while falling behind in other subject areas that are considered unimportant or dangerous by the children's family or teachers. Finally, young people may continue despite lack of support to explore and to prove their hypothetical constructions but refuse to share the results of their inquiries with other people. In hiding their spontaneous explorations from others, these youngsters deprive themselves of what Piaget and Furth consider to be *the* particularly human function — the one that provides *the* impetus to know and to understand. I refer to the young person's social identity wherein his sense of self is no longer isolated as an egocentric "me." Time and again, Piaget asserted that knowledge acquisition is bound to social relationships and the regulations which occur as people compare and modify individual perspectives. When he acts as a social "I," the youngster intentionally engages in the knowledge regulations that permeate mature and shared human thought. It is the respect for the other person that motivates the child over the course of his development to reconsider his perspective and to restructure accordingly.

A clinical focus on the importance of transitional thinking in child development would lead us to see the possibilities for insight in young people, and it would mitigate against the hazards of perceiving the child's developmental level as static. For example, in a brilliantly conceived work that attempts to mesh Piagetian psychology with psychoanalysis, Greenspan (1979) does not ignore that a child's thought level might be implicated in his learning problems. But, because he does not describe transitory phases in cognitive development, he gives the impression that children who do not learn only miss some cognitive ability and do not possess other cognitive abilities which might contribute to their nonlearning because of the connotations they attach to learning.

> It would be especially interesting to look at children in latency with learning problems who do not have clear perceptual-motor problems, but have functional emotional disorders. Do they lack full capacity for reversibility in terms of inversion or reciprocity? Do they lack full capacity for classification or seriation? With what kinds of stimuli do such limitations occur? (Greenspan, 1979, p. 192)

Concentration on what the child lacks, if it excludes what he possesses, is certain to be antitherapeutic. It implies that the child is not an actor to the vicissitudes to his own growth trends, but a reactor. However, Greenspan is correct in asking which stimuli elicit "limitations" in child thought. The stimuli that bring about a rejection of thinking are those that are associated with an affective connotation *and* a thought level — *both* of which have implications the child wishes to avoid. It is the symbolic or metaphorical meaning of the advanced thought level that I stress here because so often it is has been ignored.

Consequently, it is the nonlearning youngster's own mental activity that creates but could potentially settle these transitory disputes — intrapsychic activity sometimes put aside by those of us interested in improving the curriculum. For example, while Elkind (1981) noted that the "slow learner is fast to learn that he is slow" (p. 123), a sharp reminder of the perspicacity of the slow learner, he believed many learning problems result from the mismatch between the school's curriculum and the child (Elkind, 1979a, pp. 223–236). Although I agree with Elkind that the school curriculum is all too often "disabled," I also believe that a mismatch exists *within* the child as well. Since the young child is unlikely to criticize the curriculum, from his perspective the important mismatch consists of two opposing tendencies: one that tells him to learn (think) and the other that tells him that learning (thought) is dangerous. Although they did often criticize their teachers, none of the children in the group I studied condemned the curriculum or perceived it as something changeable (although many parents did both). Contrarily, the children often thought it was their "fault" that they did not learn—and, without blaming them, I felt they were right in a certain sense. To the intelligent nonlearning youngster, transitional phases all too often point the way to new knowledge, the implications of which he feels he must avoid. By his avoidance, he reveals constructive activity, even though to the adult it often does not appear to be constructive. Realizing that a young individual can react intelligently to a curriculum that does not match his interests credits him for his ingenuity. As Elkind emphasized, it is the adult's responsibility to revitalize the curriculum to make it appropriate for young people.

REACTIVATING LEARNING

When the children and adolescents I treated were brought for psychotherapy, they were either clearly or dimly aware that they had pushed learning aside. Often it is the youngster, not the parent, who is painfully cognizant that his natural attempts to explore the world and his family relationships are fraught with conflict. More than the parent, the young person senses it "is among the commonplaces of education that we often first cut off the living root and then try to replace its natural functioning by artificial means" in offering "special coaching for his scholastic difficulties" (Miller, 1981, p. 75). Restoring the functions of the "living root"—the youngster's energetic inquiring attitude—is the remedy for a young person who both wants and fears to know. He cannot be helped by a clinician's attention to childish anxieties only. The clinician must attend to what the child or adolescent *wants* to know, because he must use his knowing abilities to find out why he is afraid. Similarly, he cannot be helped by rehearsing situations that elicit his anxieties. Tactics such as those suggested by Bruner (1966), consisting of practice sessions that accustom a child to hearing a loud voice while learning will not restore his curiosity. A learning situation that recreates what the child most fears—a loud voice in response to his cognitive blocking—cannot possibly engender an attitude of inquiry because it requires a calm but intense, undistracted consideration of the problem at hand. The child's inquiry when carefully guided by the professional or parent flourishes in its own way and for its own reasons.

Those parents who brought their children and adolescents to me for therapy represent a self-selected group. Their request for help was a reflection of an optimistic attitude which, unfortunately, often changed to discouragement when a quick solution was not forthcoming. Initially, they thought therapy would help their offspring to become less fearful of failure and allow them to "try harder" and/or "not give up," resulting in school failure transforming into school success. But the young person did not believe I could relieve his distress because he had a better recognition of its source. Because adults hitherto had failed to pinpoint the origin of the disorder, he viewed psychotherapy much the same way he viewed attempts to teach him—distrustfully. The most he could trust of the therapeutic effort would be that it might have a Band-Aid effect: the insult would abate but its cause would be forgotten by the therapist in the same way his parents or teachers ignored the causes for his decision to fail. Even those youngsters who were unaware of their decision in regard to learning perceived all adults the same—they did not understand how a young person feels about school.

Learning in school, or more accurately, acquiring knowledge, has many meanings for those individuals who reject or evade it. Both learning and knowing have a continuously elaborated significance as these young people strive during therapy to understand how they have compromised their learning. When my treatment efforts focus on their reasons for not learning and their subsequent successes in understanding themselves, these normally intelligent "school failures" begin to learn again. As a result, their parents assume that their goal has been reached—psychotherapy has led the youngster to become less fearful of failure, to try harder, and thereby to reaffirm his learning experiences. But the young person has a different realization. He has discovered what blocked his learning in the first place, namely, his own rejection of knowledge. He uses his intelligence to detect why he found school distasteful, learning dangerous, and teachers untrustworthy. Encouraged in his attempts to explore his reasons for not learning and feeling successful as a result of his discoveries, he is now activated to learn in school as well.

CHAPTER 2

Perceptions and Realities

THE TEACHER'S VIEW

Teachers are often puzzled by the normally intelligent child who is free from specific disabilities and yet does not learn in school. As a result, they seek expert advice about these intelligent nonlearning youngsters. Thus, many of those (41 out of 60) who came to see me about their learning difficulties had been referred by their teachers for psycholinguistic screening; screening for auditory, visual, or memory skills; neurological examination; perceptual-motor screening; or projective testing. Thirty-three of the 60 children were given intelligence tests (see data in the Appendix, p. 314). Depending on the nature of the symptoms that accompanied their nonlearning, some children were screened for more than one disability. Because their teachers were often understandably uncertain about which impairment might be implicated in the child's nonlearning, they often recommended more than one test to ensure that no disability would be overlooked (see pp. 315–316). One child was given 10 screening tests; another was given 14! More children were screened proportionally in the early grades (kindergarten, first, and second) than in the higher grades (third through seventh)—61% compared to 39%. This finding suggests that teachers see one of their roles as prevention—specifically, to catch learning disabilities early in order to provide proper remediation. However laudable the teacher's intention to identify learning disabilities, it often had the unfortunate consequence of creating a disability expectation in the child and in the parents. The fact that projective testing was administered only in conjunction with screening for organicity adds to my supposition that these children were perceived as deficient.

The initial screening and test interpretations were carried out by medical or psychological diagnosticians other than me. Prior to screening, these children were generally thought to have dyslexia, mild neurological deficits or dysfunctions. The examination results were negative for the children who were screened except for two where the diagnostic results were equivocal. Their pediatricians said that the children showed "some soft neurological signs." Both these children had additional screening that revealed one child to be normal in perceptual-motor skills (Bender Visual-Motor Gestalt Test) and one to be average in reading and writing (Wide Range Achievement Test). The second child's WISC-R IQ was 123. (See listing of screening tests and Table C–1 in the Appendix, pp. 315–316. These data summarize the perceived etiology of the children's learning problems at the time they were referred for psychotherapy.)

One could argue that my group of nonlearning youngsters without specific deficits is insignificant compared to the number of children with specific deficits. I would point out that the 60 children comprised 80% of the nonlearners in my practice over a period of 12 years, including those with true learning disabilities. This is a significant proportion especially since disabled children are often referred for psychotherapy because of psychological symptoms associated with a disability.[1]

Subsequent to screening, these nonlearning youngsters who were free of specific deficits were referred to me for psychotherapy by their teachers or other professionals to relieve the child's or adolescent's distress at being a school failure. Communication with the teacher prior to the youngster's first visit with me revealed that many teachers had assessed intelligence correctly. Sometimes they were aware that one particular disability—dyslexia—is often accompanied by normal or high intelligence and thus they perceived the child as intelligent but disabled. When the screening results were negative, most teachers threw up their hands in frustration, believing their only recourse was to raise the child's self-esteem which, they reasoned, might have a positive impact on school learning or, if they still believed he was disabled, might help the alleged incapable child combat his disabilities. They were not led to conjecture that the child's or adolescent's nonlearning was in some sense a deliberate rejection of school because of the popular view that nonlearning occurs exclusively as the result of an organic or neurological impairment.

Nineteen children in the group I treated were not screened for minimal neurological dysfunction, psycholinguistic, auditory, visual, memory, or perceptual-motor disabilities. Seven of these children were believed by their teachers to have organic or neurological impairments, but they were not screened because their parents refused the suggestion. (Some parents declined to give a reason for refusing screening; others said it was too expensive.) Only 12 children were believed to be free of physiological impairments.

In addition to talking with teachers about the screening results, I asked each teacher if she had any opinions other than those already discussed about the cause of the child's nonlearning. The most common reasons given for nonlearning were hyperactivity, infantilism, and lack of ("borderline") intelligence. Others were: unhappiness in school, family problems, and elective mutism.

[1]The children with whom I worked who had specific disabilities suffered one or more of the following: congenital disease, brain damage, hearing loss, dyslexia, impaired vision, and organic speech defects. These disabled children were often afraid of learning because they experienced school failure. Although their fear of learning did not originally spring from ambivalence about knowing, quite a few of them at some point in their development began to fear learning about their disabilities and to avoid understanding their implications for future development.

Frequently, the teacher noticed a child's poor attention span which she attributed to hyperactivity or to "distractibility"—that is, daydreaming. Often hyperactivity was confused by the teacher with distractibility which led her to entertain the highly unlikely hypothesis that daydreaming could result from hyperkinesis. By citing infantile behavior, the teacher usually meant she felt that the child hung onto immature behaviors with the intention of refusing to grow up. Seven of the 10 children deemed not intelligent were viewed as mentally retarded. All but one of these children were given intelligence tests which showed them to be average in intelligence, but the teachers either did not know that the children had been tested or had forgotten this—and one teacher misrepresented the results of the intelligence test as "tester error." Understandably, teachers are confused by the plethora of diagnoses applied to young people who are not learning.

My reason for talking with teachers was to understand the attitudes of the important adults in the child's life, and how these attitudes might have contributed to the child's view of learning. I asked them to explain how hyperactivity, infantilism, or low intelligence affected the child's attitude toward school learning and school performance. Only when the teacher saw the child as infantile did she believe the child *chose* to behave in a way that influenced her performance in school. Yet by saying a child "refused to grow up," the teacher implied that exercising one's will in rejecting learning was not one of many options but an unsolvable problem. Hyperactivity, in the teacher's view, was *always* associated with minimal neurological dysfunction, and unintelligent behavior with native endowment. Other causes, such as unhappiness in school, family problems, and a few cases of elective mutism, were all attributed either to dyslexia or to neurological dysfunction as the prior link in the causal chain. No teacher with whom I spoke contemplated the possibility that, without implicating dyslexia or neurological dysfunction, unhappiness, family problems, or elective mutism might interfere with learning.

LABELING HAZARDS

Despite the screening results, these children continued to be thought of by their teachers as disabled learners in many situations and thus continued to be labeled *disabled* implicitly. Even though they trusted the diagnosticians and referred children to them for that reason, some teachers still perceived disabilities because of the children's variable school performance. Other teachers felt that the child's uneven performance resulted from low self-esteem that could be remedied only by an expert and not by the child. Even those teachers who believed the child suffered from low self-esteem reverted repeatedly to their earlier learning disability hypothesis as the result of the child's unpredictable academic performance. Consequently, parents often felt torn between the expertise and attitudes of the child's teacher and those of the diagnosticians; one expert continued to believe the child was disabled while the other had proved she was not. Because the child often expected that her teacher shared attitudes with her parents, and vice versa, she often sensed or concluded that she was still labeled covertly. The label the child sensed or concluded was applied to her interfered with her normal striving. To quote Bettelheim (1987) on the subject of striving and rivalry in the classroom:

> Teachers...are in many respects experienced subconsciously as stand-ins for parents, and doing better than other children is most desired because winning out over them gains the child parental approval and affection. (p. 244)

Because she feels unable to compete, the labeled child, then, cannot help but conclude that she is unable to gain her parents' or teacher's approval.

Rist and Harrell (1982) made the labeling hazard explicit when they asserted that teachers and parents tend to perceive truth in labels and proceed to act on the truth that the label suggests. In a mischievous way, and particularly when attached covertly to a child and/or to her behavior, labels can pervade adults' reactions semiconsciously and, in turn, influence the ways the labeled children perceive reality. Whether that label is conscious and manifest or semiconscious and implicit, we then see their responses as validating the "truth" contained in the label. Furthermore, Rist and Harrell stress that labeling has a direct impact on children's view of themselves *in school:*

> To be able to detail the dynamics and influences within schools by which some children come to see themselves as *bright and articulate* and *act as if they are,* and to detail how others come to see themselves as *helpless and inarticulate* and *act accordingly,* provides in the final analysis an opportunity to intervene so as to expand the numbers of winners and diminish the numbers of losers. (p. 158, italics added)

Nonetheless, with one important qualification, the individual child benefits when she is properly diagnosed because a sensitive appraisal of her difficulties with learning suggests proper remediation. The important qualification in the use of labels is the necessity for the clinician to monitor their application so that they do not become outdated, distortions of the child's actuality, and impediments to the child's development. That is, even when labels are correct there are hazards because of the connotation of permanence to youngster and adult alike. To say it differently, the literature on the "learning disabled" child has added one more antecedent to the already familiar variables of family dynamics and teacher expectation in the search for causes of a child's nonlearning. Labeling a child or adolescent *disordered* would contain hazards but for the fact that a learning disorder represents the child's or adolescent's *decision* to fail. A decision unlike a label appears mutable. A decision to fail implies that a child previously thought to be helpless and inarticulate can change his or her mind and behave differently.

FAMILY MYTHS: THE PARENT'S VIEW

The parents of children who refuse to learn are concerned with what school failure means and its consequences. They take their child to psychotherapy because they consider his distress at doing poorly or failing in school, which threatens the parents and the child with being held back. The parents hope the therapist can relieve the distress, which, in turn, will allow learning. Rarely do parents comprehend that they are taking the cause for the effect. When a child decides not to learn, it is this decision that causes his failure in school rather than his repeated failure that causes him to decide to give up.

It is true that school failure and the resulting anxiety can lead the child to expect failure in the future. Elkind (1981) called failure expectation "cognitive ineptitude." He pointed out that cognitive ineptitude builds up with repeated poor performance. This expectation of ineptitude is an attitude opposite to that of the normal 7- or 8-year-old who, by virtue of "cognitive conceit," believes he is capable of just about anything (p. 80). If a child repeatedly refuses learning, the self-fulfilling prophecy of ineptitude or "I can't do it" becomes ever more operative. In other words, the more the child refuses to learn, the more he believes he cannot learn.

But, my view differs somewhat from that of Elkind who has stated: "I contend that in many families, early school failure is not a symptom but the *primary cause* of emotional disturbance in the child and of familial disharmony" (1979a, p. 232). In my opinion, the suspicion or detection of a disability often does lead to emotional disturbance and familial disharmony. It is more difficult to pinpoint a primary cause in the child who has no specific deficits which may be one reason family myths are likely to emerge. In all the cases referred to me, unraveling the reasons for the child's decision to fail reveals family constellations and intrapsychic conflicts present well before school starts.

My initial concern was with how the parents had explained to the youngster that he needed psychotherapy, as well as how the parents perceived the learning disorder which, I explained, was different from a disability. In every case during the first or second interview with the parents, they described a family context that might be termed a *family myth*, and in which they saw the youngster's failure to learn related to a family failure or an imagined individual deficiency. For example, on their way to their first psychotherapy appointment, many youngsters were told by their parents, some of whom saw the problem rather differently from the teacher: "Your teacher feels you are not working up to capacity." Unlike the teacher, these parents who mentioned the child's capacity felt that there were family issues that might be related to the child's or adolescent's nonlearning, or that might actually be the cause of it; but they did not believe that family dynamics were the result of the youngster's constitutional flaws. They saw that the young person's innate potentialities were higher than the actual performance, and therefore tended to give this as the reason for seeking professional help. Explaining the first appointment, other parents told the child or adolescent: "Things are not going well in school." When a parent resorted to vague generalities, such as "things are not well," it usually meant that the parents were afraid their youngster was stupid or deficient in some way. These parents tried to protect their children by talking with them in a way that would shield them from the parents' own view that their children were unintelligent or skill deficient.

Family "myths" or belief systems, then, can be roughly divided into two cause–effect sequences. In the case of the parents who saw the youngster as not working up to capacity, they correctly viewed the problems in school as arising from the child's emotional stress which itself was related to family issues. These parents had cooperated with the teacher's request for a psychometric or neurological examination because, as cautious thinkers, they wanted to rule out the possibility of organicity before embarking on a course of action. Typically, they talked with their children about what could be done to improve their performance, which showed they believed something had interfered with a normal or superior potential.

The other group saw a different cause–effect sequence. They felt that the child's emotional symptoms stemmed from his deficiencies or lack of intelligence. Some parents believed their children to be "dumb." Others used terms like *retarded* or *not academic material.* They saw the child's distress as a reaction to having compared himself to other children and observing that he was not up to par. These parents tried to treat the issue benignly by talking in generalities, and by doing so they avoided hurting the child's feelings once again by the use of such protective phrases as "things are not going well." Although this second group of parents often did not focus on family issues, they made comparisons spontaneously between their "dumb" or "retarded" offspring and their "intelligent" or "brilliant" youngsters whenever there were other children in the family.

As relevant as these differences are to an understanding of the family from which the child's learning problems evolved, even more important was the fact that, for both groups, the family myth contained two meaning layers: a manifest meaning and a latent meaning. Reasons for nonlearning held by the parents which they presented to me or were sensed and expected by the child often hid other reasons which the parents were either unaware of or wished to deny. Sometimes, what was later revealed was directly related to the manifest meaning and only needed more specificity to be correctly explained; but in other cases the latent meaning behind the myth exposed the manifest layer as a camouflage for some unstated agenda on the part of one or both parents. The camouflage confused the child and, in turn, retarded intellectual development. Thus, it would appear correct that some parents often prefer "to handle situations with the child by secrecy, deception, distortion of reality or by other similar devices of communication which *discourage the development of cognitive modes of adaptation in the child* [italics added]" —an observation made by investigators studying a group of latency age boys with "learning inhibitions" (Brodie & Winterbottom, 1967, p. 702).

Polly, an 8-year-old girl who had been uninvested in learning for over a year when I first met her, was correctly viewed by her parents as suffering from severe anxiety spells about her parents' separation, which had occurred 2 years earlier. Her decision not to learn was directly related to prolonged periods of daydreaming in school about their eventual reconciliation. Her parents correctly attributed her nonlearning to her preference for daydreaming over school assignments. But this correct assessment of her learning problem concealed other, more important, parent motives.

Polly looked forward to therapy and talked freely about her concerns. Gradually, she became less anxious, which eventually led to renewed efforts at school. Watching his daughter's progress in therapy prompted Polly's father to admit that he had long thought his daughter's problems might call forth a joint parental effort that would heal the marriage. His hidden opinion intended to manipulate Polly into a nonlearning stance so that it would "cause" a parent reconciliation when he and his former wife got together to discuss Polly's symptoms. The other hidden and latent layer of the family myth came from Polly's mother. Her mother's behavior meant to Polly that one simply digs in one's heels when faced with a challenge. Since her mother appeared to act stubbornly about marital conflicts, Polly acted stubbornly in regard to her learning conflicts.

That family myths—the family's explanation of a child's learning problems—have two meaning layers is not surprising. Rarely is the underlying cause for a symptom initially revealed because, if it could be, there would be little reason for the symptom in the first place. Successful treatment allows causes for symptoms to stand out more clearly. When the learning-disordered child gives up old ways of thinking and is able to learn in school, a ripple effect runs through the family. Partially hidden plans or dreams come to light upon reexamination, as in the case of the father who realized that he could not depend on his daughter's nonlearning to keep the family together.

Among parents who attributed emotional distress in their child to cognitive incapacity, the manifest myth was rather straightforward. One parent said: "The kid doesn't have it." Another parent brought her 7-year-old, Rudy, to his first therapy appointment and said in his presence that he was retarded. (She probably said this in his presence because she believed retarded children do not understand such words as *retarded*.) Subsequent psychometric testing proved him to be at least average in intelligence (WISC-R IQ 101), but testing did not dissuade her or his teacher from their initial opinions. His mother's response was to compare Rudy to his older sister, whom she considered brilliant. She made the error in thinking that test results reveal two extremes only—brilliance and retardation. As it turned out, the tenacity of her view that he was actually retarded represented her wish to avoid unearthing family problems. By concentrating on Rudy's alleged innate inadequacies she avoided facing what later surfaced as irreparable marital problems.

Despite test results, Rudy's teacher insisted that he was retarded because of his extreme aversion to learning which he expressed by staring blankly and acting clumsily. He used his normal intelligence to create the charade of stupidity so that he would not have to learn in school. When he later shed the impersonation of mental retardation and only turned his head away from the school assignments when his teacher gave him word to do, she was able to see his deliberate rejection of learning. Rudy's refusal to learn was, I felt, a ruse to distract and protect his parents from ongoing marital difficulties as suggested by the fact that they stayed together as long as Rudy was not learning. His parents divorced when Rudy's 13-year-old sister entered high school one year earlier for her chronological age and Rudy was promoted to the fifth grade. It seemed to me that Rudy's brilliant sister reacted to her parents' difficulties by accelerating her learning so that she might become independent, whereas Rudy delayed his learning to keep the family together. Although Rudy was not as brilliant as his sister, his normal intelligence was more than adequate to create effects which he hoped would influence his parents to stay together and solve their problems. Put another way, today we tend to forget just how intelligent a "normally intelligent" child is because of the current focus on early advanced school learning that requires the child not only to be disability-free but also to be at least above average in intellectual potential.

Another set of parents more sophisticated than Rudy's who understood the educational assessment process steadfastly insisted that neither the aptitude test nor the achievement test results of their 8-year-old son, Kenny, were valid. Tests showed his intelligence to be "superior" (WISC-R IQ 120) and working at third-grade level (Peabody Individual Achievement Test), but his parents questioned the scientific "validity" of the tests that were used. Nevertheless, they declined to have their son tested further. Test results, like other aspects of the child's performance, thus tend to suffer distortions as they are integrated into the family myth. Much later during therapy, as Kenny continued to progress in school and tested at grade level for two consecutive years, his mother told me that she felt herself to be in a "seesaw" struggle with her son. She had always blamed her unhappiness on Kenny's poor school performance, and when he improved, she could no longer avoid facing her own problems. Kenny's improved school performance meant to his mother that he was in the "up" position on the "seesaw," while she was forced by his improvement to assume the "down" position.

Another example of how family myths often enlighten the meaning rejecting learning has for children is the case of Zoe, a 9-year-old girl, described initially as "strange," and soon after as "not nearly as bright as her [older] sister." The underlying meaning of Zoe's family's myth came to light quickly, even though it caused her parents a great deal of anguish. They soon understood that Zoe's need to differentiate herself from her popular, high-achieving and vivacious sister was related to their almost conscious wishes to have had not a daughter but a son as their second child. Zoe believed in the magic of being different from her sister. By not learning, she might somehow transform herself into the opposite sex, which would satisfy her parents' preconscious wishes and lead them to value her as much as they valued her sister.

Part of my therapeutic work consists of the important task of helping parents see how their attitudes and expectations are related to their child's symptoms. That parents generate mythical explanations for their children's nonlearning suggests that, on some level, they are aware that their nonlearning symptoms are exactly that—symptomatic and not the whole of the problem. Certainly, the parent who arrives at the correct supposition that a series of thoughts or feelings leads a child to reject learning reveals the parent's awareness that nonlearning is the end of a long chain of events. Family issues are relevant even when parents believe their child is "dumb" because they compare their children with one another. A "dumb" child is compared to a "smart" child. Such a comparison cannot fail to have an impact and leads the child considered "dumb" to believe he cannot learn, so why try. My intent is to show parents the ways in which family myths are partially correct and the ways in which they are distortions that reflect the parents' own concerns. Most importantly, therapy should pave the way for more productive myths, for a conceptualization of the child that provides him with healthier options, and which does not bind him to a fiction which is either destructive to him, or which has to do with his parents' and not his actuality.

PARENTAL REALITIES

The parents of the 60 youngsters who are the subjects of this book revealed initially or eventually that they had high aspirations for their children as students and for themselves as parents. They often wondered whether they were "good enough" parents (Bettelheim, 1987) and were thus prone to conclude that they were inadequate as the result of the child's learning problems. If they were unable to convince their children to attend school or to concentrate when there, they thought their attempts at parenting were a failure, just as their children often thought they were failures as students. The pressure to be successful or perfect parents led them to react with anger when the child did not perform well in school and to become even angrier when they understood that the child's poor performance was the result of his own decision. Then, the parents felt misused by the child. Parent–child interactions thereupon took on a destructive cyclical character wherein the child once more reinforced his determination not to learn as the result of his parents' angry criticism of his decisions. First, the child wished to avoid "learning" why his parent was angry at him. Second, he confused one decision with another. If a parent became angry because of the child's resolve to avoid learning, the child often concluded it was resolve per se which made his parents angry. Once more in the child's mind a decision to learn became as threatening as a decision not to learn.

One might ask whether the parents were threatened by their children's nonlearning because they themselves had suffered learning difficulties when in school. Of the 60 youngsters I treated, 24 had one or more parents who told me they had experienced learning problems. They had repeated a grade, had special difficulty in one or two subjects, or had dreaded going to school and were anxious while there. But the important correlation is that between the parents' school difficulties and the quality of their relationships to their children. In the 60 families, parent–child relationships were of two varieties: The child or adolescent had either formed a normal or near-normal identification with one or both parents, or the youngster had developed an enmeshed ("symbiotic") attachment to one parent in which the child lacked a normally developed sense of self which was distinct from this parent. In 11 cases of the 24 where a parent had had a childhood learning problem, enmeshed attachments developed between parent and child. But among parents who had no learning problems, only 4 out of 36 had developed enmeshed parent–child attachments (46% versus 11%). It is not clear whether the nonlearning child aggravated an already enmeshed attachment as the parent reacted negatively to the child's symptomatic behavior, perceiving his or her own problems in the child's nonlearning, or whether the child felt it necessary to refuse other relationships, such as with a teacher, or learning itself because it posed a threat to the enmeshed attachment. (I attempt to clarify what school learning and a relationship to a teacher implies for a parent–child "symbiosis" in the case of Lara, which is presented in Chapter 8.)

FAMILY REALITIES

In chapter 1, I described the three distinct types of learning disorders that I encountered: overachievers, underachievers, and school phobics. These three types of nonlearning children and adolescents came predominantly from middle-class families (the parents of 90% of the 60 young people were in professional or skilled craft occupations). In addition, two family characteristics vary among the three groups: (1) parental divorce and separation and (2) the birth order of the symptomatic child. (Social class, parental divorce and separation, and birth order are distributed similarly among the families of the over 40 nonlearning youngsters I have treated since 1985.) By "separation" I mean the parents' firm decision to live apart, maintained as long as I knew the child, but without legal settlement. Of the 60 families, 23 children had divorced or separated parents. Among the overachievers, 2 out of 11 had parents who had separated or divorced contrasted with 16 out of 37 among the underachievers (18% versus 43%). Among the school phobics, 5 out of 12 (42%) had parents who had separated or divorced. It is possible that a youngster is more likely to decide to fail or avoid the school environment in families where there is parental separation or divorce because he misses one of his parent's commitment to him or notices his parents lack of commitment to one another. That is, the child may feel inhibited in making a school commitment or in forming a relationship with a teacher because he perceives ambivalence about relationships in his parents' behavior.

The incidence of parental separation or divorce across nonlearning groups becomes even more interesting in light of the incidence of firstborn or only children in these three groups. Among the 60 children and adolescents, 29 were firstborn or only children in their families. The rate of firstborn or only children was highest in the overachieving group and lowest in the underachieving group: 9 out of 11 and 13 out of 37, respectively (82% versus 35%). The rate of firstborn or only children among the school phobic group was in between (7 out of 12 or 58%). Comparing the overachieving group with the underachievers and the school phobics, it is plausible to say of an overachiever that his eagerness to learn occurs because both parents are present and thus provide models for him as knowledgeable persons at the same time that his status as the firstborn or only child reinforces his strivings to be similar to adults rather than to siblings. In other words, the oldest or only child in an intact family uses learning to consolidate his identification with his parents which is not modulated by the presence of older siblings whose behavior could suggest to the child that he need not reach for adulthood urgently.

Contrarily, the underachievers in my group are more likely to have separated or divorced parents and to be a younger or the youngest child in the family. Two points can be made about the underachievers' family constellations. First, their identifications with both parents are likely to be less stable. They have fewer opportunities to observe the parent who has left the home, and they are often angry at the parent who elected to stay with them because this parent appears unable to maintain the child's relationship with the absent parent. Second, the underachievers, by virtue of being younger or the youngest, often suffer from an invidious comparison with an older achieving sibling—as though the family's belief system dictates that only one child can be intelligent.

Youngsters who are school phobic are likely to have families with characteristics similar to the underachieving group. Since separation and divorce is common in the school phobic group, the youngster might avoid school as the result of his excessive attachment to the parent who continues to take care of him. Being the younger or youngest child with separated or divorced parents might further aggravate his school phobia if the youngster perceives the parent as overly protective of the parent–child relationship at the very moment he attempts to transcend childhood and gain the necessary skills for independence.

THE RED HERRING: THE YOUNGSTER'S VIEW

The first principle to remember when treating a learning disorder is that nonlearning masks either a rejection of some aspect of reality or represents an expression of an intrapsychic conflict in knowing the self. Young people intuitively understand this because they have learning experiences when they are not in school or not surrounded by worried family members and solve problems of their own choosing to their satisfaction. Nonetheless, when they appear for their first psychotherapy visit, they present their version of school troubles in a way that is best termed the *red herring*. They do this to take the therapist off guard, to distract him or her from the underlying reasons for not learning. The nonlearner often believes if he reveals he can learn, he will be faced with his parents' anger at his previous nonlearning; or, if they are separated, he believes his parents will become angry if they realize he is punishing them for their marital difficulties; or, if they are not separated or divorced, he believes they will soon be as the result of his proving competence and independence; or he believes that his teacher will make intensified academic demands perceiving that he is capable and thus seeking to redress his previous poor performance. For these and many other reasons, the youngster desperately wishes to avoid revealing he can learn. His reasons for nonlearning, though often fuzzy but occasionally precise, can be quite different from his parents' view or they may mirror parental judgments.

Although it is important to place the young person's learning disorder within the larger context in which it occurs, especially the family context, I believe my central task is to view a refusal to learn from the youngster's own perspective. Simply to change a family myth as the primary therapeutic strategy will not activate the youngster's learning because of the meanings that learning has for him. To most young people, learning implies increasing autonomy to make a place for oneself in an expanding social and intellectual world. To say outright to him, or to imply through choice of therapeutic methods, that he is simply a pawn upon a family chessboard will neither renew his energies for school learning nor convince him that those energies ought to be applied to growing up. Therapeutic efforts ought to be aimed at the seat of the youngster's decision-making, including childhood concepts and their consequences for his thoughts and feelings. Immature concepts either feed the family's myth or are the result of it. These concepts which the young person typically uses need my attention, which means that family or parent meetings should not substitute for, but must accompany, the youngster's psychotherapy.

RUDY'S RED HERRING

Seven-year-old Rudy was a slender, wiry boy, frequently in motion, who communicated his intent through bodily movements and gestures. In conversation, he was often breathless. His vacant, wide-eyed stare contrasted with the range of his expressive actions. He pretended to be mentally retarded for the first several months of therapy. He pretended not to know the most commonplace facts, such as whether his sister was a girl or a boy, or if the written numerals on the blackboard meant six or nine. At the same time, he made fun of the adult, who, he believed, took his ridiculous statements seriously. He also surmised incorrectly that as his therapist I thought he was mentally retarded. During an early visit, he wrote with a sudden flourish the words *six* and *nine* on the blackboard, and challenged me by asking: "Did you think I couldn't do that?" He showed me how smart he could be in catching the adult in an apparent bind by implying that there could be no correct response. If I took his earlier statements seriously—that he might have reason to be confused about the gender of his sister—but ignored the accuracy with which he wrote the words six and nine, that meant I thought he was "dumb." But, if I passed off what he said as ridiculous, even if I did notice his correct writing, that meant that I, like his parents, was not interested in him or in the meaning of what he did.

Often children whose natural abilities are not confirmed by adults have an uncanny ability to entice them into situations where they can "do no right"—as one parent expressed it. The parents feel they are unable to behave in an effective parental fashion as a result of the child's intricate manipulations. Foremost among Rudy's motives (and among the motives of other children like him), setting traps simultaneously disproved his parents' view that he was stupid and proved that he was in control of them. As much as he wanted to maintain their marriage by refusing to learn, he also wished to test whether they could be effective parents by choosing not to learn or by misbehavior.

Because Rudy imagined consequences for learning which were dangerous and often life-threatening, he became distraught when I told him after six therapy sessions that he might be ambivalent about his normal intelligence. He thought being intelligent meant both parents would leave each other *and* him, and that this situation would threaten his survival. When he understood that I perceived his intellectual potential, he was propelled into an anxiety state which temporarily aggravated his symptomatic behavior both in therapy and at home. The only reason Rudy's parents continued with his therapy during this difficult ten-week phase was the sudden improvement he showed in sports performance—and, consequently, in peer relations—which his parents attributed to the impact of therapy. To Rudy, being competent on the baseball field did not implicate his intellect. So he revealed the positive impact of my statements about his ambivalence toward competence in a realm he felt was unrelated to school learning.

In Rudy's case the red herring was his semblance of stupidity. By inviting me to share his self-definition of incompetence he attempted to gain my collusion in his charade. But, by making fun of my alleged negative opinion of him, he revealed that he was incapable of resisting the temptation to retaliate. Rudy believed, I thought, as did his mother, that he did not know the difference between the numbers six and nine. Because it seemed to him that I insulted him, he revealed his cognitive capability by correctly writing these two words. This was a particularly clever revenge because it demonstrated his awareness of the common confusion young children have with six and nine which, in numerical form, consist of the same figure positioned differently. Once he revealed to me how smart he was, his anxiety increased, because he could no longer cling to the defensive strategy he had erected in order to protect his parents from discovering that their difficulties were not about his being retarded, but about their chronic marital problems. Eventually, these problems led to their divorce.

For quite some time, Rudy had sensed the disturbance in his parents' marriage. He played it out in therapy by having dollhouse mother and father dolls throw plates at supper. When I took the play seriously, he said it was "only a joke." When I told him that even jokes have meaning, he said it was a joke that he came for therapy. Indeed it was a joke that he came for therapy because of being retarded. Yet, on a deeper level, Rudy *created* a joke out of therapy to protect himself and his parents from all of us rightly focusing on his reactions to his parents' marital problems rather than on his suspected mental retardation.

After some 2 years of work, during which Rudy often heard me state how clever he was in setting traps to prove he was in control and intelligent, he gradually recognized that his anger at his parents for failing to repair their marriage was recreated by his failing in school. By failing himself, he subconsciously tried to bring their marital failure to their attention. Hearing from me that his reasons for nonlearning made sense, he did not need to flunk school to take the heat off their problems by distracting them from their longstanding incompatibilities. When he understood the genesis of his school failure and believed in his ability to "find out" or to "make sense," normal developmental trends began to assert themselves, and he began to learn in school.

Why is school nonlearning the chosen symptom of normally intelligent youngsters? To most children, learning means not just "finding out" but also "growing up." That is, the two most common thematic corollaries to scholastic rejection are the youngster's ambivalence about competence and his evasion of the growing-up process. Moreover, he confounds discovery with maturity. Children feel they can neither find out nor grow up if the manifest family myth hides some dangerous latent truth. And, since these young people find much support from their parents' attitudes that seems to hide those truths which are likely to threaten established family patterns, the youngsters fall prey to a symptomatology that subverts understanding. To consummate school failure the young person nonetheless must have developed some academic skills and cognitive strengths. By concealing the truth, his not learning reveals that the issue is one of knowing reality. The underlying pathology is bound up with acquiring knowledge—not just individual learning tasks but the learning act itself—and the results that learning, knowing, and self-understanding represent.

FAMILY AND SCHOOL

To investigate the world, the child must feel moderately independent. Thus, his first encounter with school doubtless recapitulates earlier crises he experienced as he tried at a much earlier age to separate from his parents. I am referring to the individuation process that is critical for self-development as the child struggles to learn who he is and what he can do apart from his parents (Mahler et al., 1975; Pine, 1985; Stern, 1985). Although Mahler et al. stressed the normal enmeshment between parent and infant or toddler, and Stern stressed the infant's (simple) awareness of self as distinct from his parents, all these writers focused on the infant's assertion of self in relationship to an important other person. About this inner struggle, Mahler et al. wrote:

> Here is the conflict: On the one hand is the toddler's feeling of helplessness in his realization of separateness, and on the other hand is his valiant defense of what he cherishes as the emerging autonomy of his body. (p. 222)

They further describe the ambivalence (or "ambitendency") of the infant who is not only merely afraid of strangers but also intensely curious about them. Like the toddler struggling to walk or run, school children struggling to learn experience intensely and defend valiantly what they feel they know. Just like the toddler discovering his world, the school child is ambivalent about strangers and new and seemingly strange situations, including those he encounters in school, where he learns unexpected facts and is given heretofore unknown information. But often his curiosity about these strange situations and what can be learned about the unknown equals or modulates his fears. Often, for the first time, he experiences the discontinuity between home and the world at large. He also begins to experience that he is *able* to know something that his parents do not know. School attendance and learning, similar to locomotion, hold out the promise of increased autonomy because on some level he realizes that his learning allows him to propel himself either toward, away from, or beyond his parents.

The child who has difficulties with learning misperceives the relationship between family and school. Before therapy, he often perceives a *union* of family and school but often not the *distinction* between them. If he were to happily and easily distinguish family from school and himself from his family, he would not be so reluctant to go beyond family members in what he knows. The normal child does just this: he happily and easily risks knowing what family members do not know or have little interest in. He feels it is safe to know what interests *him* irrespective of parental knowledge and/or what his teacher assigns. Because the learning-disordered child feels unsafe differentiating himself from his family or going beyond the family boundaries, he perceives a unity of family and school in order to make school safe. He feels it is perilous to learn in school what is not known by or is unacceptable to family members.

Many parents feel that the school environment, or the world at large, is a dangerous place for their youngsters. So to complicate matters even more, the parents react to their child's school problems as if they are caused either by the school or the child's reaction to the school reality. And because they are often sensitive and conscientious, these parents conclude that they need to make this perilous world safe. In doing so, they project their own anxieties about the unsafe world which clouds from view what might be truly dangerous from the young person's own perspective. When he hears from his parent what is to be avoided in the world, he becomes even more wary than he was before, which aggravates his pathology. The young person senses his parents' belief that the "bad" world ought to be shunned or concludes that he is incapable of adapting to a world which his parents characterize as malevolent. The child's learning symptoms are then reintegrated into the family system. At one moment, he tries to make school similar to home in order to make it safe, and at another moment, he fears school *might* be unsafe *if* it is different from home. Then, the parents bring their youngster to psychotherapy, expecting the therapist to make school and the world secure for both child and parent.

These cause–effect thinking processes explain how "learning problems" evolve for the child and his parent. Both perceive the relationship between what happens in school and the child's reaction but neglect to include in their explanations of the child's symptoms the relationship between what happens within the family and the child's reaction in school. Hence, they fail to locate the real antecedent of the learning problem. Another way of putting it is to say that in perceiving the origin of the child's learning symptoms as the "school's fault," the child and the parent display ego syntonicity regarding nonlearning (Coolidge, 1979): parents and children alike fail to understand that the child's problems at school reflect problems of the family at home.

In my view, the parents' rejection of school and its teachers is at once the result and measure of the school's importance in the child's development and the parents' estimate of the school's power over the child. Although the child often confuses school with home, the parents realize that the school's function for the youngster is distinct from family functions. If school and its different functions were not so important to the parent, he would have little reason to fear it. The potential importance these parents place on school is also the very reason they feel school will alienate their youngster from the family. The child or adolescent, who is sensitive to his parents' wishes and anxieties, thereupon refuses to go to school or to learn when there. He ascertains from parental anxiety that school is indeed different from home. Unfortunately, as the children watch and/or sense their parents' anxiety and frustration, they conclude: "Something must be wrong with me because it's so hard to take care of me."

When these 60 young people I treated first came to therapy, the conflict between them and their parents was apparent in their respective exaggerated behaviors. The child or adolescent would often explain that his anxiety resulted from his parents' worry that he would not succeed in school and therefore he was afraid to try. Or he explained that the teachers were incompetent so why should he listen to them. At one moment, parents would characterize the school as dangerous and claim the next moment to be disappointed that their child or adolescent refused to learn or to attend school. Sometimes the parents had engaged in more extensive maneuvers, such as transferring the youngster from school to school. Then he thought his parents expected other schoolchildren to somehow destroy him or negatively modify his learning capability. To professionals—teachers, school counselors, or clinicians—these young people appeared disabled or phobic. More precisely, the young person found his personal safety threatened by a complicated and shared nexus of school myths. As a consequence, parent and youngster preferred to maintain their agreement that school learning was dangerous and home was safe.

But when psychotherapy began to have an impact on these young people, their high-achieving goals were generally renewed. As the child or adolescent began to learn once more in school or began to attend school, he reexperienced that very sense of vulnerability that learning and going to school had originally stimulated in him. He again felt that he must learn in school and be strong or competent to prove his parents were perfect. Even when life in the classroom became difficult, he felt that he must be the consummate child whether or not his parents provided support and comfort during unstable times. Until parents *and* youngster understood the vulnerability they experienced regarding school, the rejection of and the phobic attitude toward school continued. Confronted with the double demand of meeting parent needs and school expectations, the youngster in therapy often continued to blame the school for its legitimate pedagogic requests. To him, the expectation to learn appeared unreasonable because he felt he must first meet his parents' needs, which depleted his energy and often confused him.

SCHOOL PROBLEMS AND SPECIAL GIFTS

Each of these 60 children and adolescents excelled in at least one school subject. Thirty-three revealed *giftedness* in one subject and 10 of these were *gifted* in more than one subject. Ten were gifted in art, 7 in math, 6 in sports, and 5 in building (shop, crafts, etc.). Other areas of giftedness were reading, story-writing, music, drama, dance, and biology. Many schoolchildren whom I treat but who fight learning are not especially talented linguistically or mathematically but *are* talented in those humanistic or scientific subjects less frequently acknowledged in children by adults. Unfortunately, they are not *perceived* this way. Because the primary focus of teachers and parents is often on the academic weaknesses, children often conclude that they are not gifted, or if they are talented, their special talents are of no particular importance. These conclusions are strengthened by the selective perceptions and disability expectations of teachers and parents who tend to discount cognitive strengths. In addition to what learning, thinking, and knowing may personally mean to a gifted or intelligent child, he finds another reason not to learn in the conspicuous absence of appreciation of his creative efforts at school.

It might be that the parents of gifted but nonlearning young people are more likely than other parents to bring them to psychotherapy because of some intuitive understanding that their children are gifted. The fact that none of these parents spontaneously articulated to me that there was a discrepancy between the youngster's high achievement in one subject and his failure in one or many others suggests that parents found this gap difficult to consider. They may have found it implausible that a gifted youngster would inhibit intellectual expression—a conundrum they nonetheless hoped I would clarify. Since these youngsters were not tested for creativity, their propensity to engage in creative thought could only be estimated by how they behaved with me and what they produced at home and in school.

Evidence for an individual's giftedness consisted of (1) winning the first prize in school art contests, or, in one case, having an original cartoon printed in the local newspaper; (2) getting the top math grade in class or winning math competitions; (3) being chosen captain of their sports teams, or receiving sports awards; (4) teaching themselves to read before first grade, being in the highest reading group and reading literally hundreds of books during the summer months, including advanced literature and science, as exemplified by a first-grader who read *Science* magazine; (5) having her story published in the school newspaper in first grade; (6) being chosen for the lead in plays and receiving awards for acting ability; (7) winning music scholarships; (8) being chosen to represent the school at a local science fair; and (9) being chosen as participants in crafts or shop exhibits.

When I remarked to teachers and parents that these youngsters had shown special competence in one or more subjects, teachers and parents often concluded that the gift or special area of intelligence had little importance. Teachers concentrated on basic skill learning and were less interested in creative expression. Similarly, the parents of those children gifted in art believed the talent was useless because it did not help students get admitted to college. They believed the only evidence for ability worth paying attention to emerged from the child's *problems* with learning—not from the child's *successes* in learning. Even those teachers of and parents with children who were gifted at math or sports were originally skeptical that their skills reflected intelligence or competence. Despite the well-known salience of both math and sports skills for college entrance, they could only attend to the children's academic weaknesses. In many cases, what teachers and parents had read or heard about learning disabilities by way of PTA meetings, in-service teacher training, parenting workshops, childrearing paperbacks, newspaper and Sunday supplement articles had so impressed them that they tended to equate any academic weakness with a learning disability. And who could blame them, since educators and other experts have made and still do make exactly the same error?

THE YOUNG PERSON'S EXPRESSION OF TALENT

The individual's reactions to his or her special talents varied. Some shrugged off giftedness as unimportant, others were shy, some were secretive. Sooner or later in therapy they all revealed that they were aware of and enjoyed their special gifts. For example, the math whizzes often expressed inner conflicts by setting up intricate math problems whereby they enjoyed working out their solutions. Nine-year-old Timothy, whose case narrative is presented in Chapter 4, refused to read but loved math which he revealed by doing "magic tricks" on the calculator in my office. One day he punched in an addition problem, only to follow it up with a subtraction problem, such as four plus four minus four. Or, he punched in a multiplication problem, only to follow it up with a division problem, such as four times four divided by four. Whatever was added, subtracted, multiplied, or divided never touched the original value.

His two parents were divorced when Tim was 6 years old and were represented by the paired-opposite operations: it was addition versus subtraction, or multiplication versus division because he felt it was a case of his father against his mother. The original value (in this case, the number four) represented himself which never changed. Commenting on his own behavior, Tim said: "If you do the opposite you always get the same; I like negating what I've just done." He felt protected if he kept himself the same number consistently because this maintained his identity in the face of his opposing parents. His use of the verb "negate" revealed a well-developed vocabulary when he chose to use it, and he chose to demonstrate language competence when he felt sure of his mathematical competence. He was able to display his math ability at the same time he articulated his understanding that he might pair opposites in math because he felt he was surrounded by opposites in life.

The young artists all went through a phase of expressing their conflicts through drawings and paintings. Ten-year-old Lara (whose development in therapy is described in Chapter 8) depicted herself in uncertain, wavy gray lines to symbolize the bored anxiety she felt at home; but when she finally resolved to attend school, she painted herself and her school friend in bold strokes of orange and red. Fifteen-year-old Aaron drew exquisitely during therapy while he barely passed his freshman courses in high school. Aaron was afraid to challenge his teachers or his father with his intellectual potential (his WISC-R IQ was 150). He found that line drawings of frowning and armed attackers got across his challenge more safely than conversation. Conversation would have specified to adults just how much he wished and feared to overtake them and consequently might have aroused envy or ridicule. Instead his beautiful Renaissance-style drawings only evoked astonished awe.

Five-year-old Gale, who taught himself to read in kindergarten, often read *Winnie the Pooh* stories in my office to show me what he himself was anxious about. He thought, like Eeyore, that no one would bring him a present for his birthday. Gale's mother believed he was learning disabled because he could—or *would*—not sit still in first grade while the other children laboriously worked their way through primers he had mastered a year ago. Fortunately, his mother eventually realized his resistance did not represent a deficit but rather a frustrated language gift.

Another language-gifted child, Faye, taught herself to read, completing some 200 books over the summer before first grade. Her mother refused to accept the fact that her child's reading was evidence of her intelligence because of Faye's immature handwriting. When that improved, Faye's mother centered on another deficiency as though ferreting out every last potential deficiency would guarantee her child's success in school. What all this represented was her mother's anxiety that Faye was not "strong enough" to handle the normal stresses occurring in daily life, most especially school-related stresses. Because of the insecurities Faye's mother experienced during first grade, she believed her daughter could not meet the same demands of the school curriculum.

Young people who excelled at sports also found ways to demonstrate their skills. Thirteen-year-old Valerie often began her therapy session by bounding up the stairs to my office two steps at a time with the flair of an athlete. She later expressed her conflict about learning and growing up by quizzing me on the sports skills I possessed when I was her age. I felt she was inquiring whether it was safe for her to be as skilled or more skilled than her therapist and, therefore, whether it was safe to learn in general.

Marla, who was eight years, was gifted in drama and extraordinarily adept at projecting different personality traits in dramatic scenes. She was determined to excel in school after two years of lackluster achievement. Her favorite use of therapy was to enact family conflicts through the medium of well-known fairy tales, especially *Snow White*. She was such a skillful actress that I found it difficult to keep a straight face and attend to the seriousness of her learning disorder, which had sprung from Oedipal conflicts humorously enacted in front of me as her "audience." As "audience" I was expected to respond sensitively and knowledgeably to her renditions of Snow White in which Marla said, "Snow White is just *smarter*—not *prettier*—than the Queen." To feel comfortable with a sterling school performance, she felt she must "trade in" her very real 8-year-old beauty by reversing the central theme of the Snow White story. She pretended that the Queen became more beautiful as Snow White became smarter. This represented Marla's admiration of her mother's adult competence and her wish to exchange one of her own characteristics—her beauty—for her mother's imagined genius. Only in this way could Marla accept her hitherto submerged aspiration to be an excellent student.

During the course of therapy, I often used the young person's giftedness or areas of intellectual excellence to motivate him or her to consider that he or she had a disorder and not a disability. At strategic moments, I would say something like: "If you are smart enough to win a math (or art, shop, or story-writing) contest, you are smart enough to read;" or, "If you are smart enough to read all those difficult books, you are smart enough to understand math (or science, history, or biology)." Again, their reactions varied, depending on how secretive they were about their intelligence, and how much they needed to keep from their families, teachers, or themselves that their nonlearning reflected their own decision. Some youngsters smirked and asked how I knew they were capable. Others acted as though they had not heard, but in subsequent weeks began to learn or even flourish in those particular subject areas which before had been problematic. The ways in which nonlearning children and adolescents responded to my attempts to respect their compromises with learning and to validate their subtle attitude shifts toward knowing are the subjects of the chapters that follow the next chapter, which establishes the importance for the clinician of the young person's intellectual development.

CHAPTER 3

The Importance of Conceptual Development

The normal child's approach to learning is influenced by two developmental trends: an evolving conceptualization of reality and an ever-changing intrapsychic actuality. First, the child initiates school learning with some stabilized concepts as the result of his previous exploration of reality. These concepts influence how he will perceive the teacher's behavior and the curriculum. Then, the results of his natural experimentation and his school learning affect his subsequent conceptualizations of reality. Second, his intrapsychic actuality influences the school child by the ways in which he conceives of himself as a learner. "Actuality," unlike objective reality, refers to the interaction of the developing child particularly with his human environment (Erikson, 1962; White, 1963). Of the contrast between actuality and reality, Erikson indicated that "the infant, while weak in our reality, is competent in his actuality" (p. 466) Erikson was referring to the fact that while adults discern the infant's needs, immaturities, and apparent helplessness, the healthy infant affirms his competence when he learns to cue his parents to his needs and experiences gratification. Thus, the young child's actuality is formed by his participation in the world of people in which the quality of reciprocal relating shifts as his developing needs change.

The school-aged child, too, deals in a competent yet evolving manner with those other people he expects to meet his needs around the learning situation—parents, teachers, and peers. In these interactions, he compares himself to others while reflecting on his special qualities and the individual qualities of others to build a sense of self. For example, he perceives that he is "intelligent" or "stupid," or "good at math like Dad and poor at reading," or "good at reading like Mom and poor at math." Personal experiences in school reinforce or weaken these self-judgments. Most important, the relationship *between* the child's conception of reality and his intrapsychic actuality contributes to his attitude toward learning. Important discovery of reality's features—whether it occurs in school or not—validates the youngster's self-esteem and sensitizes him to his individuality. Likewise, a confident, self-aware individual is more

71

likely than an insecure, impulsive individual to investigate and master reality in general and academics in particular.[1]

LEARNING AND AUTONOMY

In my opinion, youngsters who reject learning were, at younger ages, similar to normal children who often approach learning eagerly. When the child decides to reject some specific fact or acquired skill, he begins to engage in a two-step process which becomes habitual. He accurately apprehends some aspects of reality only to reject his own understanding. In effect, he learns how not to learn. And, when he rejects his own understanding, he fights that part of his personality which earlier had valued discovery. This is frequently observed in the youngster's conviction that because he chooses not to learn, he has become incapable of learning. The belief that he is incapable of learning inhibits further exploratory behavior which, in turn, limits the youngster's opportunity to affirm what he understands as a unique individual.

My view diverges significantly from the premise that learning problems are caused by the unacceptable affective connotations of subject matter blocking intellectual functions. Common in the psychological literature before psychologists developed skills in locating specific disabilities, this premise asserts that learning is inhibited when the child's impulses interfere with his attention to reality and/or distort significant details (Bruner, 1966; Klein, 1964; Newman et al., 1973; Pearson, 1954; Vereecken, 1965). A view that stresses only the necessity to gratify drive states underestimates the child's natural and often intense impulse to comprehend reality. And, when the clinician sets about to reactivate learning, the hypothesis that the youngster is overrun by instinctual drives leads the clinician to expect the child to be passive in regard to learning—not autonomous. Klein's (1964) view is extreme in denying the child's autonomy. She reasons that because school learning is "*libidinally* determined for everyone, since by its demands school compels a child to sublimate his libidinal instinctual energies," learning new and various subjects or the learning act itself will be inhibited by the fear of castration (p. 68). She neglects the child's impulse to know per se and focuses only on the threat a libidinal breakthrough poses for the unsuspecting child. Anna Freud (1971) offered a more productive view about the aims of child analysis when she argued that they ought to be

> in line with the known ones, i.e. to include the undoing of repressions, regressions, and inadequate conflict solutions; to increase the sphere of ego control; and, added to this, as an aim exclusive to child analysis; *to free developmental*

[1]Apart from the words we choose to designate each "world," the importance of making a distinction between "reality" and "actuality" lies in clarifying the difference between an assumed phenomenal true world and an actively experienced world. The actively experienced world in which we participate changes over the course of the life span, a process Erikson (1962, 1964) referred to as "developmental actuality." When I refer to "intrapsychic actuality," I mean to include interpersonal actualities because I believe our psychic individuality derives, in large part, from social interactions.

forces from inhibitions and restrictions and enable them once more to play their part in the child's further growth. (p. 214, italics added)

Perhaps her experience as a teacher before she became a child analyst made her sensitive to the child's "intellectual needs" and prompted her to remind clinicians that the young person's "intelligence grows naturally, as his body grows" (A. Freud, 1968, p. 429). White (1963) went even further in locating the child's autonomy when he forcefully reminded clinicians that

it is the child who strengthens his ego, actively exploring and testing a world in which, by happy design, a child's initiative and intentions are often enough efficacious. (p. 94)

Two important ways in which the youngster can strengthen his ego—whether against instinctual drives or not—is by testing his conceptions of reality and comparing them to those of important other people.

In their attempts to diagnose learning disorders, clinicians must not be tempted to focus on *the* predominant sphere of the psyche—intellective or affective. We must be attentive to the ways in which cognition interacts with emotions and attempt to unite each sphere's particular impact on the child's development in our conception of the origin of learning disorders and their remediation. In a paper that discusses the relevance of Piagetian psychology for clinicians, Anthony (1954) brought forward the union of the two distinct spheres of the psyche when he discussed about symptoms:

in every thinking disturbance, how much is the feeling at fault; and in every feeling disturbance, what has gone wrong with the thinking? and at what stage of the thinking process? (p. 34)

His view gives a sense of the individual's complexity as a person who acts rather than a person who is acted upon. Anthony's questions to clinicians appear to have had little impact on those who treat the child who decides not to learn. The premise that the young person is not using his mind when he refuses to learn illustrates a reluctance to apply Piaget's theory to the atypical learner and to the "science of education." Learning mistakes are potentially educative—even an outright rejection or evasion of the learning act. It is ludicrous to deny the normal cognizing function required by "learning not to learn." Cognizing is required to block a cognitive function.

Thought expansion can and ought to be introduced into the youngster's psychotherapy in a healing way—so that the therapist and the young person shape a mutual, articulated perspective which helps him understand his symptoms more thoroughly. Dewey (1956, 1963) proposed that the curriculum should begin with the child's interests and, just as important, with the ways in which he understands his personal experience. It is a sine qua non of psychoanalytic psychotherapy for the therapist to begin with the patient's own concerns. Like Dewey, the therapist readily admits the continuity between past and present experiences. Although Dewey's prescriptions are not generally welcomed by today's educators or perceived as applicable to the modern classroom, some are easily integrated into a psychotherapeutic intervention which starts where the youngster is with the aim of expanding intellectual functioning. Starting where the individual is means recognizing which of his experiences are conducive to growth. In other words, the youngster learns school subjects meaningfully only when what is given by the curriculum is transformed by what he experiences internally. Likewise, the individual in psychotherapy alleviates his symptoms when he transforms his restricted or distorted conceptions of "objective" reality to include newly apprehended reality features and corrects false inferences.

REALITY CONCEPTIONS AND SELF-DEVELOPMENT

It is important for the clinician of nonlearning youngsters to recognize that their conceptions of reality contribute to their resistance to learning. Conceptions of reality are formed quite early in the child's life. Piaget (1952) showed that even in infancy the child is occupied with understanding reality in that he creates effects in his environment which he reproduces repeatedly. His activity promotes intellectual development and, later in childhood, enhances a self-reflective sense when he tries to integrate the results of his activity with either stable or emerging cognitive structures. Piaget (1971) stated that an individual's ability to discover and predict influences his developing self-awareness because

> a child's spontaneous grasp of the physical world will enable [him] to succeed in predicting phenomena long before [he] can explain them...but the correct explanation consists in achieving a progressive conscious awareness of the *motives* [italics added] that guided the prediction. (p. 162)

Piaget's focus on motives brings the clinician to familiar territory. To the usual *preconscious* motives therapists investigate, I would add to their therapeutic agenda the individual's *conscious* motives for discovering and predicting. *These motives for discovering and predicting and the intellectual modes the child or adolescent uses constitute the point of origin for his blocking the learning process.* I am thus asserting that a young person's continuing learning inhibitions are informed by his particular learning experience and his reflections in therapy on the implications of what he does or does not know.

Stern (1985), too, linked self-development to the infant's earliest apprehensions of (social) reality. From infant studies he postulated an early emerging sense of self attuned to the parent in ways that reflect the infant's accurate, if restricted, grasp of reality. He asserted that the infant's social perspective suffers little distortion by virtue of the pleasure principle; instead, distortion originates in the child's developing cognitive capacities. That is, the infant's early experience reflects the impact of real, not fantasied, events. This conception of the infant's experience is consistent with Piaget's studies of infant intelligence in that the infants he observed appraised real events occurring as they created effects with inanimate objects. Distortions in the reality–apprehension process occur when the individual begins to reflect on real events—when he begins to think about what he has learned about people and things. Because of normal cognitive immaturity, he is unable to find his way out of the morass of thought connections he has built up to deal with his observations. Stern has captured the paradox that more sophisticated cognitive functioning represents for the individual when he proposed that

> from a normative and prospective vantage, the infant experiences only interpersonal realities, not deficits (which cannot be experienced until much later in life) and not conflict resolving distortions. It is the actual shape of interpersonal reality, specified by the interpersonal invariants that really exist, that helps determine the developmental course. Coping operations occur as reality-based adaptations. Defensive operations of the type that distort reality occur only after symbolic thinking is available. (p. 255)

The paradox that Stern boldly confronts surrounds the apparent contradiction in the notion that a simpler mind can "read" reality without distortion, whereas a more complex mind fabricates distortions. Normal children create distortions as way stations to understanding. The nonlearner has taken this normal process and used it to prevent understanding and to foster still additional distortions because knowing certain aspects of reality threatens him. It is precisely the point at which the child knows what he knows—and knows he is capable of understanding—that he can deliberately distort where before he unself-consciously transformed reality as the result of his attempts to represent and master it. His deliberate reality distortions in order to avoid the consequences of learning have significant sequelae for his self-development and his self-image.

REALITY CONCEPTIONS AND INTRAPSYCHIC ACTUALITY

Although the child's intellectual development is central to the clinician's understanding of the child's learning problem, his use of concepts and his relationship to reality must be placed in a larger context that includes the internal adaptations which constitute his intrapsychic experience. Some psychoanalytic theorists attempt to coordinate Piaget's studies of the child's developing relationship to reality with affective development (Greenspan, 1979; White, 1963). White's proposal that "adaptive activity appears to go under its own power" rather than under the power of instinctual drives makes his "effectance" theory compatible with Piaget's theory of intelligence as adaptation. Like Piaget, whom he quotes extensively, White stressed action as *the* requirement for spontaneous learning. And, not all learning takes place in the service of instinctual needs:

> The search for drive satisfactions will confer a considerable knowledge about the environment. But there is bound to be a certain narrowness in the curriculum devised by instincts. The push toward instinctual aims and objects means a restriction of what will be learned. Objects will be examined to see whether they are edible, breakable, or erotically gratifying, but not in the spirit of finding out everything that can be done with them. An organism equipped with effectance as well as instinctual energies will get itself a far more liberal education. (pp. 36–37)

Although White conceives of effectance as energizing intelligent interactions with reality, he awards a very different role to it as compared to impulse.

As Piaget has shown, structures evolve from "reality testing." Even though they may change and develop, structures derive from a previous stable configuration. So structure acquisition, the consequence of the individual's participation in reality, connotes continuity while instinctual energy is intermittent. Thus, the clinician of children who have learning problems is faced not just with a probable high energy level that inhibits learning (such as anxiety, panic states, angry defiance, etc.) but also with well-entrenched structures and concepts that either inhibit or prohibit learning. If knowledge develops for its own sake, the clinician must focus on why certain children reject knowledge for its own sake.

White's (1963) work anticipates Greenspan's (1979) attempt to synthesize psychoanalysis and Piagetian developmental psychology. He posits ego structures that have internal and external "boundaries" and further purports that the theoretical integration of psychoanalysis and cognitive psychology can be accomplished by considering that the same psychological processes operate at both boundaries (p. 133). That is, the intellectual edifice constructed by the child which Piaget describes, and which varies with developmental stage, operates at *both* the external reality-oriented boundary *and* the internal impulse-laden boundary. I take Greenspan's theory a step further in my account of Timothy (Chapter 4) when I assert that the two-boundary conceptualization of ego development provides a better hypothesis to explain learning difficulties than that espoused in much of the psychoanalytic literature which has it that learning inhibitions derive from the pressure of instinctual drives and/or the inhibition of instinctual aims.

USEFUL PIAGETIAN CONCEPTS FOR THE CLINICIAN

The several key concepts drawn from Piaget's theory, which guide my work with children and adolescents, illuminate my observations of them and assist me in devising interventions that speak to both the intellective and the affective spheres of the psyche. Three of these concepts—assimilation, transition, and variation—are all related to Piaget's thesis that a child does not, indeed cannot, learn unless he fits new material into an already accepted, familiar, and well-developed conceptual system. That is, the child naturally learns in the fashion Dewey described as appropriate teaching technique. Two additional concepts, egocentrism and decentering, are relevant to self-development and the symptoms that occur when self-concepts remain immature.

Assimilation

By the term *assimilation* Piaget means the individual's tendency to transform what he finds in the environment to fit an already existing system. Flavell (1963) has described it well:

The process of changing elements in the milieu in such a way that they can be incorporated into the structure of the organism is called *assimilation,* i.e., the elements are assimilated to the system. (p. 45)

Accommodation, the counterpart to assimilation, refers to the individual's efforts to adjust to objects in the environment, which means that "the organism must accommodate its functioning to the specific contours of the object it is trying to assimilate" (Flavell, 1963, p. 45). When the therapist begins working with a nonlearner, he or she must be attentive to what Piaget (1952, 1954; Flavell, 1963) calls "reproductive assimilation": the need to repeat certain action patterns or the "need to function" (Wolff, 1976, p. 177). Piaget and others use the terms *reproductive assimilation* and *schemes* primarily to describe infant development. Nonetheless, assimilation and accommodation are concepts that cognitivists use to understand the development of older children as they enlarge and refine their cognitive systems. With the repeated application of existing schemes, the probability of encountering new objects, problems, and perspectives increases because of the unexpected results that derive from repetition (Flavell, 1963, p. 55). Sometimes a surprise dislodges the child from an immature thinking mode. For example, 7-year-old Matt, who was particularly prone to "trick" or "surprise" others with impish delight, was believed by his teacher and his mother to have "spelling dyslexia." For almost a year, he used the typewriter in my office and never misspelled a word. The unexpected result for him, an individual who had repeatedly surprised others, was his recognition that he spelled correctly in one instance but misspelled consistently while writing homework papers or on spelling tests. This unexpected discrepancy in spelling performance led him to exclaim: "When I'm typing, the machine does it. When I write, I *have* to spell backwards!"

This boy, the oldest of three children, felt that to write forward meant to grow or move in a forward progression. If he progressed or grew up, he feared he would lose his harassed mother's attention. I encouraged Matt's perception of the unexpected by stating that he had many reasons for behaving which varied with the situation: "When typing, you have a good reason for spelling forwards; when writing, you have a good reason for spelling backwards." He then entertained the idea it was *he* who "made the machine work." With a flash he realized: "It's much *harder* to make the typewriter work than a pencil!" The fact that typewriting requires a manual dexterity and a sustained effort to remember the position of the letters impressed upon Matt the fact that he accomplished "hard" tasks better than "easy" tasks. Then he began to understand that spelling was not difficult because it required using a pencil. He could comprehend it was his varying conceptions of spelling that inhibited his learning—his resistance to progressing forward on the page with his own hand which stood for growing up. By way of contrast, the manual typewriter's carriage seemed to move "backward" because it moved from right to left as words were typed. Moreover, since "the machine does it," Matt did not have to claim spelling competence. But now he had assimilated more completely two actions to each other: the meanings of handwriting and of typewriting. Thereupon he could create a more comprehensive perspective which stimulated self-insight to help him stop reversing letters or letter sequences on homework assignments and spelling tests.

The unexpected has a similar impact on other nonlearning youngsters. As they begin to understand that their school learning *means* something to them, they are repeatedly surprised by the realization that schoolwork *has* symbolic meaning. Alternatively, they sometimes surprise themselves by discovering how much they *do* know. Thereafter they become motivated to try to conceptualize differently and more maturely.

Transition

By aptly characterizing Piaget's style with the remark "In Piaget's world, nothing was ready-made, everything grew" (p. 265), Anthony (1957) humorously emphasized the view that transition phases loom large in the child's intellectual development. Anthony, too, finds Piaget's work useful for the clinician despite certain differences in orientation between Freud and psychoanalysis on the one hand, and the cognivitists on the other. For Freud, who concentrated on adults, a child's symptoms were likened to those generated by the mind of the neurotic adult. But, since the child's intellect is significantly different from the adult's, it is misleading to liken a child's symptoms in using his intellect to an adult's. Moreover, to ignore that a symptomatic child may be in a cognitive transition phase is tantamount to ignoring possible therapeutic interventions.

Transition in development occurs when the fit between the child's cognitive structures and reality is workable in some important specific respects while wanting in certain other salient respects. These structures, which are organized differently by children of different ages and stages, fluctuate and stabilize throughout childhood and adolescence, for no sooner does a child or adolescent arrive at a plateau when the stage is set for another change. Transition phases can be relatively brief or arduously long, and are often problematic for learning-disordered children who tend to get waylaid as they move from one stage or period to the next.

Transitional moments often occur during the therapeutic hour just as they occur elsewhere in life. Whenever therapy has a positive impact, the child will come across bits of new data during the clinical interview or within the therapeutic interaction. When this occurs, the therapist must support the patient's ongoing conceptual organization or partial understanding in order for the child to assimilate new information. Then the therapist must help the youngster challenge his present orientation, because his pattern has often been to avoid or reject the new and the ambiguous. Since the new and the ambiguous can only enter the child's conceptual system through his own activity—behavioral and/or mental—the therapist must repeatedly support the youngster's intact cognitive capabilities. The therapist must also assess and tolerate momentary "errors." Only then will the young person stop clinging to an immature perspective because only then can he more fully understand what it consists of and then question it. In response to the therapist's respect for his intact understanding and current cognitive organization, the youngster will often reach for a more refined conceptualization of reality.

Piaget uses the term *equilibrium* to designate the relatively harmonious or "finely tuned" balance of accommodation to the environment and assimilation of it during stable developmental phases (Flavell, 1963, p. 165). Then, the individual does not feel the "perturbations" (Langer, 1969, p. 36) characteristic of the "disequilibrium" of transition phases but instead feels a smoother coordination of self and reality. When the individual experiences disequilibrium — those times when assimilation and accommodation are unbalanced and asynchronous — he tends to push ahead toward the harmony of self and reality. Too, the nonlearning child tries to find release from the often painful states of disequilibrium but equally often he cannot accept what the new equilibrated thought level yields in terms of his expanded relationship to reality. Yet, it is precisely the disequilibrations in the child's behavior which reveal that he has begun to progress in therapy.

Suppose an intelligent child aged 8 or 9 reasons: "Good grades in school mean someone is smart. I don't get good grades in school, therefore, I am not smart." Because such a child perceives the reality that good grades are the result of intelligence, he incorrectly concludes that poor grades are the result of unintelligence. His thinking remains immature regarding the coordination of grades and intelligence. Later he may observe or guess that some intelligent children get poor grades. This observation and/or guess may imply to him that *he* is such a child and thus he is at risk for disequilibrated thought. If being intelligent threatens him, he will resist a "higher degree of equilibrium" (Flavell, 1963, p. 239) because he does not want to understand why he gets poor grades. Then he will reject the thought that good grades and intelligence can be independent. This thought rejection may aggravate or actually lead to a negative self-image. The child will remain insecure as long as he retreats from mastering the disequilibrium that derives from ambiguous and/or hypothetical cause–effect relationships. The therapist's aim for such a child is to help him with those aspects of his thinking that lead to or reinforce emotional conflicts. Needless to say, this assistance must be geared to the child's present cognitive capacities.

In discussing the child's readiness to tolerate the perturbations characteristic or disequilibrium, Langer (1969) observed that

> we need to know in what way the child is able to accommodate to a given type of perturbation...for example, whether the child will passively acquiesce and mimic or actively seek to experiment and prove. (p. 36)

As the child attempts to experiment with and prove new solutions to problems, he is, in a sense, "working through" — that is, he is coordinating dimensions of his experience in a new and presumably liberating and more mature way. When his thought has become equilibrated, he is able to apply a broader conceptual base to daily life and is more open to psychoanalytic insights. The hypothetical child described before just might be able to contemplate that he is *both* intelligent *and* having school difficulties and at the same time understand that the relationship between grades and intelligence is not one of simple correlation. When he is capable of or given support to understand two-variable systems and as he wonders why an intelligent individual would wish to avoid achieving, then he might be able to raise his self-esteem.

Variation

Variation rather than rigidity in behavior is widely accepted by clinicians as a sign of mental health. Happy resolutions are more likely to occur when the child seeks to maximize solutions to problems by trying more than one alternative or by staying with an option long enough to exhaust its possibilities. A healthy response to any problem is a strategy midway between habitual and restricted choices (which may prove to be unworkable) and haphazard choices without thorough exploration of each possibility. Children with learning disorders frequently exhibit one or another of these extremes: they either adhere repeatedly to the same tired and incorrect choice or they jump from one hunch to another without understanding its logical conclusion. Neither is a true variation. That the first is not is self-evident. In the second case, the child does not stay with a hunch long enough to permit working out real alternatives.

The therapist who seeks to introduce variation in the child who dares not think will widen the "probabilistic" (Langer, 1969, p. 24) area of activity so that the unexpected can occur. A normal child, free-wheeling and curious, comes across a wide range of information through natural exploration, where serendipitous discovery is expected and where a state of equilibrium (within stages) becomes successively more probable (Piaget, 1967). Although the learning-disordered child, by himself, might on occasion seek the unexpected, he often finds himself surrounded by people or environments that inhibit his natural exploration of the world and his natural attempts to clarify confusions. He benefits little from serendipities. This sector of the natural habitat is restored in therapy, if only for 50 minutes. The 50-minute hour and all it entails for or implies to the child stands as a model of what might occur in daily life. As he comes to understand what differentiates the therapy session from the rest of life, the child is able to modify school and home situations so that they are more supportive of what normally occurs in typical development. This last sentence represents a belief that the child can, through his own efforts, change his environment; that he can jostle the expectations of his parent and teacher. After all, the child has the power to affect the parent and teacher negatively. Why not assume he can bring about attitude changes for the better?

It is important to get across to the child the idea that he can, in some important ways, "create" his environment by his own activity. As he develops, activity becomes increasingly internalized by thought, and the tendency to vary one's behavior transfers from action to thought because, from his perspective, both are ways of being. Indeed Piaget and Inhelder (1969) have concluded about child development what some clinicians know intuitively. Time and again they describe the integration of an ontogenetic process beginning with subjective centering proceeding toward a decentering that is cognitive, social, and moral. The process is particularly notable since it recapitulates what develops on a smaller scale at the sensorimotor level on a larger scale at the level of abstract thought (p. 128). Hence, if a child avoids variation in behavior, he is quite likely to avoid novel thought.

In Piaget's theory, as in Freud's, is the suggestion to therapists why they ought to begin from the child's perspective. Sigmund Freud (1949) urged therapists not to introduce an idea (an interpretation) to the patient unless its meaning has become partially conscious. Freud required of the therapist a finely tuned sensitivity when he insisted that the therapist observe in the patient's behavior a readiness to change. Freud's wisdom in teaching us to refrain from asking the patient to change before he was ready overlaps Piaget's view that the individual's own (and to him, valid) version of himself in his environment must precede an accommodation of the self to the environment and a new level of adaptation.

Egocentrism and Decentering

Egocentrism refers to the child's tendency to assume without question that his perspective holds true for others — "other" being either another person and/ or an object (thing). Although adults do not attribute perspective to objects, children often do; for example, in thinking their favorite doll or stuffed animal feels the way they feel. Decentering occurs when the child takes account of that which he cannot directly apprehend but can only imagine or construct. Then he understands that perspectives differ, interpersonal as well as spatial. What I refer to in this book as *interpersonal decentering* is of paramount importance in therapeutic interactions. In therapy the child or adolescent is encouraged by therapeutic exchanges to recognize that his view of the past and present does not necessarily correspond to his therapist's view and, with this recognition, becomes open to therapeutic insight.

One classic example of egocentrism taken from Piaget's (1963) work is that of a young child who believes that the moon follows him when he is taking a walk. The perspectives of other children can correct this immature view when the young child hears the slightly older child's surprised challenge: "Oh, come on! It only seems as if the moon is following you because it's *you* who's walking. That's like when you're next to a car that's moving forward and it seems like you're moving backwards even when your car stands still."

In a later work Piaget (1976) again demonstrates egocentrism in children when he converses with them about the effects they produce in structured-interview situations. For example, he asks children to launch an object so that it would hit a target.[2] Even though a child performs this task skillfully and correctly, he is unable, before a certain age, to perceive how he affects his environment and believes instead that a certain position of his body somehow causes the object to hit the target. He seems to believe that some specific gross motor activity magically unites him to the object and produces the effect. Perhaps he believes that because the object hits the target head-on, to achieve this goal he must have released it in a face forward or head-on position. If this is so, it shows that he does not clearly differentiate himself from the object, and that he, as Piaget suggests, attributes some aspects of the object's activity to his own actions. Thus, he might believe that the characteristics of objects in motion are characteristic of himself in motion, since he does not "see" that the object and himself are two separate and distinct entities, reasoning that because the object hits a target head-on, he or his arm and hand must be in a head-on relationship to the target. It is not so much that a younger child believes he *is* the object but that he believes the object behaves as he does and has qualities and feelings identical to his. For example, young children often believe inanimate objects (e.g., stuffed animals) have feelings just as they have feelings. Or when the child sees how an object behaves, he believes that he behaves in similar fashion. He assimilates his observations about the object to himself and vice versa.

Piaget (1976, 1978) observed that the older child understands and can explain his own successful actions. Accordingly, successful actions and self-reflections on these actions promote "consciousness" or "cognizance" of mental processes, such as the actual relationship between one's actions and their effects. The older child no longer perceives himself as blending into reality and stops indiscriminately attributing qualities of things or other people to himself or vice versa. A firmer sense of self divides him from the world, so when he is asked to explain how he achieved success in hitting the target, he is able to reflect on what he did and not just on what the object did. His experimentation with objects and his coordination of their movements with his activity inform him not only what objects are like but also what *he* is like, namely, a self-reflecting individual. A dialectic process is inherent in this view of the child's experience: repeated investigations into the qualities of things and other people leads him to reflect on the self which itself leads him to better understand the thing and the other person as distinct.

Egocentrism can be readily observed in the interpersonal world of the child when he plays the game of peekaboo. The young child believes that his perspective matches the other person's, and so he believes that when he cannot see the other person, the other cannot see him. As he shuts or hides his eyes and then opens them or removes his hands from his eyes, he is surprised that

[2]Piaget's description of this task is as follows: "The sling used in this experiment is of the simplest type: a wooden ball 5 cm in diameter, tied to the end of a string that the subject releases after swinging it around a few times, aiming at a target.... However, sensorimotor success does not always lead to accurate conceptualization (in this case, of how one aims and the object's flight path) and it is interesting to find out why" (p. 12). A successful action is hitting the target.

the other person knew all along where he was. Similarly, a young child believes that when he is angry, everyone else is angry, or he often believes that *because* he is angry, the other person becomes angry. The latter is yet another example of partial understanding in that the child's angry behavior often elicits angry feelings or behavior in another person. The error in the young child's egocentric thinking is his belief that his anger is isomorphic with that of another person, or that his perspective is identical to that of another.

The pitfalls of an egocentric attitude not only affect the youngster's behavior as he struggles to interact productively with peers and teachers but also shape therapeutic exchanges. For example, if the child or adolescent perceives his therapist to be angry just because he is angry, or believes that his angry behavior will arouse irritation in the therapist, he will be less likely to listen to what the therapist has to say or he will misinterpret the therapist's actions. Or, if the child believes that the therapist shares his understanding of natural phenomena, he will become puzzled, often mistrustful or angry, when he perceives that his and his therapist's perspectives differ. He might conclude that the therapist has not listened well enough to his version. Or, he might believe that "grownups know everything, children know nothing" and relinquish his inquiring attitude with the conviction that he will suddenly discover the truth about the world and other people only when he is finally an adult. Thus, it is fundamental for the therapist to estimate the youngster's cognitive level so that therapeutic conversations take account of the potential misunderstandings resulting from the young person's as yet unstable view of himself and the world in an interpersonal context.

Stages of Cognitive Development

Many of the 60 nonlearning children and adolescents whom I treated were transitional for concrete operations or for formal operations when they entered treatment. The term *operations* according to Piaget means organized, integrated systems of cognitions that contain definite, sturdy structure (Flavell, 1963, p. 165). The "preoperational" thought of the young child (approximately ages 18 months through 6 years), even though symbolic, consists not of operations but of intuitions and isolated partially formed concepts ("preconcepts") which do not hang together systematically. Young children form intuitions rapidly. They know something about the world and about people, but they do not question how they arrived at their conclusions, and, therefore, in an important sense they do not understand them. For example, such a child often knows his mother is angry. Since he does not question his perception he does not fully understand the circumstances leading to her anger or the intensity of her feeling, or the life-historical aspects of the angry parent–child interaction. Moreover, when a young child attempts to check his intuitions, he sometimes concludes he does not really know anything because he has not yet learned to prove his intuitions. More systematic thinking is required for an individual to reflect on his intuitions and to understand how they were formed.

As children approach systematic thought, they suspect the validity of intuiting per se. It is the uncertainty surrounding the validity of particular intuitions that propels older children toward mature inquiry which reveals to them how ideas began and how they can be verified. It might be said, then, that the difference between intuiting and reasoning is that the former gives us a glimpse of what is real, whereas the latter develops the process by which we have understood. Thus, the "concrete operational" thought of the latency age child (approximately ages 7 or 8 through 10 or 11) is characterized by concepts organized into operations that are nonetheless tied to concrete "realities" of the present rather than to a set of hypothetical events, one or many of which could have or actually did happen in the past. Because of his tendency to question the truth of perceptions and his predilection to search for the real causes of events, the older child with an angry mother has a pretty good idea what caused her angry feelings. However, such a child is primarily concerned with the present; unlike the adolescent, he does not construct a "theory" of human emotion which would explain a life history of angry interchanges between him and his mother, enabling him to foresee easily predictable, angry parent–child interactions.

On the other hand, the "formal operational" thought of adolescence elaborates abstract systems concerning the "real" and the "possible" in a continuous time frame.

> Unlike the concrete-operational child, the adolescent begins his consideration of the problem at hand by trying to envisage all the possible relations which could hold true in the data and then attempts, through a combination of experimentation and logical analysis, to find out which of these possible relations in fact do hold true. Reality is thus conceived as a special subset within the totality of things which the data would admit as hypotheses; it is seen as the "is" portion of a "might be" totality, the portion it is the subject's job to discover. (Flavell, 1963, pp. 204–205)

Assessing and monitoring the symptomatic youngster's thought level alerts the therapist to the ways in which he conceptualizes his learning problem and suggests appropriate methods of dealing with it.[3] If the child's thought is symbolic and intuitive but not yet systematic, the therapist can help the child unravel confusions by assisting him to understand what he believes to be true and by connecting disparate intuitions in a rudimentary but meaningful way. Unlike the preoperational child, the concrete operational child will present a systematic thought configuration and needs assistance in filling in the cognitive gaps or in correcting inconsistencies. Those nonlearning youngsters who are approaching formal thought are beginning to understand the difference between the "real" and the "possible" and often cease thinking abstractly because they are wary of discovering the "real." They either ignore much of what

---

[3]It is beyond the scope of this book to identify the cognitive levels within cognitive periods. Nonetheless, the reader might like to refer to Piaget (1972a, b) or to Cowan's (1978) erudite discussion of the discernible cognitive levels evident in the "early" and "late" preoperational, concrete operational, and formal operational substages. Also, Case's (1985) discussion of intellectual development expands Piaget's description of early childhood to include cognitive characteristics in addition to symbolization.

is possible so as not to test what *is* real or they maintain an undifferentiated experience in which possibilities are blurred with concrete realities. Still, these youngsters' thought systems are developed and refined enough for them to be approached by an empathic adult who presents logical alternatives. Because their attitudes are no longer uniformly egocentric, these young people can consider that perspectives may differ and can be led to evaluate the merits of differing opinions, attitudes, and beliefs. Perhaps vignettes of several youngsters in psychotherapy with me will portray the dissimilar qualities of the preoperational, the concrete operational, and the formal operational stance.

A Preoperational Girl

Five-year-old Sally came for therapy because of severe separation anxieties that occurred when her mother drove her to school. Her anxiety increased when she noticed the school day in kindergarten was longer than it had been in nursery school and concluded that her mother wanted to get rid of her. She often approached her therapy appointment sulking with her thumb in her mouth. Once she entered my office, she became lively and animated. She became expansive in both conversation and in gross motor activity as she explored how toys work or created fantasies at the dollhouse. As she spun fantasies about "growing up" and "having babies," she became frightened by her idea that growing up would cause her mother to die. At home, she said repeatedly to her mother, "When I grow up, I'm getting married. Then you'll be a grandmother. And grandmothers always die." These statements were often followed by verbal and physical assaults on her mother wherein it appeared that Sally believed she could actually cause her mother to die. By attacking her mother, she imagined ridding herself of her mother thus unself-consciously reversing her conviction that her mother wished to be rid of her.

Typical of preoperational children, Sally had developed symbols and symbolic processes that stood for often absent objects, people, or events. In her imagination, the event of a mother's becoming a grandmother stood for the event of a mother's death. Furthermore, her own growing up stood for another person's dying. Sally was not yet able to question her symbolization and instead used symbols and symbolic processes repetitively as if they were the actual events themselves. Her mentations did not possess sturdy structure because many facets of an event were left uncoordinated and, moreover, they revealed missing links in the imagined causal sequence. For example, in her statements to her mother, "I'm getting married" and "then you'll be a grandmother," she omitted "then I'll have a baby" after "I'm getting married." In her conversation she omitted *the* event which in her mind would cause her mother to die since it causes grandmotherhood.

I first attempted to alleviate Sally's anxiety and her aggressive symptoms by remarking, "Your mother grew up and had you as a child and your grandmother is still alive." This comment had no perceptible effect on Sally's anxiety although it did improve her thinking. She reacted by saying, "I know my mother will die when I have a baby." She supplied the missing link in connecting the fantasy of her mother's death with the imagined birth of her baby. But, she still could not apply my remark about her grandmother's existence to the bind her thinking created because she had developed no symbols or symbolic processes to stand for her grandmother. So far, her symbols and symbolic processes stood only for her mother or events pertaining to her mother. She had developed these ideas which were stand-ins for "my-mother-will-die," "when-I-grow-up," and "when-I-have-a-baby." Furthermore, for her to understand the meaning of my implied analogy between her grandmother and her mother, and her mother and herself, she would have had to consider and coordinate many items of information reflecting operational logic which might consist of: (1) recognizing her grandmother was alive and then (2) inferring that her mother by having a child did not cause her own mother to die, followed by (3) applying both these thoughts to her relationship with her mother as she (4) fantasized about having her own baby.

When I centered Sally's attention on her present relationship to me as we talked during her appointment, she was able to understand her reasoning better. I said, "But Sally, I have two grownup children and I'm not dead." She then became silent for some seconds and soon jumped up from the chair she was sitting in to play "house" with the dollhouse family. In this play, the dollhouse babies were first fed by their mother after which they went off to school. As Sally explained, "They got old enough to go to kindergarten!"

Sally now seemed to be saying that growing up was safe. At least going to kindergarten was safe because she easily understood my statement that although I had grownup children, I was alive. She might have thought: "She must be alive because she's talking to me." Since I was present, not absent, she did not need a symbol to represent me, which simplified the intellectual task confronting her. Then she could consider that a living mother could have grownup children. Only later did I come to stand for her mother. By then the fact that she knew I was alive challenged her view that a grown-up child always causes her mother to die. Thereupon she stopped attacking her mother and began to enjoy conversations with her about "growing up." This positive result occurred because Sally *assimilated* present interactions with her mother to the previous interaction with me in therapy in which I said I had not died when my children grew up. Piaget's theory of the child's conceptual development explains *how* Sally's transference of her problems with her mother to the therapy hour enabled her to resolve a most important conflict she had in simultaneously relating to her mother and in imagining growing up.

Four months later, she developed symbols and symbolic processes to stand for her grandmother. This occurred after her grandmother visited Sally's family for two weeks. Sally understood that her grandmother had gotten older and more frail. Although she said, "I still love Grandma," she resisted helping her out of a chair. She seemed to say, by her behavior, that, "if I don't help Grandma, then she's not old and frail." "Helping Grandma" thus stood for "grandma's old," and "not helping Grandma" stood for "Grandma's not old." When I said that she wished to stop her grandmother from being old by refusing to help her,

Sally instantly agreed and added sadly, "But that's not true." Now she was able to understand which real events stood for imagined, wished-for events. But she also implied she knew the difference between what is true and what is not.

Two Concrete Operational Children

Seven-year-old Jake had recently begun to originate operations of the sort described above. When in nursery school, he often behaved as if the school was an enemy camp and the teachers were his adversaries. Gradually, he became responsive to the nursery school's curriculum and, later, to the kindergarten curriculum. In first grade, he began to display some behaviors typical of concrete operations—by which I mean the beginnings of systematic thinking. He resolutely approached both school and therapy appointments with a prepared agenda. For example, he enjoyed advance planning for special school events, such as participating in a holiday festival, or while being brought to therapy, he discussed with his mother what he was going to talk about that day. His demeanor on entering my office was one of complacent competence. He felt sure that he knew facts about himself and about the world, and he seemed to feel equally sure that what he had learned was enormously important.

One day, by making a joke, he verbalized directly how for many years he had seemed at odds with schools and teachers. He was playing a table game in which the players must choose an occupation. First he listed the choices: doctor, lawyer, teacher, journalist, and physicist. Then when he turned the spinner, he landed on the "teacher" space. He protested this turn of events, arguing that he would rather be a doctor because "his salary is better." I intended to introduce variations in Jake's opinion regarding teachers when I said, "It's true that doctors make more money than teachers, but teachers get to work with children and many doctors don't." Then he said with a smirk, "You mean I have to be a teacher in this game? The person you fight with in school?" As he saw that I was amused by his joke, he began to laugh and added this statement: "I don't fight when I like the teacher." Jake's joke revealed organized thinking typical of concrete operations. To humorously characterize teachers as the people children fight in schools, he must have thought something like this: (1) teaching is one of many professions ("jobs") and (2) teachers seem like "enemies" to me but (3) they don't always seem so—especially when I like the teacher. His sense of humor linked these successive thoughts into a composite that consisted of three well-integrated elements.

Sometimes Jake still behaved as if his teacher was his enemy; that is, instead of making fun of this idea, he acted it out. In contrast to the past, when his acting out was intermittent and often unpredictable because it did not rest on sturdy structure, now he could with a vengeance create what seemed to his teacher to be an armed camp in the classroom. His more advanced thought processes helped him accomplish his pathological goals. But these processes also created the option for him to understand his acting-out behavior which he expressed by making light of his pathology when rapport between him and his teacher or between him and me was reestablished.

Nine-year-old Nathaniel, whose mother was "always off working at the University," picked up a compass one day and began to explore how it worked. In speaking to me about the compass, he revealed an evolving cognitive organization. First he said that if he owned a compass he would always know in which direction he was walking when he took hikes with his mother. He tested the compass by pointing it north and watching the needle turn. Then he began to rotate the compass and said, "If you turn it around, the needle will point south, in the opposite direction." He instantly recognized his error and said, "Oh, no! That's not right! The needle always points north. That's how you know which direction you're going."

In first grade, Nathaniel had reading difficulties sufficient for his teacher to suggest tutoring. His tutoring sessions helped him to overcome his reading insecurity and to reinforce the basic skills he needed for reading. When he had become an adept reader in second and third grades, often he proudly displayed his reading ability and behaved as though the printed word had tremendous significance. So when he saw the letters N, S, E, W on the compass, he not only understood that they represented the four directions but also endowed them with as much, if not more, importance than the compass needle. Because he was initially centered on the letters, and not the needle, he failed to coordinate the purpose of the letters with the needle's function. After recognizing his error, he mused, "At first I thought the letters [N, S, E, W] were there to show you which way you're going. Now I know you figure that out by which way is north!" His "transitional" thinking thus consisted of two correct but uncoordinated ideas: (1) the compass letters represented the directions and (2) the needle's movement somehow signified the direction he faced now or in which he could hike with his mother. The latter is a "preconcept" because he was unsure just how the needle indicated the direction in which he could walk. By coordinating (1) and (2) he arrived at a more mature organization of facts: (1) the compass letters stand for the directions, although (2) the needle always points north, which (3) could reveal the direction of his movement if he referenced it to the needle.

Nathaniel's cognitive struggle is a nice example of how a concept's meaning can temporarily inhibit an emerging conceptual organization; that is, the "part" can sometimes distract the child from organizing the "whole." My view is that his understanding was not impeded by the affective connotations of taking walks with his mother, but rather, his understanding was impeded by the importance he gave to printed letters (and words). Because of his hard-won reading successes, he infused the reading symbols ("signs") he had recently mastered with more significance than they possess in this context and temporarily ignored the critical importance of the needle. When he saw that the needle did not point south when he rotated the compass, he appeared to remember what he had learned in school about compasses and either generated or regenerated a cognitive organization that integrated several concepts.

Like Jake, Nathaniel acted complacent about his competence. After he corrected his error, he seemed to "forget" his earlier mistake and automatically reinstated his assured demeanor. To him, "facts" were unquestionable. When he understood that he had grasped facts and/or ideas, he became contented and acted as if there was nothing more to be learned, known, or said. He exhibited what Elkind (1979a) calls "cognitive conceit" in concrete operational children. The conceit may derive from the child's occasionally remembering the many years he worked to think systematically. Or it may derive from his anticipating the many thought mutations that he will experience in the future. In both cases, he hopes to rest on his laurels. Once the world begins to "make sense" to the child and to become more predictable, he often acts as if there is nothing more to be learned at the same time he is sure that he is capable of knowing everything—that is, facts which he has yet to apprehend. Perhaps it is the contradiction inherent in his juxtaposing "nothing more to be learned" with "I'm capable of knowing everything" and other similar contradictions which propels the child toward abstract thought. When he is able to anchor what he actually knows in the larger frame of what remains to be known, he places himself increasingly in an intellectual and social context and begins to think about his own thoughts.

A Formal Operational Boy

Sixteen-year-old Aaron, a gifted artist, had been in psychotherapy with me since he was thirteen. Like Jake and Nathaniel, he usually came to his appointments with an organized agenda. Unlike the two younger boys, he introduced conversation more systematically under the rubrics, "What happened this week in school," and "What happened this week at home." Although brilliant (his WISC-R IQ was 150), his academic performance was uneven, primarily the result of his vacillating trust in his teachers. When he trusted his teacher, he did his homework and achieved well. When he mistrusted his teacher, he showed his displeasure by refusing to study and by behaving cavalierly in class. In therapy, he became progressively more attuned to the subtleties of interpersonal interactions. He began to anticipate what I would say in response to his narratives about school and home.

Studying religion was particularly problematic for Aaron, so much so that he polarized his feelings about the subject matter and the teacher because he was personally struggling with many of the themes the study of religion aroused. When his teacher understood his personal struggles and tried to help him, Aaron became ecstatic and exclaimed that he liked studying religion after all. But when his teacher was understandably occupied with other students or with the curriculum, Aaron felt deserted and criticized himself for being fascinated with his course in religion.

A turning point in Aaron's attitude occurred one day when he came intending to talk about "humility." He said humility is a very important religious concept. Then he added, "And I bet I know what you think the reason is for its being important," thus inviting me to tell him what I thought. I answered humility could be an important concept in his religion course because his teacher, perhaps, hoped the students would act humbly. He grinned triumphantly and exclaimed, "I thought you thought that!" Out of all the possibilities which could apply to me, he had anticipated the real—my actual—reaction. His accuracy in predicting events excited him and affirmed that he could not only introspect about himself but also empathize with another person. His statements revealed the decentering trend in that he not only could think about his own thoughts but could anticipate mine.

Then he proceeded to give a lecture on those important concepts of the various religions he was studying in class. He said humility was only one of the many concepts revered by particular religious groups and that understanding religious concepts went beyond their application to individual human existence. His conversation revealed that he had realized concepts can exist apart from particular individuals who apply them to their lives. Although his own personal struggles were still on his mind, he understood that his peers, too, tried to apply religious concepts to their lives. Then he moderated his anger at his teacher for not always attending to him. Although he did not say it directly, he implied by his statements that a cultural value is thought by a society to be important irrespective of the unique importance particular individuals might give it. If so, this would be why he was increasingly able to tolerate his teacher's investment in the religion curriculum per se.

Although his more mature understanding occurred as he ridiculed my idea of humility as a strategy to socialize individuals, he did initiate a more abstract discourse with me in which he differentiated the social uses of concepts from individual uses. Most important, Aaron had a more vivid sense of who he was as he realized it was he, not I, who had expanded the discussion to include abstract concepts disassociated from individuals.

COGNITIVE MONITORING

In my work with nonlearning children and adolescents, I am as concerned with underlying capabilities as I am with an initial stubborn rejection or anxious evasion of academics. For this reason, I estimate the cognitive progress in therapy of these youngsters by using Piagetian interview techniques which serve as a partial inventory of a young person's current understanding of cognitive problems. The youngster's diagnostic evaluation thus consists, in part, of several Piagetian interview tasks (see pp. 317–322). Because I also wish to estimate whether and in which ways psychotherapy has an effect on a child's ability and willingness to think and to solve problems, I reinterview each child or adolescent after 3 to 6 months of therapy. (This reinterview is scheduled at a time other than the youngster's regular appointment so as not to interfere with his own agenda.) Cognitive progress can be the result of one or both of these factors: (1) the thinking psychotherapy restimulates or (2) the spontaneous development of new concepts outside of psychotherapy. I choose a short time interval between the inception of psychotherapy and the reinterview because I wish to estimate the degree to which both sources of cognitive progress occur. My intent is to understand more fully what the young person comprehends so I can phrase statements appropriately to his developmental level. Sometimes during interviewing or early in treatment, a transitional child or adolescent is able to arrive at a full grasp of a concept or of the relationship between concepts.[4] If so, I feel I have more options in what to say during the therapy hour. The cognitive interviews also reveal how the child or adolescent feels about the knowing process—whether he is comfortable with his competence or whether he still fears the consequences of a rational, clever, or proficient self-image.

INTEGRATING COGNITIVE APPRAISAL WITH PHASES OF PSYCHOANALYTIC PSYCHOTHERAPY

It is important for the psychotherapist of *any* theoretical persuasion to realize that aspects of Piaget's theory are potentially helpful in working with youngsters who have decided not to learn. *To promote learning in the reluctant student, the therapist must at all times keep in mind how a normally curious child behaves.* Clinical attention to intellectual development in young people sharpens technique and specifies how to achieve the aims of the various psychotherapeutic phases.

In my work with nonlearning children and adolescents, with whom I meet once weekly, I initiate four phases. These phases are distinct conceptually but often overlap in practice: establishing rapport, exploring and understanding the learning problem, conversing about the core learning conflict, and assessing progress in learning, including appraising new problems with knowledge acquisition. These phases correspond roughly to Luborsky's (1984) phase-oriented description of "supportive-expressive" psychoanalytic psychotherapy. He distinguishes between the "supportive" and "expressive" aspects of psychotherapeutic intervention and, most useful for my purposes, outlines distinct phases of the "expressive" aspect: listening, understanding, responding, and returning to listening.

Establishing Rapport

Children and adolescents who reject or evade learning are quite wary of the first therapeutic encounter that makes the early establishing of rapport

[4]In *The Grasp of Consciousness* (and in other works), Piaget reports the reactions of many children who tried to understand the relationship between their actions and the results these actions produced. For example, he quotes a girl of 7 years, 7 months who tried to mesh the success of her action with an adequate explanation: "[she is asked] Where did you let [the ball] go? Here;...*I made a mistake* (She changes her own position...and successfully releases the ball") (p. 21). This report and many others like it suggests to me that Piaget's subjects sometimes learned while being questioned—the 7-year-old girl understood that earlier she had made a mistake and tried to correct it. Piaget was not trying to teach the child but the child learned nonetheless. Similarly, the child in therapy often "learned" even though, in the ordinary sense, I had no intent to teach him.

critical. These young people are wary because they often believe that the therapist, like the teacher, will concentrate on what they do not know and will ignore
what they do understand. Even if the therapist focuses on what the child or
adolescent does understand, the youngster reacts fearfully to this empathy
because it implies that he is capable of understanding what he has sought to
obstruct or distort. In many cases, he is afraid of revealing to the therapist how
much he knows because he believes this revelation will threaten or anger his
parents. Rapport is often established by the quality of the office in addition to
the therapist's gentle, inquiring, but nonobtrusive attitude. Toys and equipment that appeal to all age groups and that invite him to participate in interesting activity coupled with after-school snacks suggest to the youngster that the
therapist respects his need to play and explore and that he will be taken care of.
By inviting the youngster to choose to explore what interests him, I hope to
communicate early in psychotherapy that it is his choices that have not only led
to his learning problems but also will lead to his resolution of them. Younger
children might choose to play with the dollhouse, Playdoh, or their favorite
table games, whereas preadolescents and adolescents might explore the calculator, the typewriter, Rubic's cube, or advanced games like chess. Whatever the
individual's choice, the therapeutic environment as well as the therapist's first
friendly greeting can be thought of as "supportive" in Luborsky's sense:

> A supportive relationship is necessary, according to the theory of psychoanaly-
> tic psychotherapy, so that the patient will feel secure enough to venture to try to
> undo the restrictions in functioning that necessitated the treatment. The suppor-
> tive relationship will allow the patient to tolerate the expressive techniques of the
> treatment...that are often the vehicle for achieving the goals. (1984, p. 71)

If the young person feels safe in revealing his natural curiosity, he will be able to
tolerate conversations with the therapist about his core learning problem. These
conversations are often initiated when the youngster reveals that he expects the
therapist to behave either like a teacher or a parent. Rapport is established
when the therapist communicates to the youngster that he or she understands
these implicit comparisons between adults while emphasizing that therapy is
different from school and home. This carries the implication that his learning
attempts in therapy will have different, more positive outcomes. And, when the
youngster realizes it is *he* who has initiated successful learning attempts—and
not his therapist or some other important adults—he can imagine broadening
his explorations in situations that are different from those made safe by his
therapist. He understands that as an individual he is a "constant" in varying
situations. To quote 13-year-old Mario, "If I can figure out what's going on in
therapy, I can do that anywhere I want to." The young person "conserves the
self as a logical thinker" (Furth, 1987, p. 77).

In my work with young people, I begin exploring their learning conflicts by
asking them to describe how they feel about the three important aspects of their
lives: home, school, and peer relationships. Then, as I listen, the youngster
often focuses on one of these aspects more than the other two. A preliminary
understanding phase is soon initiated when I converse with the child about his
chosen topic. Both the youngster and I understand even more about his learn-

ing problem during the cognitive interviewing when he reveals what he knows about dolls and houses which seriate, the appearance of small objects (e.g., beads or marbles) in differently shaped containers, and the like. The interview questions typically interest young people even though they are afraid of learning and afraid to reveal what they have learned because, unlike school assignments, the interview items are familiar and the questions themselves seem similar to their spontaneous queries. This procedure not only centers the youngster on what he does know but also anchors him in previous spontaneous explorations that have often seemed safer than schoolwork. The youngster is then prepared to understand that he and I are engaged in a joint endeavor to promote his learning. When he realizes that he and I are progressing toward the question of why would an intelligent young person choose to learn in one situation and not in another, he is ready to understand his own intentions more thoroughly. Piaget's theory helps the therapist assess the youngster's comprehension modes and thus adds specificity to technique in the "understanding" phase.

Conversing about the Core Learning Conflict

This phase of psychotherapy is also productively enhanced by attention to Piagetian psychology. When responding to young people, it is essential to speak their language. The youngster will attend to the therapist's communications only if they appear intelligible. Consequently, therapeutic statements ought to be formed in line with the child's or adolescent's thinking mode—a crucial aspect of psychotherapeutic intervention that is addressed in detail in Chapter 6. In work with young people, it is particularly important to assess the influence the therapeutic statement may or may *not* have. Therapists, even more than teachers and parents, have the responsibility and presumably an interest in finding out where and why a situation or a conversation went wrong. When the therapist respectfully tracks down miscommunications or misinterpretations based on expected adult–child or adult–adolescent thought discontinuities, it helps the young person progress toward understanding his symptoms and the ways in which he is a worthy and special person.

Assessing Progress in Learning

The last phase requires an appraisal within each therapeutic hour and over the course of treatment to assess any progress in the youngster's understanding of his core learning conflict and any additional problems with knowledge acquisition that he may have encountered or generated as the result of therapeutic intervention. Appraising the impact of therapeutic conversation— especially the interpretation—is the complement to guiding the conversation with the youngster and to forming interpretive statements (see Chapter 6). Overall progress can be assessed, in part, by comparing cognitive reinterview results with the initial statements the child or adolescent made in answer to the cognitive questions. Interview and reinterview comparisons are discussed in many case narratives in this book. A second important aspect of reassessment is an appraisal of how the young person feels about acquiring new knowledge — whether it improves his self-esteem or whether it threatens him. Sometimes nonlearning young people in therapy retreat even more strenuously from learning when they discover that they are capable of achieving because they realize their learning is often a threat to their parents. To produce a positive therapeutic outcome, it is not enough for the therapist simply to understand the youngster's problems with learning. By his or her own "learning" about the young person's conflicts the therapist must encourage him to expect that learning can be shared and productive. Because he perceives shared learning as safe, his recognition that his therapist "learns" productively about him will convince him to change his antiquated learning modes.

SUMMARY

This chapter specifies the ways in which Piaget's theory of normal intellectual development can be usefully applied to young people who often abort progressive development in their attempts to reject or evade learning. I show that a "drive theory" of learning inhibitions fails to take account of the youngster's deliberate and conscious institution of roadblocks to learning. When the clinician understands that intellectual factors — and not just affective reactions — contribute to the young person's learning inhibitions, clinical interventions can be adapted to expand and refine the youngster's thinking mode which, in turn, aids school learning. At the very least, the child or adolescent begins to think differently and more productively about what happens in school. Sometimes he applies academic knowledge creatively or his thought advances one or several steps further than the assigned material requires.

Although it is important to attend to intellectual development as well as affective development, the clinician must not lose sight of the fact that these two spheres of the individual's mentality coordinate to produce learning inhibitions. Given the difficulty of disentangling the intellective function from the affective in the youngster's psyche or in actual life situations, it is productive to consider that his problems with learning occur at two boundaries of the ego: the external boundary which intersects reality and the internal boundary which responds to impulse. This conceptualization of ego development alerts the clinician during a momentary therapeutic encounter to the locus of the young person's compromise with learning. Has he compromised his school learning at the outer boundary because he wishes to avoid some aspect of reality? Or has he compromised school learning at the inner boundary because of some pressing, chronic psychodynamic conflict? And, especially, has he compromised understanding those concepts and conflicts that are inherent in recognizing the self? Because cognitive stage theory prepares the psychotherapist to expect specific behaviors and modes of comprehension at particular chronological ages, it can assist the clinician in deciding in which aspect of his mentality—or both—the child's or adolescent's commitment to nonlearning resides.

Precisely because he is free from constitutionally determined cognitive deficits, the normally intelligent youngster who decides to fail in school has developed, however reluctantly, many typical cognitive functions and structures. When clinicians observe the operation of these functions and structures, they are enabled to hypothesize whether the youngster is capable of (1) making analogies between learning and growing up and/or (2) imagining the future. These thought processes, in turn, often intensify his ambivalence about school learning because he correctly reasons the competence gained from his school experiences assists him in behaving in a more grown-up fashion. Assessing the youngster's thought level also reveals whether he is likely to make comparisons between himself and his parents or his siblings. Then clinicians may hypothesize that the young person's decision to fail derives primarily from his preconscious ambivalence toward family members whom he wishes to emulate but also to vanquish. Hypotheses regarding the origins of the youngster's learning disorder and the ways that learning compromises unfold can be interpreted to him productively only when statements or other therapeutic interventions are geared to his thinking mode.

Last, but certainly not least, Piagetian psychology helps the clinician transcend the thought discontinuities between adult and child as the clinician endeavors to understand and respect the child's perspective. The clinician's efforts during the therapeutic hour to respect and to comprehend the youngster nourish his idea that the therapist is "learning" about him. Since this "learning" seems safe to the therapist (even fascinating) the youngster quite likely concludes that learning can be safe—maybe even captivating.

CHAPTER 4

Ambivalence about Knowing
Timothy and Annie

My purpose in devoting this chapter to 9-year-old Timothy's reasons for reject-ing reading and 7-year-old Annie's reasons for rejecting math is to show that similar psychological processes were at work to explain their learning problems and their treatment progress. Both children were brilliant and exercised what Elkind (1987) calls a "structural imperative" in conflict-free subject areas but were nonetheless underachieving in one particular subject. Tim often appeared alexic or dyslexic, whereas Annie appeared to suffer from acalculia. With psy-chotherapeutic treatment, the two children overcame their learning problems and sometimes even excelled in the subjects they had avoided before. Their progress in therapy reveals how partial understanding—"transitional" thought—creates the necessity to reject school learning but permits especially the brilliant child in psychotherapy to surpass the confusion that contributes to his or her thinking process.

Partial understanding is best understood by considering that the child attempts to master and to bring together the two important aspects of his experience—reality and intrapsychic processes. Timothy's and Annie's re-sponses to the school curriculum helped them generate ideas about a reality they at one moment accepted and at another moment rejected or distorted. That children can generate ideas on their own is a view which, fortunately, com-mands increasing attention among professionals who deal with children. For example, Greenspan (1981) found that children's fears are often related to the ideas they themselves create. Later, Kagan (1984) made the same point about a different sphere of the child's experience when he noted that a small child is capable of concocting standards by which he and other people predictably behave:

> I do not suggest that exposure to adults who praise the proper and punish the improper is irrelevant, but I believe that all children have a capacity to generate ideas about good and bad states, actions, and outcomes. (pp. 130–131)

Respecting the child's capacity to originate ideas is one important compo-nent in helping children trust learning.

Tim and Annie generated ideas about the good and the bad aspects of knowing and not knowing, and they cogitated about the personalities of their teachers and the meanings of their homework assignments. They reflected on the symbolic and affective meanings these realities had for them and were vigilant about the potential outcomes of knowledge acquisition. As a result of their cogitations, they became increasingly attuned to themselves as unique individuals and began to perceive themselves as intelligent and capable of learning. When this occurred, they were able to separate themselves from other family members and *their* motives and affective reactions. Then they no longer needed to hide from others the fact that they had acquired skills and information. In effect, Timothy and Annie placed themselves in a larger group of distinct individuals whose goals, motives, and personality traits were not identical to their own however similar they sometimes seemed.

TIMOTHY'S PRESENTING PROBLEM

Timothy had refused to read for nearly three years when his mother brought him to me for psychotherapy. His rejection of reading symbolized his rejection of the knowledge contained in the books that he was assigned to read in school. Tim's mother understood this, so she suggested that he read the comics "for fun." She became upset when she perceived that he not only refused to read in school but also refused to even look at the comic books at home.

When I first met Tim, I thought he knew intuitively that books tell the reader about important aspects of life. Later, I realized that his was not simply intuitive knowledge. On the contrary, Timothy could read all the words and understand the ideas they refer to. Some of these ideas he wished to avoid because they touched upon inner or family conflicts. But he also reacted to the act of reading per se which is why he even rejected comic books.

I also realized that Tim's refusal to read diverted everyone from his eager acceptance of the school subject he excelled in—math. What impressed him about math was the power in knowing which contrasted with the risks of knowing he experienced in reading. Math symbols and processes did not tell him anything unexpected. His knowledge of math symbols and processes, which he had gained primarily through playing with the calculator or working math puzzles, revealed that knowing something well makes one's experience more predictable. On the other hand, reading books convinced him that knowing something well only increases the likelihood that one will be confronted with innumerable variations in story narrative. Tim felt that mathematical processes always led to "right" answers whereas literature not only had no "right" answers but also raised questions, many of which he wanted to avoid. Because learning math did not involve word mastery nor did it imply unpredictable story meaning, he knew he could control math and its symbols better. Thus, the risks he saw in reading came from two sources: his understanding that books often tell the reader the unexpected, and his understanding that he refused to read, which led him to believe that he *could not* read.

TIMOTHY'S FAMILY HISTORY

Tim was a winsome, interesting boy who often peered out at others from behind his very long hair. His face was extremely expressive, often changing within seconds from an angry scowl to a mischievous grin. His parents were divorced when he was 5 years old. A year later, his father dropped out of medical school and moved away, although he visited Tim monthly. Five months after Timothy began therapy, when he was 9 years, 5 months, his father returned to where Tim was living and began seeing his son more frequently.

After Tim's father left school, he was beset for several months by anxiety and depression which the family members often referred to as "Dad's nervous breakdown." Timothy's mother was worried that her only son, who strongly identified with his father, would turn out "crazy" if he continued to model his behavior on that of his father. She also believed that her son's nonreading was the result of his father's lack of interest in him. His mother's opinion of school learning seemed in direct antithesis to his father's. Tim knew she wanted him to learn. But he surmised that his father did not want him to learn by virtue of his own exodus from school. Even though Tim wished to please and emulate his mother, which he occasionally did by getting perfect scores on math tests, he also wanted to please and emulate his father. Since he was equally loyal to both parents, he felt caught between his mother's demand for learning and his father's prohibition of learning. He refused to learn lest he overtake his father academically. For his mother, he feigned helplessness lest he be accused of disloyalty to her especially if she knew he deliberately chose not to read. Nevertheless, he did try to appease her sometimes by performing brilliantly in math.

Timothy was trapped in a maze of opposing tendencies that stifled many attempts to know the world or to know about important people. If he recognized and understood his father's behavior and motives, he felt he must block out the meaning of his mother's behavior and motives. He was perfectly capable of reasoning: (1) my mother and father are different personalities; (2) therefore, my mother's behavior in regard to me will be different from my father's; (3) furthermore, their motives for behaving a certain way toward me create very different reactions in me. But before therapy, Tim regularly declined to think in this systematic fashion primarily because he was afraid his thinking ability would embarrass or threaten his father. Moreover, intermittent understanding of his family's dynamics saved him from the painful recognition that he believed he could not please both his parents simultaneously. What eventually helped Tim was his realization that he could dare to learn and his relationship with neither mother nor father would be sacrificed. When he began to understand that his successful school learning could be safely distinguished from his father's learning attempts, he was able to disconnect school learning from family problems. He no longer needed to prevent his father from perceiving that he achieved in school to please his mother—and to please *himself*—nor did he need to prevent his mother from knowing that he admired his father. Then he no longer hid from his parents that he was capable of doing schoolwork.

TIMOTHY'S INITIATION INTO THERAPY

When Tim first began therapy, he tried to conceal his positive feelings about schoolwork from me. His rejection of reading can be seen in his repeated statements, "I hate reading," which were often followed by his murmuring, "but I love math." His statements that he hated reading led his teacher to wonder if he was dyslexic or if he experienced some other language disability. In therapy, he centered his conversations on the fact that he did not read because he was "stubborn." Nonetheless, being stubborn worried him because he knew that reading skills were the basis for all other school subjects (except math). As a result of his rejecting reading, he thought he was or would be a failure in his other subjects (except math) and concluded therefore he was generally a "school failure." The thought of being a school failure became most painful when he realized his nonreading would prevent him from investigating his favorite school subject other than math—science.

When I turned our discussions away from his hateful feelings about reading to his loving feelings for math, he was delighted. I first proposed that he felt differently about math than reading. He smiled broadly and eagerly confided that he knew he was stubborn, and not stupid, because sometimes he got 100s in math. When I suggested that math knowledge would help with his scientific interests, he got closer to his aversion to reading when he said: "Reading is about people, girls and boys, families—what I don't want to think about." He added: "Math is just numbers which do what you want them to." I remarked that he might also make reading do what he wanted it to do by adding his own interpretations to story themes or his own ideas to science texts. He smiled again and said—admitting that he *could* read—"I do that all the time, but I keep it to myself." Timothy had thus masked a brilliant intelligence by simulating a learning disability. Since the story themes in his storybooks were often about families ("what I don't want to think about"), he pretended he couldn't read—a "disability" that left him free to show off in math class.

For quite some time Timothy continued to be ambivalent about reading and about acquiring knowledge from schoolbooks. He become confused by his own attitudes toward reading expressed in therapy, particularly his reluctance to do what he wanted with what he read. This ambivalence peaked whenever he remembered his father's panic at studying for final exams. He often remembered his father's panic as he tried to answer my question: "What is so terrible about reading?" Reading, even about science in which he was interested, was "so terrible" because it was the very activity that would reveal both to him and his father that he was acquiring the "special" scientific knowledge required by a medical degree. Since he had recognized he had made a decision about reading—he said he was stubborn (not disabled) when he did not read—he also thought reading was terrible because reading mistakes might reveal that his stubborn attitude had actually led to a reading disability. Thus, he was afraid of the very event he wished for: to remain subordinate to his father by becoming reading-disabled, which would assure his father's love and attention. His ambivalent attitude toward reading continued to be expressed in therapy when he began to compare me and therapy to his teacher and school.

EARLY TREATMENT PROGRESS

Teacher and Therapist from the Child's Perspective

Since his past conflicts with learning continued to overwhelm his perception of school events, I was not surprised when Timothy soon began to call his therapy appointment his "special class," which suggested that he wished to find out whether I was similar to or different from his teacher. He often implied by calling therapy a "class," and some weeks later by asking me to go to a school picnic, that he wanted therapy to have a direct and positive impact on his school life, either by transforming therapy into a school (and a "special") class or by actually bringing me into the school environment. By merging therapy with school, he understood it was his school learning that needed my help. Like many other similar children I worked with, his reasoning went something like this: What better way to get support for the learning he needed than to transform therapy into a class and to bring the insights he gained there back to school? By calling therapy a *special* class, he also revealed his secret wish that therapy would enable him to enjoy reading, not hate it.

Timothy also wanted to know how the therapy classes differed from school classes, and how I, as therapist, was different from his teacher. He chose to test interpersonal differences between me and his teacher by revealing some of his secrets to me (those he ordinarily kept to himself) so that he could observe my reaction. Two more issues surfaced as he tried to find out how therapy was different from school. These two issues, holding secret knowledge and acquiring knowledge on the sly, often recur with those children I treat who either fight learning or are intensely ambivalent about it.

Timothy's Secret

Tim's biggest secret was his ability to read, and related to this secret was the connection he made between the act of reading (knowing how) and the act of stealing. Since he often felt that he was not supposed to find out from books, when he emulated his father (who seemed to panic at studying) he felt there was a certain relationship between what is known and what is stolen. These thoughts and the underlying metaphors they represent came to light when he told me repeatedly that he "got into trouble" at school. He soon began to notice that he got into trouble particularly on the days he came to see me. He told me he had been reprimanded by his teacher because he and some friends were planning to "pick pockets." When asked what he had in mind to pick from his classmates' pockets, he answered smugly, "pencils." Here Tim presented still another antithesis. To him it seemed contradictory to get into trouble for trying to procure the very item that could lead to learning, or reveal by his handwriting that he had learned something. On the day he came to see me, he intended to pick pockets to find pencils because he wished to dramatize to me the polarities he sensed in his behavior. I told him that choosing pencils was indeed significant, since he well knew that children's pockets were usually full of all sorts of other more interesting objects. He was surprised when I said this because he had assumed that I, like his teacher, would disapprove of picking pockets for pencils. Yet he saw that I reacted differently than she did. His intent to steal the pencils showed how much Tim both wanted to learn and feared the consequences of his behavior. Learning seemed acceptable only if he stole it. But stealing, even if he stole only pencils, would surely get him into trouble. Stealing pencils also suggested that he wished to write his own stories to better control what he read. Or, since he had rejected learning to read, perhaps he intended to obstruct other children's working in their reading workbooks by stealing their pencils.

Tim soon set up another contradiction: he could read only in my presence but not in school. He revealed how well he could read, for example, by reading the signs by my front door to me. When he came for his fourth appointment, he rang the bell three times, long and loudly. When I greeted him he said, "Did I 'press the bell hard' like the sign says?" He then pointed to the "no solicitors" sign and said, "I'm not one of those [solicitors]." Although he read the word *solicitors* silently, so I could not be sure that he read it correctly he showed that he knew what the word meant by the conversation that followed immediately. By saying he did not want to "bother" me, he implied that he recognized one connotation of solicitors which he did not want applied to himself. He also revealed by this incident that he had attributed to our interactions the contradictory meanings that differentiate the two uses of the word *solicitor*. He implied he did not bother me the way he had bothered his teacher and his mother by not reading. Yet he also implied that he had begun to feel he was soliciting my help. By his reading the no-solicitors sign, he showed he had solicited enough of my help in the past to safely read in my presence. By this simple act, he revealed his biggest secret—that he could read and had gained knowledge by reading. When he did not suffer any drastic consequences as a result of his reading or learning the meaning of a difficult word—I neither pushed him to read more nor did I become threatened by the fact that he knew how to read—he began to disclose still more how much he understood the reading process. He did not limit his behavior to the passive act of reading, but in subsequent weeks revealed how much he knew about the activity that is required to teach reading which he had learned by observing his teacher.

CLINICAL ISSUES

The Pitfalls of Partial Understanding

Timothy's behavior communicated that his nonlearning stance was not the result of never having learned but rather the result of ambivalence about learning. When he pretended to be incapable of reading, his simulated reading "disability" functioned to protect him from intensely ambivalent feelings regarding his father. As he tried to learn and not to learn, he often only partially comprehended what was taught. Partial understanding is not solely the result of the affective sphere of the child's psyche dominating the cognitive sphere. It is just as much the result of the child's confusing society's rationale for learning with his own reasons for either approaching or evading learning. That is, the young person who apprehends a subject must integrate the reasons for doing so given by his teacher (who, in some sense, represents society) with the intrapsychic reasons for his curiosity. But he may experience discontinuity between his "external" and his "internal" worlds when he compares the accepted motives for learning given by his teacher (who represents society) with his often unexpected motives for either learning or not learning.

Thus, the question to ask when attempting to remediate a functional learning disorder is not whether emotions dominate cognition but rather where the child's investment in learning lies—whether in his inner intrapsychic world or in his understanding of reality. For example, the girl who saw the letter *t* as "mommy waiting to hug me" made the intrapsychic need of mommy hugging as important as the letter *t*. Since she could recite the alphabet, its primary significance in her inner world meant that the letter *t* had been integrated into a stable cognitive system. She responded to the reality of the alphabet by imbuing the letter *t* with added affective significance. It was yet another way for her to express her need to hug her mother. Just because she momentarily saw the letter as a symbol representing mother does *not* mean her symbolic use of the letter will prevent her from apprehending it as part of a particular word. Some days later, she found an additional and an entirely expected cognitive context for the letter *t* as she said, "t is in tea!"

Partial understanding was conspicuous in a conversation I had with Tim during his second month of therapy. His incomplete understanding derived from his focus on an intrapsychic issue at one moment and on reality the next moment. He began a series of discussions by telling me to answer the question "Are birds mammals?" In the next breath he informed me that in school he could only see the little word in mammal and not the whole word mammal, and asked if I could guess what that little word might be. Before I could answer either question, he went on: "Birds are mammals because they are warm-blooded, they have hair, and one more thing I always forget...Oh!...they feed their young!" Then, he added: "I couldn't read 'mammals' in school because I kept forgetting if mammals feed their young." I thanked him for telling me how he reacted to a certain word and was about to inquire why he had forgotten that mammals feed their young, when he said abruptly: "I kept seeing the little word in the big word, the little mamma in the big word of mammal, and I couldn't read mammal and couldn't remember which animals *are* mammals."

At the suggestion of his parents, I soon had a conversation with Tim's teacher who, on many occasions, gave generously of her time to talk with me about his academic progress and the problems he continued to have with learning. She told me that asking her students to "see" the little word in the big word was one of her favorite teaching strategies when children blocked the whole word. When I told her, with Tim's permission, that his understanding of the science lesson was influenced by his "seeing" the little word "mamma" in the big word "mammal," Tim's teacher was surprised and then laughed, saying, "I guess he's too smart for me!" She went on to explain that she had witnessed him on numerous occasions turning a teaching strategy into a learning "defense," and that he was so clever at misusing her teaching methods that she often felt distracted by his behavior. She summed up by saying: "But I *do* really like that kid. Sometimes I still believe he's 'dyslexic,' but other times I think he's a smart aleck, yet it's always fascinating to see what he will come up with, even though he's usually frustrating my goals as a teacher." I explained to her that while her teaching strategy might help him on some occasions, in this case it did contribute to his misunderstanding because of what he brought to the science lesson. I tried to get across that it was precisely his previous learning and thinking about mammals which led him to expect the lesson would tell him what the characteristics of "mammas" might be. He hoped mothers were "warm" (warm-blooded) and knew they certainly had hair but he had an off-and-on awareness of their capability to feed their young. And since he knew mother birds feed their young, he ignored the difference between hair and feathers and asserted that birds were mammals because he wished to assert that mammas feed their young. Tim's teacher listened to this explanation but again voiced her anxiety that perhaps he was "too smart" for her to teach because of his complex thought processes, which often led him to make deductions she could not follow. As an afterthought, she exclaimed, "And, anyway, I don't have time to follow the original thoughts of all 33 children in my class!" We ended the conversation by my describing the less complex example of the little girl who saw the letter *t* as "mommy waiting to hug me," which Tim's teacher readily understood, and by my saying that the ways in which children perceive school assignments and reason about them ought to be part of a teacher's education.

Like the little girl who imbued the letter *t* with personal significance, Timothy's perception of the little word mamma in the big word mammal did not exemplify emotions crowding out cognition. However, it did disclose his blending two contexts as he struggled with a taxonomic problem. The science assignment about mammals represented real, educational expectations which acted upon his "external [ego] boundary." He moved from that outer context to his inner, intrapsychic world where the affective significance of mammals feeding their young overtook his mind with such intensity that he did not thoroughly consider the various ways in which animal mothers could feed their young. In trying to understand the science assignment, he repeatedly switched from the mammal subgroup to the animal group, perhaps because he had recently observed mother birds feeding their young in his backyard. *Tim's cognitive sophistication facilitated this switch in contexts.* He understood that he saw two set problems and two subset problems. Big words (the set) have little words in them (subsets) just as animals have subgroups (one subset of which is mammals). He understood that his earlier focus on the little word *mamma* in the big word *mammal* reflected his personal need to know his mother would react to him: Would she react only to the errors he made in school and then refuse to take care of (feed) him or would she react empathically to his temporary misunderstanding of the science lesson?

Initially, Tim did not understand that none of the mammal subgroups includes birds. Important to him at that moment was the fact that mothers, as a group, would nurture their young, not whether this nurturance is gained by the infant's suckling. It was *precisely* his cognition that permitted both his error regarding which animals are mammals *and* his understanding of his mothering needs. Cognition told him, for example, that animals could be classified as either warm-blooded or cold-blooded—classes that are connected in some way to the surface characteristics of their bodies (e.g., whether protected by hair, feathers, scales, etc.). His question to me "Are birds mammals?" led to his more explicit understanding that while birds feed their young, they are not mammals because, for one thing, they do not have hair.

Tim's insights broadened when I reassured him that while he had not understood every word of the science lesson, he had understood a great deal. As he located the critical distinguishing characteristic of mammals which he now recognized his mother possessed—he said he knew his mother had nursed him as an infant—he understood his anxiety about his mother not taking care of him if he did not understand school assignments, including science lessons. In conversing with me, he began to understand that his mother cared very deeply about his learning. Furthermore, he recognized he had understood so much about classification that it was difficult for him *and* me to unravel all the cognitive connections he had made. Realizing how difficult it was for me to understand Tim's thought processes made me more empathic with his teacher who, indeed, was faced with many more children at any given moment than I, many of whom were undoubtedly reacting intelligently to the curriculum. As Tim perceived that we both struggled to understand what he made of the science lesson, he sensed that he had become activated and motivated to clear up his confusion himself. He probably also understood that I was active in trying to understand what he communicated and approved of his attempts at clarification. This meant that as he sat thinking and talking with me he felt safe in expecting his mother's love because he felt sure my approval of him meant he *was* learning.

Timothy's challenge to me shows how he was at once an "underachiever" and an "overachiever." Initially, like a typical underachiever, he turned away from the critical point of the lesson: that mammals can be distinguished from other animals by the fact that they suckle their young. At first, he ignored the fact that any animals nurse their young; but minutes later, he was less satisfied with the outright rejection characteristic of the underachieving stance and, like many overachievers, readily apprehended and gave personal significance to part of the lesson. In perceiving *mamma* in the word mammal, he vacillated in his understanding that the class of mammals is a subset of the animal group which includes birds as members of another subset. In order to rescue himself from this abyss of partial understanding, he repeatedly applied his teacher's advice of breaking up words into their little word parts to his classification problem. Probably because he easily saw the *mamma* in *mammal*, he thought of the correct analogy: the word *mamma* is to the word *mammal* as mothers (humans) are to the class of mammals. If so, he would be sincerely trying to understand the lesson rather than to escape learning by outsmarting the teacher. But whichever way he used to ferret his way out of confusion, he was confronted with his own psychology, which told him about mammas but which did not consistently assure him that mammas feed their young. Initially, he was centered only on the fact that *bird* mothers feed their young. Since he kept "forgetting" that mammals feed their young, the only way he felt safe imagining his mother would nurture him was by asserting that birds and mammas belong to the same mammal class.

Our conversations helped Tim become increasingly thoughtful about the opposing tendencies underlying his partial understanding, tendencies he eventually termed *my opposites*. As Tim became increasingly comfortable talking with me, he brought many more details of his daily experience and observed that I was attempting to form generalizations that might help him. This prompted him to use his intelligence to create his own hypotheses and to correct me if what I said was imprecise. Together we understood that math had been opposed to reading, mother was opposed to father, and whole words seemed opposed to little subwords. He tried to bring these opposites together by bringing learning into therapy and me into school so that he might close the gap between what he correctly understood and what he did not understand. He also tried to close the gap between his tendency to make fun of the teacher and to make light of learning with the utter seriousness with which he contemplated acceptable learning in therapy. It then became clear to me that it was irrelevant to Tim's future learning and treatment progress whether his teacher or I were as brilliant as he or whether we could follow his every thought to its logical conclusion. More important was Tim's understanding that important adults, such as his teacher and his therapist, engaged in observation and deduction. This gave him permission to observe and deduce and, even more significant, to *admit* that he had been observing and deducing all along.

Reading and Interpersonal Understanding

When Timothy began therapy, he felt that he did not do well in school, which often led him to react defiantly when his teacher tried to help him. When in therapy he began to understand that he had learned much more than he formerly realized, he began to perceive his teacher differently and to react to her more productively. Although before he had been aware of some of her characteristics, such as her favorite teaching strategies, he had not viewed her as a unique individual with personal values and goals. He had seen only some of her characteristics in the same way he partially comprehended the mammal characteristics. As a result of his awareness of human individuality, he began to reflect differently on his relationship with his teacher. He had decentered to the degree that he recognized his teacher as an individual capable, like him, of individual motives, values, and goals. He considered that what went wrong might exist in their interaction rather than simply in her. Previously it seemed to him that she thwarted *his* values and goals.

Another clash that helped him understand his typical mode of interacting with his teacher surfaced during his fourth month of therapy when he described what often happened in reading class: "When I don't read well, my teacher wants me to read faster and louder, so I read slower and more quiet, and mumbly." He meant to express his inner opposition to her outside expectation, which resulted in his doing the opposite of what she wanted and expected. In this way, he reacted to his teacher much the same way he reacted to his mother, who wished him to achieve in school so that he would escape the problems plaguing his father. But Tim felt he had to oppose these expectations because to give in to them meant giving up his prized identification with his father which, unfortunately, included memories of his father's "school failure," his withdrawal from final exams, and his subsequent drop out from school. For Timothy's compliance with his teacher's and mother's expectations meant he would be disloyal to his father *and* to himself since had chosen his father as a model. Hence, he *had* to oppose other adults.

When Timothy began to voice his feelings about reading and learning and when he heard himself articulate why he felt the way he did, he began to make reading and learning safe by putting limits on what he read and learned. He comprehended his teacher's goals and knew he could not change her wanting to teach him to read. So he began to take control of his learning by changing his attitude and becoming active in choosing what to read and what to learn. His choices almost always reflected his personal interests and hobbies. A week after his decision to read slower and "more mumbly" when asked to read faster and louder, he said quietly to me, "I would like to read if the story was about batteries." He implied that if stories were about scientific topics, their content would be as predictable in their outcomes as were mathematical operations. Because he had gained a wealth of information about batteries by way of spontaneous exploration, he therefore could predict much of the story line. These "predictions" made scientific stories safe in contrast to those about "people, boys and girls, and families" — what he did not want to think about. He implied as well that if he were permitted to read quietly (more mumbly) he would consent to do so. Choosing what he wanted to read and the way he read meant that he could enjoy reading. In fact, he would "*like* to read" (emphasis added) and no longer "hated" reading. Making reading safe also had the effect of separating learning and his feelings about it from important people and his feelings about them.

One week after choosing to read about batteries (after looking up and reading about batteries in a children's science dictionary in my office), Timothy asked if he could look up some words assigned for homework in Webster's dictionary. He told me that when his reading teacher assigned a biography for homework, he substituted the word *autobiography* for *biography* in his assignment book. Admitting his confusion, he understood how his word substitution represented an attempt to make reading safe. If he read only about himself, or more precisely only those aspects of himself which he might choose to write about, he could control the material he was expected to learn. Learning to read in therapy (or his conviction that he was learning to read with me) gave him the feeling that it was harmless to learn in the presence of adults. He felt free to read slowly and quietly with me—I respected not just *how* he read but *what* he read. I was pleased when he chose the subject of batteries, with his reading the dictionary, and most of all with his preference to read his autobiography. Tim's handwriting slip and confusion of the two words demonstrated to me his recognition that therapy requires the telling of one's own story. Since he had become much more attuned to the other person, he probably noticed that I was delighted with his behavior, not disappointed, because it revealed that my therapeutic efforts had had a positive impact on him. His understanding of his handwriting slip helped him to understand that his particular problems in reading and writing could be solved by his writing about himself, that is, by examining his own motives. Moreover, by focusing on his autobiography, he was able to separate himself from his family since he imagined his story would focus on his unique characteristics and would not be permeated by his parents' conflicts which had previously overwhelmed him. By increasing control over his school assignments, he was able to separate reading and skill-learning from other aspects of his life, such as his uncontrollable need to imitate his father.

Cognitive Monitoring

Timothy's advancement in learning and knowing took many forms. By his fifth month of therapy, his teacher reported that he had made 2-year's progress in reading. His favorite books included those with technical themes, such as children's "how-to-do-it" books about making vehicles out of ordinary household items. He also loved books about magic and stories with trick endings. He imagined he was "tricking" his teacher when he read these stories in class, believing he could "figure out" the trick more rapidly than she could. Sometimes he brought trick stories to therapy and enjoyed reading them aloud to me with a magician's flourish, expecting me to be mystified by the trick as he read. No longer did the stories he chose have to be exclusively about him nor did he project his conflicts into stories as much as he did before. When storybook themes held out the promise of a product he could use, such as learning to build or learning magic tricks, he was content to allow the story to unfold as it was written, without distorting its message by expecting to see himself or his family everywhere on the page. Furthermore, he used reading to triumph over other people and thus revealed that he identified knowing how to read with outsmarting others.

Soon he began to write original stories for the first time. He wrote about himself (his autobiography), and he wrote about his father (a biography), whose carpentry he had admired for years. He became more interested in his father's successes, such as his carpentry skills, and less interested in his failures as an academic dropout. Observing Tim's renewed reading and writing enabled me to monitor his academic progress.

But cognitive monitoring consists of more than an observation of what a child is able to produce when he is expected to meet a school's curriculum. It consists as well of an estimation of what underlies a motivated child's ability to meet the demands of a curriculum. During Tim's initial diagnostic evaluation, he easily expressed his level of operativity (Piaget & Inhelder, 1969) because the interview questions did not seem to him to be at all related to his schoolwork. He felt confident that revealing the right answers to questions about marbles or dolls was safe because only right answers to *schoolwork* would dramatize his father's academic incompetence. When he was asked whether there were "more girls or more people" about an array of four boy and five girl Fisher-Price dolls, he could confidently answer, "Even if there was only one boy in the world, there would still be more people than girls." His answer showed that he understood the relationship of set to subset and could not be diverted in his thinking by the fact that one of the subsets (boys) had fewer elements than the other subset (girls). This response is to be expected for a child his age, exactly 9 years. More important was the quality of his response. By saying "even if there was only one boy" he called upon logical necessity to justify his correct answer. It was logical necessity because Timothy knew that he need not count either the girl dolls in my office or any real girls. His answer could stand as correct on the basis of logic without an empirical test.

Four months later, when he was reinterviewed, he answered similar task questions. On this occasion, he was able to correctly and confidently answer questions normally asked of children 2 or 3 years older. For example, he was asked to consider two identical glasses partially filled with equal amounts of water. The contents of both glasses were poured into a third container, and Tim was told that this amount of water would be doubled by water poured from a fourth container. Then I told him that the doubled water would be equally divided by pouring it into the two original and identical glasses. After saying this I asked, "How much more water will we have in these two glasses compared to when we started?"[1] Timothy considered the problem for a few seconds, began to grin with apparent understanding, and then changed his expression to a mock frown, as though to make fun of serious thought. He answered humorously about the amounts of water in each identical glass: "It will be double! What else *could* it be?" Piaget (1972a) indicated that such a response is not expected until a child is 11 or 12 years; Tim was 9 years, 4 months.

His precocious response to Piagetian interviewing cued me to the complexity of his learning disorder. In making fun of serious thought as he correctly answered a question that was at least one chronological year beyond him, Tim at the same time ridiculed his earlier symptom of pretending to be stupid by now mocking, but not believing, that the question was too hard for him. But as he derided his past stupidity mimicry, he was more in control because he knew the right answer; that is, he now knew he was intelligent. Earlier, he was not sure he

[1]This question was adapted from the description of a task that Piaget (1972a) originated to test the child's understanding of the mathematical operation of distributivity.

was intelligent and thus was unsure about his answers to his teacher's questions, especially reading comprehension questions. Then, he made fun of his teacher who, in turn, misunderstood his insecurity and thought it reflected the serious reality that he could not learn to read. Because Tim now knew he could learn and read, he could make fun of (pretend to frown about) his earlier attempts to defend himself. In effect, he made fun of his stupidity impersonation and, in doing so, he revealed an increased self-reflexive sense since he now made fun of what he understood about himself instead of making fun of the other person.

Subsequently, Tim broadened his "problem-finding" (Arlin, 1975) to include increasingly complex science investigations. When he invented new problems to be solved, he tested the limits of his intelligence. But he was also interested in testing the intelligence of other people, and, most important, in exploring whether it was safe to know something another person did not know. One day during his sixth month of therapy, he began his appointment by saying, "What happens if you break a magnet in half?" I was about to answer that I was not sure when he began to nod his head yes, anticipating he had asked a question which I would find difficult. He was not trying to make fun of me as he earlier had made fun of his teacher. Before, he had avoided reading by taunting his teacher and ridiculing her goals which included teaching him phonics and other "tricks" to enhance his reading competence. Now he tried to show off what he actually knew by outsmarting me. In so doing, he approached an awareness of the connection he made between outsmarting or tricking others and genuine knowing. His awareness that he might liken knowing to trickery was one more sign of his progress and a common theme among all learning-disordered children's progress. But, even though he was pleased that he had outsmarted me, he was not sure that his genuinely knowing something better than I did was safe. Nonetheless, he still wished to distance himself from an intellectual orientation represented by my not understanding magnets which he felt was characteristic of his father's school failure. Instead, he wished to expand his development as a thinker as he asked me a question about physics, anticipating that his physics knowledge would surpass mine.

Tim may also have been trying to express some ideas about the "magnetism" between people. Since he had felt so unseparate from his parents, he might have wanted to know how to break up the "magnetic field" of mother, father, and himself. If so, he would be expressing the same need he expressed earlier as he maintained himself in the face of opposing parents when he, through "negating what I've just done" (Chapter 2), retained the same numerical value (the number 4) which represented himself. But, he also might have wanted to test whether he could attract the attention he felt he needed when the original magnetic totality (the family triad) was broken. He probably meant to inquire about his parents' earlier magnetism for one another, which had been broken as the result of their divorce. Would his parents still retain some of their attraction to and for him, even if they were no longer attracted to one another? As much as Tim wished to separate himself from his parents, often he could see no positive benefit in doing so and therefore felt he must symbolically test the safety of individuation by complex math or physics experiments.

However, I did not ask Tim about nor interpret the possible symbolic meanings described which might have been inherent in his question to me. I wanted him to know that I took his question seriously when I said that I did not know what would happen if a magnet were broken in half. This gave him the option of behaving in the fashion of one who knows. He, like his teacher, knew about magnets but I did not. It might have seemed to Tim that his teacher was similar to his knowledgeable mother, whereas I was similar to his defensive father and, for once, he felt safe allying himself with the adult (his mother, his teacher) who knows rather than inevitably protecting the adult (his father, me) who does not know. I felt that my knowing, or guessing, about his motives for learning about magnets was less important than his need to prove his expertise about magnets was superior to mine. If I concentrated on his motives and revealed my superior knowledge, he might have concluded that I was pitting my expertise about motives against his knowledge about magnets.

But at that moment I did wonder if Timothy failed to appreciate the difference between the potential to know and knowledge itself. Perhaps he thought I felt tricked because he thought that I, like him, could not see any way of finding out what I presently did not know. So two weeks later I told him that I had figured out what happens if one breaks a magnet in half, to which he answered, "I know the answer, and I knew you would figure it out." Perhaps he had spontaneously understood that there is a difference between that which has been apprehended and codified by other people and the process of knowing from one's own perspective. In addition, he may have surmised that I could figure out magnets because I had figured out important aspects of his personality. Whichever way he came to understand that what is not presently known can be observed or deduced, he seemed to understand that the act of knowing and a knowledge base are distinct but become integrated by the process that makes an organization of information available to the knower.

He also revealed that he had accurately assessed the capabilities of another person when he said, "*I* knew *you* would figure it out" (emphasis added). His self-reflexive sense included his sense of the other person, a complex phenomenon he now easily and often articulated. Moreover, he seemed to link his rapidly expanding ability to reason logically to his increased attempts to participate in a social world. Before this, he could not or would not reason logically in school or in the presence of his teacher because he did not feel like cooperating with her and because he believed she did not respect him as a thoughtful, potentially "knowing" individual. But in therapy, it seemed to him that we were working together on at least two problems: a physics question and a psychological question. He was the expert on the subject of magnets and I the expert on the subject of human motivation. Since I appreciated his physics expertise, he could acknowledge my figuring out capabilities.

But Tim's statement revealed much more than a mere understanding of logical reasoning, including the "logical necessity" inherent in answering "what happens if you break a magnet in half?" From what he said, I thought he had understood the dictionary's definition of a magnet as a piece of steel or iron with a positive and a negative pole. He said, "For it to be a magnet, it *has* to have a positive and a negative pole; if you break it in half, the two pieces *have* to have both too." In addition he understood that individuals are motivated to reason logically by their desire to gain the respect of other important people. The wish to be taken seriously by others motivates us to replicate intentionally the logical thought processes of others—a manifestly social act (Furth, 1987). In stressing what he and I could figure out together, Tim seemed to understand intuitively what Piaget asserts repeatedly and in many different contexts. Social interactions are not just decisive in weaning the child from his egocentric attitude but they provide the very laboratory for knowledge acquisition. In Piaget's view, "knowledge as such does not exist, but only socially related persons who know" (Furth, 1987, p. 124). Although this may be true, undoubtedly many socially related persons who know understand there are others who know more!

Finally, and most important for his changing perception of his father, Tim revealed by his willingness to share knowledge with me that he now found it acceptable for both of us to know and to understand. Where before he had become panicky when he realized that he might know more than his father (i.e., to know how to read and study with fewer conflicts that his father had reading and studying), his interactions with me in therapy revealed to him that I, like him, was capable of learning heretofore unknown facts about the physical world which implied that he might learn to better understand the still somewhat alien subject of human motivation.

Self-Reflexive Understanding and Renewed Learning

Much of what the child learns, whether in school or not, includes what he learns about himself in interaction with other people. The emphasis in this book is on the degree to which the child or adolescent *reflects* about the qualities of the self and of other people. But, this self-reflective quality emerges relatively late in the child's development and is preceded by other important self-development phases. Stern (1985) located the genesis of the developing self in the interactions of the infant and the mother. (A child's sense of self is not inferred from the statements of adults in therapy but from observations of or from experimental research with infants and young children.) But when Stern refers to an infant's sense of self, he is quite clear that he does not mean a self-reflexive sense, only "simple (non-self-reflective) awareness" (p. 7). It is useful to consider the senses of self as Stern conceptualizes them when assessing the youngster's developmental level and planning therapeutic strategies because they "are not viewed as successive phases that replace one another. Once formed, each sense of self remains fully functioning and active throughout life. All continue to grow and coexist" (p. 11). That is, it is certainly possible in theory to differentiate the "emergent," "core," "subjective," and "verbal" selves and it is also possible in psychotherapeutic practice to observe them.[2]

Similar to Piaget's (1976, 1978) subjects who, at approximately the age of 8 or older, introspected about the reasons for their successful actions, children older than 7 or 8 and all the adolescents I treated either talked about the activity of introspection directly or they implied that they were aware of introspecting in their conversations with me about what learning and knowing meant to them. I believe this increasing predilection for self-reflection is linked to the older child's and adolescent's experience of individuality specifically in terms of what they actually know and what they guess or suspect remains to be known by the self (a theme which I elaborate in Chapters 7, 8, and 9). I also believe that a sense of self becomes more refined as the child or adolescent simultaneously understands what is characteristic of the other person. For example, a critical factor in Timothy's sudden academic improvement and expanding thought was both his increased self-reflective awareness and his sensitivity to me (as one of some trusted adults) both of which can be seen in his statement that *he* knew what *I* would do ("I knew you would figure it out"). As I observe children and adolescents develop, it is often unclear in which sequence self-reflection, academic success, and interpersonal understanding evolve. Although increased self-understanding is linked to academic success and to interpersonal understanding, these questions remain about particular learning situations with a child:

1. Does increased self-understanding lead to academic success or vice versa?
2. Does increased self-understanding lead to interpersonal understanding or vice versa?

It is clear to me that increased self-understanding results in more energetic and successful attempts to master cognitive problems or to comprehend difficult academic tasks subsequently. Once the self-reflective function is in place, the child is better able to apply his cognition to academics and to understanding other people. I often hear an initially puzzled but suddenly discerning individual exclaim: "Oh! *I* know what *I* did!" just as he is about to correct himself and rethink a cognitive or interpersonal problem more maturely.

As Tim in therapy tested his language and logic against mine and began to perceive that we not only shared values and goals but sometimes disagreed, his self-reflexive sense helped undo confusions instigated by our verbal selves. As

---

[2]Stern hypothesizes that the "emergent" self is formed during the first two months of life when the infant begins to organize the many disparate aspects of his sensory, physical, and social experience. These disparate aspects of personal experience become more integrated as the "core" self becomes more distinct from others, which permits the infant to be with another person in a way that does not threaten his selfhood. The "subjective" self, which develops next, becomes capable of being intimate with and exquisitely attuned to the other person which implies the infant's intuitive recognition that significant others also have selves. Lastly, the "verbal" self expresses through language—and in my view, the logic underlying language—the degree to which attempted communications result in shared understanding.

he increasingly saw himself as a learner and a thinker, increasingly he began to separate himself from, but become more sensitive to,the needs, values, and goals of other people. One day after 6 months of therapy, when he was 9½ years, as he rested the calculator on the back of his neck positioning it perhaps to represent his own head, he said, "The calculator is telling me how to do math." Because he knew full well that I believed it was he and not the calculator who was telling him how to do math, he proceeded to show me, with a mischievous grin, how he could multiply zeroes without looking. Not only had he memorized how to multiply zeroes when the calculator was out of his field of vision, he had also realized that to create this effect with the calculator on the back of his head (or neck), he had to mentally reverse the left-right sides of the calculator and the directions of his hand movements. In addition to this impressive mental facility, he tried to express that what had bothered him about school-work in the past was that he might make mistakes. He could more easily express this fear and make fun of it around the subject of math, since he knew he was good at it, but had always felt he was "no good" at reading. About calculators, he seemed to be saying that they were better than people because they do not make mistakes especially while multiplying zeroes, a thought that amused him but which he did not take literally. In making fun of a past anxiety, he knew I would respond by focusing on what *he,* not the calculator, could do. I said maybe he needed the calculator at the base of his head to tell him that he could read, more than he needed it there to multiply zeroes. I said this because Tim had admitted in therapy that he had "always been good at math." His immediate "Huh?" revealed he was taken aback by my attempt at humor, so I explained that since he had memorized how to multiply zeroes without even looking at the calculator, I felt he could learn anything he wanted to learn. To this his annoyed frown changed into a smile of recognition as he said, "Yes, but that's not what I meant."

Perhaps Tim felt annoyed at me because my first remark focused not on what he expected—math—but on the unexpected—reading. My remark about the unexpected seemed to create once more in Tim the antipathy he had felt all along toward reading and the unexpected contents of books. Or perhaps he felt I was not giving him the recognition he deserved for his recent advances in reading when I spoke first of his needing support in order to continue efforts at reading mastery. Whatever the reason for his annoyance, Tim's language and the thought underlying it seemed at odds with mine—in his words, "that's not what *I* meant" (emphasis added). Stern (1985) found situations like this potentially hazardous because the child's developed verbal self can come into conflict with others' verbal selves:

> At first glance, language appears to be a straightforward advantage for the augmentation of interpersonal experience. It makes parts of our known experience more shareable with others.... But in fact language is a double-edged sword. It also makes some parts of our experience less shareable with ourselves and with others. It drives a wedge between two simultaneous forms of interpersonal experience: as it is lived and as it is verbally represented. (p. 162)

And most germane to what I have described as occurring between Tim and me is Stern's assertion that

> meaning results from interpersonal negotiations involving what can be agreed upon as shared. And such mutually negotiated meanings (the relation of thought to word) grow, change, develop, and are struggled over by two people and thus ultimately owned by *us*. (p. 170)

Stern's commentary explains why Tim was immediately more interested in my meaning when I changed my words so that I talked about learning instead of reading. Then we both "owned" language and he did not feel at odds with me or my perspective. Even though he tuned out when I said the calculator might tell him how to read, he tuned in when I tried to negotiate meaning with him as I said I felt he could learn anything he wanted. The verb *learn* opened up new possibilities, including mental virtuosity, in contrast to the verb *read* which had been problematic in the past.

Tim also brought a self-reflective sense to understanding his past. He asked himself why reading, both in school and in therapy, had been so difficult. Although he now talked freely about his ambivalent feelings regarding his parents and the ways this ambivalence was tied to learning, he also focused on the learning act itself. He told me how the phonetic approach had impeded his understanding of the assigned story. Then, laughing and again mocking himself instead of others, he told how he used the process of sounding out to prevent understanding: "I used phonics when I didn't want to know what the word was." I asked him to give me an example, which he did eagerly: "Take the word marginal. If you read mar-gin-al, you don't have to think about what it means. All you think about is 'mar'...what's that?...'gin'...I'm not old enough for that!...al?...means nothing." I agreed that treating a word this way would certainly deprive it of its original meaning or impute some different meaning. Then I inquired what might have been the problem with the word *marginal*. He told me how in school he had been called "marginal" in his reading ability and added, "I never could read the word margin in your game of Sorry because I always thought margin meant *I* was on the margin, but I *did* know the number eleven means you can change places." Sorry is a table game requiring the players to follow the written instructions on a deck of cards. The purpose of the game is to be the first player to advance all four game pieces to the home position. Tim was referring to the number eleven card, which permits the player who picks it to either move 11 spaces or to exchange places with an opponent, which often accelerates one's own game piece toward home. By exclaiming about what he could not know (read) and what he could know, Tim tried to express several levels of knowing. He hated the number 11 card because its message contained the word *margin*, but he liked knowing he had the option of "changing places" even though he regularly declined to take this option. Often, changing places would have advanced him in the game, but to Tim it had another meaning: changing places with a parent who had not succeeded in school, or changing places with a parent who he saw as pushing him to avoid his father's fate.

These complex thoughts were brought to mind through Timothy's understanding of the uses to which he put phonics. He recognized he had turned a teaching strategy into a defense strategy against learning and knowing. When he explained this to me I told him he had done some important thinking, at which he pointed to the number 11 card where it said "margin men" and added this to his previous comments: "I didn't want to be one of those." He then fell silent and read the rest of the card's message: "Forfeit move if you do not wish to change places and it is impossible to go forward 11 squares." Although I could not be sure because Tim read silently, this number 11 card seemed to epitomize his learning problems which he had tried to understand, to communicate to me, and to sum up by reading the card's message silently. He had seemed to "forfeit" his own developmental progress because he did not want to "change places" with either parent. Refusing to change places with a parent, I thought, meant to Tim that it was impossible to go forward because progress in learning had always been bonded to parental progress. Tim had solved this problem by forfeiting learning and by resigning himself to an unchanged stance, similar to the game piece which remains in the same position if it is impossible to progress.

Self-Development and Egocentrism

Remember that egocentrism refers to a failure to grant either an object a position or a person a perspective other than the youngster's own. In an excellent summary of the relevance of Piaget's psychology for clinicians, Rosen (1985) has shown that this concept has profound implications for psychopathology and therapeutic intervention "Since egocentrism is a negative and limiting feature of development it provides fertile grounds for exploring psychopathological phenomena in both the intrapsychic and interpersonal realms" (p. 45). Despite Tim's progress in psychotherapy, his lingering egocentrism continued to confuse him as he tried to separate his nonlearning attitude from his father's apparent rejection of schooling. Consequently, although he had struggled laboriously to differentiate himself and his perspective from me and my perspective thereby solidifying his sense of self, his view that what held true for him held true for his father (and vice versa) impeded a more complete sense of himself as unique. It should be noted once more that even though he concentrated on the child's egocentric understanding of the inanimate world, Piaget (1981; Piaget & Inhelder, 1969) did theorize that the final resolution of egocentrism occurs within social interactions. One critical "social interaction" in which Tim resolved his lingering egocentrism was his behavior with me in therapy. Then, as he saw that I did not share his parents' attitudes toward learning, he made comparisons first between himself and me, then between me and his father, and finally between himself and his father.

I would add that the child's egocentrism often transfers from the world of inanimate objects to the intrapsychic and interpersonal worlds and vice versa. It is these quicksilver transfers that often confound the therapist's attempts to understand the child's view. When Tim, for example, began to understand more fully how differently he felt about reading and math, he could make fun of his earlier attitudes in regard to learning as he played with the calculator. In making fun of the idea that calculators, similar to people, can "tell" us what to do, he showed, whether he firmly believed it or not, that he had at least wondered whether machines can behave like people. As sophisticated and brilliant as Tim often was, he nonetheless often deduced that because *he* hated reading, it must have been the necessity to read that led his father to drop out of medical school. Thus, as he observed that he shared a learning problem with his father, then he guiltily concluded that his own panic in first grade could have *preceded* his father's decision to withdraw from school. Since his vivid memories of his difficulties in the learning situation overpowered *him*, he could only assume that his father felt the same way. The term *egocentrism* helps explain the logic that weaves the child's view to the adult's. It was difficult for Tim to distinguish between his own feelings and his father's and, worse, to decide whose angry and guilty feelings had caused their respective nonreading and nonlearning.

With egocentrism's decline, the older child recognizes and can articulate the distinction between the perspectives of self and other. This conceptual distinction between self and other, that is, "interpersonal decentering," follows the

> initial state in which everything is centered on the child's own body and actions to a "decentered" state in which his body and actions assume their objective relationships with reference to all other objects and events registered in the universe. (Piaget & Inhelder, 1969, p. 94)

Although Tim showed egocentrism around reading by believing that language symbols (i.e., "signs") were indistinct from his wishes or motives, he decentered when he said he could "make *numbers* do whatever *I* want" (emphasis added) while simultaneously he adhered to the conventions of mathematics.[3] His success at math and his cognizance that it was *he* who was manipulating the math symbols (signs) conveyed to him that his understanding of mathematical operations would permit him to do whatever he wanted with the symbols. For instance, he could invent math games wherein he remained true to his sense of math at the same time that he remained true to his own desires regarding math. Decentering, then, led to a firmer distinction between logic and motive.

Nevertheless, he still believed he had no control over words and thus revealed uneven development. Although Tim recognized that it was people who "made up numbers" and people who "made up the rules about numbers," he showed an astonishing ignorance of or refusal to recognize the fact that it is also people who make up language and its rules. Because he felt helpless regarding words that seemed to overpower him, he failed to perceive how any person could control words or originate rules about words. Since he linked his memory of his father's academic struggles to his own, he felt that no one, not he nor his

[3]From a Piagetian perspective, language consists of signs, not symbols, both of which are part of the "semiotic function" (Piaget & Inhelder, 1969, p. 57; Furth, 1969, p. 265). Signs are conventional and arbitrary in contrast to symbols, which are "motivated"—they bear some resemblance to what they signify. Even though signs are conventional and therefore social, the child often uses them for his own motivated purposes. In this book, when I use the term *symbol*, I mean the representation process by which the child chooses a thing, event, number, word, or even person to stand for other things, events, numbers, words, or persons.

father, had any power in regard to words. When he separated his perspective from his father's, words became safer because he no longer expected to "see" his father's medical school failure as he read. Finally, he began to perceive that math *and* language symbols bore the same relationship to his self. It was his very realization that people "made up the rules about numbers" which prompted him to understand that people also made up the rules about words. That is, his previous understanding of symbols was broadened to include words as well as numbers.

Tim also realized that "kids make up words all the time" when he told me about various new slang words which were popular among his school friends. He accurately reported the social basis for words as he described a group of his peers deciding by a vote what a certain slang word meant. Then he perceived that he could make words, like numbers, do what he wanted them to do without denying the conventions of language. He read what was on the printed page while he simultaneously searched for his own story interpretation or language inventions. He no longer felt helpless about written language which before he had tried to command and deny at one and the same time. And, he understood that language development in human history is not isomorphic with a single individual's wishes or perspective.

TIMOTHY'S COORDINATION OF OPPOSITES

When Timothy had been in therapy for 9 months, he became unhappy about himself in school. His complaint was no longer "I hate reading," but "I hate school." Even though before he blamed himself for not being able to read and thought his reading hatred might make him a school failure, he now, in preadolescent style, blamed the school when things failed to go his way. Like many adolescents, he tried to preserve a positive self-image in school by hating school. Tim's belief that the school ought to change, not he, meant that he was, to quote him, "okay, as is." He focused his school complaints on school rules and spent much of his therapy time endlessly arguing like a lawyer for or against specific rules or procedures.

Consider again Stern's (1985) view that as the self becomes and continues to be verbal, language usage can become a double-edged sword. (It should be remembered that Stern theorized that the several senses of self which are formed during infancy coexist simultaneously, and that his is not a stage theory in which developmental characteristics recede and are replaced partially or totally by the qualities of more advanced stages.) Tim's language ("I hate school" and "I hate the school's rules" in contrast to his earlier "I hate reading") suggested a regression. His aversion seemed to be even more pervasive than before. But, I viewed Tim's hating school as an advance, not a regression, because he no longer hated himself when he had a "bad day" at school. Nonetheless, the language and the underlying concepts he used to express his problems carried the risk of interpersonal misunderstanding at the same time that they carried the logic of preadolescence. Did he dare tell me, his mother, or his father that he "hated school"? Would we perceive his increased self-esteem, or would we focus on what might be the implied regress in his statements?

On one occasion when he had had a bad day in school, he was reluctant to come to therapy. In fact, he was about to refuse to come into my office when I asked him, "Why today of all days?" To this Timothy, who was soon to celebrate his tenth birthday, smirked and said, "My brain hasn't told me yet." I answered that I was sure his brain would eventually tell him but he remained silent for most of the hour. Just before leaving, he glanced at himself in the mirror and smiled pleasantly, quickly brushed his hand over his hair while saying good-bye, remarking that his brain did tell him after all.

During the next session he told me how "hard" it was "to grow up when grownups push you around all the time." He was referring to his teacher who had recently criticized him and to his mother who had been very worried about his intention not to come to therapy the week before. She saw his reaction to therapy and to school events as a reversion to the old symptoms, which had changed from hating reading and loving math to hating bad days in school but liking good days in school. At first, Tim's mother did not see that when he complained about good and bad days at school, he classified math *and* reading as acceptable when he said he "liked" school, whereas before he had always loved math and hated reading. He soon focused on what had happened in school the previous week to create his school rejection. While on a field trip, he had been honored by his appointment as student leader of his class, but then had been deprived of carrying out this role because he had been unable to prevent another child from misbehaving. In frustration, Timothy said, "Why should I talk to you? It wouldn't do any good [last week]."

As I listened to his explanation of week-old events, I realized that there had been a shift in the way Tim now expressed anger compared to the way he expressed it in the past. Before he had refused to *read* when angry; now, he refused to *talk*. Earlier when he said "I hate reading" he had probably meant "I won't read when I hate" (i.e., feel angry). But now when angry, he continued to learn and read in school (even though he hated school) but refused to talk to me because I had not been able to change the school rules nor was I able to prevent him from being deprived of an honor. I had failed to have the wished-for magical effect on both him and the school's procedures. Although his refusal to talk represented his intent to punish me, it also revealed an intuitive understanding that I could not directly alter all aspects of his life. By continuing to bring his school problems to therapy, he freed himself to behave appropriately and continue to learn in school.

Thereafter, difficulties in learning became substantive only. His difficulties revolved around a temporary misunderstanding of a science project, or difficulty with a particular story theme rather than a rejection of learning because it might touch upon family conflicts or it might reveal to his parents how much he knew, including what he knew about them. School was school, and family was family. His excuse of "hating reading" soon became modulated by his belief that he could make reading, and all of learning, do what he wanted it to, as he had earlier felt he could manipulate math. Rather than use cognition to avoid learning, he used it to make learning serve varied needs. Similarly, Annie, whose case narrative follows, differentiated school from family by making math do what she wanted. Since she was two years younger than Tim, she needed to understand in which ways making math bend to her wishes distorted math and in which ways it added to her expertise. Unlike Tim who had mastered math thoroughly, Annie needed both practical instruction and therapeutic insight.

Timothy's last appointment was just before Christmas. His teacher had informed his mother that he had made another gain in reading: he had progressed 1½ years so that he now read on grade level. He told me that he knew what he was getting for Christmas "because I *peeked* in the closet and *read* what it said on the package. I'm getting *just* what I wanted!" However much he still needed to "peek" in order to feel free to read, to "sneak" to steal knowledge, or sometimes to "peek" and "steal" to be pleased with his mother's gifts, he had learned that reading could lead directly to gratification or to the expectation of gratification. Now, Tim behaved toward his parents in the fashion of a normal post-Oedipal young person. He knew in which ways his mother would predictably satisfy his needs (by giving him the presents he wanted) and he knew it was safe to tease her, which he did by secretly searching for his presents and by pretending not to know how to read wherein it was obvious to both mother and son that he was only joking. Simultaneously, he continued to openly admire his father and to write original stories about him.

ANNIE'S PRESENTING PROBLEM

Annie, who was almost 7-years-old, had math difficulties sufficient for her teacher to suggest math tutoring. Although she could read above grade level and write charming stories well beyond her years, she became severely confused by the most simple math problems. In addition to her math problems, Annie came to therapy because of inattention in school and because of anxiety attacks before school which her mother said led to daily arguments between herself and Annie. According to her teacher, she began to daydream when she was faced with math assignments but instantly became attentive once more when the teacher asked her to work in her language workbooks or to write an original story. She also created stories at home and kept a journal with preparatory notes describing real events, including dates and descriptions of the people involved.

ANNIE'S FAMILY HISTORY

Annie was a thin but graceful girl with piercing, inquiring eyes and exaggerated facial expressions. She would pout or frown when she felt misunderstood by adults. Her voice, too, was often exaggerated; for example, she would cackle like a witch when angry and plan to avenge the person she was angry with. Annie's parents had high hopes for her and had themselves been good students in high school and in college, but as adults they shrugged off their adolescent achievements. Rather they affected a casual attitude toward their memories of "high marks" in school and even toward the ongoing success of their family business. But, they were not casual about their children's academic successes and wished to validate their own abilities by basking in their children's achievements. When discussing Annie's achievements in reading and creative writing, her mother minimized Annie's linguistic talents and focused on her math problems, explaining that she may have "inherited" a math "disability" from her. Annie's mother summed up by saying that she could not convince herself she had achieved because of her persistent struggles with "the simplest of math problems." Both Annie's parents might be best described as covert worriers who inspired overt worries in Annie, and in her 3-year-old brother whose precocious reading they had already begun to brag about. Just prior to Annie's referral for therapy, her parents had separated and had told me they hoped the separation would give each parent "time to think." They had talked with Annie and also with me about her math problems at the same time that they talked about their marital problems. Since Annie had overhead many conversations between her parents about math and marital problems, I wondered if she identified her own math problems with her parents' marital problems. If this were so, Annie's math problems might have been intended to signal her parents that she was having problems as a result of their problems.

ANNIE'S INITIATION INTO THERAPY

Annie came to therapy very angry at her mother who, she claimed, never listened to her or explained things "right." She asserted that her mother always forgot what she said and frequently said "uh hum" when Annie was talking "because she doesn't really want to *know* what I think." Soon she began to object strenuously whenever I said "uh hum" during her appointment. On one occasion she screamed that if she ever heard the sounds "uh hum" again she would kill the person who said them. To this I responded by asking what she would like me to say instead. She answered instantly: "Say 'okay' or 'that's good,' *anything* but uh hum!" I thought she tried to express that she was angry at her mother for doubting her intelligence and believing her to be math disabled. So she retaliated by criticizing her mother's use of language and claimed to be a language expert when she quite literally told her mother and me how to speak.

TREATMENT PROGRESS

After 4 months of therapy, when Annie was 7 years, 3 months, and so might be expected to be at least transitional for concrete operations, she began bringing her math problems to therapy (1 month later, she understood all four tasks of concrete operations). She began by showing me the math problems she was assigned in school, such as two digit addition, two digit subtraction, and beginning multiplication. She continued this phase of therapy (7 weeks) by writing math problems on the blackboard in my office which in her immaturity she viewed as "impossible." She would ask me to add digits numbering in the billions (e.g., 1,000,000,000 plus 1,000,000,000) with the intent to watch me struggle to answer. She assumed the more digits she made me add, the harder the problem was. She may have also wished to say that since her parents' marital problems seemed impossible to resolve, all other problems were equally impossible. I explained that while it did take me a long time to write the answer, adding one billion to another billion was not as difficult as it seemed. To tell me that she did not fully understand what I said, she marked wrong all the problems I had answered correctly by covering up the answers with a large X. I thought she covered up my answers with an X, and implicitly my statement, because I had said that problems were not as difficult as they seemed to be. Despite my statement, she continued to believe that problems, both her math and her parents' marital problems, would be difficult to solve. But I was not altogether sure that Annie had connected her math problems to her parents' marital problems. Later statements she made told better than any of my speculations what her problem was. Moreover, when I focused on *her* math problems instead of her *parents'* marital problems, she heard me say or imply that she was competent and could find solutions. This response became apparent by later events.

After crossing out my answers to her addition problems, Annie started to talk about the arguments she had with her mother as she waited for the school bus in the morning. She admitted that she often provoked arguments with her mother and associated the fights with her mother to feelings about school: "I felt bad about school in the morning... I got so worried about my teacher and mad that I picked a fight with Mom." When told that perhaps she wanted to make her mother feel "bad" so that her mother might know how she felt inside (when waiting for the school bus), Annie nodded her head yes in vigorous agreement.

The very next week Annie revealed what she knew about math, expressing she was ready to learn some new facts, both about math and about her relationship to her parents. Thus, it appeared that her math difficulties in school might well have been related to an "arithmetic" with her parents (Greenspan, 1979, p. 237). First, she demonstrated an understanding of commutativity by writing "3 plus 1" and "1 plus 3." She promptly provided her own answer: "They're both 4, they *have* to both be 4." After erasing these problems, she wrote "3 plus 3" and "3 plus 3." Watching my face, she broke into laughter at this attempt to make fun of an adult, which might have related to her feelings about her teacher, who had tried to teach commutativity because she believed Annie did not understand what, in fact, she did. Since I was at that moment engaged in forming some hunches about Annie's core problem, I did not interpret that she might be making fun of those adults who thought her stupid, in this case possibly her teacher, or even me. Instead, I said, "The way you wrote it, you couldn't tell which problem was which," a statement that remained very close to the concrete details of her behavior. That is, when illustrating commutativity, she had switched to the concept of identity which further suggested to me (but which I did not say to her) that she was unable to distinguish which problem was her mother's and which was her own. To my statement she laughed even harder, possibly responding to the auditory similarity of "which" and "witch," and challenged me once more in asking what all the numbers she had just written on the board added up to. After some calculations I answered that the total of the numerals written (3, 3, 6, 3, 3, 6) was 24. With a flourish she set up the same problem but in a more organized fashion:

$$3 + 3 = 6$$
$$\underline{3 + 3 = 6}$$

Then she asked, "How'd you know the right answer?" To this I said the answer was twice 12. I felt that an organized response to her question "How'd you know" was called for because she had shown a keen math understanding in arranging the numbers on the blackboard. Seeming to go onto something else, she played quietly with marbles for 10 minutes and then suddenly burst out: "Oh! I *know how* you did it, because 4 3s are 12, and 6 and 6 is 12, and two 12s are 24!"

In organizing her math problem, Annie showed a math ingenuity that had remained dormant as she struggled with intrapsychic conflicts and with the myth that she was "math disabled." First, she arranged the numbers (3, 3, 6, 3, 3, 6) in two groups; four 3s were arranged on the left side of the equals sign and two 6s on the right side so that she might understand more easily the total of the 6 numbers. Second, if she had followed through in correctly answering the math problem implied by the straight line beneath the numbers, it would have looked like this:

$$3 + 3 = \quad 6$$
$$\underline{3 + 3 = \quad 6}$$
$$6 + 6 = 12$$

By her number arrangement, she ingeniously posed two math problems: the one asking for the sum of all the numbers and the other consisting of one subset of numbers which could be added horizontally and the other subset of numbers added vertically. Although she declined to write the answer adding vertically, she showed by her excited exclamation to me ("Oh! I *know how* you did it...") that she understood her math problem could be segmented into at least two sub-problems which she could solve: she could add four 3s and add two 6s and follow these calculations by adding the two sums to get her answer. In playing with numbers and number arrangements, she discovered the intrinsic appeal of math and cleverly generated her own "math problems" which helped her understand math logic better.

Developments with Annie the following week (the third session of this therapeutic sequence) illustrate how complex it can be to pay attention to both spheres of the psyche at once, which might be one reason in working with children that a clinical interpretation rarely reflects both. When her mother reported that Annie had come home with schoolwork containing the single error of a small "i" for capital "I" (she avoided writing the personal pronoun *I*), it appeared to me that at school she felt unworthy of being herself (the "I") because of the confusion she experienced regarding math, confusion which was readily cleared up when she was permitted to play with numbers at her own pace and instigation. In response to what her mother told me about her substitution of a small i for capital I, I told Annie we can still always call ourselves I even though we sometimes make mistakes in math.

When she came for her next appointment, Annie remembered how she had successfully understood the reasoning in my adding up to the number 24. This remembrance implied she was aware that she, too, could solve the problem. Then she tried to take this interpretation further. She revealed that while she heard me say she could always call herself I, implying she was a unique individual, she had not integrated this understanding with certain specific math problems which still gave her difficulty. It might be said that Annie heard my remark within the context of her inner, intrapsychic world but for the moment could not apply it to logical problems or to math as she dealt with the reality of the external world. She explained her reasoning by saying, "You can always get the right answer adding two columns [of numbers] like 14 and 12 if you think of the problems as separate problems." By this she meant that a two digit addition problem, such as 14 plus 12, was easier for her to solve if she thought of adding 4 plus 2, and then 1 plus 1. As she told me this, she put the problem 95 plus 56 on the blackboard. I answered by saying that while what she said made sense, it worked only for problems such as 14 and 12 or 33 and 33, but would not work for 95 and 56. She listened attentively and did not make fun of my attempt to help with understanding, as she had before, probably because previously she had understood a math problem through her own efforts or perhaps because she felt I truly believed in her capacity to solve problems.

Indeed, it made sense for Annie to solve two-digit addition problems her way. The most obvious reason behind her method was that attention to two easy problems, such as 1 and 1 or 4 and 2, is much easier than adding 14 and 12. But the following week she revealed how her math solution had been overdetermined. She said sadly that her father had left home because "he was mad at both of us [herself and her mother], and he doesn't want to be with either of us." It then became clear that when she heard me say she was an "I" although she might make mistakes in school, she wanted even more to separate herself from her mother. She acted out her increased need to be a separate person by conceiving of two-digit addition problems as being two different "problems." Annie was thus *not* as concerned with her parents' separation as she was with separating herself from her mother. The impact of the interpretation ("You can be an 'I' ") stemming from interpersonal difficulties between Annie and her mother transferred to math problems and displayed a vivid illustration of the relationship between cognition affecting the inner and outer ego boundaries. Even though she was wrong mathematically, she was right psychologically. The reason for her father's departure *was* a different problem for her compared to her mother. But her mathematical calculations were incorrect nonetheless. A near concrete use of intelligence, then, was combined with a motive to produce the math error. She could not easily add 14 and 12 but she did find it easy to coordinate 1 and 1 with 4 and 2. Easier calculations restimulated her desire to separate her problems from her mother's.

CLINICAL ISSUES

Psychological Discontinuities

To understand the complexity of learning problems such as Annie's, the therapist must recognize that more than one discontinuity can exist in the child's experience as she struggles with a core problem. This occurrence has been called "dyssynchronous development" (Greenspan, 1979, p. 229). Although the child may show "ideal" operativity because she understands how the inanimate world works, as Annie did when she solved those math problems unrelated to her conflicts with her mother, cognitive activity at the "internal boundary" may crumble as the result of psychodynamic pressures. One important aspect of Annie's math problems, for example, is that an interpretation aimed at the child's inner world ("You can still always call yourself an 'I' even though you make mistakes in math") does not necessarily clear up the child's misunderstanding of logic or facts of the external world. As Greenspan has suggested, in therapeutic work it may be helpful to begin with the ways the child relates to the external world and has problems with math and then to progress to themes of the intrapsychic or inner world, such as a negative parent identification. But therapeutic work can also move in the reverse direction from the inner world to the outer. As the child works through an internal problem, adaptation may continue to be compromised or even worsened in the child's external world. A situation like this occurred with Annie's "arithmetic" with her mother, which meant that any two-digit number must be separated in order to add it to another two-digit number. Every time Annie was presented with a two-digit number to add to another two-digit number, she felt she must separate the digits. Internally, she felt she must separate her problems from her mother's because she knew her problems were not the same as her mother's. She had heard me say precisely this and seemed to react as though the truth in her personal "logic" was as compelling as her mathematical logic. It then became apparent that Annie needed to know that the logic of math *always* holds true while the logic of her inner or "psycho-logic" world is independent of math. Helping her with the remaining problems she had dealing with reality (e.g., ways to successfully add 95 and 56) helped her understand the difference between the world of people and the world of math.

A second discontinuity can exist between the two spheres of the psyche: affective and intellective. For example, Annie was brought up short by her recognition that in math she must attend less to how she felt about her mother and more to the logic of math. But the very logic of math sharpened her feelings about her mother because in recognizing she must consider two-digit addition problems as two two-digit numbers together when separating the two digits in each pair, she became even more in touch with the togetherness of the two digits and the fact that they had to be considered in tandem. The logic of the math problem thus impacted Annie's affect. That is, progress in the intellect may retard progress in the affective sphere or disequilibrate affective schemes (Piaget, 1973a; Cowan, 1982). When she experienced discontinuity between the intellective and affective spheres, she tried to deny what she already partially knew about math. My attempts to show her that she could not rely on her heretofore immature math logic was intended to coordinate the intellectual and affective spheres. I stressed that her attempts to resolve all her problems via math logic "made sense" at the *same* time I stated that her problems in math and the problems she had with her mother were entirely different.

A week later (the sixth session), Annie quickly calculated the number of days it had been since she had seen her father by multiplying the number of months (2) by days (31 days of the two months). With relish, she added the remaining days of the present month to get her answer. When praised for her quick thinking and good understanding of how she felt about her father's absence (that it was much too long a time), she answered that someone in her class had gotten "thirty math problems wrong and only one right." She then captured a visual image on the blackboard of what she had just said, revealing her understanding of multiplication. The configuration looked like this:

$$
\begin{array}{ccccc}
 & & C & & \\
X & X & X & X & X \\
X & X & X & X & X \\
X & X & X & X & X \\
X & X & X & X & X \\
X & X & X & X & X \\
X & X & X & X & X \\
\end{array}
$$

When told this was a good way to write the number 30, she answered, "Yes, six rows of fives [five X's], and one more C [correct] makes thirty one!"

Follow-up information on the work she had done came from her mother who reported before her seventh session that Annie had consented to show a family friend how well she had learned two-digit addition. Moreover, Annie's mother spontaneously confided: "I've finally become convinced that she's bright," and with this statement revealed her initial doubt about Annie's learning ability. Annie's mother had doubted that Annie could learn math not just because she shared an alleged math disability with Annie but also because she doubted that she could be an effective parent following her separation from her husband.

Inhibitions: Unconscious and Conscious?

Annie's math difficulties resulted from inner or interpersonal conflicts expressed by way of mathematical symbols or processes that came to stand for some other object, event, or person. In Annie's mind, the tools of math and its processes symbolized a central problem that she experienced in dealing with her parents. Put another way, her use of math symbolized her confused attempts to understand the Oedipal triad. But, math inhibition—or any learning inhibition for that matter—is not simply the result of blocking an unconscious impulse. That unconscious impulses may exist is not at issue. Of more concern is what the child who decides to evade learning is aware of in regard to the assigned material. To undo the inhibition which stands in the way of understanding, the therapist must acknowledge what the child has understood. This will activate increased learning attempts and credits her for this activity.

In a paper on acalculia, Vereecken (1965) attributed difficulties in the learning of math in a 6½-year-old boy to inhibitions of an oral-aggressive nature. Piaget's concept of *reversibility* (the ability to return to the starting point in one's thinking) is discussed in this paper, but it is not directly integrated into the discussion of the child's symptoms in a way that either clarifies their nature, or validates the child's decision about an intellectual problem. Ideas derived from the Piagetian tradition (mobility, reversibility) are used to suggest only what the child lacks, despite the possibility that cognitive psychology could shed light on what the child actually knows. The implication is that the child senses enough about math and its relationship to oral-aggressive fantasies to avoid math and by this avoidance submerges certain math facts or calculations. It also implies that the child does not know enough to avoid the results of his or her learning. (Since the author does not write that the child may be avoiding the results of learning, i.e., math knowledge itself, the reader cannot speculate what specific resistance this may have been.) Thus, the child is seen as remaining passive with regard to drives or to developmental trends. In assuming that children are *not* autonomous—that they act *without* their own good conscious reasons—we are more likely to fall prey to inconsistencies in reasoning, such as the child is somehow capable of pushing aside fantasied or expressed oral-aggressive impulses but cannot choose to avoid math knowledge as the result of resisting math facts. We must ask why the child chose math learning to symbolize an inhibition of expression when he could have chosen any other school subject or a segment of life less obviously related to academic learning (e.g., peer relationships). The clinician's inattention to the child's choice masks the meaning of his behavior.

The child described by Vereecken behaved at least some of the time in an autonomous fashion, as revealed by the fact that his math errors required more complex calculations than a direct route to the right answers. The boy declined to add the 2 two-digit numbers of 42 and 30 directly, and instead added 3 tens to the number 42. Reversibility can be seen in the child's understanding of the number 30 can be returned to 3 tens. The process the child chose over the correct one involved more steps and consequently more mobility than the latter. As one developmental psychologist (Elkind, 1979b, 1981) has stated, the more steps required, the harder the task for the pre- or concrete operational child. Dividing the second number into 3 tens before adding it to the first number, requires just that "free mobility" called for by reversibility, which Vereecken found wanting in his 6-year-old patient. An equally plausible explanation would be this young boy's desire to show off how smart he could be in adding four numbers instead of two, or in dividing and adding simultaneously. The boy could have been told, for example, how clever he was in knowing that 3 tens are the same as 30 or in dividing and adding at the same time. Perhaps he wanted to show everyone who was worried about his math problems that he did not have them anymore.

This is not to say that this boy attributed no submerged meaning to math symbols. The point is that he understood quite a bit about math or he would not have chosen this subject to represent less than conscious impulses. The question *why math?* helps clinicians understand the relationship between symbols and their meaning as well as ways to communicate this understanding to the child. To Annie, two-digit numbers meant herself standing close to her mother. But it also meant that she wished to separate herself from her mother because she wished not to have her mother's math problems or to have the same problems in regard to her father as her mother did. She chose math because she had heard adults talk about math problems at the same time they also talked about marital problems. Communicating these ideas to Annie in her words and terms helped her understand what I understood and helped activate her math ability.

It appeared to me that our conversations brought Annie to a transitional stance regarding knowledge of math and of other persons. It was not that I introduced new math facts or cognitive disequilibrium as I talked with Annie, but rather that I watched and waited for agitations to occur with Annie's own perspective. Even if I could have succeeded in bringing about a transitional moment by making pointed, didactic statements, Annie might then have believed that her recovery was in my control and out of her hands. Although I did try to promote doubt, the balance in activity shared by me and Annie was critical, since a therapeutic interaction consists of a watchful adult and an active child. Of course, there exists the peril that letting the child bring about her own perturbations might take longer than those perturbations provoked by the adult, but the benefits of helping the child survive a self-initiated transitional moment far outweigh this danger. The reason for this is that the new level of adaptation reached by the child by her own efforts is more likely to be longlasting.

SUMMARY

The symptoms of Timothy and Annie and their progress in psychotherapy serve as a paradigm for the main thesis of my book. From the child's perspective, learning and knowledge acquisition require risk-taking. Because the non-learning child often perceives only the dangers of understanding and often omits its benefits, distorted modes of knowing surface in his development and in his treatment. These modes of investigating include attempts to gain knowledge on the sly, to keep secret what is known or that the knowing process has been set in motion, to equate what is known with trickery or cheating, and to cling to confusions that seem safer than rational thought. The nonlearning child, then, tends to confuse gaining academic knowledge with other phenomena. Partial understanding runs rampant between the past and the present of these children as they begin to understand the power of insight but fail to disconnect *knowing* from *reasons* for knowing. Or, when they recognize what they *do* know, they understand they must temporarily endure the effects of partial understanding. Their longing for certainty at that moment can only be frustrated. For all these reasons, nonlearning youngsters try to make what they learn safe, often by insisting on choosing what is to be learned and how it is to be learned.

Psychoanalytic commentary might point out, and correctly, that Tim's Oedipal need to peek at or sneak from his parents was one underlying cause of his symptoms. Similarly, one underlying cause of Annie's problems with math was her Oedipal need to preserve her father's affection. Both Tim and Annie felt that to learn meant giving up an important relationship within the Oedipal triad. Certainly, Tim felt that to learn by reading meant he was overtaking or replacing his father in order to gain more of his mother's attention. Annie's partial understanding of math made her realize that she was afraid of having the same problems with her father as her mother did. Being "the same" as her mother, or even similar to her, threatened Annie's relationship to her father. Both children might also have felt that to "know" anything was equivalent to "peeking" at what occurred in their parents' bedroom before parental separation.

Nonetheless, I would argue that this formulation does not do justice to the ways knowing for its own sake is bound to Oedipal fantasy, nor does it specify ways of activating the child to learning or even stress that activation could be therapeutic. Often a child is rendered passive when the therapist understands all too well the nature of Oedipal fantasy and how it might be related to the underlying cause of many symptoms, including nonlearning. Furthermore, an interpretation of the Oedipal fantasy, which implies that the childhood wish is doomed, could mean to a child that understanding what he wishes from his parents is equivalent to understanding that he cannot have from them what he desires. Knowing, then, becomes united with a deprivation. Particularly problematic is the psychoanalytic interpretation that children fear they will be punished for wishing to overtake or replace a parent. The therapist should not base his or her statements only on the probable guilt and anxiety children feel when they understand their motives for learning include competing with the same-gender parent. Such statements increase their guilty and anxious reactions and thus their attempts at "not knowing" if they do not include with equal force that it is safe *and* legitimate to know.

Sometimes it is wiser for the therapist to focus on what the child *can* have and *can* know. Because a breakdown in learning requires the child to activate new ways to learn so he may proceed toward inquiry, it is prudent during the therapeutic exchange to facilitate the child's reach for knowledge *qua* knowledge. That is, in order to overtake a parent by competing with his knowledge base, a child must gradually learn the principles of scientific inquiry. But if he does so, he is no longer so preoccupied with Oedipal fantasy because he has become engaged in learning for its own rewards. Tim's rejection of reading and Annie's math problems were not undone by my telling them they wished but were afraid to overtake their parents. They both needed to understand that their particular learning would not threaten their self-development.

Thus, it was more important for Tim and me and Annie and me to focus on *thinking* rather than on peeking, sneaking, stealing, confounding, threatening, or placating, and to understand that their search for knowledge affirmed their sense of self which, for once, did not merge into that identity perceived as "father" or "mother." When Tim and Annie concentrated on thinking, they could decide whether they *were* peeking, sneaking, stealing, confounding, threatening, or placating—or whether they were purely learning. Then, they could enjoy school assignments because they neither feared being identical to nor estranged from a parent. Their greater self-understanding told them that they were unique individuals who had developed clever ways of knowing. A stronger sense of their knowing selves helped more than would an interpretation given by their therapist concentrating on the threat they imagined they had been to a parent every time they learned in school.

Tim's and Annie's compromises with learning reveal that a child's distorted forms of knowing are often the result of competence ambivalence. Compromised learning attempts do not represent true inquiry but are only quasi-scientific. Ambivalent attempts to know are thwarted by the very unpredictable nature of these attempts; yet they can be improved by the child's use of introspection which reveals to him his motives for knowing and his capabilities to reason *despite* his ambivalence. But like authentic knowing, these distorted forms of inquiry take place within the two realms of exploratory activity: the interpersonal and the physical. A third realm is activated as the self-reflective child cogitates about intrapsychic themes—which might have existed all along but which the child "suddenly" discovers. These self-revelations mean to him that he need not be as dependent on his parents as he once thought.

But, before the child has become self-reflective, he often confuses the inanimate, the interpersonal, and the intrapsychic realms and concludes that the results he produces in the physical world automatically apply to the interpersonal world, or vice versa. Or, he concludes that what is true intrapsychically applies indiscriminately to others, and vice versa, or that what is intrapsychically actual for him dictates how he should relate to others. Again, his understanding is partial in that he may accurately apprehend the impact of his activity on objects but underestimate the impact of his behavior on other people. Or, he may believe the way his actions affect people is just as effective as the way he affects objects. Finally, he may comprehend only vaguely that there is a difference between his cogitations about himself and about other people.

Thus, older nonlearning but self-reflective children are different from young nonlearning children. While older children might ask, "What did I do to make that work?" or "What did I do to achieve success?" younger nonlearning children ask this question less often because it does not occur to them to question themselves or their reactions. They have yet to become fully introspective. However, both younger and older children need support as unique persons. It is thus essential for therapists who work with nonlearning children of all ages and stages to concentrate on that which the child has understood accurately. Having a sense of success, of having known some aspects of a problem all along, strengthens the child's sense of self and sense of autonomy, both of which are required for continuing inquiry.

When left to his own devices, the child, whether in school or not, tends to investigate the whys and hows of his own experience, and thus to personalize his school assignments. Although the school curriculum may not always accurately reflect principles of inquiry the way Dewey (1956, 1963) hoped it would, the child does learn more easily the more the curriculum matches his interests. In much the same vein, Piaget (1971) urged teachers to foster the "spirit of experiment" (p. 50), which takes the child's own penchant for exploration into the world of controlled investigation. As he pointed out,

> the child spontaneously acquires between the ages of eleven to twelve and fourteen to fifteen all the intellectual instruments necessary for experimentation properly so-called. (p. 51)

Child inquiry is related to scientific inquiry. With the help of education, the developing child is enabled to conduct inquiries in the scientific sense. These inquiries are aided by what he knows about himself, and, as a result of these inquiries, he comes to know more about the self. The nonlearning child is no exception. As he comes to believe he *has* known, and has known without untoward effects, he can resume his journey toward the unknown.

CHAPTER 5

Overachieving and Underachieving
Two Misunderstood Children

The learning styles of overachieving and underachieving youngsters deserve close study. Although many similar psychological processes contribute to these two very different learning styles, the psychotherapist must begin with the child's manifest behavior and must empathize with the different routes to approaching and retreating from learning that overachievers and underachievers select. Both children described in this chapter created impersonations. One child began to take on the characteristics of an adult, whereas the other took on the characteristics of a fool. The compelling question about children like this is by what cognitive processes do they manufacture fake self-presentations to satisfy projecting family members? And by what processes do they keep their knowing selves secret from everyone? These two questions also apply to the case narratives of the school phobic youngsters that will be presented in Chapters 7 and 8.

It is fairly common for children to impersonate stupidity in the classroom. Less common is the child who strives to appear more competent or mature than he is. Jeremy used his average intelligence to impersonate maturity because to him adulthood was safer than childhood. Betsy carried her underachieving stance to the extreme as she sought to model her behavior on what she knew of younger, "foolish" children and mentally retarded children. Caroline, Robin, and Maisie, who are subjects of Chapter 7, and Lara, the subject of Chapter 8, dramatize the school phobic's fear of knowing. Because Jeremy and Betsy feared knowing, their attitudes toward knowledge acquisition had by and large preempted intellectual development. They faked maturity or stupidity and were more likely to retreat from transitional phases of intellectual development as they attended school but failed to process what was taught there. Even though a deliberate rejection or evasion of knowledge is common to all non-learning children and adolescents, those whose pretense permeates most of their behavior tend to mimic earlier or alien developmental levels and those who respond by becoming phobic as the result of an acute sensitivity to what schools and learning are all about tend to engage in suppression, momentary forgetting, or repression. School phobic youngsters are also often encapsulated in transitional cognitive phases, but typically they contend with these phases more openly and with greater anguish than those children who pretend not to know or who are certain that learning is the same as growing up. Overachievers focus not on learning for its own sake but primarily on the growing up process which they believe occurs especially in school.

JEREMY: AN ACADEMIC OVERACHIEVER

Presenting Problem

Jeremy, a 6-year-old overachiever, who was the oldest in a family of three boys, had excelled in kindergarten. He had a friendly smile and an eager approach to other people, and often gazed affectionately at his mother when she brought him to therapy. His teacher had asked him to be a "teacher's helper," and to instruct other 5-year-olds how to count and to recognize the colors. He also excelled in first grade and was months ahead in his workbook, so much so that his teacher often asked him to help other students. But when Jeremy came to me for an evaluation, his answers when questioned during the interview about logical reasoning tasks were average, not precocious (see the Appendix, pp. 317–322 for a discussion of these tasks). Eugene, his younger brother, had many developmental problems, such as separation anxiety and poor peer relations. Their mother had preferred spending time with Jeremy and dreaded the time she spent with symptomatic Eugene. Much like Jeremy's teacher, she saw Jeremy as her "pet." The mother's attitude caused problems in both boys; she fed Jeremy's wish to be an adult and to reach for intellectual maturity beyond his chronological age and she helped Eugene's wish to stay close to his mother at all times.

A family crisis ensued when the third child was born because for the first time Jeremy created a fuss in the family by trying to persuade Eugene that he was "too sick" to go to nursery school. Jeremy reacted to the new birth by reaching for adulthood even more urgently as he simultaneously tried to keep Eugene infantile by persuading him that he should not attend school. Jeremy could tolerate, even welcome, Eugene's staying home with their mother because he imagined that, while he was at school, "Mom likes me better because I'm smart in school." This difficult mental feat was aided by his belief that his presence in school was the same as being the preferred smart child, whereas Eugene's presence at home was the same as being the unpreferred, stupid child. Since he regularly used the phrase "the same as," he could imagine something like "being in school is the same as being preferred by my mother." Or he could bring about the same imagined result by thinking "being at home means not being preferred by my mother." His ability to successively coordinate the meaning of "the same as" with himself at school and his brother at home is expected of a 6-year-old child (Jeremy's age) and is consistent with his just barely concrete operational stance soon after he presented for therapy. Most important, by convincing Eugene to remain infantile, Jeremy preserved his cherished image of himself as the smart, grownup child.

Jeremy's need to grow up quickly and achieve well had multiple meanings. His father had been the middle child in a family of three boys. He described his older brother as high-achieving and his younger brother as a school failure who finally dropped out of school. In his determination that Jeremy not repeat his younger brother's failure and to relieve his own anxiety, he pushed Jeremy to prove to his family that his son was different from his nonlearning brother. Jeremy admired his father and tried to meet his needs by protecting his own position as the high-achieving son. From his childish perspective, he could become even more competent were he to stand in the way of his younger brother's learning by persuading him to avoid the very environment—namely, school—which leads to learning.

But, what he replayed of his father's experience was not an exact copy. It was not so much that he thought he must mimic every aspect of his father's high-achieving behavior to avoid his uncle's failure and thereby reduce his father's anxieties. He added to his father's agenda the idea that he could accelerate his growing up by behaving in a smart and mature fashion, a thought consonant with his cognitive development. Likewise, he believed he could retard Eugene's growing up which seemed to threaten his place in the family especially when the new birth occurred. Jeremy generated his own ideas and fashioned his own actuality like his father had done in childhood and in adulthood. Thus, the child is not the passive recipient of the parent's view but constructs his own view, however related the two views of child and parent may seem on the surface. Jeremy thought he could and indeed must accelerate his own growing up, while his father only wished Jeremy would achieve as a child.

Jeremy's Initiation into Therapy

My work with Jeremy, and later, with Eugene, began with an evaluation of both boys followed by family therapy meetings to deal with the crisis created by the birth of the third child and the meaning of this event for the family. Family therapy helped Jeremy's parents to understand how they and their children felt about each other and the birth of their third child. But Jeremy, and later Eugene, needed an intervention more specifically geared to their developmental status. I soon began individual work first with Jeremy, and when he had been in therapy for 6 weeks, I began to work individually with Eugene, whose symptoms of immaturity had not created a family crisis but were nonetheless chronic and interfered with his adjustment to nursery school. Since I had seen both boys in family therapy, I did not refer Eugene to another therapist. I felt that my referring Eugene elsewhere would mean to Eugene *and* Jeremy my agreement with the family myth that Jeremy must be grownup and preferred and that Eugene must be infantile and rejected. (Of the 60 nonlearning youngsters whom I treated, 6, including Jeremy, had symptomatic siblings whom I also saw in psychotherapy. Of these 6 children whose siblings I also treated, 3 had completed their therapy before I met with their siblings. Seven nonlearning youngsters had symptomatic siblings whom I referred to other therapists.)

Therapy with Jeremy had to be geared to his cognitive orientation. He would not have heard such statements from me as (1) your brother will not catch up to or overtake you, or (2) it is impossible to make yourself grow up faster. I had to penetrate his cognitive system in order to make clinical statements "stick" — to take hold in a way consistent with his view of the world. His beliefs, created in part by his cognitive orientation, produced symptoms in Eugene, thereby strengthening Jeremy's immature view that Eugene's not learning in nursery school would retard his growing up. Jeremy's "theory" of learning and growing up was fostered by his teacher's calling upon him to be a "teacher's helper."

TREATMENT PROGRESS

Jeremy and His Brother

Jeremy's explanation for being in therapy was "I need to help my brother." His statement was a "red herring" in that it hid his wish to impede his brother's growing up at the same time that it implied he was fully grown and capable of helping a small child, as would a parent. He showed his need to stretch for maturity by reaching for competence which was quite beyond him. For example, when he failed to get 10 out of 10 bull's eyes on the dartboard, he said, "I'm not good enough," and set the standard even higher as he tried to get 12 out of 12. He did little else but try to reach for perfection until he was told: "You're a bright boy, but you'd probably also like to play." Then and in later weeks he relaxed his vigil somewhat about growing up prematurely, and his parents reported less tension at home and school, as well as fewer attempts to persuade his brother that he was too sick to attend nursery school.

Subsequently, Jeremy revealed in therapy that he had missed the pleasures of early childhood. He took the permission contained in my statement "You'd like to play" literally by behaving in the fashion of a much younger child. For example, he began to crawl around the floor imitating his baby brother and also tried to capture his attempts to make sounds, comparing them to the articulation difficulties he had noticed in Eugene. He soon expressed his anger that as much as he had aspired to be an adult, he was equally convinced his younger brothers had it better. He focused especially on his brother Eugene when he took into account that although Eugene did not work as hard as he did, he had gained many prized moments of his mother's attention as the result of his reluctance to grow up and attend school. Jeremy's view of reality had expanded so that he could no longer maintain that it was only he who was close to his mother when he showed off in school; he began to imagine that Eugene might be close to his mother by remaining home.

Permission to be a child and behave in a way typical of a 6-year-old paved the way for the interventions that more closely captured his dilemma. My conversations with Jeremy required that I balance statements addressing his emotions with those appealing to his cogitations. However grownup Jeremy often appeared, and however well developed his imagination was, his thinking was often prelogical. When his thinking became logical, such as coordinating two situations (being at home or being at school) with his mother's varied affective reactions to her sons, Jeremy's more mature thought processes were at risk because he often did not want to understand that Eugene could be intimate with his mother by remaining home. So he soon began to experience a difficult transitional phase in cognitive development. By this time, Eugene came to therapy for the problems described earlier, some of which had been exacerbated by Jeremy's omnipotent belief that he could control Eugene.

Jeremy revealed his dilemma by objecting to taking turns with Eugene, who sometimes had his appointment first. When it was Jeremy's turn to be second, he repetitively "exploded" the dolls and furniture in the dollhouse to show that his anger was so explosive it might harm the entire (doll) family, or it might harm the very play equipment which at other times helped him reveal his conflicts. When Jeremy's appointment preceded Eugene's, Jeremy did not act out any explosions, but instead built beautiful structures with Legos, which I often praised. To my praise, he once answered, "I know I'm good at this. My Mom thinks I'm smart, too." Being second meant to him that Eugene had not only overtaken him, but also had replaced him as the oldest boy in the family (his greatest fear) which precipitated his overachieving symptoms. I told him that he was always first (in birth order) whether he had his appointment first or second. Although he appreciated my intent to reassure him, the statement did not change his attitude; all it did was begin to unravel his worldview. He reacted by complaining that, at certain times of the year, he was older than his brother, and, at certain times "less older than him." I told him that he was always the same number of years older, which again fell on deaf ears. He reacted by saying: "My brother's birthday is in October, and mine is in June...so in June I'm three years older than he, but in October I'm only two and a half years older."

Since Jeremy was predisposed to believe he could change his age and accelerate his growth, he became prey to the hazards of his own wishes. The clue to his confusion was the way he combined relatives—"Right now you are seven and your brother is four"—with absolutes—"You are always the same number of years and months older than your brother." Jeremy's parents had tried to straighten out his confusion by explaining that he was always older, but Jeremy could not comprehend their meaning.

Until the child has become concrete operational, he does not differentiate time from space, or separate the concept of time from other concepts, such as number or quantity (Piaget & Inhelder, 1969; Cowan, 1978; Elkind, 1981). Jeremy was just 7 years and 4 months and so it was not at all surprising that he struggled with the concept of time and had not mastered its applications to various areas of his life. What was surprising was the advanced level of his thinking in some instances which was apparent by his ability to imagine his mother's closeness to him when she was actually absent, and by his determined and successful attempts to master first-grade subjects so that after 4 months of school, he had exhausted the first-grade curriculum. But, even though Jeremy might succeed in speeding up his learning (and, in his mind, his growing up) by engaging in impressive memory feats or overworking himself in school, and though he could repeatedly remind himself while in school that his mother was proud of him, he could not speed up all aspects of his logic. Its transitional quality was revealed by the ways he discussed his problems with me.

My understanding that Jeremy had good reasons to reach for maturity prepared me to say to him about the age gap between him and his brother: "But that happens every year, though; it never changes. Every year for part of it, it *seems* as if you're two-and-a-half years older than Eugene, and every year for part of it, it *seems* as if you're three years older than he is." I phrased my remarks as closely as possible to the preconcept that gave rise to his confusion; that the age difference between him and his brother actually fluctuated. Jeremy sat still and thought for a long time. He then said, trailing off doubtfully, "Yes, but Eugene's just had his birthday...." When I said, "Yes, but you're *always* first, and *every* year it seems as if you're *either* two-and-a-half years *or* three years older, so you see, Eugene will never catch up to you," he began to nod his head, assenting. Then, he seemed to reconsider what his parents had said before. While earlier he had strenuously objected to the statement that Eugene would never catch up to him by saying, "What do you *mean* he will never catch up to me?" he at last acknowledged that the intervals "two-and-a-half" and "three" could repeat themselves every year. He began to conserve some time intervals, the critical one being the birthdate of his brother in relation to his own.

Jeremy's Understanding of Time

Gaining this concept was the key to Jeremy's understanding that Eugene would never overtake him. Now he wondered if he could preserve his mother's affection for him as her first son if he did not reach for adulthood prematurely. He also tried to understand other problems of time that were generally related to the one just described. While he could understand that he would always remain 28 months older than his brother, he still thought that the person who came to the appointment first had a longer time with me.[1]

[1]Because both boys wanted to be first to see me, I tried to arrange their visits on separate days, a plan which to the parents seemed impractical or impossible because they had to travel a considerable distance to get to my office. Since their parents were eager to continue both boys' therapy, I suggested they take turns in having the first appointment. Jeremy may have thereupon brought to therapy more problems regarding his understanding of time because he trusted I would not react with anger if he complained that Eugene sometimes had the first appointment. If so, his trust that I would accept his complaints helped him understand more fully those dilemmas which still remained.

When he had to wait to be second, Jeremy asked, "*Why* does Eugene get to stay here longer?" Then I began to explain the 50-minute time period which was consistently adhered to whether it was he or his brother in my office. His conviction that his brother stayed longer for his appointment reflected Jeremy's core conflict and revealed, at the same time, that gaps continued to exist in cognition. But now Jeremy brought to bear a more developed self-reflexive sense as he sought to understand his conflicts. The week before he had searched for his reasons for exploding the dollhouse when he said, "I only explode the dollhouse when Eugene comes to see you first." On another recent occasion when I had tried to put into words why he might be exploding the dollhouse and said, "Maybe so I'll be sure to notice you?" he had answered a vigorous "Right!" Similarly, he explained why he thought the person who came first always stayed longer. He reacted to my explanation that he and Eugene both had 50 therapy minutes by saying: "It's *so hard* to wait. The time goes slow when Eugene comes first."

The importance that Jeremy attributed to time going slow because he wished to be with me, and wished his brother was not, confused him and momentarily retarded his otherwise rapidly developing sense of time and his sense about using it. Jeremy resented that I seemed to have actualized his worst fears in that I now seemed, as his mother might have seemed in the past, to enable Eugene to overtake Jeremy's prized status as the oldest, smartest, and most "caught up" boy of the family. As he struggled to understand my rational explanation of the uniformity of the 50-minute hour, he pointed accurately to a change in his actuality which I had not noticed initially. It was true that he and his brother had equal time with me, but there had been changes in his experience of therapy and a shift in his relationship to me which Jeremy perceived as just as important as the uniformity of the 50-minute hour. While before Jeremy had 50 minutes with me and continued to have 50 minutes, his brother, whose initiation into treatment followed Jeremy's, now had 50 minutes with me where before he had had none. To Jeremy, Eugene had "caught up" to him because, although younger, he now had the same number of therapy minutes.

But Jeremy's resentment also activated him to understand what I said about the constancy of 50 minutes. He tried to understand that one's subjective feeling of time is independent of time itself. My therapeutic statement to him, "Of course you are angry at me because I no longer only see just you in therapy, but also your brother Eugene" did not give him the concepts to figure this out for himself. Sensitivity to Jeremy's anger and resentment had to be coupled with assistance in his use of cognitive concepts.

I showed Jeremy my watch, and counting by fives, which was a skill he had proudly showed to me the previous week, counted once more the number of minutes he and Eugene stayed with me. This brought into clear focus that time's elements (in this case, 5-minute intervals) can be tallied, and that this process yields very different results from the feeling of time in one's imagination, where time can be speeded up or slowed down.

Jeremy now tried to and succeeded in bringing together two aspects of his understanding. When he understood that the minutes of his appointment could be identified and always added up to 50, he contemplated why it felt as though time "goes fast" and "goes slow" depending on the situation. Where before he had brilliantly applied his imagination to the task of keeping his mother with him in school when she was physically absent, but clung fast to a prelogical thought which said "the faster you learn, the faster you grow up," he now brought together the psychological and the logical aspects of one concept. As he began to imitate me by counting the minutes of his appointment by fives, he said with sudden insight, "Oh, it just *feels* like Eugene has more time. . . that's because it's *me* who's waiting when he comes first!" He now understood that the passage of time is independent of the activity of waiting. Then, he was able to get to the core of his overachieving need because he understood how he tried to overachieve by having more time with me: "I wanted you to help me to get better more quickly than my brother!" By saying this, he implied that his advancement, whether in therapy or in school, served the purpose of preserving his mother's affection by creating increasingly larger gaps between his successes and those of his brother. His distinction between what time is and what time feels like revealed that he had successfully mastered transition (at least in regard to one concept) and is a nice demonstration, not just of the problems of children, but of their developmental resilience. Despite serious conflicts, in the course of three appointments he had replaced his preoperational understanding of time with the more mature differentiation of "what time feels like" and "what time is."

Three months later, Jeremy told his mother that he no longer wanted to be his teacher's helper. Thus, he relinquished the role of overachiever by truly understanding its origins. After three more months of therapy, during which both family and Jeremy's own needs were addressed, Jeremy had become self-confident and normally achieving in school. He told me: "School is better because we are reading books now. It's not boring like last year when all we did was the same old stuff—workbooks!" I asked if he meant the stories were more interesting than workbook drill to which he responded: "Yeah, and it's not *so hard* to stay *so long* in school!" In combining the phrases "so hard" and "so long," he once more likened a feeling state to the passage of time. But his cogent pairing of "so hard" and "so long" communicated as well that he separated affect and time. Otherwise his positive statement about school would have taken a simpler form: "It's not *so hard* to stay in school!" Moreover, he made the transition between home and school personally meaningful by saying: "The story I read today was about Chinese people and there is a Chinese family in our neighborhood. I walk past their house every day when I go to school." I thought he meant to express that school learning was no longer the empty reach for basic skills solely to grow up faster. Reading about Chinese people in school helped satisfy his curiosity about the people in his neighborhood who were different from him. Discovering the intrinsic value of academic learning—its link to his natural curiosity—helped Jeremy strengthen his heretofore shaky conceptual orientation.

Although Jeremy still liked coming to therapy, he said, "I don't have much to talk about because I don't explode anymore." In his second-to-last appointment, he made fun of his earlier magical thinking regarding time, while he also expressed pleasure in spending time with me. When his mother was late picking him up from his session, he said, grinning alertly, "Oh good! Now I *really* get to stay here longer!" This statement represented two triumphs: mastery of time's regularities since he now knew that to stay longer required adding on more minutes to the number 50; and triumph over adults who always said their time with him and his brother must be fairly distributed. He knew enough about time to make fun of his earlier anxieties and of those cognitive misconceptions that fed them.

CHARACTERISTICS OF UNDERACHIEVERS AND THEIR FAMILIES

By far the greatest number of nonlearning youngsters whom I treat are underachievers: 37 of the 60 nonlearners who are descibed in this book were underachievers. Many were younger or the youngest child in the family, such as Eugene who as a younger child countered his brother Jeremy's overachieving by underachieving. The younger or youngest child often sees many virtues in delaying growing up. Betsy, whose case narrative follows, was the youngest child in her family. She had concluded by the time she entered treatment that it was only babyhood that attracted her mother's attention.

Underachieving can be considered a collusion on the part of the child and the parent in some cases. The child enjoys her special status as the younger or youngest, and the parent wishes to "keep the baby at home" in order to continue the pleasures of parenting, namely, nurturing, playing, talking, and being with the remaining children or child in the family. Or perhaps the parent feels guilty about sending a reluctant child to school or expecting an indifferent child to learn in school. In situations like this, both parent and child view the child's not learning as a way to protect her.

As I noted in Chapter 2, separation and divorce were common in the families of underachievers. In some families, the underachievers suffered also from an invidious comparison with an achieving sibling—as though the family's myth dictated that only one child could be intelligent. Other circumstances that led to a child's underachieving in school included: (1) a death in the family during a critical stage of knowing in the child's development; (2) a close parent–child relationship in which the parent felt that he or she was unintelligent and the child concluded she must be like the parent in that respect; (3) children whose parents felt competitive with them and sought to inhibit school success; and (4) though rare, cases of children who erroneously connected the brilliance of a family member with medical symptoms or a congenital defect of that person. A brilliant 7-year-old boy exemplified this by believing that high intelligence was somehow the cause of his brilliant father's heart attack. Another very intelligent boy believed that he would suffer medical symptoms because his brilliant uncle had a congenital defect. The underachieving stance of both boys was designed to deny their expected illness by denying their intelligence.

There were several instances of children who impersonated mental retardation — Elkind called it "pseudostupidity" (1979a, p. 92). Although Elkind described such pseudostupid behavior in adolescence, I have seen instances of it in latency-aged children, although the intellectual processes whereby these children carry out an impersonation of severe mental deficiency must differ from those of the adolescent. Some children had succeeded in fooling parents, siblings, other family members, teachers, peers and neighbors into holding the uniform opinion that they were undeniably deficient in mental ability. At certain points in their treatment, they even caused doubt in my mind about their intellectual potential. In the cases of Betsy and one other child, I found myself checking their IQ test and interview results to make sure that they had performed normally. This fact may serve to illustrate how skillful the children were in simulating the behavior of the mentally retarded.

BETSY: AN OVERCONVINCING UNDERACHIEVER

Eight-year-old Betsy's father died suddenly a few months before her fourth birthday. Betsy's story illustrates how not learning and not knowing can be stubbornly bound up in an unexpected and traumatic event. Her fantasied consequences of intelligence predated the development of her capability to reason logically. Thus, she was prone to irrational associations or cause–effect constructions that proved very difficult to alter because they captured a family dilemma which had great meaning not only for Betsy but also for other family members. She was the one child in the group who persistently aroused in me the query: *Is* she *really* intellectually deficient? That she was *not* is the special thesis of the remaining sections of this chapter.

Betsy's Initiation into Therapy

Betsy's teacher and mother both thought she was dyslexic. At the age of 8, she could neither read nor do simple addition problems. Betsy's mother hoped a psychological evaluation would shed light on what Betsy was actually capable of — both then and in the future. She had failed third grade, had left public school, and had been placed in a private school for learning-disabled children. Her brother, who was 2 years older, was a brilliant student and was described by Betsy's mother as "another parent to Betsy." Betsy's father had been a successful scientist before his death. Her brother modeled himself on what he could remember of his father, and seemed to peg his own brilliance on these vivid and cherished memories.

When Betsy came for her first appointment, she was friendly and eager to come into my office, but once there, became shy with a searching gaze, apparently wondering what I expected of her. Initially, body movements and gestures were clumsy and inept; her shoes were often untied and her hair unkempt. Her voice was high-pitched and her speech became mannered as she enunciated words and sentences in a precise but artificial fashion. She seemed to expect that I, as listener, would misunderstand what she said. Or perhaps she felt she was on stage, playacting a view of herself before an audience. Her mother had been concerned about her "infantile" behavior, which she traced to Betsy's fourth year when she had lost her father. In describing her daughter's playacting a baby, Betsy's mother said, "She seems to turn the baby stuff on and off at will." When Betsy would overcome her shy or "fake" demeanor, her stiff manner would dissolve and she would become charming and outgoing.

Early in therapy, Betsy chose, of all the games in my office, to play the game of Clue. The game involves guessing the identity of the "murderer" as well as the weapon and the room in which the murder was commited—all of which are shown on cards which have been placed in the "secret file." The typical strategy is to deduce the identity of each card by the process of elimination from guesses made to other players. Betsy revealed a potential for normal cognitive functioning by quickly learning how to play the game and by winning. After the game, she gazed at the box cover on which the game's characters are pictured and said: "The ones who look innocent are really guilty, and the ones who look guilty are really innocent." Her remark revealed that she knew what appears on the surface is not necessarily what lies underneath. This revelation had two implications. First, it demonstrated that she understood the difference between what appears to be and what is—a cognitive milestone in children who are or are becoming concrete operational (Bruner, Olver, & Greenfield, 1966; Piaget & Inhelder, 1969). Switching an appearance (they "look" innocent or guilty) with a reality (they are "really" innocent or guilty) for what might have been defensive reasons revealed that Betsy was not stupid. Turning innocence into guilt (or vice versa) suggests that Betsy might have even felt guilty about some aspects of her experience, perhaps her father's death. Her game-playing suggested that she had moved normally in a general way for an 8-year-old through typical developmental stages, at least in regard to conflict-free situations. Although the game of Clue may not have been conflict-free since it suggested death, game-playing as an activity was conflict-free because it did not imply to Betsy that she knew or was expected to know anything.

The second implication of her response to Clue was for her fake presentation of stupidity and infantilism. Since she appeared to be retarded or babyish, underneath she must be the opposite—smart and grownup. If this was so, then Betsy's retarded behavior was a sham that stood for her ambivalence about intelligence itself or what she might come to know as the result of using her mind. It was not so much that she wished to achieve other specific gains, such as those suggested by Mahler (1942) in a paper in which she described some children who used their "pseudoimbecility" to spy on the sexual activities of adults. Mahler suggested that the dumb act of smart children helps them find out what goes on in their parents' bedroom, a discovery which is facilitated by the adults' belief that a dumb child cannot understand what is seen. By way of contrast, I have focused on what a child might want *not* to see because of the imagined results of what might be understood.

At first, Betsy could only reveal indirectly that she was intelligent by talking in riddles about how she came to the solution of playing dumb. This she did by engaging in a complex series of play enactions of school. She was the teacher and I the student. She told me I was in second grade (her grade) and that I was "still doing easy math, like one plus one." She carefully set up a math paper consisting only of this simple math problem and then instructed me to answer it correctly. When I completed her assignment, she carefully and in mock seriousness marked a star next to the correct answer. In so doing she brought to light the inadequacies of a reward system for a child who impersonates. The star, in association with an easy math problem usually given to much younger children, actually rewards stupidity and its impersonation. In this way, she implicitly blamed teachers and schools for her complicated defense system, which was intended to fool everyone around her into believing she was unintelligent.

Much later, in a moment of great distress, she said, "They think I'm *stupid*...Why did they ever think that?" She had temporarily forgotten that it was she who had concocted the impersonation of stupidity because she wished to hide its cause from herself once more—her father's death and her feelings about it.

Cognitive Monitoring

As in so many cases of underachieving children, Betsy's "basic skills" were poor for a second grader. She had mastered math and reading at a low second-grade level. Still, 5 months before, she had done no academic work whatsoever. Despite her astonishing ability to finish 1½-year's work in 5 months, her teachers continued to view her as unintelligent. One teacher characterized her as "of limited ability," adding that "She probably will have to take a menial job when she grows up."

Betsy revealed the ability to reason logically in her first experience with Piagetian interviewing. At 8 years, 5 months, she understood two out of four interview tasks (conservation of number, and classification); even though these results do not suggest brilliance, neither do they suggest mental retardation (Inhelder, 1968). Betsy's ability to reason logically improved during the time she was in therapy as revealed by her answers in her second interviewing, which occurred 4 months after the onset of therapy. She understood all four tasks of concrete operations and had begun to understand one advanced task of formal operations (see pp. 317–322).

She even became interested in one of the task questions, "More boys or more people?" She calculated silently and answered, "Five is not very many. Nine is more than five." Her answer led to a discussion of other classification schemes. She asked, "What about Indians and New Yorkers?" Similar to some of Piaget's (1963) subjects, Betsy may have been "making fun of the psychologist"! I asked if she meant all the kinds of Americans—to which she nodded affirmatively. So I asked the classification question in the abstract (without reference to the Fisher-Price dolls): "More Americans or more people?" Grinning she answered, "More people, because there are lots of people, like English, Chinese, and Spanish."

Since she had shown interest in the classification task, I decided to ask her one advanced question. I showed her a rubber band with a mark on it and asked her to put her finger on the mark before I stretched the band.[2] She put her finger directly on the mark but then immediately withdrew it and began to give ridiculous answers, such as putting her finger quite far to the right or left of it, while she watched my face. Perhaps she tried to guess the answer by reading my face or perhaps by her behavior she made fun of the question. Struck by her originally correct response, I asked her once more to comply, to which she suddenly remarked, "The rubber band just stretches and the mark doesn't move." All the while she was rubbing the mark off the rubber band so that by the time she finished answering the question, the mark had almost completely vanished. As she answered the classification question, her smile had turned to a frown as she watched how I would react to the mark's disappearance.

It seemed to me that her face-reading meant the answer was safe only if it came from another person (me) and not from her own thought processes. As such, her unself-conscious face-reading was analogous to her use of prelogical thought in that it helped her avoid thinking more maturely. Perhaps she made the mark vanish to avoid her own and my evaluation of her (incorrect *and* correct) answers to the task question. Or perhaps she wished to express symbolically that the problem with thinking centered on a disappearance (her father's death). Nonetheless, her performance had improved, a fact which I attribute to her growing, if still ambivalent, determination to communicate to others that she was a normally intelligent person.

But Betsy continued to be labeled *mentally deficient* by family members and teachers. This evaluation of her mental capacity cannot be explained as the sole result of her earlier low-basic-skills performance. That she activated and improved her basic skills should have suggested to everyone who knew her that she was capable of learning to learn, and in short order. The adults who knew Betsy best were misled time and again to think that she was mentally deficient as a result of the strength of her impersonation, not the lag in basic-skills learning. What convinced me that she had normal cognitive capabilities, apart from normal test results and progressive intellectual development, was the realization that she must have these abilities or she could not have projected so convincingly a fake personality. Thus, her behavior was very similar to Rudy's (Chapter 2), who demonstrated his intelligence by his intent to catch me in an erroneous diagnosis of his intellectual potential; the very act of foolery showed the intellect at work. To repeat: We tend to underestimate the shrewdness of "normally intelligent" individuals.

---

[2]This task is taken from the description of questions Piaget (1972a) originated to ascertain the child's understanding of the mathematical operation of distributivity.

TREATMENT PROGRESS

The Interplay in Therapy of Intellect and Affect

Betsy's turning point after 6 months of therapy came when one of her pet gerbils died in school where she had taken it for a science project. Its death was one of those unexpected happenstances that helped Betsy understand her central dilemma—the close connection, in her mind, between learning in general and learning about death. When she began to talk about the gerbil's death, I wondered if she thought its being in school somehow caused the gerbil to die. But Betsy focused on other of her concerns and only later made an explicit connection between school learning and dying.

She focused primarily on how the surviving mate isolates itself, and out of "loneliness" and isolation from its partner, eventually also dies. Of the surviving gerbil, she said, "It goes away, hides from everything, because it doesn't want to *see* that its mate has died." When told that eventually the gerbil might come to accept it, she answered, "How *can* it accept it? It doesn't even *know* what happened." Although before she had asserted that the gerbil reacted to its mate's death by "going away" and "hiding from everything" she now said that the gerbil could not—or need not—accept its mate's death because it didn't *know* what happened. Pretending to speak for the gerbil and probably for herself, she seemed to span logical and prelogical thought. She asserted correctly that gerbils are different from people in that they only react but do not conceptualize what has happened (they "see" but do not "know"). But, she also implied that what is not known does not exist and therefore need not be accepted. Therefore knowing, unlike perceiving, might have meant to her to accept the fact of mortality.

Betsy may have intended to describe her mother's mourning behavior when her father died. Initially, she seemed to focus on the isolation and loneliness of the surviving "mate," a focus which was different from her mother's attitude as she described the death of her husband. When Betsy's mother brought her to therapy and told me about her father's death, I inferred that her mother's protective complacency was intended for Betsy's benefit. If so, her mother's denial provided a way for Betsy not to know about her father's death, which, in turn, could mean that neither she nor her mother could afford to know (learn) anything. She was predisposed to come to these conclusions because she positively identified with her mother. Therefore, she might have reasoned, "If this is the way Mom deals with Dad's death [by acting as though it hadn't occurred], that's the way for me, too."

This session was a turning point in Betsy's treatment progress because for the first time she revealed it was just an act that she knew only the most basic facts. Although minutes before she had mimicked prelogical thought in asserting that one can reject mortality by not knowing about it, she now revealed, by reading a difficult word, that she was only playacting underdeveloped reading skills. She had set up one of her favorite games, Monopoly, during which she had earlier read only such simple words as "go," "free" (in "Free Parking"), "Park Place," and the like, when she suddenly and apparently out of the blue read the word *mortgage*. Taken by surprise, I praised her, telling her that mortgage is indeed a difficult word to read. It was easy for Betsy to discuss the fact that she could read this word because of its special significance. Her mother had just that week gotten approval for a mortgage on a new house, which signified to Betsy (and probably to the rest of her family) a move away from the past, and from the connotations which reminded her of her father. It probably also meant to Betsy that her mother had faced the traumatic event in a new way, had more completely resolved her feelings about it, and quite literally had taken a "new lease on life" in planning to move to a new home.

To Betsy also the new house and its viable mortgage meant a new life. Living in the old house where her father died had meant to her that she must remain 4 years old, because staying at the age at which he died meant retaining the time of her life when her father was alive. Betsy's willed retardation probably had the same meaning for her mother and brother. It was not so much that Betsy's identity was tied to her father as a person, but to the time when he existed. She was positively identified with his existence and negatively identified with his death. This meant she had to remain 4 years old—behaviorally and intellectually—and had to avoid growing up which, as we will shortly see, became stubbornly associated with death. And, remaining 4 years old, meant that Betsy, before therapy, had decided to continue thinking in the fashion of an individual who has

> engaged in symbolic reasoning for some time, and sometimes she is right, sometimes not. But at no time is her reasoning stable, adequately communicable and justifiable, and at all times there is an admixture of irrelevant, if not illogical, elements. (Furth, 1987, pp. 130–131)

Yet, 4 weeks later, she was reading at grade level, if a little laboriously, and with a demeanor that communicated, "This is not quite me yet." Betsy's increased willingness to learn resulted from both the prospective change in her home environment and from her thoughtful conversations with me. She began to tentatively embrace concrete operational thought and became increasingly comfortable with herself as a "human knower" in a group of similarly knowing individuals (her therapist, her mother and her brother) who regulate interpersonal relations and thereby adapt cognitively *because* they have adapted socially. No longer did Betsy use face-reading as a favorite method to attain knowledge. Now she actively participated in the knowing process by generating original ideas and comparing them to the ideas of others.

To take her recognition of the word *mortgage* as an example, when hearing from her mother about the house mortgage, she might have connected this word with her understanding of the words *mortal* and *mortality*—both of which she had discussed before with me. Although the meaning of the root subword "mort" was probably not uppermost in Betsy's mind when she correctly read mortgage, the idea that mortgage meant a new life, in that it was essential to her new home, was distinctly available to her. She had readily linked her liberated reading with the event. It is unknown whether the root meanings of the word were known to her mother or to her brilliant brother. But, Betsy's sudden reading of this difficult word, and the startling release of cognitive activity, powerfully impressed me as I attended to both the conscious and preconscious meanings in what she said and did. The thought that occurred to me was that "mort" might stand in Betsy's mind for death and that "gage" means a pledge. I thought—but did not say—that mortgage might mean the death of a pledge to the dead, that is, a "dead pledge." Because her idea-generating capacity was still tenuous, I did not want to flood her thought systems with my tentative, hypothetical but complex interpretations. Nonetheless, my hypotheses regarding her behavior surely influenced the way I handled the rest of this therapeutic hour and many subsequent hours in which Betsy realized she was not only a clever girl but also that she could put her cleverness to use in figuring out why she had turned off her mind.

During our Monopoly game, Betsy correctly read the word *mortgage* when my landing on one of her properties forced me to mortgage one of mine. Soon after, she began to make a mess of her property cards as well as of her stack of money, so that when I again landed on her expensive property, she could not find the appropriate card. It was hidden under some five-hundred dollar bills, and she could not find it in order to read how much money I owed her. Her correct reading of mortgage prompted me to say that she had two choices: one was keeping her property cards and money organized so she could charge me, and the other was losing the cards, which meant she would neither have to read nor charge me large amounts of money. Her correct reading of a difficult word emboldened me to state with conviction that when she did not permit herself to find out or to read (to find or to read the property card), there must be powerful reasons behind her behavior, since she had just revealed her innate capacities by reading the difficult word *mortgage*. Compared to an abstract discussion, wherein I analyzed the possible symbolic meanings of *mortgage*, within the structure of the game I was certain Betsy could easily grasp my meaning.

At this Betsy said if she did find the card and read to me the sum of money I owed, we would have to end the game, since I had little money and no expensive properties. In this instance, reading and finding out meant bringing the game to an end, which might have stood for terminating an interaction with me, reminding her of the end of her interactions with her father. But, as I put the choice to her of charging or not charging me (or of keeping her cards in order or stacking them haphazardly), she made her choice confidently, and with some contempt in her voice, "I'd keep the cards and money straightened out, of course!" As we continued the game during the next session, her attitude seemed to have shifted somewhat. She played normally and did not behave as though she felt the need to protect me against the inevitable bankruptcy I was to suffer, and announced matter-of-factly, "I won."

As Betsy played games in therapy, it became clear that together with her pretense of stupidity she had developed a capability to protect others. Similar to Jeremy, her skills had developed unevenly. In Betsy's case, interpersonal knowing was highly developed in comparison to basic skills or academic knowing. Although she now welcomed a new life (the house mortgage) she nonetheless wished to protect herself and me from future tragedy (the Monopoly mortgage which threatened our game interactions). Those who evaluated Betsy's intelligence estimated it solely on the basis of academic skills and ignored her sensitivity to people and the cognitive concepts she had developed to find out about and to interact adroitly with them. Her intent to protect me most probably recreated past attempts to protect her father from his illness and her mother from her feelings of grief about her father's death. It may also have meant that by having little money in the Monopoly game, I was similar to her mother who, for so long, had seemed to be bankrupt with regard to buying a new house, which meant finding a new life for the family.

But, reading and understanding the word *mortgage* may have had an even more complex meaning for Betsy, and, if so, made it all the more impressive that she was able to read this word freely. Mortgage may have meant at one and the same time a beginning and an ending: a new life separate from her dead father may have been joined in her thoughts with her game competence and forcing our game interactions to terminate. But, my putting the choice to her of behaving competently and charging me what I owed her in the game surely meant to Betsy that I was a strong and perhaps a healthy person who would survive her competent actions. This released her from the hold her stupidity impersonation had on her.

This vital session is one more demonstration that psychotherapy consists of an interaction between patient and therapist. As I thought about Betsy's sudden reading of a difficult word, I thought she might be willing to reconsider her father's death in a more liberating way. If she did so, it would enable her to allow the "pledge" to "die" which had kept her 4 years of age. This seemed to be why she brought organization into her behavior which allowed her to become competent in winning instead of protecting me, the sure loser in the Monopoly game.

Thus, what is at issue is not just what the patient is specifically conscious of, but, more importantly, that the therapist's vigilant attention to preconscious as well as to conscious levels of meaning gives the patient permission to understand. If the therapist is first pleased and then cogitates about the child's sudden reading of the difficult word *mortgage*, the child is pleased and encouraged to contemplate the reasons for her behavior, including, and most especially, the belief that she dare not learn or think. The child who begins to understand herself in therapy realizes that in one part of her experience (the preconscious), precisely the unexpected can be true. Then, as she rationally evaluates those previous preconscious thoughts which have become conscious, irrational ideas and rational explanations appear to the contemplating mind with equal force and seem to clash. Because the unexpected can be *true*, she then wonders if everything can be *known*. The leap from a conviction of the truth to a conviction that facts can be known stems from the child's belief that the truth and the known are synonymous. Because children want to know the truth, their equation of the truth and the known confers the act of knowing an extraordinary significance. This idea is especially healing to the child who is afraid to know and who has been led to believe that she cannot know. Precisely because it deals with such hard-to-know aspects of the preconscious, the anything-could-be-true hypothesis is particularly powerful because it puts therapist and child in the same boat. Both therapist and child seem to the child patient as allies who seek the truth. And since to the child, adults "know" the "truth" about everything, the fact that adult and child together are in a search for the unknown comforts the child who becomes convinced that with the adult's help she will find it.

Betsy's Beliefs and Wishes: The Hazards of Conversation

Although Betsy's choice of games, such as Monopoly and Clue, suggested that she tried to express her feelings about her loss, it was not immediately obvious what lay behind her choices. One possibility was that she might have thought that her father had been murdered, insinuated by the murders in the game of Clue. Still it would have been incorrect to interpret to Betsy that she might have felt she was the murderer—that she had by "bad" wishes somehow "caused" her father's death, or that because her activity in the Monopoly game caused me to lose, she had brought our interactions to an end. To say everything that occurs to one's mind without first screening out those thoughts characteristic of adults but not of children contaminates the potential benefits of ruminating, such as those benefits which accrued to Betsy as she heard me say she was indeed clever when she chose to read the word *mortgage* in therapy. Just as they often confuse what is known with what is the truth, young (and sometimes older) children confuse what is said to them with what is real. Young children are not able to understand fully what making a *guess* about the motives for human behavior (or any other phenomenon) really means. Their cognitive abilities do not yet include a paradigm that says to them that out of a range of guesses (possibilities), there might exist a reality. The therapist who does not carefully consider what might be understood or misunderstood by the child patient risks suggesting an idea that has not occurred to the child, and thus risks that the child will confuse an interpretation with reality. I have found that younger children do not even understand the statement, "I *wonder* if you think such and such is true," which reflects the therapist's intent to guess about a truth but seems like *the* truth to the child when the "such and such" is as highly charged as a parent's death. The child might hear an interpretive statement like this as an accusation, which can only aggravate any emotional conflicts about a parent's death. It is not necessarily so that the single statement that appears to make the child most anxious is the correct one. The child may have been made anxious by the multitude of statements, all of which are confused by her with reality. They are not seen by the child as merely guesses, but that which is undeniably "true" because the adult has uttered them.

Even older children and adolescents become confused when presented with a series of guesses precisely articulated to evoke some reaction from them in order to verify the therapist's hunch. To the older child or adolescent, the therapist often seems like an authority; whatever is said by the therapist carries a certain aura even though older children and adolescents are capable of understanding the difference between a guess and the truth.

Although Betsy was 8 years old when she came for therapy to deal with the causal connections she had thought up to explain her father's death, she remained in some respects similar to a preoperational child aged 4 in her use of prelogic and preconcepts. This was apparent in her statement that the gerbil (which might have represented herself) could not accept its mate's death because it did not know about it. Betsy had only briefly considered the fact that the gerbil's self-imposed isolation represented "knowing" (i.e., reacting) and had centered on "what is not known is not." Prelogical thought was especially evident as she was reminded of those events, such as her father's death, which so deeply troubled her. Since she continued to think prelogically in regard to some themes, she might have reacted irrationally to my statement that an "innocent" child could have the guilty fantasy of harming a parent; that similar to the faces of the Clue game's characters, she might be afraid that she harbored real guilt behind a look of innocence. The clinical data that follow, provided by Betsy's talk and play enactments, gave the specifics needed to understand more clearly how she conceptualized the cause of her father's death.

Betsy's Oedipal Experience

Betsy first revealed that she did not believe she was responsible for her father's death or for the onset of his illness. She did believe she was responsible for not curing him. She played this out during her 9th month of therapy by pretending I was sick and telling how she must find the magic medicine which would save me. It was easy to say to Betsy that I might not be the only person she would like to give magic medicine to. She smiled and went on with enactments, but suddenly switched from play involving me to scenes with puppets, where the (grand)father puppet refused to let his (grand)daughter marry the handsome prince, and instead banished her to the "dungeon" (which probably represented an underground coffin). Since she had a strong attachment to one of her living grandfathers, Betsy may have wanted to talk about what his old age meant to her. I said that maybe the grandfather wished to keep his granddaughter with him. Betsy nodded in assent, so I went on to say that the granddaughter need not be kept in the dungeon because the grandfather would never lose her as a granddaughter. I continued by explaining that only a grandfather can be a grandfather, so he would still be the granddaughter's grandfather even if she married the prince. At this Betsy started to talk about the grandfather puppet, made a slip of the tongue and called the grandfather a "father," thus revealing she was more preoccupied with fathers, and not grandfathers. When told it was her feelings about her father, and not her grandfather, which was her problem, Betsy began to talk directly about him.

She said that although she did not remember her father's death, she remembered some events that had happened the year before. She recalled how she had "followed my father around all the time," thus indicating she had felt profound love for him, which is a normal occurrence in Oedipal children. She did not feel guilty about harming him but remorse (and perhaps guilt) about not saving a loved parent. Even though it was clear to me that she wished to join her loved, but deceased, parent, I did not tell her this. I felt if I said she might want to be with her father in the coffin, she would react as though I spoke "the truth"—that she *must* be with her dead father because she often *wished* to be with a living father. Instead, I attempted to express that although her father was not alive, in her memory he would always be her father. I told her that she need not limit her future but might expand it by suggesting that she accept the fantasy, which she initially rejected, of the (grand)daughter puppet marrying the prince—and reconsider the other fantasy of the (grand)daughter puppet being banished to the dungeon. By doing this, I hoped to suggest to Betsy that mature cognition was safe: it would tell her that she would always be her (deceased) father's daughter which meant she might marry the prince rather than go to the dungeon. My aim was not *just* to create a safe atmosphere in which Betsy could hear and understand an interpretation which was *both* retrospective *and* prospective, and which therefore offered her a neat resolution to her dilemma. My aim was to encourage Betsy to deduce that her future need not be overwhelmed by the past. If Betsy was encouraged to *reason*, she might thereafter help herself to feel safe and to understand.

Further revelations came in the ensuing weeks when Betsy enacted dramas which showed that in therapy she once more experienced Oedipal conflicts. She said the mother puppet died and the daughter felt "guilty" about leaving the (grand)father puppet to marry the prince. Now she sometimes felt free to imagine a communion with her (grand)father without her mother present. But she understood that a (grand)father–daughter communion would make her feel guilty about marrying the prince. At the same time, she expressed that she felt guilty, without knowing exactly why, about her anger at her mother, the living parent. She perhaps wished that her mother, not her father, had died, and then felt she must "cure" me—another woman—lest I retaliate by not curing her.

Betsy revealed through her puppet shows that her thoughts were becoming increasingly complex. Yet, to have suggested to Betsy that her guilt feelings resulted from "bad" or angry wishes she may have had toward her father *or* her mother would have convinced her that adults do not understand children. This suggestion would have contradicted the remorse she felt for not saving her father and it would have proved to her it was unsafe to imagine her mother's absence. Most critically, an interjection of this sort would have served to strengthen her belief in the safety of prelogical thought. She might have deduced that thinking must be avoided at all costs since only a terrible person would wish both parents dead.

Betsy was almost 9 years old when she understood that her learning disorder originated with her fear of what can be known. She felt rather comfortable with the unknown; the less she knew, the better. Her reasoning about her conflicts harked back to prelogical thought—to the time when she was 4 years old—when coincidentally, her father died. When she attempted to think about her father, causal connections suddenly began to have a "logic" of their own.

Without therapeutic intervention, Betsy probably would not have achieved the formal thought required to unravel the connections which expressed and perpetuated her feelings about her father's death.

SKETCHING BETSY'S COGNITIVE DEVELOPMENT

My intent now is to reexamine Betsy's symptoms when she was 8 years old in light of normal cognitive development. In what behaviors typical of early childhood did Betsy's mental retardation impersonation originate? Her arrest in reasoning spurned by her father's death when she was four was preceded by normal intellectual functioning as described by her mother when she recounted Betsy's early history (e.g., age of talking, vocabulary usage, ability to follow directions, interest in and competence at drawing, peer interactions, information acquisition, such as color and number names, counting, her address and telephone number, etc.).

Imitation and Play

The ability to imitate at an early age, sometimes in extraordinarily accurate and voluminous detail, lies behind the impersonations of a child like Betsy. As Piaget (1962) showed, infants and young children progress through stages of imitation and its counterpart, play, beginning in the sensorimotor period. Imitation and play represent, respectively, the young child's attempts to reproduce reality or to manipulate aspects of it. The infant first reproduces events of the present and the immediate past and later expands imitation to include what Piaget refers to as "deferred imitation." "The child reproduces an absent model through memory" (Flavell, 1963, p. 126). In the early stages of play, the infant has no end goal and play tends to be, to quote Piaget (1962), "a happy display of known actions" (p. 93). By the time the child is preoperational, her play intends to make reality bend to the child's wishes. At approximately the same time when deferred imitation appears in her behavior, play is also no longer tied so closely to the present or to the original stimulus. The child playfully reenacts the past by using "inadequate," inventive, or unexpected props "*as if* they were adequate; that is, by treating them as symbols of something else" (Flavell, 1963, p. 128). Play and imitation are in later childhood (beginning at about 7 or 8 years) reintegrated into intelligence as a whole, which explains, in part, the greater stability of the concrete operational (the latency) child's view compared to that of the preoperational child. Together the two processes form the basis for a more mature adaptation — where imitation, an accommodating process, and play, an assimilating process, balance in a fortunate state of equilibrium. But the integration of imitating and playing is a lengthy course that does not result in a permanent equilibrium until the emergence of concrete operations when imitation becomes "deliberate" and play becomes "constructive" (i.e., permeated with "rules" and other aspects of games) (Piaget, 1962, p. 274).

Betsy's Impersonation

Piaget's view of imitation and play, more simply said and applied to Betsy, details how the young child attempts to come to terms with reality. Through playing, the child comes to know what she wants to or can do, and through imitating she comes to know what is given by her surroundings. Betsy's normal development prior to the age of 4 means she had the capacity for genuine "as-if" pretense and make-believe and for deferred imitation. When at age 8 she was brought for therapy, her ability to project behaviors or attitudes which were not her own suggests that imitation and play after the age of 4 had come together in such a way as to permit her the as-if identity of a stupid or mentally retarded person. For several years, she had attempted to fortify her identity as a 4-year-old—her age when her father was alive. Her imitating behaviors had the aim to project the personality of a "foolish" child and were overly developed as she tried to maintain the time of her life when her father lived. Because she so desperately wished her father was alive, she sustained a mode of thinking wherein "the universe appears. . . to be at the beck and call of their [children's] actions" (Furth, 1987, p. 27). Betsy hoped her father would reappear at her beck and call.

But, her need to project an impersonation of mental retardation meant imitating was out of balance with comparable playing predilections because the results of her playful explorations—childhood knowledge—would challenge the results of her imitations—her mental retardation charade. Although her imitations had become mature and "deliberate," nonetheless she frequently experienced play disruption when she was behaving competently in therapy (e.g., articulately describing a dollhouse scene; winning a table game). (*Play disruption* is Erikson's, 1950, term to describe the sudden or gradual cessation of play activity brought about by anxiety. It is roughly analogous to the child's anxiety dream and perhaps to the blocking of an adult patient.) Her "asynchronous" development suggests that anxiety may have foreclosed the full development of play throughout the preoperational subperiod following her father's death, where imitation became overdeveloped for reasons already discussed. The mental retardation red herring she had created inhibited play sequences because through play she might be confronted with her own intelligent exploration or explanations of play phenomena. Or, she might hear me comment about her intelligent uses of play.

It is unknown whether Betsy had ever witnessed the behavior of a child who was actually mentally retarded before her admission to a school for learning-disabled children. It *is* known that she was often compared to her brilliant brother and so might have concluded that to differentiate herself from him she must behave stupidly. Or she might have concluded that she could never compete successfully with him. In any case, she behaved in a way contrary to what she knew was consonant with her own identity and took on the characteristics of an identity foreign to her own. Moreover, her description of some of the learning-disabled children in her school suggested that they were mentally retarded and thus misdiagnosed as only learning disabled. And lastly, she had ample opportunity to refine her impersonation of the retarded as the result of observing television characterizations of this population (such as cartoon characters who were manifestly mindless, and a program Betsy told me about depicting the life of a mentally retarded person). As she progressed in therapy, she used her imitative skills in creative drama, and her interest in theater continued after her therapy terminated. Behavior that originally had been pathological thus became a redirected part of Betsy's repertoire as she approached adolescence.

When Betsy was 8 years old, she entered therapy at just the age most children become concrete operational. But she was caught in the preoperational subperiod that immediately precedes concrete operations. She resisted checking her impressions of herself and reality by resisting a stable system of thought. Piaget (1924) has lucidly described the quality of the preoperational child's relationship to reality:

> play cannot be opposed to reality, because in both cases belief is arbitrary and pretty much destitute of logical reasons. Play is a reality which the child is disposed to believe in when by himself, just as reality is a *game* at which he is willing to play with adults and anyone else who *believes* in it. (p. 93, italics added)

This quote aptly captures the playful 3- or 4-year-old who enacts past events as she wishes them to be and produces effects she wishes to create. The young child's "reality" (more accurately, her actuality) is based on whimsical ideas that often remain uncorreced and, as Piaget noticed, the child welcomes collusion in her "game of reality" from anyone who suspends belief in a more mature worldview long enough to join in.

Betsy's impersonation was exactly that: a suspension of belief in a critical detail of her identity—her native intelligence—for specific reasons described earlier. She was so skillful that she managed to entice the cooperation of all who knew her. Since the age of 4, she had remained preoperational by making the reality of her unintelligence a game which she was willing to play with anyone who believed her to be stupid.

Learning about Death

At 4 years of age, Betsy was aware of her father's death but probably not the process whereby she came to understand that it had happened, nor what it meant. Perhaps she adhered to immature reasoning to avoid reflecting on those learning and thinking processes that might lead her to understand the circumstances of her father's death. Because it appeared safe, she became expert at "transductive" reasoning, usually for the purpose of arriving at conclusions which suited her. Unlike deductive or inductive reasoning, transductive reasoning connects one datum with another by coincidental associations, or by reversing cause–effect sequences. In both cases, the child reasons from particular to particular, tending to juxtapose data rather than to connect facts or events through logical necessity or causality. According to Flavell (1963), "centering on one salient element of an event, the child proceeds irreversibly to draw as conclusion from it some other, perceptually compelling happening" (p. 160).

On entering school 2 years after her father's death, Betsy might not have known that school and teachers are supposed to transmit knowledge but she surely knew school is a place for learning and where concrete skills are taught and information transmitted. It was probably at this point that she spontaneously associated the act of learning with what is learned, a transductive connection she expressed in therapy by saying: "Learning in school is two and two, and learning in school is t-h-e." It seemed to me she was saying learning is the same as a *product,* not a process. She seemed to say that since learning leads to knowing facts, learning and the known are equivalent (A→B, therefore A = B). Learning of the death of her father, then, symbolized general learning because learning is the same as what becomes known. Note that Betsy's choice of benign subject matter in proposing to add 2 and 2 and in spelling "t-h-e." About the word *the* as a product, nothing much can be said, and Betsy declined to supply the result of 2 added to 2, perhaps because it was the very nature of the "products" of learning which she tried to avoid. She could articulate what "learning in school is" by imagining safe consequences, such as the word *the* or by wondering about the sum of 2 and 2 but not venturing a guess. These results of learning were safe. But she could not afford to develop her thinking processes if these led to an unsafe product, such as understanding the unwelcome event of her father's death.

During therapy, Betsy developed an incorrect syllogism linking learning and dying which nonetheless represented a positive step in reasoning. She now knew that learning and growing up were somehow related, but she inferred incorrectly that they were equivalent. Since her father had learned, grown up, and died, learning thus led to dying. This syllogism also reminded her of the earlier idea: since I "learned" about my father's death, learning *is* or *is like* dying. The symptoms of not knowing and nonlearning were so stubborn in Betsy's case because by her reasoning, she was engaged in a struggle for survival. A full year after she had begun therapy, she told me: "I'm sad about my father, but I don't let myself think about it."

A statement such as "I don't let myself think" is often misinterpreted by the therapist, who might assume it reflects the child's resistance to fully experience the particular feelings linked to a past event. Therefore, she cannot think through the conflict because of her wish to repress some unpleasant associations. But critical attention to what Betsy said and how she said it revealed that one appropriate affect—sadness—had been experienced. Since the intellect tends to reconstruct or construct anew the traumatic event, a reexperience of affect will not overcome the distortions created by the immature mind which anxiously resists maturity. Even if the therapist suggests that other feelings in addition to sadness, such as anxiety, are attached to her memory about a parent's death, this will not necessarily assist the child in understanding her problems with thinking. In conversation with Betsy, I focused on the fact that she was able to talk about and even experience sadness but, more important, she was still unable to *think.* When I asked her what was dangerous about thinking, she said, "If I think, I'll know what I don't want to [know]." If knowing meant dying, the "logic" of transduction, she *would* have to know what she did not want to know. Who would want to know if knowing leads to death?

Betsy did not deny the reality of her father's death nor did she disavow her feelings of grief connected to it. She did attempt to disavow the anxiety associated with the thinking process because the very process of thinking suggested to her that she would be similar to her parent who had died. It is unfortunate that therapists in many such situations with an anxious child strive to bring about repeated affective experiences without examining how the child's mind is working and without recognizing the anxiety she experiences is coincident with a mature thought level. Betsy needed help in understanding that it was *precisely* her thinking that could lead to insights which would *liberate* her from the ideas which brought about and perpetuated her symptoms. I tried to communicate to Betsy that her thought processes could have more productive outcomes. I meant to suggest that the knowing process is not the same as what is known. By talking with her about the differences between thinking about an event and the actual event, I hoped to communicate to Betsy that neither growing up nor thinking maturely are equivalent to dying.

TRANSITION PHASES AND THERAPEUTIC INTERVENTION

In telling Betsy's story, I concentrate on her experience of the two transitions to more mature thought: that which occurred at 8 years when she entered therapy and soon became normally concrete operational, and that which occurred almost 3 years later when she appeared to straddle the abyss between concrete and formal thought. At 11 years of age, Betsy was not expected to be completely formal operational when she began to understand her own thought processes about her father's death and when her anger at her mother intensified in therapy. But had I accepted such phase-approriate reasoning as fixed, I would have missed opportunities to help her. Within stage inconsistencies usually mean that a transition phase has come about, which ought to enlarge rather than restrict therapeutic possibilities.

The wisdom of aiming therapeutic efforts directly at thought immaturities, such as magical thinking, is questioned by Elkind (1979a): "A therapeutic approach aimed at their [children's] feelings, rather than at their magical thinking, would probably be most helpful" (p. 215). Nonetheless, Elkind accurately describes how such thinking aggravates the original affect which adds to the child's symptoms (e.g., the guilty child who believes his parents divorced because of his angry misbehavior). It is not clear why Elkind rejects a strategy which has a double aim: to alleviate the bind magical thinking creates for the child as well as to free the child from intrapsychic conflicts.

Greenspan (1979) also noted the hazards of concrete operational thought in the child's attempt to deal with the presumed anger of a parent. He contrasted the reasoning capabilities—and presumably the therapeutic possibilities—in the formal operational youngster who perceives parental anger as compared to the concrete operational child. The argument runs that the younger child often has no (cognitive) recourse but to deny mother's anger because the logical possibility of the inverse is the only one the child is capable of that does not overly threaten him.

> Thus, in observing that mother is angry at him, the concrete operational child can feel: "I don't love mother," or "I love mother," or he can change it to the inverse, "Mother is not angry with me" (a denial). "I don't love mother" may be too strong a feeling, and "I love mother" too painful, to accept. Within his two-variable system he may have only one possible correlational feeling—the inverse. (p. 215)

The older child capable of formal thought has more logical options open to him. He can use the reciprocal and thus conclude that if his mother is angry at him, he is angry (or has been, or can be) at her. He is not bound to a logical system where the inverse (denial) appears to be the only way out because other possibilities are either too painful or do not occur to him.

Although these points agree with many that I make in this book and illustrate the necessity to attend to the child's level of reasoning in any attempt at remediation or cure, the therapist may also promote doubt in the child's mind about some aspects of her perspective. If the child is already doubtful (transitional), the therapist can help her understand, for example, that she need not deny what her intuition told her about other people and their feelings.

When she began to understand that her magical thinking regarding her father's death was limiting and unnecessary, Betsy, at age 11, once more became painfully transitional in thought. She was not quite sure that new thought would serve her better and was reluctant to but finally did understand that her uses of the inverse were aimed at helping her deny her anger at her mother for not having been the parent who had died. When she admitted to anger at her mother, she defended herself from the implications of it by telling herself, similar to what Greenspan describes in hypothetical fashion, that she did not love her mother, or that her mother did not retaliate by becoming angry at her (despite Betsy's wish to have had her mother die, and not her father).

Betsy's search for a more mature perspective took a turn for the better when she realized that it was often her own beliefs which created her problems. Her belief that what one wishes to happen does happen had led to many anxious moments when she feared that her death wish toward her mother would lead to her demise. Since there would be no one left to take care of her, she tried to defend herself against this anxiety by the use of the inverse ("I am not angry at mother"). As before, I told her that she was making connections between events which were not necessarily so. Immediately, Betsy recalled having erroneously thought that growing up, or academic learning, had led to her father's death, and she added a new thought saying that the problem was her father's work itself: "I thought he died because of all the hard reading and hard paper-writing he did at his work. I thought if I learned to read and write the same thing would happen to me." This thought seemed similar to her earlier attempts to avoid reading and knowing how much to charge me in the game of Monopoly. Competence meant the demise of someone.

Yet a close look at how she arrived at her conclusion reveals complex thought processes. In order to express what she used to think, she had to have differentiated magical thought and logical thought. Magical thought suggested to her that in the past her father died because of growing up and/or learning. Observation and deduction told her that her father died when he happened to be a certain grown-up age and contracted a terminal disease. Because she sensed that differentiating logical from magical thought processes would constitute a very important learning experience for her, she became inhibited in making this differentiation because learning something new had always meant dying. Thus, the very act of understanding tempted her to fall back on immature thinking. But she responded positively to my statement that this particular learning would not threaten her because she would understand why her father actually died and would realize that learning and dying have nothing to do with each other.

She then recognized that she had felt that her mother was out to get her. When she explained the reason for this, she said, "because I wanted her out of the way." This was the affective core of her individual version of the Oedipus complex, wherein one parent was missing by virtue of his death. She had wanted her mother out of the way so that her father could be present. She then said that she felt her teachers "were all out to get me too," providing a higher level variation on the theme that school would somehow do her in. New connections were thus embedded in Betsy's remake of a past which continued to cause her difficulty. But her introspections revealed that she was struggling with many more aspects of situations than before and that she might be approaching the capability for abstract thought.

Formal operational thought is most likely to be revealed in therapy when the young person examines his own motives in the presence of an empathic adult. The quality of self-understanding and interpersonal exchanges vary dramatically during the youngster's transition from concrete to formal thought. The older youngster not only cogitates but she thinks about what she "used to think" and in regard to many variables. Cowan (1978) has described adolescent introspection well:

> The ability to coordinate four dimensions [instead of the merely three dimensions typical of concrete operational thought] and operate on the results of operations means that adolescents can 1) think about 2) their thoughts about a complex combination of variables (3, 4). For example, they can criticize their own ability to understand the relation between what they do and how others react. (p. 289)

Betsy engaged precisely in this introspective process when she coordinated her previous thoughts about her two parents: (1) she recognized what she *had* thought (2) which was different from what she *now* thought (3) regarding her father (4) about whom she felt differently than her mother. When she explained that she wanted her mother out of the way and connected this wish with her perception of her teachers, she revealed that she was capable of projection. Despite their paranoid nature, these projections reflected higher level thinking, as Elkind (1979a) discusses. Her projection onto the school of her feeling that her mother (or her earlier mental retardation presentation) would do her in depended on an attribution of her own feelings or those of family members to someone outside the family. But because Betsy had begun to doubt her mentally retarded self-image, she did not create a union of school and family, but instead projected only some feelings onto the school and teachers—the residue of her negative identity. Elkind (1979a) described projection well when he says, "but such attribution must, of necessity, wait upon the child's ability to conceptualize the thoughts, feelings, and impulses of others" (p. 217). The fact that Betsy was often *wrong* about the thoughts, feelings, and impulses of others does not detract from her maturing ability to *conceptualize* what these might be.

As insight piled atop insight, Betsy's reconstruction (or more accurately, her construction [Spence, 1982]) of the past became more complex. Each of her reworkings led to a better understanding which, in turn, led to greater adaptation because as she struggled to understand why knowing had threatened her, she gained a more intense sense of who she was and how she had come to be the way she was. Betsy and her mother discussed the possibility of fewer therapy visits with me. These discussions were permeated by Betsy's expected ambivalence—her pride in her academic and therapeutic achievements and her remorse in forsaking her relationship to me. Her graduation to the 5th grade did not represent just renewed academic learning, but reflected as well a more mature, flexible, and reliable conceptual system which enabled her to understand herself and to construct a theory of her past and present. Also to be expected was her pretense of stupidity during her last several appointments. She gave the reasons for it all on her own: "I thought I'm stopping [therapy] because you thought I was stupid. That's because I *made* my mother think I was stupid so she wouldn't know how angry I was [at her]." As a final summation, she said: "I knew if I passed all those tests [at school] my mother would find out that I'm smart, and so would my teacher, and then I would *have* to read hard stuff in school." At this moment in Betsy's life, as she tried to piece together remembered bits of her past, she implied that if she were smart it meant she was capable of anger. In Betsy's mind, anger had worse consequences than stupidity. If she were smart, she would be expected to behave in the fashion which, in her mind, led to her father's death, and she would have to admit how angry she had been at her mother, the living parent.

To end this account of Betsy's progress in therapy and in thought development, it might be of interest to the reader that she continued to struggle both with her feelings and with her schoolwork. She became particularly enamored of reading joke books, probably because the result of this "knowledge" made her laugh instead of feel sad or anxious. It might also be useful once again to quote Greenspan, whose remarks highlight problems in development which were true not only of Betsy, but of all those children who suffered disorders in learning. Deftly tying together the two strands of affective and intellective development, Greenspan (1979) observed that

> children who have been exposed to traumatic separations or to highly inconsistent patterns of response, particularly around heightened emotional states of neediness or anger, often have difficulty maintaining a consolidated and differ-

entiated representation of their primary nurturing figures and the world they represent. Extreme separation anxiety, manifested by a refusal to go to school and accompanied by stubborn clinging and negativistic behavior patterns, is not infrequently observed in such cases. Equally important, however, is that such children maintain magical patterns of thinking, not only in relation to their internal world but often at the external boundary, and thus have difficulties at school. Under emotional pressure, logical thought (concrete operations) may be compromised. (p. 170)

Betsy's logic had been compromised by her deliberately clinging to those immature thought processes which seemed safe.

SUMMARY

The overt behavior of overachievers and underachievers in regard to learning differs dramatically. In fact, most overachievers are not perceived as having problems with learning. As students, they are often welcomed by teachers and praised by parents. Their achievements seem to come easily and thus validate the expectations and hopes of teachers and parents. Overachievers are referred for psychotherapy only when parents and teachers notice undue tension associated with a "perfectionistic" attitude toward school assignments or when they have difficulty with one particular subject. Because parents and teachers respond to the overachiever by striving to promote excellence in all subjects, they seek the therapist's assistance to understand and correct the youngster's single academic lapse.

Contrarily, underachievers are all too conspicuous and often frustrate the goals of teachers and parents or, at the very least, exasperate them during their arduous attempts to convince the youngster to apply himself, to retain what he has learned, and to maintain his precarious knowledge base. But, both overachievers and underachievers use learning and knowledge for extrinsic purposes. Overachievers use the act of acquiring knowledge to implicitly assert that they are fully grown. Underachievers use the lack of knowledge to assert that they cannot or must not grow up. The learning process is implicated in the overachiever's reach for maturity and in the underachiever's recoiling from it. In both cases, the therapeutic task is to disconnect learning and acquiring knowledge from growing up, however related learning and maturing are. The child must understand the flaw in reasoning: because adults have learned more than children, the more I learn the more mature I am. Both Jeremy and Betsy eventually understood that learning and understanding occur throughout the life span and are influenced by the learner's own trustworthy activity. When freed from the burden that the identification of learning with maturing places on the youngster, he or she can enjoy acquiring knowledge without wishing for or dreading adulthood.

CHAPTER 6

Cognition and Communication

In previous chapters questions of communication with young people have been the implicit or explicit topic when I discuss therapeutic intervention. The subject of this chapter is that proposed ways of talking to a young person ought to intersect his thinking mode. Any statement a clinician makes, especially the interpretation, must be phrased in words that young people can understand. Incomprehensible statements will not catch their attention or influence their thoughts.

Often it is assumed that young people experience resistance when they fail to hear an interpretation or other statements when it may well be that the thought level in the interpretation is inappropriate. Rosen (1985) remarked that

> it would be a mistake to view the patient's behavior as resistance in the traditional psychodynamic sense, as the explanation would actually reside in the patient's cognitive inability to assimilate and accommodate the interpretation in its presented form. (p. 203)

Special attention to the ways youngsters view the world frequently paves the way for their understanding affective meanings. The young person will consider more easily what the therapist says when conversing about his affective life if he feels the overlap of their perspectives is sufficient for communication to continue.

Harmonizing communications with the youngster's thought level is *not* "talking down" to them. Note that we would not call it *talking down* when we try to make ourselves understood by someone who is not fluent in our spoken language. Similarly, we are no longer fluent in the youngster's thinking mode— nor is he fluent in ours. Yet the theory that there are thought discontinuities between adults and children must not tempt clinicians to speak condescendingly to young people. If we show other people that we are interested in understanding their reasons and how causal connections go together, it is an act of respect and perceived as that. Talking down is neither respectful nor does it reflect consideration of a child's or an adolescent's often inventive use of concepts. To see the youngster as childish in only some respects and to alter our behavior accordingly means to him that we take him seriously. And, in some instances, we must "talk up" to the child—specifically, in those instances when he has, through development or therapy, become ready to approach and resolve a transitional phase in thinking. Although it may be important for the therapist's *psychological* expertise "to be at a higher level than the patient" (Rosen, 1985, p. 202), therapeutic communications ought not to seem to the patient to be condescending or arcane. Furthermore, the therapist must often promote the young person's reach for a higher level comparable to that or even beyond the therapist's, exemplified by several conversations between Timothy (see Chapter 4) and me when he understood physics better than I did.

Shapiro (1979) is also concerned with the misunderstandings that may occur between children and adults in clinical settings. When therapists use technical (metapsychological) language to speak to young people, it suggests to the patient not only that we do not understand him but also that we intend to remain distant from him. According to Shapiro,

> We certainly should avoid speaking to patients in metapsychological terms or in the argot of our particular theoretical framework. So why should we use one of the many pretentious codes unless our aim is to further distance us. Instead, we should substitute for classic Latinisms the lingua franca that dominates the therapeutic milieu. Furthermore, since the patient should be doing most of the talking, it ought to be his brand of the lingua franca. (p. 132)

Shapiro's discussion of how to talk to children and adolescents is based on his conviction that a psycholinguistic analysis of how we communicate in general and to patients specifically will sharpen our therapeutic technique (pp. 52–54). Consistent with Piaget and Inhelder (1969), I believe that linguistic development is best understood as one aspect of cognition (as the "semiotic" or symbolic function). Although attending to a patient's language usage (his vocabulary and his syntax) is very important, clinicians must not forget that there is thoughtful activity which is not primarily language-based, for example, sensorimotor behavior, images, symbolic play, art, music, dance, athletics, dreams, etc. The point is that cognition more than language pervades behavior and that verbal *and* nonverbal behavior becomes interpretable by the therapist when he or she considers the cognition which underlies it. The point is not the dispute about which is preeminent in development—cognition or the logic of language—a dispute that Piaget and Inhelder (1969) referred to in this passage:

> Unlike images and other semiotic instruments, which are created by the individual as the need arises, language has already been elaborated socially and contains a notation for an entire system of cognitive instruments.... The individual learns this system and then proceeds to enrich it.... Must we then conclude, as has been suggested, that since language possesses its own logic, this logic of language constitutes not only an essential or even a unique factor in the learning of logic...but is in fact the source of all logic for the whole of humanity? (pp. 86–87)

In psychotherapeutic exchanges, it is the particular and often enriching meanings the patient brings to language that concern the therapist and inform him or her of choices for interpreting meanings. Therefore, it is not just our understanding that surface language features vary with developmental stage which is effective in communicating with individuals and in catching their particular meaning. We can expect, as Shapiro has pointed out, that the child will often misuse grammatical structures or the adolescent will often pierce his conversation with the prevalent slang. But it is our knowledge of the cognitive organization which produces the child's immature grammar or the adolescent's slang and the connotations associated with his speech which is effective in communicating. Attending to the meaning behind what appears on the surface and which is permeated by the patient's cognition is more comprehensive and provides more options for the therapist at the same time the patient's cognitive level restricts how a statement ought to be made.

Shapiro also advises the therapist to supply the appropriate word to the child to make a connection between her behavior and the presumed affect leading to it or accompanying it. This advice is important for clinicians to consider because it illustrates just one more reason why an appraisal of the child's cognitive functioning—and not only those typical linguistic utterances used by children—is more comprehensive. Concentrating on what the child knows, and not just on what she says, helps the therapist avoid telling her something she already knew as if she did not know it and prevents a communication breakdown between the therapist and the child. Shapiro (1979) has noted correctly that his suggested procedure is "didactic" rather than "analytic" (p. 134), but more important than this distinction of style is that the child often knows what affect accompanies her behavior. The therapist who says in situations like this, "'You always become quiet and silent and stop playing when you feel angry'" (p. 134) might appear to tell the child the obvious. It would be more accurate to say that the child doesn't know what to *do* with either affect or established behavior patterns. The child sometimes even knows what affect has led to the behavior, but again, she does not know how she can *change* the affect, her behavior, or her future. And, if the child does not know that she falls silent when she is angry, supplying the word *angry* will not necessarily connect the affect with the behavior.

Suppose it is true of a child, as Shapiro has described, that "doing" is used sometimes instead of "thinking about things" (p. 135). A child who acts without thinking or feeling, one who "acts out," is quite likely to be subject to more than one affect. "Doing" instead of "thinking about things" or "doing" without "feeling" often occurs when the individual cannot find the words to express a complex affective state—and adults, not just children, often find themselves in such a situation. If the child is not just angry but is also jealous, sad, and distraught, the therapist's offer of the word *angry* will seem inadequate to describe her emotional state—or even wrong. If the word *angry* seems incommensurate to describe her intense feelings, she has no recourse but to reject it because she is not mature enough to mentally list (therefore separating) multiple affective states, and then to select *the* name which correspondes to just one feeling—anger. Consequently, she cannot agree with the therapist's choice of the word *angry*.

If, on the other hand, the child is subject to the single emotion of anger, and the therapist has accurately selected this name for her affective reaction, she is likely to perceive that the therapist has searched for the correct word to connect the heretofore unconnected feeling of anger and the angry behavior. She could conclude that the therapist means by saying the word *angry* to validate not just her angry feeling but also her angry behavior. The therapist might then observe an escalation and not a reduction of angry behavior as the child tries to show the therapist precisely how accurate the word choice is in describing her behavior. Even if the therapist was fortunate enough to have correctly understood the child's affect, as the result of symptom escalation, the therapist could conclude that the word choice was *in*correct. Or, if the therapist does recognize that the word *angry* is correct to describe the child's affect, the therapist must now painstakingly explain to the child that thinking, feeling, and doing are different. What Shapiro ignores is that supplying a single word for affect is often either inadequate or increases the therapist's tasks.

In the long run, what will connect affect and behavior productively is the youngster's *own* ability to form reliable concepts and to make distinctions between feelings and actions, thought and behavior, and to reflect on the motives of the self in an interpersonal context. Since only the youngster can know which affect or affects he is experiencing—the therapist merely guesses what they are—only the child can assign names to affective states. This fact makes the "therapeutic" activity of naming affects superfluous at the very least and distorting—thus damaging—at its worst.

Nonetheless, a psychotherapist in just the right interpersonal context can create the conditions that lead especially the older child or adolescent to make important connections between discriminated facets of his experience. For example, Pine (1985) reported an important therapeutic moment between him and 16-year-old Robert. Robert said about a high school dance he had attended but not participated in: "All the other guys were dancing with girls except me...but I wasn't angry" (p. 139). As Robert's therapist, Pine asked himself whether he ought to have remarked to Robert that he was denying anger. Let us now consider what Robert's therapist actually said. "Perhaps as you say, you weren't angry. Perhaps you were envious; perhaps you were wishing that you could be dancing too" (p. 139). Pine continues by saying that his patient responded positively to this interpretation ("he lit up") and analyzes this positive response as being the result of therapeutic "teaching" the names for the different affects of anger and envy—affects which presumably became distinct as Robert listened to his therapist.

The therapeutic benefit Robert received does not seem to me to be the result of Pine's "teaching" Robert in a literal sense. It seems to be rather that Pine created a situation in which Robert could learn by his own efforts; that is, the balance in Robert's learning and Pine's teaching seems more weighted in favor of Robert's learning. First, Pine validated his patient's spontaneous differentiation of anger and envy as he responded empathically to Robert's statement "but I wasn't angry:" "Perhaps, as you say, you weren't angry." This therapeutic statement implies that some affect *other* than anger may have accompanied "all the other guys were dancing." Equally important in the interpretive statements was Pine's triple use of the word "perhaps." *Perhaps* means uncertainty and invites the youngster to articulate his own ideas about his feelings and his behavior. Most important in Pine's therapeutic endeavor was his linking an affect's name—envy—to a vividly remembered detail of Robert's experience: "You were wishing you could be dancing too." This is not simply "naming affects." It is putting a young person more deeply in touch with what he himself has just remembered. It is adeptly creating a relationship between newly differentiated affects (anger and envy) and the experiences in which they originated. Moreover, this complex therapeutic effect, in my opinion, was built on Pine's repeatedly saying "perhaps" in conversing with Robert, which led him to contemplate which actual affect he perhaps *had* experienced.

Contrarily, adult statements that supply the youngster with the names for her feelings appear manipulative to her especially if these statements contain the word *always* or other words which imply unquestioned expertise emanating from the therapist (e.g., "You *always* become quiet and silent and stop playing when you feel angry" [Shapiro, 1979, italics added]). Such statements are especially offensive to young people who *do* understand they are silent—or are behaving in some other way—because they are angry. The child suspects that the therapist wishes her to use the word *angry* rather than be silent, or use the word angry instead of hitting. If a child does not easily distinguish actions from feelings, she may conclude that she ought not to act *or* feel in a certain way.

When the child is ready, able, and willing, she will spontaneously use the correct word to describe the feelings which accompany her behavior. When a child is not ready to name affects, the therapist's lesson will be lost or resented. In the former circumstance, the therapist can express appreciation for the child's accurate connection of behavior, affect, and language, such as "you are showing *and* explaining to me how you feel." If the child tells the therapist what he or she is *not* feeling, the therapist can proceed from there as Pine did when he suggested some affect *other* than what his patient appropriately denied as explanation for his experience. When a child is not ready to name feelings or remains silent rather than deny what the therapist suggests, the therapist must deal with the child's wordless behavior in a way that respects her and keeps her safe.

Finally, the psycholinguistic attempt to alter overt phenomena contradicts the psycholinguistic view that language consists of a covert system with grammatical rules and semantic meaning. A psycholinguistic approach to therapeutic communications should show why encouragement in therapy to instigate or change a youngster's language code allows her the use of correct names and, most importantly, why the corrected language reduces her symptoms.

Although it is never correct to ignore the intellect's work in the child's understanding of her conflicts, at any given moment the therapist might concentrate on one or the other sphere of the psyche. The therapist might ascertain how the child has reasoned in her attempt to master certain school subjects, or might focus on what affective themes would cause the blocking of understanding. Nevertheless, during the critical intervention, when the therapist wishes to communicate his or her understanding *of* the child *to* the child, a statement must not only reflect empathy with the child's affect but also reflect the child's mode of thinking. Only in this way can the therapist bring about an understanding of affective conflicts in the child.

INTERPRETATIONS

Critical interventions in psychotherapy, of which the interpretation is the penultimate example, imply that events for the patient will be different following them as compared to what was likely to transpire before. An interpretation, whether offered to an adult or a child, refers to the "verbal expression of what is understood about the patient and his problems" (Levy, 1984, p. 4). If actually heard by the child, an interpretation can lead to a turning point in the child's therapy. Of course, these interpretations are built on the work that preceded them; but in concisely capturing the essence of that work which simultaneously points to the potential of change or a new development, they can be powerful energizers for that change or development. Schafer (1983) has called these important interpretive statements "creative redescriptions" (p. 130). Some portion of what the patient in the past has already known or sensed becomes what the analyst in the present has to say to the patient. What is new is the transformation inherent in the analyst's often more organized rendition. The analytic organization condenses critical aspects of the past and because it is an abstract summary, it is more easily seen by the patient as a prospective suggestion compared to his often repetitious behavior which tends to be retrospective.

A beautiful example of a critical interpretation which presumably represented a turning point in the patient's analysis is quoted by Spence (1982) in his book *Narrative Truth and Historical Truth*. I have deliberately chosen an example from the therapy of an adult patient to begin this discussion because as I have noted before, critical interpretations to children are harder to formulate. The difficulty stems from the discontinuity between the child's and the adult's perspective. Thus, the appeal of a critical interpretation made to an adult can be immediately obvious. The "of course!" or "that's it!" reaction is instantaneous on reading a passage such as this:

> in what is perhaps [the analyst] Viderman's most famous clinical example...one of his patient's reported the following dream: "My father and I are in the garden. I pick some flowers and offer him a bouquet of six roses." Viderman, in an attempt to bring out the patient's ambivalent feelings toward his father, tried to combine the positive connotations of the gift with the negative feelings he may have had about the fact that the father died of alcoholism. He took advantage of the phonetic similarity between the six roses of the dream and the father's fatal illness—cirrhosis of the liver (the similarity in sound connecting *six roses* and *cirrhosis* is particularly evident in French)—and made the following reply: "Six roses or cirrhosis?" (p. 178)

The analyst took advantage not just of the phonetic similarity in French between "six roses" and "cirrhosis" but also of the patient's mature cognition which doubtless permitted instant aesthetic understanding of his analyst's ingenious pun.

The efficacy of the interpretation to the patient can be gauged by the "corollary" to the interpretation—the patient's own reactions. In emphasizing the patient's expanding self-knowledge, Levy (1984) has commented that

> what the therapist says to the patient comes to define a way of thinking about
> things together, establishes a mode of communication between them, and deter-
> mines, to a large extent, what form the patient's new self-knowledge will take. In
> fact, it can be said that the patient and therapist together interpret the patient's
> inner and often hidden mental life, in that the patient often amends, corrects,
> and amplifies on what the therapist says. (p. 4)

Although the psycholinguistic and the psychoanalytic views converge on the point that interpretations ought to be drawn from the patient's language, the psychoanalytic view stresses as well the necessity to observe the effect of the interpretation. The importance of the patient's reaction in assessing an inter-pretation's impact is noted by Loewenstein (1951) who said, first, that it is important to "use the idiom of the patient's individual experience" (p. 9). Sec-ond, many of the patient's reactions show how close to or far from the mark an interpretation has been as in this comment from a patient quoted by Loewen-stein: "You missed it by a hair's breadth."

Similarly, Ernst Kris (1951) has reported a series of therapeutic exchanges between him and a patient who did not respond productively until Kris more nearly approximated the patient's perspective. He accomplished this by simply changing one word: the exchange of the word *need* for *demand* in the phrase *demand for love* made all the difference. Even though as Kris suggests the ex-changed words might reflect a shift in emphasis from assertive to passive, it surely could have been seen by the patient as a shift from unreasonable to reasonable. A "demand for love" might characterize someone who is basically unreasonable, while a "need for love" is generally accepted as true for everyone. Perhaps feeling at one with humanity, the patient could hear about his need but not about his demand. Theoretical credibility should not be the sole criterion by which we evaluate an interpretation. The patient's response must also be appraised.

Kris (1951) further advised the therapist to use his intuition in forming interpretations and suggested that the therapist's use of his imagination is not incompatible with rational thought. Often "playing on" (p. 29) one's own thoughts and associations helps the therapist arrive at a sentence which more nearly approaches the patient's experience compared to single-minded rational search. Especially in work with children, such free associating particularly when focused on "how it must have felt to be a child," or "when I was a child, why would I have behaved a certain way," helps the therapist form a perspec-tive similar to the child's and to make appropriate statements. In this way, the discontinuity between adult and child is partially overcome. Although an adult might say "You missed it by a hair's breadth," a child will simply ignore a statement which does not fit his experience, including how he thinks about the world, and not just how he feels about it. Wording is critical because it reflects a conceptual level; the therapist's "level" as revealed by the words chosen and the syntax of the statement cannot seem alien or too difficult for the child to understand.

Erik Erikson (1950), the renowned analyst of children, has put a skillfully formed interpretation to 3-year-old "Sam," who made many transductive con-nections between critically important events of his life. He perceived a link between his grandmother's death and his own symptoms of "idiopathic epilepsy" (pp. 21–22). Since Sam's precocious mind was busily occupied connecting his violence to his grandmother's death, Erikson tried to separate the events surrounding his epileptic attacks from other, unrelated events. During the therapeutic hour, Sam began to build with dominoes as he had repeatedly built with larger blocks in nursery school. His therapist noticed that the domino blocks he built all had the colored dots facing inward so that the observer could not see them. Erikson's series of statements skillfully began with one very close to a vivid aspect of the child's world, and thus with what the child knew or felt. Erikson's statements also concretely joined the child's perception to its symbolic meaning: "If you wanted to see the dots on your blocks, you would have to be inside that little box, like a dead person in a coffin" (p. 25). Erikson continued to make connections, but then specifically between Sam's having hit him (during the same hour) and his presumed fear that he would have to die because of this violence: "This must mean that you are afraid you may have to die because you hit me," to which Sam breathlessly answered "Must I?"

There is an apparent precocity in Sam's use of "must" in "Must I [die]?" since most children are more likely to have said, "Will I?", "I would?", or "Do I have to?"—assuming a child chooses to ask these questions at all. The upper layer in this 3-year-old boy's use of must reveals a facility with language which permitted his therapist to continue the therapeutic dialogue. But it also contains a statement of necessity. Erikson's statements which made ample use of what might have seemed to Sam like necessity in saying "this *must* mean" or "you *must* have thought" (emphasis added) might have momentarily confirmed his fears, namely, that whatever he thought or felt must have been so. Erikson's rescuing statement and elaboration of the interpretation only reveals the problem when he says: "Of course not. But you must have thought that you did make your grandmother die and therefore had to die yourself" (p. 26). Sam's facility with language thus helped him attend to the word *must*, which he, in turn, reinterpreted within his 3-year-old system of meanings. To the child *must* means an event will definitely happen.

Sam was predisposed to hear what his therapist had to say not just because Erikson understood the conflicts of such young patients, but also because he painstakingly expressed from the child's perspective how he came to understand these conflicts. Starting with the dots on the inside of the domino box, Erikson oriented the child to his own behavior. Erikson appealed to Sam's imagination when he told him that in order to see those colored dots—a visual image all children might be expected to enjoy—he would have to be in a different place. This statement carried the implication that things can be seen from different perspectives, at one moment from the inside and at another moment from the outside of the box. This is a cognitive strategy (although possibly unintended as such) that laid the groundwork for Erikson's kernel message; namely, the same event can be looked at differently. To Sam, it might have meant: "You can see your grandmother's death in another way." According to the clinical data given, Sam was left to come to this conclusion on his own rather than having it spelled out explicitly by further statements made by his therapist. (See Erikson, 1950, p. 28, for a description of Sam's improved status as the result of psychotherapy.)

The problem in what Erikson communicated to Sam was the statement "this must mean that you are afraid you may have to die," which in the use of the word *must* suggests a connection in reality between an anxiety and its source; a connection young children are prone to cast in an unchangeable cause–effect relationship. Furthermore, Sam may have understood another common meaning of the word *must* as it appears, for example, in a parent's statement "you *must* behave" or "You *must* clean up your room." Even the use of the word *may* (in Erikson's phrase "you may have to die") probably would not mitigate the impact of the word *must* on a young child because *may* often connotes permission. Indeed, it is one very important word in the childhood game "Mother, may I?" To any young child in Sam's situation, *may* could mean that he had permission to die.

Sam's poignant "Must I [die]?" captures his affective reaction to a probable thought error as he may have misinterpreted his therapist's intention. Subsequent conversation with Sam might have considered his immature reasoning or tendency to transpose meaning. Erikson's "of course not" could have been followed by an elaboration of the interpretation which sought to embrace Sam's intellectual perspective. The reply to Sam could have included his belief in the efficacy of prelogical reasoning at the same time that it pointed toward more mature reasoning: "Of course you *believe* what you fear will happen. But, as you can see, that's *not* so, because you've just hit me and you're *not* dead and *neither* am I." At 3 years, a child may not be able to hear all the words of this sentence, but he might be able to hear the word *believe* and understand that it implies uncertainty, suggesting what he believes may not be true. The stress on the words *not* and *neither* would mean to a child that it is certain neither he nor his therapist have died. In this imagined version of what might have been said to Sam (or to other 3-year-olds in similar circumstances), replacing the word *must* with the word *believe* could have replaced the feeling of necessity with something more tenuous. A necessity cannot be changed, a thought which brings about the child's symptoms, whereas a belief suggests something one wishes or fears.

Whether a child understands the word *believe* as meaning he wishes or fears something or, rather, that he holds an opinion must be estimated by an assessment of his cognitive functioning. His understanding of the words we use must be checked against his reactions — both in behavior and in speech — as he listens to and cogitates about what is said to him. At later stages in the child's development, it can be productive to discuss the similarities and differences inherent in the words *believe* and *must*. For example, *believe* and *must* have similar connotations of certainty if the belief, like a conviction, is strongly held; or *believe* and *must* are different if we recognize that a belief or conviction can never be identical to a certainty in science because beliefs and convictions do not always depend solely on empirical evidence. But, it is erroneous to burden a 3-year-old with such thoughts. And it *is* important to encourage doubt in the 3-year-old's mind about the automatic or certain connection between an anxiety and an event.

Several pages later Erikson's remark about interpretations to children that "such things are hard to say" (p. 28) is precisely right, but he continues by saying "wording is not too important" (p. 28). The bulk of this chapter is concerned with the importance of wording for young children in therapy. Words—both the therapist's and the child's—link more than those disparate elements of the child's life (such as affect and behavior, or affect and events). They also link elements of two often discontinuous worlds as the therapist attempts to form sentences appropriate to the child's cognition, and the child attempts to communicate with elaborated or new concepts. Correct wording can make the difference between a heard interpretation and one that goes unheeded because the child cannot hear the meaning embedded in adult language. It is Sam's poignant "Must I?" which catches our attention. It reveals how hard 3-year-old Sam tried to hear his trusted therapist, and, at the same time, how doomed part of the message was. Even though an adult patient might understand, for example, the pun of "six roses" and "cirrhosis," the thought processes of even a precocious 3-year-old do not permit the easy understanding of a series of such complex sentences as

> But you must have thought that you did make your grandmother die and therefore you had to die yourself. That's why you built those big boxes in your school, just as you built this little one today. In fact you must have thought you were going to die every time you had one of those attacks. (Erikson, 1950, p. 26)

Maybe these sentences cogently capturing Sam's core problem appear this way in the text to clarify Erikson's message to Sam for the adult reader. But as clinicians we ought to keep in mind that sentences such as these contain many themes. In this particular passage, these themes imply (1) inference versus empirical evidence (what Sam *must* have thought versus the real reason for his grandmother's death); (2) the past in relation to the present (Sam's grandmother *had* died which may have meant to Sam that he *now* must die); (3) big compared to little; (4) nursery school compared to therapy (big boxes in nursery school and little domino boxes in the therapy hour); and (5) the possibility that death could follow physical illness (Sam's epileptic attacks).

Thus, interactions between adult and child, even more than those between adult and adult, fall prey to misunderstandings, and not just those that reflect misreadings of the patient for the therapist's personal reasons (countertransference), but also those that arise out of the inability of the therapist to comprehend the child's mode of reasoning, or his or her inability to play back this mode when making an interpretation. However, the discontinuity in thinking modes between adult and child does not make him "anti-analytic" as Anthony (1982, p. 346) has suggested. Although Piaget may have seen children as antianalytic in that they are incapable of abstract reasoning until the early years of adolescence, it can still be said that the child *is* "analytic" in that he can think out problems in a way which can be predicted by his operative level. Anthony suggests further that we divest ourselves "of the idea, strongly engrained in some, that nothing will happen unless or until it is made to happen or helped to happen" (p. 342). What this means is that if the therapist can resist the temptation to exert the power contained in his superior knowledge, which is more complete than the child's, the child will act on and gain from the concrete lessons embedded in the adult's statements. Our refraining from making things happen for the child will help him make interesting things happen—just as when the child was an infant, he "made interesting sights last" (Piaget, 1952, p. 153). By watching interesting things happen as the child attempts to come to terms with the world and with his symptoms, the therapist is shown by the child's activity how he might be helped.

THERAPEUTIC STATEMENTS: CONCEPTS, CONTENT, AND WORDS

What are the criteria by which we judge an interpretation to be correct? All that has been said up until now implies the requirement that it be geared to the child's level of intellectual functioning, or just a bit beyond. But there are surely other criteria as well, requirements that would probably apply equally in working with adults. It was said earlier that an efficacious interpretation captures the essence of previous work and points to potential change. The essence of previous work is usually the nature of ambivalent feelings and predominant themes inherent in the patient's conflicts. As mentioned earlier, it is probably also true that for both adults and children the efficacy of the interpretation is at its apex when it springs from the concepts or words that the patient has used and the specific behavior that the patient has engaged in.

Dillon (see Chapter 1), who was 9 years old when he first came to see me, was a tall, slender, gawky boy who often assumed bizarre postures. His demeanor was very intense and, while he had a full range of facial expressions, he restricted his voice to a narrow range of monotonous pitches. He rejected learning because he wished not to know the reasons surrounding his natural mother's desertion and his parents' adoption of him. He became symptomatic in therapy because he became aware of both the prelogical and preconscious connection he had made between having been adopted and his view that there was something wrong with him. He said to me after 11 months of therapy: "There was something wrong with me when I was a baby; I can't read or spell very well and she [his natural mother] must have known that." He believed that he was given up for adoption because his mother knew there was something "wrong" with him and had concluded that whatever was wrong would impede him later in life. (Dillon's natural mother had given up her infant because she was unable to take care of him.) His imagined version of the desertion and the adoption was more threatening than the reality, and he sought to avoid what he thought he knew and other related facts which he thought would be even worse.

Dillon repeatedly used the verb *deserve* which expressed his anxiety brought about by a prelogical, but now conscious, thought. The repetition of the verb *deserve* helped me form an interpretation which Dillon could hear easily. As he tried to express his ambivalence about the merged desertion-adoption, he vehemently said about his adoptive mother, "She does not deserve me." In response to this, I said: "Why shouldn't she deserve you? She picked you from all the other babies, didn't she?" (Dillon's mother had told me during the initial parent conference that she and her husband had actually selected Dillon to be their adopted child.)

Before asking Dillon why his mother should not deserve him, I had asked him to explain what he meant by saying his mother had not deserved him. He answered: "She deserves a better son. She deserves someone who does his homework." Only then did it become apparent that Dillon did *not* mean that he was more virtuous than his adoptive mother deserved. His statements conveyed his meaning and did not require a discourse from me on every last possibility contained in his choosing the word *deserve*.[1] He felt unworthy (undeserving) of his mother's attention—and probably unworthy of having been adopted—because he misbehaved. He refused to do his homework. And because his natural mother had deserted him, he thought his adoptive mother would also desert him. His refusal to do his homework can be seen as a test of his mother's strength to withstand his symptoms.

But, it was not just the word *deserve* that alerted me; it was Dillon's use of concepts. He had made a cognitive connection between his natural mother's desertion and his adoptive mother's imagined desertion. Since he thought his natural mother deserted him because "there was something wrong with me...I can't read or spell very well and she must have known that," he concluded that his adoptive mother would surely desert him if he could not or would not read or spell.

On hearing that his mother indeed "deserved" him, a message Dillon instantaneously processed as could be seen by his broad grin, he began to search my office for something to build with. He decided to construct a wooden puzzle upright rather than to assemble it in the usual horizontal fashion. Balancing each piece carefully atop another, he successfully completed his self-set task, sighed heavily, and declared, "This is my best session yet!" I thought he reacted so excitedly because I had affirmed the positive aspects of "his story," which occurred as he visualized his parents selecting him to be their child. His building behavior is all the more remarkable considering the puzzle he chose to erect was of an old-fashioned schoolhouse.

The very next session Dillon took the interpretation further all by himself. He did not need to hear how his anxiety about his adoptive mother (based on his fantasies about his natural mother) impeded school learning and homework because he was enabled to come upon this discovery himself: "Homework was

[1]The auditory similarity of the two words, *desert* and *deserve*, probably had unconscious meaning for Dillon who felt deserted and underserving at the same time. Such a connection remains speculative, however, since he did not reveal during conversations that he realized this despite his increased inclination to play with words. An example was the way he played with the words *tyrant* and *tyrannosaurus*. He recognized that these words come from the same root when he said to me during the same session he talked about *desert* and *deserve*: "Tyrannosaurus...tyranno...sounds like tyrant...saurus?...sore us [laughing]...what does 'rex' mean?" I took this to mean that he understood his interest in dinosaurs was related to his having behaved like a "tyrant" when his mother asked him to do his homework.

easy for me today because I don't hate myself anymore." He now thought he was worthy because his adoptive mother had picked him out from all the other babies. Feeling deserving and that his mother *did* deserve him, he could finish his homework instead of provoking rejection by leaving it unfinished.

Although we can imagine that generally there might be a correct meaning embedded in those interpretive statements about commonly difficult core problems (such as the meaning of adoption, or of the affect associated with gender, the meaning of an ambivalent relationship with a parent, or the ambivalence inherent in the Oedipal triad, or the meaning of a sudden death of a parent, etc.) if they reflect understanding of and empathy with the patient, we cannot make such a statement about the conceptual base and the language of the interpretation itself. That is, though we may say that a good interpretation has general application in terms of shared connotative meanings, its denotative structure has little general application because of the variability of conceptual systems possessed by the persons to whom the statements are directed. The connotations that might be shared will not be heard if the words used (their denotative meaning), as well as the structure of the sentence in which they appear, are beyond the child's level of understanding. Interpretive statements made to children cannot be assumed to be correct even if they embody the correct affective nexus because there is little chance of their applicability to a broad homogeneous population. The fact, then, that some themes are so common that they may be thought of as universal in modern Western society does not mean that the words and sentences used to express these themes will follow with automatic regularity of form—nor does it mean that form is unimportant. What ought to determine form is the child's use of concepts, or the cognitive homogeneity within developmental levels. The interpretation will be heard by the child only if it is said to him in a way that captures his mode of thinking. A mode of thinking is more than a catalog of those words or that syntax ordinarily used by the child at a given age and cognitive stage level. Moreover, interpretations are less likely to be heard if the therapist asks the child to substitute adult words for child words or to talk instead of act. The child's developmental readiness to be interested in an interpretation is the topic to which I now turn.

VERBAL EXCHANGES WITH YOUNG CHILDREN

Interactions between me and two bright boys, one of whom was not quite 5 years old, and the other who was just 5, will serve as a basis for this discussion about the difficulties inherent in an adult talking with a young child. The first boy, Harry, came for therapy because of disruptive behavior in school, a suspected learning disability (which never materialized), and numerous phobias, often about monsters or movie characters such as Darth Vader which, according to his teacher, so preoccupied him that he could "not even learn the alphabet." He had taken utterly seriously the events of cartoons and horror movies, which he had watched since the age of 2, and believed that because an occurrence was portrayed on television, it would happen to him. His parents, who were intelligent and hard-working professionals, believed that because Harry was bright and responsive in conversation with them, he could easily understand the difference between television's fictions and life's realities.

Although anxiety intruded everywhere in Harry's thinking, his phobias became most conspicuous in school where he was required to concentrate. To Harry the more he found out, the more he had to fear. For example, his parents had thought that watching the television show "Sesame Street" would help him learn the alphabet, but to Harry "Sesame Street" only showed him what he wished to avoid—knowing about monsters. Since school, like television, tried to teach him the alphabet, he was sure school would also teach him about monsters.

Harry's Initiation into Therapy

Harry was a small but well-built boy with a curious facial expression. Like a sleuth, he often investigated every aspect of my office. When conversing with me, his eyes would light up and open wide as he understood what I said, especially if I responded to his statements with a slightly new idea. Sometimes he reacted as though a conversation about and/or a description of a past event was the same as an actual present event and would react by fixing his gaze on me or on some aspect of my office as though watching a film.

When he came to therapy, Harry believed it was possible to know whether a person was good or bad by the place he resided. He based this conclusion on his understanding that "bad" people go to prison. This meant anyone in prison was bad. From his earlier reasoning, Harry developed the generalization that a specific place could make people bad. From what he said, I thought Harry did not know that sometimes good people are wrongly sent to prison. Rather, he reasoned "a good person lives in a good place," or the reverse, "a good place means the person who lives there is good." To have talked with him from an adult perspective that there is, in fact, some truth to the notion that places, such as prisons, make people "bad" would have missed Harry's point. Even though in some cases a transductive connection can be shown to contain an underlying empirical truth, that fact does not necessarily reassure the child. Furthermore, transductive reasoning, whether partly true or not, is often a contributor to the child's anxieties because he does not know in what ways his reasoning holds true—in which specific ways a place (e.g., prison) might make a person bad. If a prison could make someone bad, Harry might have reasoned, then any place could make someone bad.

Although he was phobic about monsters and bad people (represented in children's stories, television, or in the movies by "bad guys" such as Darth Vader), he was nonetheless fascinated with the props of the bad guys, notably guns. After three appointments, he noticed that I did not have a toy gun in my office and asked: "Why don't you have a popgun in here?"

The psychodynamic meaning of "popgun" will doubtless be crystal clear to any clinician. Nonetheless, a statement connecting *popgun* to *pop's gun*, which makes complex use of concepts, words, or syntax, will not enable the young child to understand, no matter how convincing or even clever it might seem to the adult. Moreover, statements made to children who are Harry's age, which include the word *penis* or the names of certain other parts of the body, sometimes appear provocative to them because they do not clearly distinguish the name from its referent. Older children who are aware of this distinction and who are capable of telling in more detail exactly what they mean do not invite inappropriate communications as frequently. Since Harry had previously thought that it is the place which makes a person good or bad, he wished to find out if I was a good person. Although he might have wanted to play with a toy gun, it was his hope that I did not have one in my office because in his view good people did not possess guns. If so, this means he believed toy guns actually have the power to cause injury.

Because I wished to separate the toy gun from the real gun without giving the impression that I took his question lightly, I said, "That's a good question because toy guns don't really hurt people." At this, Harry looked surprised and fell silent with an expectant air that led me to believe he thought I was going to continue. Aiming at the wall and *not* in his direction, I pretended to shoot with a Lego gun which a few minutes before he had made and pretended to shoot with. I said, "That doesn't really hurt anyone." He continued to watch with interest, so I explained further that "pretending to shoot might not actually hurt but might make someone think I was mad." His face wrinkled into a frown, which might have meant that he was puzzled by what I said or that he understood I was talking to him about anger and its potentiality to hurt someone. His frown prompted me to try again. I explained that if a person pretends to shoot, it sometimes means that they are mad and wish to hurt someone. But it does not always mean that, because at that moment I was not mad at him. After a very long pause Harry answered, "Yes, I get mad."

We can only speculate what thought processes occurred during the long pause, but it was probably something like "she shoots (in pretend) when she is mad, so I shoot (in pretend) when I am mad." If so, these would have been the thoughts which enabled Harry to connect the pretense of shooting with his own anger as he made the statement "Yes, I get mad." But, in addition, he may have had to sort out the difference between pretense and reality as he heard me say that, although I pretended to shoot with a Lego gun, in reality I was not mad at him.

Reality and Fantasy

This critical conversation I had with Harry illustrates the importance of beginning with what a young child knows or feels. Although Harry may have attributed symbolic meaning to the Lego "gun," Piaget's (1962) careful analysis of the development of symbols in the child suggests that a just barely 5-year-old would find it difficult to understand why or in what ways a Lego gun could stand for something else; for example, a boy's penis. Children do unself-consciously attribute symbolic meaning to objects, but Piaget observed that they do not question these meanings nor are they always aware of them. For this reason, a young child cannot understand an incorrect interpretation of symbolic meaning. In his confusion about the therapist's intended message, he might become mistrustful of the therapist and probably would not be able or wish to correct the therapist. For example, I felt Harry would find it difficult to understand a statement I might have made which centered on his imagining me resenting not having a "gun"—a possible interpretation of his statement to me, "Why don't *you* have a popgun (pop's gun)?" (emphasis added). More important was Harry's increasing ability to distinguish between a pretense of shooting, which might be accompanied by anger, and a pretense of shooting without anger. Furthermore, popguns have a denotative as well as a connotative meaning: to the child, the word *popgun* refers to a specific toy wherein what is shot out is returned to the shooter—an appropriate toy activity for a child whose developmental level predicts concern with more than one kind of bodily loss (Bettelheim, 1967; Erikson, 1950). When Harry first asked me about a popgun, I was not sure whether he was interested primarily in the activity of shooting, typical of the phallic stage of development, or whether he was interested primarily in the activity of retaining, typical of the anal stage. As therapists, we might be predisposed to a certain theory or interpretation of the child's behavior, but we ought not to forget that the meaning the child imputes is quite likely to be different from our own. The closer the therapist approaches the child's meaning pervading his statements and activity, the more likely the child will respond with trust and be able to correct the therapist if he or she is slightly off the mark.

Theory and interpretation impede our observing children accurately especially when we assume that the child has paid no attention to reality and only fantasizes. I am referring to the psychoanalytic view that the pleasure principle precedes the reality principle in the individual's development and is reality-distorting. Stern (1985) questioned this ontogenetic sequence and has sketched a dialectical relationship between the pleasure principle and the reality principle: "The evidence weighs far more on the side of a simultaneous dialectic between a pleasure principle and reality principle, an id and an ego, all operating from the beginning of life" (p. 239). Again questioning psychoanalytic theory and hypothesizing from recent research findings, Stern asked

> If current findings from infancy studies fly against the notion that the pleasure principle developmentally precedes the reality principle, then why must wishes and defenses against reality be given a privileged and prior developmental position? Why must the sense of reality be seen as secondary in time and derivation, growing out of the loss of the need for fantasy and defense? (pp. 254–255)

The therapist's presumption that impulse and fantasy constitute the child's experience or are the only important aspects of it prevents him or her from noticing what portion of reality the child has reacted to and thus from making statements which support or elucidate the child's actuality. Then our statements become overly focused on a presumed childhood fantasy when many times the child has apprehended reality correctly and is only confused by his own cognitions about it.

By way of contrast, Klein (1964) claimed that the child does not attend primarily to reality but rather seeks through fantasy to satisfy libidinal impulses. Thus, while she presents clinical data similar to what I report, she interprets her data as evidence for the castration theory of learning inhibitions. She does recognize that children create symbols by imagining one thing can stand for another. And she accurately observes that children attribute meaning to objects; for example, to the letters of the alphabet. But then she ignores what they have apprehended about reality in order to imagine that one thing can stand for another.

> For Fritz [not quite 7 years old], when he was *writing*, the lines meant roads and the letters ride on motor-bicycles—on the pen—upon them. For instance, 'i' and 'e' ride together on a motor-bicycle that is usually driven by the 'i' and they love one another with a tenderness quite unknown in the real world.... The 'i's' are skilful, distinguished and clever, have many pointed weapons, and live in caves, between which, however, there are also mountains, gardens and harbours. They represent the penis, and their path coitus. (p. 73)

For Fritz to have used letter symbols ("signs") so inventively, he must have vividly perceived the many reality details of weapons, caves, mountains, gardens, and harbors. Furthermore, he clearly understood the ways vowels are often adjacent ("ride together") in words. Yet Klein (1964) concluded

> I endeavored to show that the castration-fear was the common basis for these early and for all subsequent [learning] inhibitions. ... It is the consequent repression of the active masculine components—in both boys and girls—that provides the chief basis for inhibitions of learning. (pp. 82–83)

Klein wrote before Piaget documented fully what children are capable of apprehending, understanding, and articulating about reality. But she nonetheless describes in her article how accurate the children she observed were in using symbols to express their observations and understanding of reality. At the same time that she assumes the child's wishes are determined by the pleasure principle and precede his grasp of reality, she reports the child's accurate understanding of reality details (including coitus) and how to symbolically represent them. She thus attributes either too little or too much understanding to the young child. Even though the child Klein describes obviously had a vivid grasp of certain reality details (weapons, caves, mountains, gardens, and harbors), he probably did not possess a clear, mature understanding of adult sexuality which would mean that this could not possibly be the basis for his learning inhibitions. If young children do not fully understand coitus, why should they imagine being punished (castrated) for the impulse to engage in this act? Although driven by Oedipal impulse, his childish view of coitus could not support the symbolic use of letters that Klein attributes to him. And Fritz may have used the letters for some *other* and maybe *even* nonsexual purposes, such as to express his wish to be close to another person in the same way that the letters i and e are close in certain words. Similarly, Harry had apprehended enough about reality to know that there is often a correlation between a person's residence and his or her moral conduct but, being 5 years old, did not understand the difference between the possibility of such a correlation and the reality. Since it is not obvious at any given moment which aspect of his experience he has understood, it is risky to interpret the young child's behavior without careful consideration of what has been perceived accurately but misunderstood and what has been misperceived.

Harry's Differentiation of "Mad" and "Bad"

Whichever way Harry made connections between my not having a popgun toy in my office and his own concerns and accurate perceptions, he revealed he was ready to take the next step in thinking when he considered what I said about shooting and a feeling of anger. His own feeling "mad" had remained unstated by me since I referred to "someone" or to myself and not to him in regard to feelings. This makes it all the more impressive that he was able to talk about himself and his feelings because it meant he had made a critical inference—that because a certain connection between behavior and affect was said to exist for someone else, it might also exist for him. The critical thought and new development for Harry was his understanding that while the pretense of shooting exists independent of but often associated with affect, it is *not* associated with being a bad person. It was this realization that liberated Harry from the thought that toy guns are equivalent to real ones and that pretense is equivalent to reality. He seemed to understand that bad people shoot (and hurt) with real guns, but good people might pretend to shoot with toy guns whether mad or not. Feeling for the first time that his pretend shooting did not mean that he was a bad, but merely a mad person, he could then process information given to him by adults that pretense is different from reality.

I do not mean to suggest that Harry's thoughts proceeded the way I have just presented them. What Harry probably understood was the difference between *mad* and *bad* and possibly that one can pretend to shoot in anger and playfully. At the age of 5, he could not be expected to coordinate these two thoughts, just as Erikson's patient Sam probably could not have coordinated the series of statements made to him (see p. 172). But young children *do* attend to certain telling reality details, such as the colored dots on Sam's domino boxes, or the emphasis in spoken language on *must* and *believe*, or on *bad* and *mad*. Another example is a 4-year-old girl who thought that because *bad* and *mad* rhymed, they had the same meaning. She expected to be punished every time she became angry and protested vigorously when I said that she was not bad because she got mad: "But," she said, "*mad* rhymes with *bad*!" Since bad and mad were remembered in a graphic pair, she could disconnect the pair when she understood my statement that just because they rhymed did *not* mean they were the same.

Two weeks after Harry and I talked about shooting his Lego "gun," he told me that "cookie monster [on television's 'Sesame Street'] isn't scary, he only eats cookies." Reality and pretense were once more distinguished in Harry's search for rationality. He now knew that impersonated monsters in actual television stories were different from imaginary monsters in his fantasies and dreams who eat people! In effect, he separated his "real" experience of television from other "real" life experiences which included fantasies and dreams.

That same day he soon revealed why he had been so interested in the Darth Vader doll, which had been put in his Christmas stocking. Originally unable to understand how a "bad" toy (a doll representing a "bad" story character) could be given on a "good" occasion or come to him in a "good" Christmas stocking, he was now more adept at making distinctions and could imagine how he might transform the bad into the good Darth Vader. In doing so, his behavior resembled that of some of Anna Freud's (1968) child patients whose "dangerous" toy animals nonetheless protected them. He explained that he took his Darth Vader doll to bed because the doll would scare away monsters, like the Sesame Street puppets who used to appear in his dreams, and unlike those on television, always ate people. On leaving the office, tucking Darth Vader carefully in his pocket, he said, "Now, Darth Vader, are you all right in my pocket?" I told him that since he was taking such good care of him, perhaps the Darth Vader doll was not so bad or so scary after all.

From "Popgun" to "Nerf Rocket"

When Harry noticed that I did not have a popgun in my office, he decided instead to play with a "nerf rocket"—a shooting toy which expels a foam rubber missile that is shaped very much like a penis. It then became clear to me that he was preoccupied with phallic not anal themes. He had complained for seven consecutive appointments, "This nerf rocket doesn't work!" But when he heard that perhaps Darth Vader was not as "bad" as he once thought, Harry suddenly grabbed the nerf rocket toy and said, "This rocket works!" When told "it sure does!" as he sailed it through the air, he announced his concern, and in typical child language, generalized it in saying: "I need help *fixing* things!" I thought he meant to say that he had fixed the nerf rocket so that it would sail impressively through the air because he now felt his use of toys—and his body—had no unsafe consequences. He may have felt safe imagining that toys or toy parts—representing his body or body parts—functioned properly because I had said earlier that, because he had decided to take care of him, Darth Vader, residing in Harry's pocket, was "good," not "bad and scary." His deciding to take care of Darth Vader meant either that he had changed his mind about Darth Vader's qualities or that he recognized taking care of someone, represented by the toy doll, is likely to make him behave properly. Perhaps to demonstrate the impact on him of my statement "it sure does [work]" regarding the flying nerf rocket, on leaving the office that day he asked to use the bathroom to urinate, a request he had never made before.

His behavior as much as his language told what was bothering him. When he heard me clarify what is pretend and what is real, what really hurts and what does not, what is mad and what is bad, he got to the problematic core in his request that I help him fix what might not be working in the future—either toys or parts of himself. I was able to fix this state of affairs by sharing his pleasure in the act of shooting a safe rocket. This meant the rocket *did* work, which might have suggested to Harry that a part, or all, of his body worked. If so, that meant that his head (brain) worked—since one part of his body was working, all body parts were functional. Such a conclusion in Harry's thinking could only have reassured him, because in school he got the feeling that his brain did not work as he struggled to master the alphabet.

Harry's apprehension of reality often came about as he sat watching the portrayal of events on television. While watching television, it had appeared to him that the body parts of the cartoon personalities had not functioned properly when, for example, they became "traded" among several television monsters, as in a dumb monster in a cartoon Harry told me about who "lost his head" and borrowed the smart heads of other monsters. Harry's parents had permitted and sometimes encouraged him to watch television at the same time that they shrugged off as "unrealistic" the anxieties that the shows caused. They engaged in many long talks with Harry about the fact that what he saw on television was not real. Although the psychoanalytic theory of castration or genital injury anxiety might go part of the way to explain the source of Harry's problems, it was his reactions to television which gave his anxieties specificity. It is possible, though unknown, that 2-year-old Harry worried about his body before he was introduced to television, just as Klein's patients might have been uneasy at age 3 or 4 about some aspects of their erotic life before being introduced to the alphabet (or other learning tasks). What is important is that Harry understood the television story themes but became confused about the story's implications for him. If a story character suffered a physical trauma or found himself temporarily trapped, Harry often believed that he would be injured or trapped. This cannot be explained solely as the result of the anxieties he brought to watching television. It is more accurate to say that his sensitivity to story themes helped him elaborate his normally childish predisposition to worry about his body or his achievements.

With each developmental step, the child reacts to inner experience and outer reality sensitivity and uses whatever concepts he has developed to comprehend inner and outer worlds. Even more important in Harry's case, there is a difference between anxiety about the loss of a body part and anxiety about a body part's malfunctioning. On the television show a monster lost his "dumb" head because it could not think but then regained (borrowed) a "smart" head. To Harry, a loss of a body part did not occur without reason. It occurred when a body part did not function or functioned unsafely. In safely shooting the nerf rocket which was an experience I appeared to enjoy with him, Harry got the feeling that a toy representing a body part functioned well and had no bad consequences. Furthermore, he was able to distinguish between the symbol (the toy rocket) and its referent (his penis) which is why he could enjoy separating the rocket from its base and why he felt safe urinating. And, if his body functioned properly in urinating, that meant his entire body was functional. This, in turn, seemed to include his head—that specific body part which had in the past been said to be malfunctioning by his parents and his teacher when it came to distinguishing between the fantasies television stimulated and reality in regard to the alphabet. It might be said, then, that Harry was as worried about using his head as he was about using his penis. Using his head for imaginings began to appear less dangerous to Harry when he realized his brain had been struggling successfully all along to understand his fantasies.

Austin and His Friends

Like Harry, Austin was convinced that having mad feelings was the same as being bad. Both Harry and Austin arrived at this conclusion because often they had witnessed other children doing "bad" things when they became angry. Since young children are not yet able to control their behavior which springs from angry feelings, it seems to them that "bad" ipso facto follows "mad."

Austin was a sturdy, good-looking boy who literally marched into my office. A sense of purpose exuded from his posture, his gestures, and his facial expressions. A little tall for his age and physically quite strong, his demeanor communicated a direct approach to life's problems. He was referred for psychotherapy because to his kindergarten teacher, he appeared tense and fearful, and had problems relating to peers because when he became fearful, he attacked others.

Five-year-old Austin tried hard to emulate his conscientious parents who both worked full-time. Anything less than complete success in both kindergarten and in 1st grade made him angry, which caught him in repeated cycles of affect and explosive behavior. When he felt angry, he assumed the person to whom his anger was directed must have been equally angry and that this caused his own angry feelings. These thoughts frightened him and made him even angrier and led him to behave in such a way as to elicit angry reactions in his peers, which repeated the cycle endlessly. His beginning attempts to learn in school were permeated by his merciless competitive strivings to be the best student in his class.

Eventually, Austin was ready to hear that people are not bad however mad they sometimes become and that boys might like to play with each other even though they got mad at each other. However, he was still unable to apply such general statements directly to himself, only to others, probably to test whether acting on such important premises was safe. He began to talk about a "special friend," a boy in his class whom he would have liked to have as a special friend. He complained that Sammy, who sat near him in class, "does not know how to make friends yet," thus voicing his own anxieties. I told Austin, "You know what? If Sammy really wants friends, he will find a way, like riding bikes, maybe."

Austin began his next appointment by saying: "Did you know that Sammy is my friend now? He wanted to be friends with me." Because I wished to make explicit the connection between a child's motivation to make friends and the increased likelihood of the occurrence, I said to him, "Wanting friends would help you do it, all right." Then I asked him to explain how he thought it happened that he and Sammy became friends. He answered, "I wanted to be friends with him. We're going to build a playhouse and you need lots of people for that." His friendship with Sammy was corroborated that day by Austin's teacher, who was excited and surprised by the change in Austin.

My statement to Austin did not tell him how to make friends (which probably would have insulted his ability to imagine his own solution). So it was met by him with renewed vigor in attempts to originate friendships. But my statement did contain the conviction that a child can find a way to make friends as well as one small suggestion—riding bikes—which was at once a familiar activity and an invitation to finish the thought by adding other activities. Not only had Austin become convinced that Sammy liked him, but he also differentiated Sammy and his motives from himself and his own motives, even though Sammy's motives were similar to Austin's. Motive overlap did not tempt Austin away from the decentering trend. He began with what was to him the most salient fact, because it helped him with his feelings of vulnerability in interpersonal relationships: "He wanted to be friends with me." Then, he could feel safe admitting "I wanted to be friends with him." As though that were not enough progress for one week, he widened his social circle further by planning to build a playhouse (not just ride bikes) where "you need lots of people."

Austin's Use of Concepts

Austin grew more determined to figure things out for himself. Although transitional in thinking when he presented for therapy (he failed to understand the classification task), over the course of 4 months he became concrete operational (he understood all four tasks of concrete operations, tasks which usually are not understood until the child is about age 7). Moreover, when my statements fell short of the mark, instead of tuning out he began to listen carefully before correcting me. For instance, I had suggested that his fighting could be that it is hard to have two friends simultaneously (he had had a long-term, intense friendship with another child in his neighborhood who was not in his class). He thoughtfully considered it for some minutes and then carefully said, "No, that's not it."

Austin's use of concepts could best be seen in his monster phobia which reflected not just age-appropriate imagination, but also an ability to draw intelligent conclusions from facts however misguided some of his conclusions were. Moreover, he was able to embrace a more mature perspective by coming to terms with some of these faulty conclusions and, in doing so, arrived at a thought level which reduced his anxiety. He said he knew that some monsters were only "pretend" and thus seemed to have differentiated reality from fantasy. But he consistently pronounced the word as "be-tend," which suggested that for him pretend still contained an element of reality in that a monster might actually "be." He also told how he had been afraid of the Loch Ness monster for some time, and introduced me to this anxiety by way of commenting that he could see deep puddles in my backyard from the window in my office. He added that there must be frogs in these puddles, or perhaps even bigger animals. When I responded, "What about those monsters?" he again corrected me that it was not monsters, it was "*the* Loch Ness monster." He was told how intelligent he was to be afraid of *the* very monster that some grown-ups believed existed. To this Austin smirked in enjoyment probably because someone appreciated the intelligence underlying his anxiety. Shortly thereafter, his parents reported that Austin was no longer so difficult to get to bed. About this positive change, Austin said, "I don't see monsters in my dreams anymore." While he may have been repressing his dreams or denying that they were about monsters, he was nonetheless no longer afraid of going to bed. Perhaps my focus on his intelligence suggested to Austin that he could use it to deal with scary dreams when they occurred.

YOUNG CHILDREN AND SPECIFIC STATEMENTS

It has been my intent to show that it is effective in working with young (preoperational) children to start with the cognitive system the child has constructed. Although respect for the child's view is very important, this respect must be expressed in ways the child can understand. Otherwise, it seems either incomprehensible or condescending to him. Interpretations made to young children can aim to stretch their thinking, but only a bit. When this is done, the child moves forward both in understanding the reasons for his phobias (or other symptoms) and in understanding the school curriculum: his thought is no longer focused solely on self-protection and becomes attentive to school activities.

Moreover, the child senses that he has "figured out" his reasons—or that his mind is capable of "figuring out" reasons—and he applies this insight to other areas of his life, such as school learning or social development. Harry began to learn the alphabet as he learned in therapy that using his body *and* his mind had fewer dangerous consequences than safe ones. Austin's teacher noticed increased ability to concentrate on his 1st-grade work. She attributed this to greater relaxation in this tense young boy who now understood that other people's anger was not necessarily his fault.

It is probably true that therapeutic work, especially forming an interpretation, is most difficult with preoperational children. The interpretation or other statements must rest on concrete details which are salient from the child's perspective, such as the dots on the inside of Sam's domino box. When the adult bases statements on fitting details, it unites child and adult in a common world both can understand. Even though it may be hard for the adult to select that it is merely some dots, a popgun, or the Loch Ness monster which is meaningful to the child, or to identify the meanings these things might carry, understanding how childhood symbols reflect a cognitive system is critical in communicating to the child that meanings are shared. This fact often results in the direct expression of affect and in the cessation of symptomatic behavior. These young children cannot be fully rehabilitated simply by advising their mothers how to take care of them or how to respond to their symptoms (Brazelton, 1976; Greenspan, 1981). They are just old enough to require an intervention aimed at the concepts they have built up, but just young enough so that the discontinuity in thinking between child and adult is at its height.

THERAPEUTIC STATEMENTS AND OPERATIVITY

Children in therapy who are operative in their thinking are quite different from children who engage in prelogical reasoning. It is not just that they have greater control over their behavior, but also that the quality of their overall reasoning helps them understand their emotions and their motives. Indeed, greater control over behavior often derives from the ability to reason. Interpretations given to children whose thinking is operative but not yet abstract (formal) ought to be formed in line with one or both of the following considerations. The first is the necessity to clear up the child's thinking errors. This can be done directly in conversation with the operational child. One no longer needs to embrace in near totality immature prelogical connections because the older (latency) child's thought has become to some degree systematic and thus can correct flaws in reasoning or fill in gaps in the cognitive system. It is this logic which the therapist can call upon to assist the child in understanding herself. Without insulting their intelligence, conclusions that latency-aged children make can be assessed and refined.

The second consideration is the necessity to remain literally true to many details of the child's experience when forming interpretive statements. Conversing accurately with the child about the reality minutiae she brings to the therapeutic discussion encourages her to reorganize them into a more complex and parsimonious structure. The therapeutic progress of two 8-year-old girls illustrates these principles. They were referred for psychotherapy because both their teachers and their parents felt that low self-esteem had led one girl to refuse to learn and the other girl to daydream so that she had learned very little the year prior to coming to therapy. The first girl, Jamie, was transitional in her thinking (she had understood all but the seriation task during the cognitive interviewing) while her age-mate, Gwen, was solidly concrete operational (she understood all four tasks).

Jamie's View of Birth Order and Intelligence

Jamie was large for her age and a little clumsy. Initially, she was uncomfortable using language and instead expressed herself by gross-motor movements and facial expressions. Often she would make expressive sounds, such as squealing with delight or grunting in disgust. During her appointments with me, she appeared angry and would brood silently. Jamie's mother had told me that no matter how well Jamie achieved, she could never admit she had achieved and always described her accomplishments in the most negative terms. This disturbed her mother who felt that her bright daughter was falling prey to a negative self-image by virtue of being female. Jamie had two brothers, one older and one younger, who were equally intelligent but who were proud of and not cynical about their achievements.

Jamie readily revealed her innate ability by winning every game in my office and often with great flair, even difficult games like chess and backgammon. But just as predictably as she would win, she repeatedly made little of her game prowess and, like refusing to learn in school, she refused to discuss why she felt she was "no good" or "so down on" herself.

After exactly 1 year of therapy, during which Jamie remained adamant that she never did anything right while simultaneously trouncing me in game after game, she did something conspicuously different. She said she would "let" me win the "easy" game of Hi Ho Cherrio—a game which requires primarily luck and little thought. Without my having the slightest idea where it would lead, I thanked her for her good intentions, but reminded her it is impossible to "let" someone win this game. I also reminded her that the other games we had played, such as chess and backgammon, were not "luck" games and that she had won through hard work and not because I had "let" her win. What was clear to me was that she had shown some variation in behavior, which I wished to encourage by thanking her for her good wishes toward me. Before, she had never shown one trace of remorse that I always lost. From this I surmised that she was not interested in whether her opponent lost but only in depreciating her winning.

She reacted by setting up the game Clue during which she began to talk about the fights she had with her brothers. Extrapolating from her intense need to win at games while playing with me, I said perhaps she is fighting with her brothers about who is the smartest at games or in school. Jamie first rejected this interpretation in shaking her head no, but then looked briefly at me with a smile. I continued by saying that she must be just as smart as her brothers because, if not, she would not be winning so many games with me. To this she said, "Yes, but he's older," concentrating not on her younger but her older brother. The fact that I was older than she but nevertheless lost the games did not appear to occur to her, although demonstratively she was motivated to win games in therapy. It was as if through winning at games with me, she was winning with her older brother and thereby proving she was just as smart as he, or even smarter. Jamie was on the verge of structuring her experiences in a way that would both advance her cognitively and help her with her problems with her brothers.

As the result of this conversation, it became plain to me that her refusal to do schoolwork was based on her belief that she was not as intelligent as her older brother who, she assumed, was more intelligent because he was older. From what she said, it appeared that she had constructed the following syllogism: people who have more experience are smarter; my older brother has lived longer and therefore has had more experience; hence, my brother is smarter. And, since she could not change the fact of her birth order, she assumed a stance of resignation—that nothing could be done about what so preoccupied her. That she nonetheless wished to do something about it was enacted in therapy by competing with and winning at games with a person older than she.

Acting on this hunch, I said, "Well, maybe your older brother knows more because he's lived longer, but that doesn't mean he's smarter." In response she told me some minutes later how she could do things when she was her younger brother's age that he could not do now, thus implicitly revealing she had begun to doubt that being older means being smarter. She seemed to say that she was smarter at her younger brother's age than he was. Her statement thus revealed that she heard me make a distinction between the potential to know and the amount known which accrues with experience. Perhaps then she questioned her earlier resignation regarding helping herself with her feelings about her older brother. If before she could see no way to compete with his having been born first, now she might have perceived that she was "smart" despite being younger than her older brother.

But Jamie never said (as an adult might), "You're right, that's why I resent my brother" or "You're right, why should I work in school if I can never be smarter than he"; nonetheless she indicated through taking the role of the older sibling in regard to her younger brother that she was ready to understand there is a difference between the potential to know and the amount known. By her behavior, she seemed to say that she thought she was smarter than her younger brother. But now this thought did not reify her earlier conclusion that being older means smarter. Because she understood she knew more at a younger age than her younger brother did at this same age, she revealed she understood the difference between a capability to understand and the age of understanding. Feeling as innately capable as her older brother, she now understood she only required additional experience to be comparably intelligent.

It may be unfortunate that it took a full year before Jamie was ready for something different in therapy that would lead directly to a therapeutic inter-change; nevertheless, it should be said that acting on adult knowledge of Jamie's problems before she had communicated her view of them probably would not have worked. For example, her parents thought correctly that Jamie was upset about her brothers, but their correct thought was not specific enough. Only Jamie could express that it was an incorrect syllogism that was at the root of her feelings of resentment—at least of her conscious feelings. Had I spoken of her jealousy or anger at her brothers without taking into account her feelings about her older brother in contrast to her younger brother, or how she reasoned about age and intelligence (that birth order determines intelligence), I would have shown her that I did not understand the basis for her feeling helpless to change her situation. Adult talk—"You need not feel you can do nothing about it"— when the child knows she can do nothing about birth order only convinces the child that adults do not understand her. Once the incorrect deduction was uncovered, Jamie, like Harry and Austin, began to move rapidly in therapy. She came upon many healing insights and moved ahead in development. Her symptomatic behavior at school stopped, and she was put in the advanced reading group and began to admit and enjoy her successes at home.

Gwen's Reactions to Television

An opportunity to form a critical interpretation came earlier in Gwen's therapy because she used language adeptly and comfortably. She was a shy but willowy, graceful girl who typically conversed with her head lowered. Rarely did she become openly angry, and she spoke softly, confidentially, and intensely about "social causes." Retiring in her demeanor, she would articulately advocate people's "rights," such as the rights of children.

Gwen's father had left her and her family 3 years earlier. She was brought to therapy because her feelings of loss interfered with her ability to concentrate in school. Gwen's mother described the many fights between herself and Gwen, especially those fights about Gwen's wish to watch television instead of doing homework or playing with neighborhood friends, which her mother perceived as a tendency to escape, like daydreaming.

One day, Gwen told me that her father's work involved television advertisements, although she was careful to say that he was never visible on the TV screen. It was easy to tell Gwen, "Maybe that's why you're fighting with your mother about TV. You want to hear your father's voice." Since my statement to her involved only an appeal to concrete thinking and did not require the correction of reasoning errors (such as transductions or flawed syllogisms), Gwen's capability to hear this interpretive statement and make it part of her own thinking was quickly evident. Her mother reported that an entire month went by without a fight because, as her mother put it, "Gwen doesn't want to watch TV all day anymore." The marked cessation of symptoms led Gwen's mother to request that Gwen reduce the number of therapy visits—a request which required much therapeutic work because fewer visits reminded Gwen of the desertion of her father.

The statement "you want to hear your father's voice" was not intended to clear up Gwen's thinking, but it remained literal in its connection to the detail of her wish to watch television. It was not phrased in more formal language, such as "perhaps television reminds you of your father because that is his work," or the even more abstract and hence removed from the facts: "Maybe you think your mother is interfering with your relationship to your father so on hearing your father's voice you believe you might see him or feel that you are with him." The latter would have been wrong because it would have implied that she wanted to have more to do with her father than her behavior and language indicated. She did not want to see him, only to hear him. This reflected the intensity of her continued ambivalence about him—in her anger she might be able to tolerate his spoken voice, but not when coupled with his image. An adult patient might correct the therapist if he or she is inaccurate in speaking of the patient's desire to see a parent rather than just hear him. A child who is Gwen's age is less likely to correct the therapist because she has not yet constructed a thought system that would coordinate the differences between only hearing a parent in the present with having simultaneously seen and heard a parent in the past with the possible differences and similarities inherent in relating to her two parents in the present.

My agreement with her mother's request to meet with Gwen only twice a month became a complex measage to Gwen. First, it meant that while she had earlier wished only to "hear" her father as she sat watching television, she now wanted to continue to "see" me in therapy. Second, it meant that I would tolerate her mother's suggestion of an interruption of an important relationship at the same time that it meant Gwen had done well in therapy. This was uncomfortably similar to a situation in Gwen's past when it had seemed to her that her mother had suggested that her father interrupt his relationship with her, since her mother (whom Gwen trusted in other situations) had been unable to keep the marriage together. In order to fully understand this complicated situation and to fully hear what I might say about it, Gwen had to have an equally complicated and formal system of thought—or at least the beginnings of one.

Gwen's Metaphors

Connections between two logically or empirically unrelated, but psychologically associated, events or situations are common in work with adults, and become ever more common and articulated in work with children as they approach adolescence. These connections do not represent errors in thinking. On the contrary, as-if connections reflect metaphorical thoughts which provide useful arenas for further therapeutic work. Therapy itself is an as-if situation. It was Gwen's simile "my therapist behaves as if she is my father" which enabled her to understand that she had wanted to continue to "see" me just as she had earlier wanted to "hear" her father. It was not so much seeing or hearing us that led to her symptoms, but the need to continue a relationship in which she sought love (first from her father and later from me). Thus, the earlier interpretation that she wanted to "hear her father's voice" helped initiate Gwen into transition for formal operations. Thereupon, she became capable of constructing, understanding, and articulating a metaphorical comparison between my threat to leave her (to reduce visits, and later to terminate therapy) with the source of her symptoms—her father's desertion. As the clinical data which follow show, she understood that relating, whether past or present, involves both seeing and hearing the other person and that those other persons, whether her father or her therapist, had an attraction for her which varied. This complexity of thought reflects formal operational logic.

In response to my suggestion that I see her every other week, Gwen became once more angry and sad about her father's desertion, but she also heard me say that just because she had improved and was almost ready to leave therapy did not mean I had stopped caring about her. My reminding Gwen of the differences between me and her father, who could not tell Gwen that he cared about her, was a process different from convincing Austin that there were no monsters in my backyard, or explaining to Harry how a person's residence might be related to his moral character. Gwen could hear what I said about her, me, and her father because her logic overlapped mine. She found comfort in being reminded that I was not her father, however similar we sometimes seemed, whereas Harry and Austin came across logic as the result of being helped to better understand their prelogic. It should be said that as-if thought does contain potential risks of reasoning. If Gwen had not fully understood the metaphors she used to compare and later, to differentiate therapy discontinuation from her father's desertion, she might have concluded that I did not care about her. Then, her symptoms might have worsened—she would not have successfully "worked through" the termination process.

Fortunately, Gwen's mother did not see Gwen's reaction to stopping therapy as a regression. And indeed it was not. Gwen talked about the fact that while she knew she and I would "have to leave each other," she also knew that I would "always be someone out there who cares about me." It was her thought that I would always care, even if she could not hear or see me, that enabled her to differentiate her father's desertion from my decision to stop seeing her in therapy. As a young child, she could not imagine that her father would "always care" when he was absent. Now she could liken my caring to her mother's at the same time that she differentiated me from her mother: "You're like my mother because you always care; but different because I have to leave you and I will never leave my mother." Gwen could now conceive of me as "always caring" about her while she could not conceive of her father as "always caring" when he left her—not *just* because her father found it difficult to express himself, but *also* because Gwen had not developed those concepts that are required for abstract thought.

THE APPROACH TO ADULT THOUGHT IN THE CHILD IN THERAPY

As the youngster reaches for abstract thought, he or she becomes ever more cognizant of symbolic meaning and becomes able to put this growing awareness to use in therapy. Preadolescent children even enjoy playing with symbols and metaphors in therapy; or they become deeply involved in telling their dreams to the therapist. Mario, a 12-year-old, enjoyed punning while he was in therapy which revealed much about his conflicts, a fact he was aware of and that amused him. At other times, preadolescents become resistant to the suggestion that symbols and metaphors have meaning and to what the particular meaning might be. But, like adolescents and adults in therapy, they usually reveal through their defensive maneuvers much about the nature of their conflicts: "the act of resisting and its motives are intimately bound up with the material being warded off" (Levy, 1984, p. 78).

More important, in my opinion, is the preadolescent's and adolescent's desire to reveal how much they understand about the therapeutic process, which is often aimed to get behind or beyond the manifest, so that they can join the sophisticated and valued world of the adult therapist. Clinicians ought to heed Furth's (1987) observation that logical operations "belong" to the individual "only insofar as the self is socialized into the community of other 'knowers' who are respected on a[n] equal level" (p. 99). This statement implies that the clinical dialogue, a highly focused conversation, has significant potential for change in the patient's *thinking*—not just in his feeling. Consequently, we ought to respect the logical operations the patient uses to become a "knower" in the community of other inquirers and most especially acknowledge the patient's attempts to become a "self-knower" in the company of his "knowing" therapist.

Katherine's "Perfectionism"

Self-reflexive awareness and resistance to knowing the self can be the explicit subject for discussion in older children, as can be seen in some conversations I had with a brilliant 10-year-old girl, Katherine. She understood several tasks of formal operations during her evaluation (see pp. 317–322).[2]

Katherine was a beautiful, tall, slender girl with long, wavy hair. She was a serious dance student and an expert ice skater. Although she was shy, she frequently smiled impishly when describing her triumphs over friends whom she endeavored to "trick" or "trap" by her clever interpersonal manipulations. She seemed aware of her natural beauty, but she did not spend hours primping and instead dressed casually. She presented as a healthy, rosy-cheeked, handsome young lady. Her parents told me that she was a "perfectionist" in school. She concentrated so intensely on being perfect that she often ignored much of what her teacher tried to teach. She seemed to feel that she had to know what the teacher intended to teach in advance of being taught. The necessity to be perfect or to have advance knowledge created distance between Katherine and the curriculum because she felt compelled to reject sight unseen what the teacher presented. When she spent hours daydreaming or many times blocked on the meaning of school assignments, she often confused her daydreaming and blocking with an incapacity to learn and to know. When she was attentive to what was assigned, and complimented by her parents, her teachers, or myself on her thorough understanding of difficult material, she habitually upped the ante and answered, "It's not bad, but less good than perfect."

Katherine, like Austin, had two working parents with whom she strongly and positively identified. She also had a brother who was 8 years younger, and her mother was pregnant with a third child. She may have felt that she must be a

---

[2]Some children in the group that I treated became transitional for formal operations at the ages of 9 or 10. Although Piaget and Inhelder (1969) have said that formal operational thought develops in children at ages 11 or 12, they always stress that their age expectancies obtain on the average. In the group of 60 children I worked with, 6 of those children who also showed superior intellectual potential on IQ metrics became transitional for the next developmental period—concrete or formal operations—at least 1 year earlier than Piaget suggested. Of these children, two became transitional for formal operations at age 9, 2 years earlier than expected. An additional two children who were not given IQ tests became transitional for formal operations at age 9. I should add that I am not linking high IQ scores to advanced development. This is an empirical question about which I have little data. See Cowan (1978) for a lucid discussion of the problems inherent in comparing IQ metrics with the results of Piagetian interviewing.

grownup to consolidate her alliance with her parents and to strengthen her identity as a "third parent" to her younger brother and to her as yet unborn sibling. Knowing everything in advance of being taught was, I surmised, Katherine's conception of adulthood.

After 5 months of therapy, during which her perfectionistic attitude was discussed with her, she understood that her attempts to be perfect in school and a parent at home were related to her need to be close to her parents, who took very good care of her and of her much younger sibling, and who were about to do the same for a third child. In therapy, she was willing to try a game (Stratego) she had never played before. Now she did not reject something new because she needed to know facts or to be perfect at skills in advance of being taught. As I explained the rules of Stratego and told her it was not as hard as chess, and about as hard as checkers, she said, "Ugh, I'm horrible at chess." But she continued in her attempts to learn something new and grasped it rather quickly, while, at the same time, she minimized her understanding. She repeatedly said as she would make a clever move, "I don't know what I'm doing." After ten good moves, I said, "For someone who doesn't know what she's doing, you're doing very well." She countered this statement with: "I'm just moving, not thinking."

Since it was her first experience playing Stratego, Katherine was delighted she was able to win the game. Her winning proved that she could succeed in trying something new without advance preparation. It turned out she had put her flag, the piece which the opponent must capture to win, not in the back row of pieces as most children do, but in the second row, and thus more within my reach. She explained that she did it purposely to "surprise" me. She implied that she fully understood not only the purpose of the game, but its typical strategies which, as she tried to win, she deliberately flouted to take me off guard. Then I said that maybe she told me she did not know what she was doing to surprise me in another way. By this I meant to suggest that she tried to keep me from understanding what she did understand. She thought awhile, then smiled and answered it must mean she was trying to "surprise" me in two ways.

The implication of my statement, which was that she must have known what she was doing or she would not be doing well, was a direct appeal to logic. In other words, her behavior did not reflect random choices. Our conversation enabled her to become aware, or perhaps to admit, that she was aware of thinking about thinking—to analyze her own theories, which is the hallmark of formal operations (Inhelder & Piaget, 1958). When she said she did not know what she was doing, she revealed she was capable in the abstract of knowing what she was doing, but in this instance she denied that she did. What I hoped to do was strengthen her newly won formal operational stance as well as focus on her core problem—that she resisted knowing what she was doing at the moment of doing it when she was afraid of the outcomes of her actions. Since she was ambivalent about success, she was alternately afraid she might not be doing well or that she might be succeeding.

On hearing my attempt to articulate the contradiction in what she did successfully and what she claimed she did not know, Katherine was able to make her own interpretations about herself, which were reflected in her statement that she had surprised me in two ways—which took my comment a little farther. She had surprised me by placing her flag in an unexpected position, revealing that she did know what she was doing—that she was thinking about the thought behind her actions—and by the statement that she did not know what she must have known.

Six weeks later, Katherine told me how excited she was with a book report assignment on *Little Women*. She was particularly fascinated by reading "Jo's journal" which linked school assignments to her own private thoughts. Much like Jeremy (see Chapter 5), she continued to find meaning in school assignments through reading and later chose Shaw's *Pygmalion* to present for an oral report in class. She told me that she had found the book on her father's bookshelf and, in reading her notes for her report, described how much she "loved" and understood the personality of Eliza, the main female character. It seemed to me that she had become closer at age 11 to her father who was a professor like Shaw's Professor Henry Higgins. By now Katherine's second brother had been born, so she allied herself with her father in making learning more meaningful while her mother temporarily concentrated on taking care of her small brothers.

Bridget's "Lazy" Mind

Consider a second example of this developmental level. At 11 years of age, Bridget had been described as having a "lazy" mind since the first grade. Although she got poor grades, no specific disability could be found. As a result, she was thought to be "socially immature." This diagnosis of social immaturity was at odds with her social vigilance as described by her parents and observed by me. Like Betsy (Chapter 5), Bridget seems to strain to understand what was expected of her and was especially adept at reading people's facial expressions. Those who perceived her as socially immature mistook a sensitivity for an immaturity. As a result of her social sensitivity, she had developed a slapstick humorous style which she used to express intrapsychic conflicts and to describe her peer relationships. For her age, she was physically well-developed and, rather than displaying social immaturity, consistently revealed that she thought she was intellectually deficient because of laziness.

As a preadolescent in therapy (she had no psychotherapy previously), Bridget worried about her long history of a "lazy mind," of having declined to use it as the result of rejecting school the same year her parents separated: "My parents rejected each other, so I rejected school." It seemed to me that Bridget felt she must reject someone or something since she had witnessed her parents' rejection of one another. That "someone" was her teacher and that "something" was school.

Bridget became increasingly aware that she sometimes deliberately refrained from thinking when it touched upon unpleasant topics. She also became aware of the implications for her and her future of her habitual pattern of "turning off my mind." She admitted this process was at work when she momentarily tried to elicit it in me by telling me there was something she did not want to confide in the therapeutic hour. I had asked for her permission to guess, which she granted, but as I got closer to the topic she wished to keep secret, playfully Bridget told me to stop guessing. When I became silent, she remarked correctly that I must still be guessing in my mind. Laughing, she told me to stop that as well. I then said that the only way I could stop guessing in my mind was to turn it off. Smiling with a knowing head nod, Bridget said she was an expert at that.

In Bridget's case, *that* she could turn off her mind was as important as *what* she turned off. Although it was important for her to understand her attempts to keep from me what was on her mind—her new boyfriend—it was more important in her recovery for her to become aware of her tendency to reject thinking. This helped not just with sexual feelings, but with thoughts about her past, when she had gotten into many difficulties because of her lazy mind. For me to have focused on her boyfriend without attending to her feelings about thinking would have been less curative. It would not have knit past with present, nor would it have provided Bridget with a new context to deal with future problems.

On becoming an adolescent, Bridget became more fully enabled to understand the origins of her pathology. Reconstructions, or more accurately constructions, of the reasons for her having turned off her mind did not consist only of piecing together memories, but of viewing her present behavior in a new way, which she related to her memories of her past. Her formal operational perspective appeared to explain events of the past. But it is probably more accurate to say that her greater maturity gave these events more elaborated meaning than they originally had because when they happened, her thinking had not developed sufficiently to construct comprehensive systems to explain them. Earlier, it had seemed to Bridget that events just happened, or worse (from her perspective), they happened because of a magic which was beyond her control.

Interpretive statements made to children who have become formal operational in their thinking need no longer be geared to literal details of reality as much as they do in the case of concrete operational children, although the closer the adult's use of context and perspective is to the child's or adolescent's the more understanding is facilitated. Even though it is true, as Greenspan (1979) has pointed out, that the new cognitive abilities of the formal operational youngster permit her to consider a wider range of issues—the young person can consider what is "possible" in addition to what is "real"—the message the therapist wishes to deliver must mesh with the words, concepts, and symbols the youngster has used spontaneously, although the translation of her behavior inherent in the therapist's interpretation need not be literal. She benefits from the therapist's language "search" because she feels valued as an individual. The therapist's efforts to find just the right concepts to help the young person's understanding reveals quite a bit to any young person how the adult mind works, which aids the patient's thought development.

Finally, the interplay of defensive reactions with a youngster's accurate and sensitive appraisal of the therapist's interpretations begins to be seen clearly in those patients who are capable of abstract thought. Fluctuating understanding of the therapeutic message can be seen particularly in the young person's facial expressions. An eager, wide-eyed comprehending look often alternates with a vacuous stare or an interruption of communication when the young person drops his head or lowers his eyelids. Such an individual might wish to elude the therapist's gaze to avoid the particular therapeutic appraisals that inform therapeutic communications. However, sometimes what appears to be defensive as young people avert their faces or become unresponsive actually reflects the absence of a cognitive concept or structure needed for them to understand some aspects of reality or their reactions to it. (The important therapeutic issue of differentiating defense from the absence of cognitive concepts and structures is discussed in Chapters 7, 8, and 9.)

THERAPEUTIC DISCONTINUITIES AND REMEDIES

Some summary remarks are in order regarding the interaction of the child's or adolescent's level of cognitive development and the clinical interpretation. The major theme of this chapter is that the dialogue between therapist and child or adolescent will differ according to the developmental progress of the patient. This implies that it is not sufficient for the therapist just to hear the youngster differently, depending on whether he is 4 or 5, 7 or 8, 11 or 12. The therapist must speak to the youngster according to his thinking mode.

Two components can be varied in what the therapist says to the child: the actual words of a sentence, and the ideas that are embedded in the sentence and expressed by the words which make up the sentence. In therapy with prelogical children (those aged 4 or 5 and younger), the therapist must use the same words or many of those that the child uses. He or she must also use the same symbols, since the adult's understanding of what the symbol means to the child helps the child understand what it means to him. Lastly, the therapist must understand and express those critical ideas that are embedded in the child's statement— whether they are about the world and natural phenomena or whether they are about the child and his family—so that the child comes to know what it is he believes to be true. Then, the child can consider whether it is, in fact, true, an event which helps thought development. Understanding and expressing to the child in his own words what his prelogical thinking consists of leads him to some small attempts to use logic or to embrace a more mature view in regard to a small but significant portion of reality.

Reconsider Austin's belief that a deep puddle might contain the Loch Ness monster, but a shallow puddle could not. Austin likened the depth of puddles to the depth of lakes or oceans. His reasoning made sense from his prelogical perspective and it also made sense from a cognitive-developmental viewpoint, since likening things to other things is a cognitive process that holds great promise for knowledge acquisition as the child matures. When Austin heard me say, "You're right that the puddle is deep and so could have a bigger animal in it, but it still is not as deep as a pond," he could finish the thought and be led toward mature reason. He said, "The Loch Ness monster is too big for your backyard.... I guess it's still in Scotland." Even though Austin entertained the idea that the Loch Ness monster might actually exist, he no longer believed it existed in either my or *his* backyard—an understanding which reduced his anxiety.

As children become concrete operational, the therapist can vary more fundamentally one of the components of a message to the child—the ideas. Accurate phrasing can become the medium by which to introduce new ideas as long as these ideas are not too far removed from the child's own. The child often shows the therapist what she is ready to hear, as Jamie did when she listened to my statement that chronological age and the capability to understand are not the same. Transitional phases in children and adolescents as they approach the two levels of operativity—concrete and formal—often lead them to entertain slightly different or new ideas.

One might ask why varying only one component in the messages sent to the 7- or 8-year-old cannot be accomplished the other way around. Why is it not just as effective to vary the words and yet stay close to the ideas? One reason is that it is the intent of the therapeutic statement to modify the representational system which underlies the youngster's behavior. Since it is ideas or systems of ideas that often lead to behavior—words are one of the means by which these ideas become known to others—it is more efficacious to have as a long-run goal a change in the ideas themselves. A second reason is tied to the first and, like the first reason, reflects an underlying premise of this book. Words are reflective of representational phenomena that lie hidden beneath the surface—such as concepts, what symbols mean, a worldview, etc. This statement may seem to contradict all that has been said in this chapter, particularly where it has been stressed that phrasing is critical to a challenge of and change in a child's conceptual perspective. Although the latter is true, we might ask how much of the truth do these words tell about the phenomena that are partially hidden but give rise to them? An analogy might clarify my view of the relationship. A word or sentence is to an idea as a system of water ripples is to the pattern of ocean swells. The relationship is not always revealed directly, which does not mean that no relationship exists. What the therapist aims to understand and to change is the pattern of what happens on the symbolic or representational level, a pattern which can often be seen on or suggested by the surface.

An effective therapist works from the surface phenomena to the depths—which is why verbal communications with children and adolescents are so important. To the youngster, if the therapist appears to understand his overt behavior, this means the therapist will understand most of his experience, including what he has tried to keep secret. This, in turn, reduces the risk in communicating with the therapist. Since the therapist remains empathic at the same time that he or she apparently understands, it seems safe to the youngster to reveal even more. When the child or adolescent reveals more, the therapeutic process has "moved further toward community of meaning" (Leavy, 1973, p. 323), which is the goal of both good communication and good therapy.

Formal operativity brings the youngster quite close to the therapist in terms of reasoning predilections and capabilities. In work with some preadolescents and with most adolescents, the therapist has the luxury of varying both the words and the ideas they contain, although an interpretation will be heard more readily by the patient the more it captures both. It is an act of respect to stay close to the patient's phraseology as well as an act of interest in the patient's skill in manipulating concepts and symbols. A direct appeal to logic can now be made as long as the patient feels that the therapist is respectful of the patient's ongoing and earlier attempts to know the world and himself. But certain over-determined flaws may occur in the adolescent's more rational structuring. These flaws can be corrected by the patient's understanding of his motives for a particular conceptual lag in what is otherwise a fairly well-defined and comprehensive thought design. It should be pointed out that much of the inconsistency in the adolescent's use of logic results from his lack of experience in using and correcting abstract ("formal") systems.

Although the watersheds of logical thinking, namely concrete and formal operational thought, provide added impetus to therapeutic progress, and are thus a boon to the therapist, they are also potentially hazardous for symptomatic children and adolescents who remain untreated. Once pathology entangles with the systematic thought of concrete operations, usually long-term psychotherapy is required especially in cases where the child's symptoms are severe. Similarly, if the youngster has gone untreated until he or she has reached formal operations, treatment is usually long-term for the simple reason that pathology tends to solidify in the adolescent's thinking. Adolescent thought is more stable even if not fully formal operational. An adolescent's behavior is more organized, and even more critically, his thought processes encompass more of the world and those who people it. This may be one reason why it is often difficult to introduce psychotherapy into the adolescent's life if it is the first experience he or she has had with it. Since more of the world is formalized in his thinking, the therapist sometimes instantaneously becomes a "player" in the adolescent's drama, where negative transferences set in before the therapist has understood what the problem is all about.

The implication for pathology of intellectual development is one more reason why treatment for young people should begin as soon as symptoms appear. It is not just the necessity to remediate the psychodynamic effects of the more severe pathologies that can devastate progressive development. Clinicians must also consider the shifting nature of thought levels in the developing child, a recurrence which leads the more severely pathological and older child to include the therapist in his grim world perspective which he crystallizes more systematically. Self-set impediments in thinking, which originate in family interactions or in school experiences, can only give subsequent psychodynamic conflicts a more tenacious hold on the personality.

CHAPTER 7

Cognition and Escape
School Phobia

Intact cognitive processes enable young people who are afraid to attend school to elude the very situation in which they are expected to learn or acquire knowledge. The quality of the young person's escape attempts varies with developmental level and so must therapeutic statements. Furthermore, school phobic children and adolescents tend to be more painfully aware of their cognitive dilemmas than the over- or underachieving youngsters. They avoid that specific environment in which they have ascertained that important learning is possible and in which they have actually learned in the past. More than the overachievers and underachievers, they are aware of the self's capability to understand. Unlike underachievers, school phobic youngsters do not shut down cognition in order to avoid learning—precisely the reason they feel they must avoid school. And, unlike overachievers, school phobic young people do not consistently attribute a special *positive* meaning to school learning. If they identify the learning process with the growing up process, they reject both processes because, unlike the overachiever who reaches for learning because he wishes to grow up, they are often afraid of growing up. To illustrate the dilemma school attendance creates for them, I present the treatment narratives of three school phobic young people: Caroline, a 17-year-old college student; Robin, a 6-year-old first grader; and Maisie, a 4½-year-old who became phobic in nursery school about attending kindergarten.

Most discussions on the subject of school phobia assert that anxiety about school attendance springs from particular family constellations, especially enmeshed relationships with a parent, usually the mother. A youngster might wish to avoid going to school because she fears what will happen at home during her absence. For example, her mother will take care of a sibling. To the child this means that while at school she will have sustained the loss of the most important person in her life to a rival sibling. Coolidge (1979) differentiated between primary school phobic symptoms and secondary school phobic-like symptoms. According to him, the primary symptom

199

is characterized by a strong reluctance to go to school as the result of morbid
dread of some aspect of the school situation. The specific fear may be of a
teacher, another child, the janitor, toilet, eating in the dining hall, or almost any
aspect of school. (p. 453)

School phobic-like symptoms do not manifest as a morbid dread of school but
may be milder or they may accompany psychophysiological symptoms, such as
asthma or colitis. Also, they may be the precursor of psychotic disturbances.
Although 3 of the 12 school phobic children and adolescents I treated had
"mild" symptoms, none showed psychotic symptoms.

The child who is afraid of separating from the parent is *also* afraid of
approaching something. As a result, many children who are afraid of going to
school because they fear separation from a parent will suffer this separation
when they go to play at a friend's house. Moreover, often they are *not* afraid of
approaching places other than school, such as grocery or department stores,
the theater, or vacation sites—whether their mother accompanies them or not.
Unless it represents some major anxiety about knowledge acquisition, why,
then, would the youngster have a phobia about school? In my view, the school
phobia centers on the meanings knowledge acquisition has for the young person and not just on pertinent family dynamics. Robin, for example, said, "I
don't want to sit still in class and think." An even more articulate rejection of
thinking came from Caroline who had achieved well in high school but refused
to attend certain college classes and often threatened to drop out of college
altogether. About her resistance she said, "I don't want to find out what I want
to know." A rejection of thinking might well reflect the youngster's view that
acquiring knowledge will lead to a loss, either of the parent or her nurturance.
But the act of knowing often touches us very deeply, so the rejection of it is
remarkable and significant. Therefore, a youngster's rejection of school because
he or she rejects understanding must be just as energetically and conscien-
tiously addressed during treatment as an enmeshed relationship between parent and child would be, or any other significant aspect of the phobia, such as
fear of another child, the teacher, or of the rooms in the school building.

COGNITIVE COMPROMISES

A normal child often expects that school learning will have an impact on
aspects of his life. This reveals his implicit (but perhaps unself-conscious)
belief that school and teachers exist to benefit him, which is reminiscent of the
preoperational child who thinks the sun exists to keep us warm. Contrarily, the
youngster who is afraid of school or college reverses the trust because she fears
that an educational setting might reveal something of substantial importance
that she wishes to avoid. Furthermore, school phobic young people often believe that if they learn nothing in school they have not learned or will not learn
elsewhere or that the only safe learning is their own spontaneous discovery
outside of school. Avoiding the school's physical plant serves to assure some
youngsters that they need no longer fear learning because all learning—includ-

ing understanding themselves or their parents—takes place in school. For example, Caroline concluded correctly that college would show her why she feared college learning. She might be required to take psychology courses and psychology, she knew, would reveal to her why she felt the way she did about her mother. Avoiding college, in effect, helped her avoid knowing why knowledge threatened her. At other times Caroline pursued psychological understanding, especially when she initiated investigations, because then she felt she could control the outcome of systematic inquiry.

From a Piagetian perspective, it is ironic that school phobic young people often believe knowledge acquisition is only imparted by school attendance and has little to do with their own efforts. Or, if they recognize their spontaneous discovery attempts in therapy, they sometimes minimize their own thought processes. This finding is exemplified by two school public children with whom I worked who perceived self-motivated discovery as "mere curiosity" or "just exploring." The use of the words *mere* and *just* reveals the attitude of these intelligent and often inquiring youngsters who needed at the very moment they explored reality to deemphasize the significance of investigating it. Those school phobic youngsters who do admit to originating ideas often insist that this is the very reason they avoid school; only their *own* ideas are safe and *not* those which originate in the minds of their teachers or other students. These youngsters do not retreat from thought itself but from the place (school) where thought is expected by others and shared.

CAROLINE'S COLLEGE PHOBIA

Presenting Problem

The oldest in a family of five children, Caroline was a very pretty but unpretentious young woman who approached therapy cautiously. She was serious about her therapy appointments, and her facial expressions were often contemplative. When angry, she withdrew into many silences, often brooding about "the state of things," such as her future, that of her family, or national and international problems. When relaxed and self-confident, her face radiated affectionate, intense feeling for the other person and she tended to the needs of her family and friends with care and understanding.

Caroline's parents had worked fulltime both before and after she and her siblings were born. Her mother had entrusted enormous responsibilities to Caroline in a correct assessment of her brilliance and early social maturity. Although she knew before therapy that she was angry at her mother, she did not know exactly why she was angry and referred to her reasons as a "secret." Her secret was that she was too bright and mature to be a protected child. Discovering this secret meant not just getting in touch with her anger at her mother, but also a realization that she had needed protection in her growing up years. Such need for protection was evidence in Caroline's mind that she was not intelligent.

She was anxious about the imagined consequences of protection as she discussed with me her angry feelings that she had not felt protected. As she began to feel increasingly safe with me, she sought to reestablish her intelligence by logical sparring. In this tangle, college attendance was implicated because her brilliant success in high school had proved that she was a genius as well. This meant she had surpassed her mother and left her without ever having been a protected child.

Because of its seduction in promising advanced knowledge and the opportunity to leave home, college even more than elementary or high school was problematic for Caroline. She assumed college, as the (perceived) final setting for learning, would yield more "facts" about her family and her role in that family than she could afford to recognize. She wished to conceal the reason for her college phobia (her anger at her mother) because she wished to protect her mother. She understood she was angry at her mother and so avoided especially college psychology courses to avoid being reminded of her anger.

Early Treatment Progress

Caroline looked to the other (parents, teachers, college) to more thoroughly define herself. In therapy, she began to do the same with me. She vacillated between believing there was no efficacy in being intelligent, if indeed she had admitted that she *was* intelligent, and challenging me with her repeated statements, "If I'm so smart, why can't I change them [her teachers and parents]?" Her adolescent syllogism consisted of the notion that she was not smart if she could not change another person or an institution (college). When she observed no wished-for change, she concluded she was not smart. This erroneous conclusion (if A does not lead to B, then A does not exist) derives from the adolescent's cognitive sophistication which includes a self-reflexive awareness that differentiates self and other. But, when she compared herself to other people, she realized she was indeed smart; she often used her intelligence to poke fun at my reasoning ability as well as to challenge it. The block that kept Caroline from comfortably accepting her intelligence was her adolescent imperative to change the other person, or the world. Even though a self-reflexive sense might on occasion tell her that she *was* intelligent, it had yet to reveal to her that a change in the other person or in the environment is independent of intelligence.

As the result of our discussions, I realized that in childhood Caroline felt flattered by her mother's trust in her and tried to suppress her anger at not being cared for. She supposed that her mother's view of her as worthy of being an adult meant that her relationship to her mother ought to be purely positive. She created a kind of "logical necessity" in thinking that her relationship to her mother *had* to be, or *must* have been, free from ambivalence. Her imagined "perfect" intimacy with her mother was a "rational" support for her early entrance into adulthood.

Once she became an adolescent and understood the difference between a wishful "logical necessity" and a real logical structure, a feeling of psychological "necessity" took over this brilliant girl as she tried to understand why as a child she had been an admired "adult" and not a protected child. "Mom *had* to expect so much of me because I was *so* smart she thought I *could* be an adult." Rather than giving her a logical reason, Caroline now tried to give her mother a valid *psychological* reason for not protecting Caroline as a child. Her wished-for interactions with her mother merged in her thinking with rationalizations that served to make her mother's behavior appear reasonable.

The resolution of her conflict in which protection was opposed to intelligence came about one day in therapy when in a moment of insight she said to me: "Why should I do the stupid thing of cutting classes [in college] if I have a smart therapist?" It seemed to me that for once she felt smart and protected. She felt protected because she perceived *me* as smart and thus (momentarily) unsurpassable, which meant that I would take care of her. But *she* also felt smart because I took her hard-to-answer questions seriously. Had I seen her precocious essays at logic as only self-defending, she would have defensively concluded that I felt threatened by her unfolding brilliance. This would not have been curative but a mere replay of her earlier experiences, since her teachers had often reacted defensively to her defiant use of logic. Thus, my going to great lengths to answer her conundrums, which she felt I thoughtfully considered, meant to Caroline that she finally *deserved* to be protected.

Later Developments in Therapy

As Caroline gradually began to feel intelligent and protected in her relationship to me, she began to tolerate and understand her anger at her mother. She expressed her anger by saying that when she was a child, her mother was "stupid" for not protecting her. She now contrasted her experience of the present where she felt intelligent and protected with her past in which she felt intelligent but unprotected and called this situation or the person who created and perpetuated this situation "stupid." Youngsters often say of people they do not like or events which do not turn out the way they wish that they are stupid. It is as though the word *stupid* avenges their having been made angry by either a "mean" or "insensitive" person or by a "bad" event. It becomes apparent in this context how the youngster must react when he or she is treated as if or thought to be stupid. This is one more reason why the term *disabled*, which has similar connotations, can be harmful and should be used with great caution, if at all. To the sensitive, intelligent, and especially older youngster, the word *disabling* is the direct opposite of the word *enabling*. To Caroline, her mother was "unable" to both protect and trust her. Because she appeared unable to combine the two acts of protecting and trusting, Caroline "disabled" her mother—she called her "stupid."

After a year of therapy, Caroline decided to transfer to a college which she hoped would meet her specific academic needs. She had become interested in education and biology, and much of her conversation toward the end of therapy focused on her need to make what I felt was a premature decision about which subject to pursue. She reacted positively to my statements that she need not attempt, once more, to be prematurely adult and fully decided about her future. Three years later, she finished her undergraduate work and was accepted to medical school, where as a first-year student, she got the top grades in her class.

THE EXPERIENCE OF CONTRADICTION AND THERAPEUTIC POSSIBILITIES

Before therapy, school phobic youngsters like Caroline contemplated ambiguity and did not retreat from it the way other nonlearners did when they perceived learning as dangerous or when they equated it with the growing up process and had to be reoriented to normal thought contradictions in therapy. A direct appeal to logic could be made to Caroline in the therapeutic hour because of her advanced intelligence but also because of her tendency to confront ambiguity. Her combative stance and spontaneous understanding of her dilemma were at one and the same time responsible for her escape attempts from college and for her determination in therapy to resolve an accurately conceptualized contradiction. When she wished to escape knowing about her competence on the one hand, or to know about her motives for denying her competence on the other hand, she recognized the incongruity of these two efforts. Furthermore, she recognized that her attempt to escape psychology classes contradicted her desire to attend her psychotherapy appointments where she learned about herself and her mother. It might be said, then, that Caroline became college phobic precisely because she could imagine contradictions; yet imagining them created intense affective reactions which led her to wish to avoid those situations which seemed to confront her with paradoxes. But, when she heard me attempt to get beyond her paradoxes as I said, for example, "You'll find out in therapy what it is you don't want to know," she instantly understood that getting behind or beyond her thought contradictions would not only help her in therapy but also in college. Young people like Caroline experience intense anguish about the accurately conceived aspects of phase-specific contradictions (as expressed, for instance, in her statements "I don't want to find out what I want to know" and "If I'm so smart, why can't I change them?"), so that in therapy they are enabled to resolve transition phases readily. Because they do not retreat from them but attempt to conceptualize what these phases mean, they only need therapeutic support to help them complete their partially formed resolutions.

One of the many important aspects of Piaget's theory is his supposition that continuity obtains across developmental levels. This is because functional qualities of the child's development are invariant even though structural qualities are not (Flavell, 1963, p. 408). In book after book, Piaget has demonstrated that equilibrium and the disequilibrium characteristic of transition phases occur throughout development while the concepts and structures used by youngsters vary. For example, the concept called "reversibility" does not appear in the child's thinking until he or she is 7 or 8 years. Thus, the same contradiction–apprehension process of transition could be seen in the remarkably different personalities and developmental levels of Caroline, Robin, and Maisie. It was the accurately and anxiously perceived aspects of contradiction that helped all three youngsters in therapy to overcome their problems. Even though Robin and Maisie were much younger than Caroline, their phobic attitudes made them similar to one another because they tried to master problem-solving phases where initially something appeared to be "wrong" with their spontaneous attempts at resolution. If a sensitive comprehension that "something was wrong" with themselves in school had led to attempts to deny the school's existence by refusing to attend, nevertheless, their ability to tolerate contradictions and often *discover* them in therapy made my statements focusing on finding out in school readily accessible. Caroline, for example, was delighted when I said she might as well learn in college because she was "learning" about herself in therapy. Although 6-year-old Robin and 4½-year-old Maisie were not capable of advanced and intricate thought construction, like Caroline they faced in therapy the incongruities that they found in their experience where before they had tried to deny the school reality and to repress the affect that school attendance aroused.

ROBIN'S ESCAPE FROM SCHOOL

Presenting Problem

Robin was a handsome, carefully groomed, and extremely appealing boy who readily revealed intense emotions in what he said and by facial expressions and bodily gestures. Well-coordinated and sturdily built, he showed athletic promise. He had given up trying to make himself less anxious in school and to make school safe. His parents had separated shortly before his sixth birthday and 4 months before his therapy began. When unable to calm his anxieties about their separation and its association in his mind with school attendance, he would get up from his seat, leave the classroom and wander "aimlessly" around the halls or out into the playground with, according to his teacher, "no apparent goal." When he realized that he was still anxious in the halls or on the playground, he refused to get on the school bus or to be driven to school by his mother. He told his mother he was "sick to my stomach" or that he had "a sore throat" in an attempt to persuade her to let him stay home. His choice of physical symptoms to dramatize his feelings about school was sustained by the fact that his mother was a nurse; he imagined she would either stay home from work to take care of him or take him to the hospital with her.

His mother told me that he had had severe separation anxieties during his early childhood. He was unable to tolerate her absence for even a few minutes. His separation anxieties had resurfaced when his mother seemed to take him away from his father when she and Robin moved into an apartment. From his mother's report, I thought he had concluded something similar to: I am male like Dad, so I will turn out like him. Robin often made statements in therapy about himself and his father in which he specified that he was "like Dad" — for example, "I am good at soccer like Dad" and "My Dad can do *everything* — so will I [do everything] when I grow up!" Since his mother left his father, he deduced that it was his father's competence, his being able to "do everything," that caused his mother to leave his father. That his mother did *not* leave him seemed contradictory to Robin. Her staying with him and her continuing to take care of him sometimes caused him to wonder if he *was* a boy, that is, a male "like Dad" or whether he *was* a competent first grader. He neither denied his parents' separation nor the fact that his mother stayed with him. This aroused anxiety in Robin not just because he thought about the future and wondered if at any moment his mother might leave him. He was also anxious because he could make no sense of his thoughts.

When Robin left the classroom or later refused to attend school, he had no goal in mind except not to be there. Robin's behavior baffled his parents because they did not comprehend that in an immutable fashion he connected his presence in school with his mother's imagined desertion. The fact that his parents separated just before his birthday may have strengthened Robin's conviction that growing older brings about some disaster. Magical thinking told Robin that knowing nothing was the same as not growing up and the same as remaining helpless. Then, his mother *must* take care of him even though he *was* male "like Dad." But this attempt at resolution confronted him with an additional problem: his "helpless" behavior contradicted his mother's wish that he achieve well in school.

His teachers thought Robin's behavior was "infantile" or "rebellious." One teacher thought he was behaving "defensively" lest a suspected learning disability be discovered, as if a child of barely 6 years might be capable of fully understanding a presumed disability diagnosis. Other teachers mistook Robin's self-protective absences from school as an inability to learn, when it is more correct to say that his learning ability had only partially developed and was centered on solving the confusions resulting from his own cogitations about an equally confusing life situation which he accurately apprehended.

Robin's Cognitive Compromises

When his mother brought him to see me, he refused to leave her lap because he believed his evaluation in my office to be somehow similar to what happened in school. He thought correctly that if he sat there, she would not be able to leave him. Knowing where she was permitted Robin to interact with me. His willingness to interact with me allowed me to understand the ways in which he had unevenly applied his intelligence. Initially, he appeared confused about the most common childhood perceptions; for example, he described a bright red color as a "big" color. Yet, four weeks later, he systematically tested which objects in my office would adhere to a magnet, which suggested that he often thought clearly. He also soon confided that he thought he must be "fast" at everything. When asked what advantage being fast held, he answered, "Being fast is being good." His occasional success on timed tests in school suggested to him that it was rapidity itself that led to success and, since his success assured him of his mother's love, "fast" meant "good."

Later he elaborated this transductive connection by commanding me to time him as he raced down the street while he waited a few minutes for his mother to pick him up from his therapy appointment. In explanation he said, "Running makes your heart beat faster, and if your heart beats faster, your whole body works faster." When asked what would happen then he said, "Well, if your whole body works faster, so does your brain." As an afterthought he added, "Sometimes I make my heart work so fast that my heart hurts"—a poignant statement reflecting his ambivalence about competence as well as an awareness of his behavior's painful effects. Sometimes he was made anxious by a rapid heartbeat, the result of his own sprinting.

Robin's gross-motor activity in the classroom was intended to speed up his brain which, he may have reasoned, would enable him to learn—more magical thinking which held potential clues as to how he conceptualized his learning problem. Furthermore, his thinking revealed a dim awareness that something was wrong with his escape solution to school problems. I thought his efforts to speed up his brain rested on the contradictory impulse to slow down his brain. He wished to slow down his brain's functions to avoid something he would rather not know. Slowing down in school, he knew, would get him in trouble with his parents, particularly his mother who then might not take care of him, so he defended against this underlying wish by speeding up. It might be said that Robin's cognitive compromises consisted of one self-protective maneuver on top of another. The more he avoided learning by speeding up his behavior when he hurriedly left the classroom, the more he sped the activity of his "nonlearning" brain by his own cogitations that speeding up one's body speeds parts of it.

Early Treatment Progress

When attempting to understand the knowing process in children, Robin's story is of particular interest because, like Caroline, he revealed that his phobia and his recovery rested as much on self-knowledge as it did on school knowledge. Clinical statements to the youngster often appear to have a cumulative effect when they are geared to his developmental level because either his mind can become reactivated or its spontaneous functions supported by a correct statement. The reactivated mind or supported mental functions resume their progressive development in knowing the self which adds to the impact of subsequent interventions.

Thus, Robin's story can be understood as an interaction of two progressive trends: one that was the result of his resolving his ambivalence about school learning, and the other that resulted in his definition of self as distinct from his father. Although he often talked about his mother, his primary interest in doing so was to compare and later contrast himself and his father in the context of his mother's reactions to both of them. As Robin got to work in therapy, he revealed not just what he had learned prior to therapy, but the fact that he was now ready to learn in ways different from the past. Because he became more self-attuned, in effect he changed his learning process while in therapy. His increased self-reflexive sense told him that in some situations he *did* know facts, and that in certain other situations he *did not*. About the latter he still often behaved defensively as if he felt, as he defined himself on progressively more complex levels, that he *ought* to know apart from the context or his developmental capabilities.

At first Robin found it difficult to let his mother leave the building while he spent time with me. His first therapeutic challenge was to reveal that it was his capability to know about his mother's comings and goings which was important to him, and that predicting her behavior—or his feeling that he could *not* predict her behavior—was somehow implicated in his wandering out of the classroom. Anxiously, he watched his mother leave at the inception of his third appointment, and then he refused to enter the office. When told that his mother would return, he said emphatically: "I *know*, I *know*! Don't most kids *know* their mommies will come back?" Dawdling about coming with me, he picked up a tiny plastic cup on the table next to which he was standing, but when I invited him to bring it into the office, he immediately came with me. Thus, it became clear that this symbolic act—the bringing of an object with him to the office which might have stood for his mother or the nurturance she provided—was instantaneously helpful as he sought to separate himself from her to begin a relationship with me.[1]

It is important to understand what Robin's stress on the verb *know* means. In regard to his mother's expected return, he could have said "I think" or "I hope." Why choose *know*? It might be concluded that saying *know* means a child has yet to get in touch with his anxious feelings about his mother's absence or a possible delay in her return. Contrarily, the words *think* or *hope* might connote to the therapist that the child recognizes he is anxious. But do children fully or at all understand the distinction between knowing and feeling? To a child it is often ridiculous to hear from the therapist that he can know without feeling.

Predicting whether his mother would desert him based on her own feelings was to Robin an issue of knowing and not knowing. His adamant statement "I *know*, I *know*" meant that he thought by my remark I did not know what he

---

[1] A question of commanding interest to psychotherapy students has been what to do if the child refuses to go into the office. The beginner often focuses on the *fact* that the child refuses but not on *how* he refuses. Concentration on the fact inevitably leads to a power struggle between therapist and child—an antitherapeutic event. But, attention to how the child refuses often reveals significant data that also bind the therapist's anxiety and anger which is evoked by the child's behavior. In my experience as therapist, investigating with the child how he refuses to come into my office or to do anything else has always resulted in his eventual cooperation. Especially in a situation which threatens to become a battle of the wills, there is nothing more powerful than the feeling of being understood. When the child feels understood as he asserts himself, he becomes cooperative, either immediately or soon after.

knew; that is, if I was unclear about what he understood, that created doubt in him about what he knew. Although he was fairly sure that his mother would return to pick him up on this occasion, he was not sure he knew she would *always* return, which is why he did not want her to leave at any time. Since he had accurately observed that his mother felt happy when she left him with me and that she had cordially greeted me (indicating she liked me and so would return to talk to me), he had painful memories of her interactions with both himself and other adults, primarily his father, when she was unhappy or angry. At those times, he feared she would desert him because he was male "like Dad." In what to the child is an uncertain situation, the mere expression of a feeling like anxiety does not help. In this situation, knowledge is more certain; the child reasons that if he could only figure out how to predict his mother's comings and goings, his future would rest on more solid ground. It is ineffective to point out that the child is anxious ("You are afraid that your mother will not return because you are afraid that she is mad at you") just as it is ineffective to reassure the child about reality ("If your mother said she would be back at 11:00, she will be back then"). The child needs most to hear that *he*, and not the therapist, might gain some control over both reality and his anxiety. The question then to pose to him is "You want to know what your mother will do. How can you find that out?"

Robin's *modus vivendi* in my office was to involve me in playing a set of table games. His set of favorites included games he called "hard" (Sorry, Battleship, and Stratego) and those he called "easy" (Winnie the Pooh and Candyland). Playing these games with Robin permitted me to understand both his conceptual level as well as his ability to signal when he felt life was too difficult. On these occasions, he chose an "easy" game whereas on other occasions he felt ready for "hard stuff."

Initially, he was afraid he did not know how to play games, or that he would lose. While being instructed, he repeatedly asserted that he *did* know, as he had previously done when he said he knew his mother would return. Because he wished to appear competent so that his mother would love him and praise, not criticize, his behavior, he asserted that he always knew. But he also feared competence because in his mind it was connected to his mother's having "deserted" his grown up and competent father. Thus, he repeatedly and emphatically presented in our therapeutic interactions the thought contradictions which so deeply troubled him. I thought Robin was afraid that if he were to become competent *and* his mother stayed with him, his competent but "deserted" father would envy and therefore reject him. He did not realize that a father's insecurity more than his competence would more likely lead to the rejection of Robin as a competent individual, believing only that competence was bound to distance him from either one or the other parent.

Robin thought that the way to play games successfully was to cheat. Although Piaget (1965a) showed that it is common for a child of 6 years to cheat in games, Robin's cheating had special meanings in terms of his past. In the first months of therapy, he began cheating outrageously. Then, he cheated only when he thought I was not looking. And so it happened that I sometimes had a phase of winning because he thought I was watching him and he therefore did not cheat. However, he had not yet realized that what he did was not automatically the same as what I did. He therefore assumed, I thought, that when I was winning, I must be cheating as well. This thought propelled him into a severe anxiety state for it meant I was like the parent he was so afraid would desert him. The reasons for this are explained henceforth.

The Transition from Ambivalent Knowing to Genuine Knowing

When Robin had been in therapy for 4 months, I learned the reason for his parents' separation. His mother had had an extramarital affair the previous year. If at 5 years Robin possibly sensed his parents' marital difficulties, he did not *know* about the extramarital relationship until he was 6½. But it seemed to me that Robin had sensed before being informed his mother's attachment to someone other than his father. If so, he was caught whichever way he played his chosen table game: if he won, he was the cheater and a bad person; if I won, I had "cheated" like his mother, which brought a flood of feelings he found difficult to accept.

Coincident with Robin's game-playing in therapy, his parents tried to discuss with Robin the reasons for their separation. To him, the conversation with his parents appeared only to reveal their heretofore unacknowledged sins: his mother's affair and his father's anger and withdrawal from her. At the same time that his parents talked with him about the reasons for their separation, he began to feel the age-appropriate impulse toward game mastery which carries with it the temptation to cheat. Thereupon his new solution in therapy while playing games was to compulsively admit *his* sin of cheating after each game win. He would say, for example, "But the *only* reason I won the game of Sorry is because I cheated." In response, I first attempted to show him that he was often thinking, not just cheating, to win the Sorry game. Next, I tried to explain that in order to win this game, the "luck of the draw" was required in addition to thinking and cheating. Initially, my statements did not convince him that he had not always cheated because he was focused temporarily only on the suspicion of "cheating" —either his own or another person's. What helped him handle his overwhelming feelings was my statement that he was at least honest about cheating, if he *had* cheated. In Robin's outer world, this held the implication that some day his candor might transfer to game-playing. In Robin's inner or intrapsychic world, my statement gave recognition to the impact of his parents' forthright attempts to deal with what their separation meant to them and to Robin. They had been straightforward in their conversation with him about his mother's "cheating."

Robin's anxiety and cheating behavior soon subsided and, instead, he used cognition to comprehend the requirements of each game he chose to play. He also told me that if he won, he would "only win by a little" so as not to make me "feel so bad." His cogitations about winning reflect still another thought contradiction. He tried to express the antagonism he perceived between two very different events: (1) the logic of the game which differentiates a win from a loss without gradations and (2) an opponent's desire to modify the other's defeat. If so, this would imply that he understood if he won "only by a little" his opponent might be permitted to save face. He seemed to say that saving face would be important to me because he saw me as his opponent similar to his parents who often appeared to be opponents. Perhaps he believed his mother "won" in her arguments with his father, just as he had won in the game with me. Then, he might have assumed that I "felt bad" which he hoped to mitigate by saving me from a conspicuous and traumatic game loss which stood for either his imagined traumatic loss of his mother or his father's actual loss.

Robin's Use of Symbols

In his 5th month of therapy, Robin's mother described in front of him a prolonged argument that she had had with his father. After describing the argument to me, she left, and Robin immediately grabbed the Sorry game to begin his interactions with me. By then I was convinced that the reason games held such fascination for him was his expectation that he must share his parents' problems which seemed similar to those of game opponents. By choosing the game of Sorry, it was as though he implicitly asserted *he* was "sorry" about some aspects of his family situation. What Robin needed at that moment was to understand what *he*, not his parents, brought to situations—both those in therapy and those in school—so that he might find alternative ways of behaving which did not replicate what he observed in his parents.

Shortly after choosing the Sorry game, Robin began to confuse the numbers 5 and 11 as he picked up the Sorry cards and misread 5 for 11. This confusion puzzled me because the numerical confusions that had appeared in earlier appointments had consisted of those with graphic similarities, such as 3 and 5, or 11 and 12. It thus seemed that the confusion of 5 and 11 had to do with the meaning in relationship to each other that 5 and 11 had for Robin. The numbers 5 and 11 as they were flipped up in the deck of Sorry cards remained unintegrated: they were not consistently used as elements of a numerical sequence, but could on a whim stand alone as symbols which had special, personal meanings. Since he had been 5 years old when his parents separated, it seemed to me that the two 1s in the number 11 might have reminded him of two people—his parents standing close together. I said to Robin, "When you were 5, your parents were together." To this he answered, "Yup, 6 take away 1 is 5. Yup, they were together a year ago." From then on, he never confused the number 11 with the number 5.

The statement "When you were 5, your parents were together" integrated the number 5 with the rest of the numerical sequence, as can be seen by his spontaneous subtraction of 6 minus 1. His confusion was the result of a partial but not total absence of a cognitive structure; he knew the numerical system sufficiently to differentiate between 5 and 11 because he knew 11 was "bigger" than 5. In the game of Sorry, he also knew the numerical sequence before 5 (he counted accurately and recognized the numbers 1 through 4), and from 5 through 10 and after 11 (12, being the highest number in this game). The idea that numbers have a constant identity and group themselves in sequence thus remained intact which helped him reintegrate the number 5 into a seriated sequence. In fact, he reintegrated the number 5 by "taking away" 1 from 6, which suggests that he had brought together the special meaning subtraction had for him with the mathematical operation of subtraction. To young children, subtraction often means deprivation; that is, an entity is "taken away" from another entity wherein the imagined deprived entity is often the child himself. The number 1 which was taken away from the number 6 (Robin's age when his parents separated) most probably represented his father who no longer lived in the same home as Robin. Thus, the fantasy of one person (his father) who was taken away from 6-year-old Robin became united in Robin's activity of correctly subtracting 1 from 6. As Robin listened to what I said, the number 5 could no longer be so easily lifted out of sequence. Eleven probably fell into place at this point because its symbolic equivalent, 5, had just fallen into place. Five was now 5 and therefore could not so easily substitute for 11. To say it another way, numbers were numbers, and not substitutes for some other event, thing, or person.

Robin won the game of Sorry without cheating and was pleased, but became momentarily worried that I might be angry at losing. When I assured him that I was happy because I knew he had understood his substitution of 5 for 11, a slow smile spread over his face and he asked to play the "hard" game of Stratego. He had come to feel safe using his mind to discover why he might have made the "mistake" of substituting one number for another. When he heard me say how happy I was about his using his mind, he no longer worried about my being angry at the game loss.

Symbols versus Symptoms

Did Robin's particular use of numbers ("signs") mean that his symbolic expression was symptomatic? The confusion of 5 and 11 surely represents more than a disabling mistake as Robin sought to understand his problems. The fact that he *did* understand his problems by confusing 5 and 11 means that it was an "enabling" mistake. It would be ludicrous to say that Robin's exchange of 5 and 11 is symptomatic of a disability. At the moment he transposed those two numbers, they were "motivated" symbols (Piaget, 1962), which had a highly charged meaning.[2] The remaining question is why the interpretation ("when

[2]In his book, *Play, Dreams and Imitation in Childhood,* Piaget (1962) came very close to psychoanalysis in his attempt to deal with the "motivated" or "overdetermined" aspects of symbol usage in the child. That play or dream symbols are motivated was obvious to Piaget because he recounted specific play sequences or dream reports of the children he studied in which he connected a motive to the child's choice of a symbol. For example, he descibed an angry 5-year-old who made up a story about cutting off her parent's head, hurriedly pretending to glue it back on. Piaget concentrated as much on the child's motivated rush to glue the head back on as he did to her egocentric lack of self-awareness.

you were 5, your parents were together") brought about the shift from idiosyncratic to shared in Robin's use of a "signifier." How did the number 5 come to have for Robin that restricted meaning which represents what 5 means to most people? To ask the question another way, how was the shift from "symbol" to "sign" accomplished in Robin's thinking?

When Robin heard that the numbers 5 and 11 were associated in his mind with a specific situation, he no longer needed them as symbols to stand for this situation because he could talk directly about it. He agreed with me that his parents had been together when he was 5-years-old. The back and forth switch of the two numbers meant to him that when he was 5, he was able to keep his parents standing close together which brought to his awareness the sad fact that at age 6 he seemed no longer able to do so. This thought led to his ability and willingness to discuss that his anxiety derived from the idea that he had either caused his parents to separate or had failed to keep them together. But, numbers were not robbed of their meaning, they were just put to different and often more conventional uses.

Using numbers conventionally does not mean diluting the symbolic medium by restricting the meaning of numbers to a seriated sequence only. Robin found that he could use numbers as symbols or signs depending on the context. Eight weeks after he had understood his exchange of 5 for 11, he told me that the number 1 on the Sorry card "looked sad." He said this after he had won the game of Sorry by picking a 1 card; this card had permitted him to advance his last game piece to the "home" position. He then began to play with the symbolic possibilities of what he had just said. "That number 1 is the 'sad one'...or maybe he is the 'sad won'...because he *won* the game of Sorry!" Although it was not immediately obvious why the act of winning with the number 1 was a sad event for Robin, nonetheless he continued to play with numbers in a way which helped inform me about his problems. More importantly, he brought a greater self-reflexive awareness to his symbolic play, which helped him understand what he sought to express. As he expressed ever more clearly through symbols and direct statements what was on his mind, he needed to hear from me how clever and often gifted he was in his use of symbols and direct statements because his sense of identity as an intelligent individual had not been fully formed. The identity of all children fluctuates from moment to moment. What fluctuates particularly in nonlearning children is their sense of themselves as intelligent persons.

ROBIN'S CORE PROBLEM: KNOWING AND CHEATING

Robin came to therapy with the view that to know how to win a game meant he was cheating. But I did not see Robin's game-cheating as a replay of his mother's "cheating." Rather, I saw it as a normal developmental trend which had a special connection to knowing in Robin's mind. Since he thought his mother left his father because he was grown up and knowledgeable, Robin avoided attending school. He did not ask himself why his mother chose to leave his father for another grown up and knowledgeable person—still one more example of partial understanding in children. At the young age of 6, he was centered only on one aspect of contradiction—that which told him that while his mother wanted him to learn in school, she appeared to reject that family individual who *had* learned in school—his father. When Robin began to understand the differences between knowing and cheating, he then concluded that cheating was safer than knowing because it was not really knowing and, therefore, would not like knowing lead his mother to desert him.

Much meaning was thus condensed for Robin in the act of cheating. When he felt he had cheated, his behavior seemed much like Timothy's (see Chapter 4) when he talked about sneaking, stealing, or peeking to gain knowledge. Both of these boys needed to know how their learning compromises revealed a yearning for knowledge at the same time that such yearning was ultimately frustrated by their own inhibitions. My conversations with Robin focused on the ways in which he did know, including how to gain a game advantage by cheating. By way of contrast, if I likened his normal game cheating to his mother's "cheating" behavior, he might have concluded that he would continue to cheat throughout life because his adult parent had. Such a statement would have ignored the general tendency of children who were Robin's age to cheat in games. I wished to avoid casting Robin's behavior in an unchangeable mold given by his unique experience which could have suggested to him that because he had once been a game cheater, he could never be honest. By showing Robin how he had learned through cheating, I hoped to give him a sense of his competence and to motivate him to refine and enlarge his knowing capabilities.

At the same time that I began to discuss with Robin what his cheating meant, I also reinterviewed him. His reinterview responses after 6 months of therapy were distinctly more mature in that they often contained such phrases as "I thought you meant...and so I said..." which showed he had begun to reflect on his own activity. It might be said that the child "takes" consciousness (Piaget, 1976, 1978, 1985; Bringuier, 1980) as he tries to understand himself. Piaget's (1976, 1978) subjects, who struggled to answer interview questions, often "took" consciousness as they tried to explain why they had either said or thought something. Because he was not sure he wanted to understand himself or his reasoning, Robin became more anxious as he simultaneously gave more mature, precise reasons for correct judgments compared to his first interviewing experience. For example, during the first interview, he thought there were more girls than people and, to justify his incorrect response, he began to count all the dolls in my office—not just the interview dolls—and started as well to count all the toy cars. In other words, he answered a "question" very different from the one I asked him.

Two of his reinterviewing responses follow to show the dual developments of cognitive maturity and the change in affectivity (the other interview tasks given to Robin are described on pp. 317–322).

Robin was presented with two strings of different lengths, one curled and one straight, where the end points of both strings were contiguous. He was asked if the strings were the same or different lengths. After he had correctly answered that they were different, I curled the longer string even more. Robin was then asked, "What about now?" Robin first pointed to the longer and curled string and said, "You can always do this to it," as he straightened it out. When asked how he knew [the correct answer], he said of the string, "It grew." A pause ensued. Then, "It was longer to begin with so it will always be longer." Then he began to curl the string around his finger so tightly that it turned white—the blood circulation to his finger was curtailed.

Next Robin was shown some Fisher-Price dolls, five of which were girls and four boys. He was asked, "More girls or more people?" At first he said, "Girls...there are five girls," but he quickly added, "Oh, you mean everybody...there's more people, nine people." Then he said, "I thought you meant more girls or boys and that's why I said that." I asked him if he thought he had made a mistake before, which would be why he had wrapped the string around his finger. He answered, "No, that's not it," and hurriedly asked me whether he had answered the question about strings correctly. I said he had answered the questions correctly, but this seemed to increase his tension, and he asked me to stop questioning him because he wanted to play a game. He chose the Winnie the Pooh game and, though he had never done this before, he chose the rabbit game piece to represent himself, the one piece of this game whose head had been broken off [by someone other than Robin]!

As Robin and I played the Winnie the Pooh game and he symbolically became the headless rabbit, I told him again he had done well during the interviewing, that he had used his head just as he now was using his head in counting while playing his chosen game. Robin won the game and then asked to play a thinking game in contrast to Winnie the Pooh which requires minimal thinking. He chose Battleship, which invites the child to coordinate two items of information (a number and a letter) to locate the opponent's ships. In winning Battleship, he implicitly asserted he was capable of winning thinking games as well as luck games, and, moreover, that it had become safe to do so. When he then won the game of Stratego, the hardest thinking game in his repertoire, I said, "You're really using your head today which is what you have to do in these games." Anxiously Robin responded, "I didn't cheat, did I?" His question referred to his fluctuating anxiety that ipso facto winning signifies a cheating activity.

As I thought about his statement, "I didn't cheat did I?", which followed a win at Stratego, I said: "Cheating is using your head too, so there's no way for a bright boy like you to avoid using your head." He then admitted for the first time that he put limits on what he let himself understand. He had come to his appointment bearing a flashlight, explaining that his mother had used it to look at his inflamed tonsils. He said, "I have a cold right now, and I *can't know* why they take tonsils out." I said that while doctors still do remove tonsils sometimes, it is not as common as it used to be. I went on to say that perhaps he wished not to know in this case because he was afraid he might lose his tonsils.

Robin's saying "can't know" instead of "don't know" should not be interpreted as a linguistic mistake. Robin meant precisely what he said: that he could not afford to know because of the risk involved in understanding tonsillectomies. Although there was the possibility that tonsils might have represented some other part of his body, in my statments to Robin I did not make an analogy between tonsils and other body parts but rather stayed close to what he told me. His choice of the headless rabbit convinced me that his earlier twisting the string around his finger meant his anxiety centered on his mental, not his sexual, functioning. Without heads, one cannot know and one cannot reflect on what one knows.

Robin's solutions which were geared toward the single aim of not recognizing what event had caused his parents' separation—because he thought he already knew it was something he did or didn't do—reflected clever and often involuted thought patterns. From his behavior, it seemed plausible to hypothesize that he believed the only way to avoid behaving in a socially unacceptable way such as cheating was to stop using his head altogether; to become a headless rabbit or to refuse school learning by escaping the school environment. And perhaps he believed he was behaving in a socially unacceptable fashion by being a game cheater because he thought the equilvalent of: "In order to avoid Dad's fate, I must make myself like Mom." But his clever and increasingly complex thought processes often brought about more problems than they solved. Although he realized how much fun it was to know (to win) without cheating, he nevertheless continued to confuse winning, learning, and cheating. Winning at games revealed he "knew how" to play games, but Robin understood winning could also occur if he cheated. The outcome of a win seemed to link the two very different activities of "knowing how" and cheating because a win can follow both. And the more deliberately he confused not knowing (cheating) with knowing (knowing how to play games), the more anxious he became, once more, he could make no sense of his thoughts.

A turning point in Robin's therapy came about when I suggested to him that cheating requires the use of one's head. This statement refocused him on the ways in which knowing and cheating are similar and different. This uncovered for Robin his belief that one way to avoid knowing was to cheat. In his zeal to understand the differences between winning through cheating and winning through understanding, he had ignored that thought is involved in cheating. My saying to him that he was "using his head" to play games and that there was no way for a bright boy like him to avoid thinking after he chose a headless rabbit in the "Pooh" game appealed to a maturing intellect and intended to clarify the thinking errors inherent in his previous attempts at problem resolution. I meant to confront Robin with the contradiction inherent in the following: an individual cannot choose a headless "nonthinking" rabbit without thinking about this choice.

Although I never phrased it this way, Robin was brought by our therapeutic conversations to the implicit question: What is the threat in knowing? Conversing about each aspect of understanding which he brought to the therapy hour helped him go to school and to begin to sit still in class without wandering around the room or out of it. His teacher reported that his learning improved and his mother told me that he finished his homework papers. After six months of therapy, during which Robin often heard me say he was a "bright boy" capable of learning but also afraid of it, he began to bring self-consciously to therapy those problems he still found with learning. He felt freer to attend school and to learn since his anxiety about school could be brought to a place other than school. Knowing he could use his therapy appointments to both express his acute anxieties about school attendance and to clarify his contradiction-ridden thought processes reduced the risks Robin perceived in going to and learning in school. The complexity of his learning disorder and the intricacy of the thought processes he developed to understand his school phobia necessitate a general discourse on the several theoretical issues raised by Robin's treatment progress.

THEORETICAL ISSUES AND CHILDHOOD ACTIVITY

Three developmental controversies addressed by writers who have considered how cognitive-developmental psychology and psychoanalysis might be synthesized (for example, Furth, 1987; Greenspan, 1979; Piaget, 1962, 1981; Pine, 1985; Stern, 1985) are germane to Robin's progress as he played table games and conversed with me in therapy. My discussion of a child's spontaneous activity required by game-playing, or by his investigating childhood interests and hobbies, intends to intersect these important theoretical controversies. Many children reveal their conflicts while talking about their special interests, such as sports, music or art lessons, their favorite books, movies or movie characters, television shows, their pets, or their collections of stamps, dolls, postcards, coins, seashells, and the like. Robin revealed his conflicts in therapy as he narrowed his focus on what was to become his favorite game—Sorry.

The first theoretical issue is the child's relationship to reality. The child can be observed either turning absorbedly toward or actively away from those aspects of the world which are salient from his perspective. The controversy is over whether the child has paid attention to reality and if so, which details has he integrated and which has he submerged. A differentiation of his "unselfconscious" absorption with reality from his "unconscious"—a differentiation to be discussed shortly—helps clinicians observe and decide what the child's incomplete understanding and incomplete awareness mean. Second, turning toward or away can reflect activity in one or both spheres of the psyche, affective or intellective. Here the controversy is whether one or the other sphere predominates. Third, turning toward or away can occur in regard to two different content categories: people and things. The controversy occurs when developmental psychologists assert that child psychoanalysts have omitted a significant portion of the child's experience from their purview—his experimentation with inanimate objects *for its own sake*. I will begin with the ways in which Robin turned absorbedly toward reality. Then I will discuss how affectivity and intelligence can be joined in children like Robin to produce the results that the children wish to create. Finally, I will illustrate the child's attraction to both things and people and show that it is the importance of his actions on things which allows him to use them as symbols for people or for feelings about people.

COGNIZANCE OF THE SELF AND UNSELF-CONSCIOUSNESS

To understand the meaning of the child's behavior in therapy, it is helpful to remember that child and adult are different in the ways in which they understand reality and in which they are unaware of it. As the child turns absorbedly toward aspects of reality, certain contents of his mind are unself-conscious because he is often unaware of exploring while doing so and, before 7 or 8 years, does not question his conceptions. Contrarily, when the adult is unaware, it is more often correct to speak of "the unconscious." This is not to say that children never experience unconscious motivation or that adults are never unself-conscious. In noting Piaget's (1962) attempt to discuss Freud's theory of the unconscious wherein he adapts his findings to Freud's theory in some respects and challenges the theory in others, Furth (1987) commented that

> It is not easy to draw the exact line between the conscious and preconscious. Are you conscious of what you are doing when you walk to the door? Certainly, but only to a degree. A vast, an indefinite amount of possible perceptual material is only preconscious. (p. 57)

What Furth referred to here as "preconscious" I prefer to think of as "unself-conscious." The reason we may not be conscious of walking to the door is that our attending to our purposes in getting to the door, through it, or beyond it commands us more than the "perceptual material" along the way. Similarly, children become keenly occupied with some aspect of the total situation they are exploring, a self-occupation which, paradoxically, blots out an awareness of the exploring self. The individual is not unaware in these situations; on the contrary, he is so sensitive to particular aspects of his environment that he suspends an awareness of the cognizing function. Even though such unawareness might overlap what Sigmund Freud meant by the "preconscious," it does not seem to me to be identical to what he meant by that term—an issue I will return to later.

Because the adult has decentered to the degree to which he is more fully aware of a well-defined self, his unconscious motivation will reflect a capability to maintain an actively warded off sphere of the psyche because of the capability to recognize more fully the noxious meanings of events. By way of contrast, the child's self is less developed, most importantly his self-reflexive sense, so he can therefore be unaware in two ways: (1) he can be unself-conscious and thus unaware of the self's activity (for example, symbolization) or the results of the self's activity (the varied meanings he attributes to symbols); or, (2) he can have suppressed or repressed ideas, feelings, and motives, which seem alien or threatening to a fluctating sense of self. In turn, repression often leads to increased symbolization in playing and in dreaming which in the aforementioned two profound ways the child tends to remain "unconscious" of.

Piaget's (1976, 1978) works show how the internal sense of self, or the sense of one's own logic, becomes more acutely developed in childhood by virtue of the child's actions on external objects—a statement that seems paradoxical because something outside ourselves can make us aware of something inside.

In a rare moment of expansive theorizing, Piaget remarked in his concluding passage to *The Grasp of Consciousness* that

> the subject only learns to know himself when acting on the object, and the latter can become known only as a result of progress of the actions carried out on it. This explains the circle of the sciences, of which the solidarity that unites them is contrary to all linear hierarchy. Furthermore, and most importantly, this explains the harmony between thought and reality, since action springs from the laws of an organism that is simultaneously one physical object among many and the source of the acting, then thinking subject. (p. 353)

The child's repeated self-questioning by which he comes to know *which* of his actions causes the desired effects builds his self-reflexive sense because he becomes sensitized to his own behavior. When Robin would race down a street, he would repeatedly ask himself what he did to make his heart beat faster. His self-questioning sensitized him to his motives and permitted him to understand that by making his heart beat faster, he wished to make his whole body function faster which he hoped—and feared—might speed up his brain and learning ability. Essentially, his self-questioning and self-understanding led Robin away from his egocentric perspective because eventually he was able to imagine that *anybody* could race down a street to make their hearts beat faster.

Despite their egocentrism young children quite likely have an intuitive sense of self which later becomes conceptual by way of repeated attempts to validate their unique qualities as they understand their investigations of reality. For example, I have observed young children of 2 or 3 years admire themselves before a mirror, and they are not usually surprised that it is themselves they see in the mirror. When looking into a mirror with me, young children have pointed to their and my image and said, "That's me and that's you"—and in the next second have looked directly at me (not the mirror image) to verify what they have said. Important in this context is Kagan's (1984) assertion that children as young as five can identify their own drawing style. About this apparently precocious behavior, Kagan writes that the children have "unself-consciously abstracted from all of their prior artistic products a prototypic schema that represented their unique style" (p. 207). Although it is impressive, a prototypic schema in a 5-year-old, in my opinion, is based on many immediate experiences from which many palpable (art) products have resulted. Similarly, the young children I observed *acted*—they pointed—as well as talked to verify the self-other experiences which occurred as they observed themselves before a mirror.

The observations of Secord and Peevers (1974) seem to contradict Kagan's and mine. About kindergarten children they asserted that "a view of self is either absent or of the most rudimentary nature. The question 'Now tell me what *you* are like?' drew a total blank in a few instances" (p. 133). The total blank might be the result of the young child's inability to contemplate the whole self in an abstract manner. He might recognize his image in a mirror or his drawing style. But, when asked what his whole self is like, he is unable to answer because he lacks the concepts with which to think about or express the fact that his self has many attributes which make him distinct from others. In this sense, the child can be called "unself-conscious." In my opinion, he becomes self-conscious as the result of his attempts in his growing up years to coordinate various aspects of the self, such as his personal drawing style or his mirror image. Also important for his self-concept are the results he produces while investigating reality, including conceptualizing the reactions of other people to him.

Robin's Cognizance of the Sorry Game

Robin took many forward strides in thinking as he played his chosen game of Sorry. Increased advanced and introspective thought helped him to realize how much he knew as he played this game and observed his own and my reactions to what happened. By his 8th month of therapy, he understood, for example, that an authentic game win was not the result of cheating. He knew he could depend on his mind to engage in those processes that bring about a legitimate win, processes which he had engaged in before but had remained unaware of. He became aware that he could silently add to the correct number in the game Sorry; he knew he could calculate in his head whether the number on the card he picked was too large or too small to return a piece home with; and he knew without counting that if he picked a card with a four on it (which in this game means to go backward) he need not do anything with his game piece if he was at the end of a slide arrow (because the number of steps backward is the same as the number forward). All these behaviors were accompanied by a broad, proud grin or by exaggerated shrugs and other comical gestures which communicated that he found the game Sorry easy.

In spite of the more mature and varied cognitive activity, Robin nonetheless resisted the idea that sometimes a 4 backward can be good—in the event that one's game piece is in a certain position near the entrance to the final steps toward home when the player can then enter the last stretch of the game without having to travel all the way around the board. His resistance to knowing in this case revealed his ambivalence about forward and backward progression. He realized that going forward was better than going backward and so he thought that backward could not be good because it represented his old belief that growing up (moving forward) and knowing were dangerous. Since knowing (learning how to play the Sorry game) had moved him ahead by giving him the opportunity to refine certain cognitive abilities, it still contained certain hurdles, such as having to think of one and the same thing (backward movement) as being on some occasions good and on some others bad. On a conscious level, this thought appeared contradictory to Robin, and in declining to struggle with it, he kept it from awareness. It might be said that he ignored or "repressed" those "easily observable features" (Piaget, 1976, p. 345) which were required to win the Sorry game because of the affective significance of backward versus forward progression. For the moment, he remained unself-conscious of the fact that it was he (or people in general) who had determined what an event such as backward movement can mean.

Six weeks after he repeatedly asserted "going backward" was "bad" and after many experiences in which he heard me explain that while going backward to win games may not make sense, sometimes in this game it *did* make sense, he was able to coordinate more aspects of this intellectual dilemma. Now, he eagerly took advantage of a 4 backward to advance his game piece nearer the home position. At these times he habitually said, "I love you, 4!" At other times when a 4 backward meant an impediment to winning, he said with equal intensity of feeling, "I hate you, 4!" When Robin began to understand the double meaning of the 4 backwards card and could use it symbolically and often humorously, but most important, *deliberately* to communicate ambivalence, I began to cogitate how this advanced thought process came about as I simultaneously talked with Robin about it.

During our games of Sorry, Robin and I often discussed the meanings growing up had for him. That is, he was not just concentrating on mastering and winning the Sorry game but also in investigating what this game's processes meant to him. Earlier, he had centered on the symbolic meaning backward progression had for him—that moving backward means growing down instead of growing up, and had concluded that a 4 backward card was always bad because growing down was. As much as he wished to return to the age of 5 when his parents were living together, he nonetheless recognized that remaining a childish and nonlearning person held risks for his relationship to his mother (she might fail to praise him). Furthermore, being between the ages of 6½ and 7, he found it difficult to return simultaneously to the original thought that a 4 backward was bad to resolve his ambivalence about growing up, and to hold in his mind what he heard me say when I attempted to show him the occasions on which the 4 card was good. Perhaps his talking about ambivalent feelings regarding growing up while he was playing a game that permitted him to represent symbolically his ambivalence helped Robin get in tune with the fact that he could *be* ambivalent. He had certainly gotten in touch with a particular ambivalence as he grasped the contradiction inherent in the 4 backward card and had, furthermore, resolved one more dilemma which through his activity in therapy he had confronted; that is, he vividly expressed his understanding that people can feel two often contradictory ways about the same event (or thing or person).

If Robin's emerging triumph represented a collusion of affectivity and intelligence in that he understood ambivalence at the same time he understood game logic, his progress in understanding the Sorry game was also the result of his reorganizing cognitive concepts. For example, his understanding of the Sorry card 4 required, first, his return in thinking to his original thought ("reversibility") which was that the 4 backward card is bad because it tells the player to move farther away from his goal. In order to change his attitude and game strategy toward the 4 card he had to evaluate his previous thoughts and compare them with what presently occurred to him—that, for example, his therapist might be correct in stressing that going backward in this game is not always bad. Being 7 years, he might then have been able to juxtapose two game plans and decide which of these served him better. That is, his inner coordinations of the multiple aspects of this problem probably derived from coordinating the differences in opinions he and I held about effective game strategies: he knew that I disagreed with his game playing not just because I explained how he might use the 4 card to his advantage, but also because he repeatedly observed me play the game differently from him. That he was not merely copying me was obvious because of his forceful, deliberate, and often humorous demeanor as he announced how he felt about the 4 card—affect and statements which he never observed me display. I thought he did not simply shed an earlier and immature behavior but rather opposed his previous behavior with the more mature conception he repeatedly observed me project, contemplated their relative merits, and made his own decision about a new game strategy.

Unself-Conscious Intelligence and Preconscious Affectivity

It is very difficult to analyze intelligence and affectivity separately. Yet clinicians can refine their therapeutic methods by attending to the different ways a child can be unaware. It is often the child's or adolescent's affective expressions that can help clinicians differentiate between what is unself-conscious and what is suppressed or repressed. Affects in addition to anxiety accompany a child's immature unself-consciousness, and these varied affects help me discriminate between an unawareness resulting from an immature cognitive perspective and/or a rejection of transition phases in intellectual development and that unknowing stance resulting from suppression or repression. The nontransitional child or adolescent is more likely to be complacent rather than manifestly tense, nervous, or anxious because he does not question his perspective or his solutions to problems. But the unself-conscious child or adolescent does become anxious when he is propelled into transition and finds the unexpected or the threatening. Or he becomes anxious when he thinks that I expect him to be fully knowing of his self when he is not. Thus, the youngster who becomes transitional in therapy begins to doubt that familiar perspectives are always correct, and this causes anxiety. Such a child or adolescent might even react with anger, because the mature view may seem to challenge his statements or intimate to him that he is not telling the truth as he sees it. Thus, a youngster's anxiety in therapy is not only associated with a dawning preconscious awareness of repressed mental content but it is also the result of intellectual disequilibration.

Embarrassment in addition to anger and anxiety may occur especially in older children and adolescents when they become aware in therapy that they lack self-understanding. Initially, these young people are not anxious but embarrassed because self-understanding is the perceived goal of therapy. Anxiety may be brought about by the youngster's realization that in therapy he ought to know himself at the same time he discovers he does not. Then anxiety is not the original affect but is a reaction to the embarrassed and annoyed feelings the young person experiences when he realizes that he has not fully understood himself in the presence of his psychotherapist. In such a situation, clinicians nevertheless watch frequently for what they consider deeply repressed anxious memories. Thus, they miss therapeutic opportunities when they interpret embarrassment or annoyance as less important and believe that the expression of anxiety connected to repressed memories is the *only* therapeutic release. These missed therapeutic opportunities are similar to those missed by professionals who try to assist competent nonlearning youngsters if, despite evidence to the contrary, they believe the heretofore undetected disabillity will eventually be found. In other words, the supposition that a psychological condition exists when it cannot be observed often leads therapists and other professionals to ignore what can be observed: an embarrassed or angry young person is perceived as anxious or potentially so as the result of repression, and an intelligent but insecure or stubborn young person is perceived as disabled.

In a similar vein, Stern (1985) has written that what occurs in psychoanalytic psychotherapy does not always reflect repression of earlier events or distortions:

> It is certainly true that repression and distortions can hide an earlier edition [of the patient's experience]; that is often the case in clinical work. It is not always the case, however, and even if it were, the unmasked earliest edition is rarely where theory predicts its origin point should be. To rescue the situation, theorists postulate an even earlier edition, hidden yet further in the past by repression and distortion. There is no end to the chase. (p. 262)

I am suggesting that the "chase" to which Stern refers can be diverted productively if clinicians look at those varied affects which are likely to accompany the "editions" of the cognitively nontransitional compared to the transitional child. The nontransitional child who remains unchallenged by therapeutic intervention is likely to be complacent, whereas the transitional child is likely to be anxious, embarrassed, or angry about what appears to him to be an incapacity to resolve problems. If we as therapists perceive anxiety, we must also attempt to discern between that anxiety which results from the partial understanding of transitional phases and that anxiety which is associated with repression. (I make such an attempt in Chapters 8 and 9.)

Levels of Awareness in Understanding Things and People

To return to Robin's increasing game successes, his game behavior often revealed his present state of logico-mathematical knowledge and the cognitive development in his use of symbols. But just as much as his game behavior reflected preoccupations with important people, it also reflected preoccupations with things. His confusion of 5 and 11 is a case in point. Because learning the numerical system had been important to him, at one significant moment in his life Robin could express his feelings about his parents' separation in the substitution of one number (his age when his parents were together) for another (the two ones in 11). Yet he was very matter-of-fact about the transposition and initially did not question his "mistake" nor did he feel that he had to explain it to me. However, he may have observed me cogitate about the transposition and attempt to put into words why he confused the two numbers, which may have led him to question his behavior—he might have approached an understanding of himself as a "subject" among many. Certainly, his subsequent symbolic use of the Sorry card 4 was replete with self-awareness when he expressed often humorously that he either loved or hated the 4 card which represented another important person.

But the fact that fluctuating levels of awareness might exist in both an intellective unself-consciousness and an affective preconscious does not mean that one type of unawareness is easier to overcome or to undo than the other. As Piaget (1976, 1978) has shown, it is very difficult to bring to the child's awareness that he has neglected some aspect of reality which he presently cannot explain or integrate into his current system of meanings. As clinicians, we tend to discount this type of unawareness because we are so sensitized to the unawareness that springs from repression. For example, at first Robin did not appear to have repressed the conspicuous connection between the game's name of Sorry and an individual's feeling sorry about an event for which he assumes responsibility. He simply ignored a conspicuous aspect of the therapeutic environment—the name of the Sorry game—rather than consciously apprehend the name Sorry, which would be followed by relegating Sorry and its associated meaning to his unconscious. Although he later analyzed the meaning the name the Sorry game had for him, initially he concentrated on his parents' marriage and on his wish for their reconciliation in his transposition of 5 for 11. The symbolic meaning of the game's name Sorry was initially ignored because he was not so much focused on their separation as on their imagined reunion. Only later did he understand that he might use the Sorry game to express his sorrow about their separation. And then he did not need to repress this understanding because he knew his feelings about his parents were acceptable to me.

Moreover, it is sometimes rather easy to bring repressed material from the preconscious to the surface of the youngster's psyche. This most often happens, as Sigmund Freud (1949) noticed, when the patient is already partially conscious of the conflict and for this reason brings it to the therapist's attention. Robin was almost conscious of the meaning contained in his repeated statements "I hate" and "I love" regarding the number 4 card; he understood without a moment's hesitation that 4 stood for an important person—his mother. When I started to say that his statements of hating and loving the 4 card sounded like hating and loving some important other people, Robin interrupted me and supplied the name of the particular important person by abruptly exclaiming, "Oh! My mother!" His behavior shows that sometimes repression can be rather easily undone and contrasts with the difficulties he had had earlier in either returning to the starting point or in freely leaving it to understand what 4 backwards meant, which reveals how difficult cognitive repressions—more accurately, an unself-consciousness—can be to overcome. If the thrust from awareness occurs as the result of both a cognitive unself-consciousness and preconscious motives, it might be especially hard to overcome and to undo. Robin had struggled to master that reversibility required to understand his thoughts had begun somewhere and to consider simultaneously the two pre-conscious meanings of 4 backward. He was dimly aware that 4 backward meant both growing up (i.e., getting closer to one's destination) and growing down (i.e., returning to infancy). The supposition of a return to childish activity made it all the harder to master a return to the starting point in thinking because then he would be confronted with his central conflict. Because going backward suggested infantile helplessness, he wondered did he dare relinquish dependency and in its place risk competence to maintain his parents' affection?

LATER DEVELOPMENTS IN THERAPY

Temporary Discontinuation of Robin's Therapy

When Robin had been in therapy for a year, his mother decided to stop his visits because his behavior at school and at home had improved. She also decided to move out of the immediate area in which she and Robin and Robin's father lived, in the hope that fewer contacts between herself and Robin's father would reduce the impact of their disagreements on Robin. But to Robin, the move meant that he would be prevented from knowing what went on between his parents. He was unhappy about his mother's decision to move because he did not want to move farther away geographically from his father and he wanted to continue therapy, which his mother said was unnecessary and im-possible because now they would have to travel for over an hour to get to my office. He was openly angry with his mother as she brought him for his last therapy visit; later, during the hour, he expressed anger at me for agreeing to stop his visits. (I agreed to his mother's plan of stopping Robin's visits with the condition that she bring Robin either to me or to another therapist closer to their new home if his symptoms recurred as the result of the school and home changes.) He pointed to the Sorry game piece I was using and said, "I hate you, you're dumb." A little later he said, "I'm mad at you, you're dumb, you're winning and I'm not." He once more used the Sorry game's piece to express affect about an important person (me) but, as we shall shortly see, he could now converse about symbolization directly.

Many themes were condensed in Robin's statements, "I'm mad at you, you're dumb," and "You're winning and I'm not" — statements which I thought were aimed at me as a person more than they were at my game piece, although Robin remained reluctant to admit it. First, he seemed to make a connection between his anger and my being dumb. And he seemed to make a second connection between winning at games and winning at battles with adults. He may have meant to liken my imagined win in the Sorry game with his mother's triumph in moving him away from his father and from therapy. Perhaps he even thought I agreed with his mother that his relationship with his father should be disrupted and that his therapy should be terminated. I told Robin: "You can hate me, and be angry at me, but I'm not dumb; there are no dumb people in this room." To this he answered, "I'm not angry at *you*, I'm angry at your [game] piece, you're going to 'sorry' me, and I don't want to say goodbye to you." I thanked him for explaining more thoroughly what he meant and said I knew he did not want to say goodbye, and that I knew he was angry he had to say goodbye. I also reminded him that in the game I was not in a position to "sorry" him (I had no game pieces in the "start" position which I could have exchanged with one of Robin's margin game pieces in order to send his game piece back to the start position).

In calling the person he was angry at dumb, I thought he implied that when he became angry the other person would seek to defend against anger by projecting a dumb act. This seemed plausible because I knew from previous conversations with Robin that it was the presumed anger of someone important to him that made him act dumb. For example, he said about his mother's anger, "I'm too dumb to know why she's angry!" So he assumed that when he was angry I must either be dumb or acting dumb in self-defense. A dumb person cannot know that the other person is angry, nor the reasons for it. And even if a dumb person is aware of reasons, the implication of mutism in the adjective *dumb* can render the dumb person speechless. In this interaction with me, he thus approached understanding one more reason for his dumb act and his anxiety about school attendance. He preferred to be thought of as dumb to protect himself from knowing the reasons for his mother's anger.

What Robin referred to in saying that I was going to sorry him is one more demonstration that the interpretation of symbol meanings does not discourage the child from future symbolic play. One meaning of the verb *sorry* in the game's context was that Robin thought I was going to make one of his game pieces return to "start." He might have been wishing that I return him to start—the beginning of his life when his parents were still together, or to the start of his therapy so that he could avoid ending it. He also probably meant to say that he would be sorry if I said goodbye to him. Finally, in his differentiation of his anger at me in the game (his anger at my game piece) from his anger at me as a person, he articulated the difference between the "signifier" (the game piece) and the "significate" (me). Although this differentiation may have been set in motion by his need to restrict his anger at me to the context of the game— because being angry at me as a person was still too dangerous, it was a clear demonstration of Robin's developing skill at using symbols—symbols he very much needed because a direct expression of anger as he was about to leave therapy was quite unsafe.

Resumption of Robin's Therapy

Robin's therapy was interrupted for 8 weeks, a short-lived termination which his mother soon recognized was premature. As she returned Robin to therapy, it became clear that his recent move to a new home meant, first, that he had to give up one of his teachers who had become a trusted friend (his male gym teacher); and second, it aroused anxieties associated with separation from his mother, and now from his father as well, who lived farther away and who saw him only rarely. It was as if the old anxiety which meant being in school is being away from mother transmuted into: because I'm now in a new school, I'm farther away from both mother *and* father, and things are even worse than they were before. In school, Robin became distraught about "losing" his father, blamed the loss on his mother whom he accused of not being his mother at all, which was illustrated by his repeated statement: "I have no mommy." In saying of his mother "she's not my mommy" Robin tied his fate once more to his father's, since he well knew that she was not his father's wife anymore. He reasoned, If I am like my father who has no wife, in that likeness I have no mother.

Robin's statement "I have no mommy" was viewed by his parents and new teacher to be a symptom of childhood schizophrenia (a loss of contact with reality) when it represented the faulty logic inherent in his view that he would suffer the same fate as his father. Although schizophrenics often reason this way, immature or faulty reasoning is not always a symptom or the only symptom of the disorder. For us to mistake faulty or immature logic for a "thought disorder" represents transductive thinking. In many cases atypical reasoning accompanies severe psychopathology; but in other cases, especially in children, it represents simply an immature thought level or delayed thought development. In the latter case, the therapist ought to attend to how the child's mind has reasoned rather than try to bring about a return to reality.

Since it seemed to me that Robin was reacting to an accurately perceived reality which recently had changed drastically, I told him that although his father had no wife, he had a mommy with whom he must be very angry, since she did not let him see his father. To this he said, looking straight at my face in the first direct gaze that day: "Why did I always play 'Sorry' here, what do I have to be sorry about?" Now he attributed conscious significance to the Sorry game. Where before he had been preoccupied by fantasies of parental reconciliation, his new question to me revealed that he had assumed he was to blame for his parents' separation. He had reorganized previous therapeutic conversations and arrived at the hypothesis that he had earlier taken his parents' problems as his own and felt he must have done something for which he was very sorry. It also seemed to me that he was sorry for his ongoing anger at his parents and might have confused his anger at them *after* they separated with his anger at them *before* they separated. Because parental separation had aroused anger in Robin, he might have concluded it was this anger that led to their separation, a plausible conclusion since he had witnessed how angry his parents had been at each other before their separation. Robin may have thought that because the anger his parents had experienced before their separation had caused it, his own anger could have caused their separation whether his angry feelings occurred before or after it, especially the anger directly connected to the separation.

During Robin's final 6 months of therapy, he was able to ask himself questions and give himself answers. He continued with the theme of "What do I have to be sorry about?" and said: "What *was* I sorry about. I didn't do anything to you. What were *you* sorry about? You didn't do anything to me." With these statements he revealed he could disconnect himself and his interactions with me from the interactions he observed between his parents. Although he guessed his parents were still sorry about their failed relationship, he now knew he and I had a different relationship, one about which we were not sorry. Now he implied he did not feel sorry (i.e., blameworthy) about his parents' divorce and he no longer tried through playing the Sorry game to make me feel sorry for his parents' divorce. In his own words, he stated he had worked through the transference of family problems to therapy.

He soon added to these statements the following comment: "Remember when I couldn't remember the two ones in eleven. . . that's because they always won!" He began to laugh about his pun on the number 1 and the verb won. When I asked him to explain his pun, he said, "Higher ones always win out over lower ones." He seemed to say that the two 1s of 11, or "wons," would win out over lower ones—the number 1 which has less value. His explanation suggested that as angry as he had been in blaming his mother for his parents' separation and divorce, he was also angry at his father for going along with it. He had been angry at his two parents—those two 1s who won against him, the one 1—as they decided to separate and later to divorce.

Remembering in Therapy and Increased Self-Understanding

Early in Robin's treatment, his behavior and statements reflected either the absence of or only partially developed concepts and cognitive structures. He had neither denied his parents' separation nor repressed affect associated with it; it was his very awareness of the separation which produced his symptoms. His immature reasoning told him that if his father had been rejected by his mother, then he also would. But in his 14th month of therapy (when he returned after a 2-month hiatus), Robin gave evidence of having repressed and evidence that he understood that repression (or "forgetting") was part of his experience. As he struggled to understand why he had been brought back to therapy, he said: "Sometimes I have been forgetting things." When asked what things in particular, he said, "Like how to play games, the things I *learned* here." Similar to Tim (see Chapter 4) he seemed to say that what enabled him to learn in school was his learning in therapy. He seemed to say he knew from his therapy experience that he was capable of learning in school because he was capable of learning in therapy. But now, he was afraid the therapeutic impact had been lost as he complained that he had been forgetting what he had learned with me.

I told Robin he would eventually remember what he had learned, that all of a sudden those things he forgot would come into his head again. He sighed in relief and began to talk of an impending trip to see his paternal grandmother. But, in his telling of this anticipated event, he once more forgot. In forgetting that his father would be accompanying him, he became anxious that he was to travel by himself on the train to meet his grandmother. In later conversation with Robin's mother about the trip, it became clear that indeed Robin was to be accompanied by his father, although Robin had asked to make the trip alone. As he listened to what his mother told me, Robin suddenly exclaimed, "See what I mean, I forgot again!"

Robin's request to make the trip alone and his later forgetting his father was to accompany him might represent a shift in affect regarding his father about whom he had recently experienced increased ambivalence. In an interesting paper on momentary forgetting, Luborsky (1967) described some instances of this phenomenon in his work with adults. Sometimes the patient recaptured the forgotten thought and sometimes not. In reviewing his data, Luborsky attempted to establish connections between the forgotten thought and other themes in the associations of his patients. Of interest for my purposes was the frequency with which momentary forgetting centered on the Oedipal triad or themes which revealed that the patient was about to adopt a new attitude or behavior. Similarly, Robin expressed feelings about the Oedipal same gender parent as he forgot, and it seemed to me that, as he forgot, he was about to experiment with new behavior. It felt safe for Robin to reconsider his Oedipal experience and to become angry at his father because he now knew his mother would not leave him. He knew she would not leave him because she *did not* leave when he started to learn in school. Convinced that his mother would stay with him, he could imagine getting angry at his father. Feeling safe in his anger at his father in what had been until very recently an unresolved Oedipal situation led Robin to forget his father as he momentarily wished to dispose of this parent by imagining his absence on the train trip. Then, Robin probably got in touch with his positive feelings for his father, and the heightened ambivalence which ensued the next moment might have made him wish to get rid of the whole complex of thoughts and feelings.

But just as Robin could have reexperienced a more intense Oedipal complex, he might have felt increasingly sure of a resolution. The thought that his father would accompany him on the train was forgotten because as Robin felt increasingly safe in his mother's presence, he felt increasingly safe imagining his father's absence. "Knowing where his mother was"—that she was psychologically "with" him—permitted him to feel safe *both* in his father's presence and in his imagined absence: he might someday become independent of his father as his father recently appeared to become independent of his mother. Robin told me, for example, that "Dad's not so upset" about living "farther away" from his mother because he had a "new [girl]friend." Robin's forgetting was thus the result of an attempted change—he could imagine himself being independent like his father. Robin's statement that he had forgotten what he once knew also revealed he had become aware of his momentary forgetting. The attempt to remember something one once knew probably supports a self-reflexive sense. The child asks himself: "How can I not know something I used to know?" Understanding and the recovery of forgotten material seemed connected in Robin's mind with learning in some instances and not having "really" learned in others—his central problem. Once again, he seemed to say that his experience of therapy was a matter of using or not using his head.

AN OVERVIEW OF ROBIN'S THERAPEUTIC PROGRESS

Once Robin began to progress in therapy, each statement I made to him about the activity of knowing built on previous statements. As he expressed his conflicts about his parents in his revealing confusion of the numbers 5 and 11, I focused on what he knew of numbers and his parents in speaking of his age (5 years) when his parents were together. The activity of knowing was part of my statement to him that his cheating required the use of his head. And finally, when I told Robin that there were no "dumb" people in my office, he heard me say what he had already understood—since both boys (Robin) and girls (me) were people, we were both smart. When he later said, "What was I sorry about?" he self-consciously questioned previous thoughts and feelings. He expressed that he now knew he had felt guilty before about having "done something" and, in a moment of self-reflexive awareness, decided that this thought was wrong. His thinking about his own previous thoughts liberated him from feelings of guilt and anxiety connected to his parents' separation.

Robin's beginning attempts to think about his own thoughts should not be confused with the adolescent's "thinking about thinking" (Inhelder & Piaget, 1958, p. 340). Although on occasion a bright child like Robin might question previous thoughts, this self-questioning is not the same as the intricate logico-mathematical thought systems the formal operational adolescent is capable of constructing. Self-questioning especially in an interpersonal context might nonetheless be a latency-aged forerunner of the adolescent's abstract (formal) thought. About Robin we can say that he questioned his earlier opinion that he had caused his parents to separate because he knew I did not share his opinion; that is, he had decentered to the degree that he caught the discrepancy between his and my judgments. The decentered individual who is open to opinion and judgment discrepancies between himself and others undoubtedly would be more educable. The pedagogy that Dewey and Piaget espouse would promote the development of rational thought by progressively elaborating what the child already knows to what is known by society. On the topic of socialization and operational thought, Piaget (1971) observed that

> this general coordination of the actions [which constitute logic] necessarily includes a social dimension, since the inter-individual coordination of actions and their intra-individual coordination constitute a single and identical process, the individual's operations all being socialized, and cooperation in its strict sense consisting in a pooling of each individual's operations. (p. 71)

By this statement I understand Piaget to mean that since individual and interpersonal cognitive adaptations arise from the same processes, the individual is open to education when he willingly replicates and extends his internal coordination of actions by adapting to the internal coordinations of others. Writing about the lengthy psychological course in which the young child's symbolic thought becomes socialized, and continuously emphasizing the importance of the child's symbolic thought which is what makes us human, Furth (1987) remarked that symbolic knowledge is at first "I-want-my-object" knowledge and will remain so for many years to come until the "I" is sufficiently socialized to incorporate the desires and viewpoints of others into itself. When adults use what Piaget calls operations, it is no longer the single "I" who acts but the social "I" (Piaget's "epistemic" subject), who as participant of the group has identified with the knowledge regulations binding on all humans. (pp. 126–127)

Earlier, Robin had exercised his will to avoid knowing; it might be said that he took the easy way out as he left the classroom and wandered about. But like Timothy, he soon tried to exercise his will in very different ways: he tried to know and not to know at the same time. Cheating at games was seen by Robin as a way of finding out but not revealing what he understood. But gaining one's goals by not thinking fed Robin's insecurities in regard to his intelligence. He felt he had come upon knowledge as he began to be sure that he knew certain facts and feelings, which as a person he was still not supposed to know. The knowing process itself still seemed forbidden to him in his particular family constellation. Knowledge seemed forbidden to Robin because his mother had moved him away from his father which seemed to prevent his knowing about their continuing disagreements.

In Robin's case, what knit the will to learn in school with his enhanced awareness of self (he had "learned" about himself in therapy) was the connection he perceived between his intent and the results of his behavior based on that intent. With more developed concepts and cognitive structures, he had a fair idea that the consequences of his behavior were somehow related to his intent. His learning attempts in therapy could then be reproduced willingly because he understood which cause led to what effect. He could distinguish between those events he had brought about and those he had had no part in. As he understood he had learned to do his homework but he had *not* brought about his parents' separation, he became symptom-free. And, as he left therapy for the last time, he gave voice to self-reflexive awareness in saying, "I wonder why I am not playing Sorry anymore?" When he was told, "Maybe it's because you're not sorry anymore," Robin smiled and went about building a complex structure with blocks which had many paths for marbles, as he put it, "to gain momentum to get where they want." Although he may have attributed intention to the marbles, he may have also meant to distinguish between inanimate and animate bodies. He may have meant to *liken* the marbles' momentum with his own momentum as he, for example, raced down a street. Momentum and marbles may have stood for wishes and people, who by understanding their motives "get where they want." Because he no longer inhibited his intent (he no longer felt "sorry" about the gaining of his objectives) he could make an analogy between the marbles' getting "where they want" and his own goals which increasingly included school learning.

If he was making precise distinctions and sophisticated analogies, Robin showed that he had successfully overcome a difficult transitional phase in which he relinquished prelogical thought, adapted to the logic of concrete operations, and readied himself for the abstract thought of preadolescence. His progress in therapy illustrates the substantial cognitive shifts that occur in young children who receive long-term intervention which is aimed at the thought contradictions which often accompany cognitive immaturity. As the case narrative of Maisie which follows demonstrates, a positive therapeutic outcome can be produced with prelogical children in short-term psycho-therapy. But the therapist will not witness the sturdy cognitive changes in very young, short-term patients that he or she is likely to perceive in slightly older long-term child patients when their therapy is geared to facilitating cognitive development as much as it is geared to resolving affective conflicts.

MAISIE AND WHAT SHE KNEW

Presenting Problem

Maisie was a beautiful, graceful, 4½-year-old girl with a winning smile and bright, sparkling eyes. She often displayed a comical streak that was remarkable in such a young child. Maisie found both a startling contradiction and an escape route in "hearing" the little word "no" in the very different word "know." The *no* in *knowing* signified to her that negation was the same as apprehension. Like Caroline and Robin, she was afraid of growing up and associated the growing up process with the beginning of kindergarten. When she became anxious about kindergarten, she became even more convinced that knowing represented the act of saying no ("no-ing").

Before her mother brought her to see me, she told me that Maisie repeatedly "shook her head" when faced with the expectation that she attend school or when she was asked what she had learned in school. Her mother focused on one particular incident when Maisie shook her head no defiantly as she said to her mother, "I know the ABC's." To fortify her escape attempts which had begun with "no-ing," she began to assert that she could not learn because she always forgot. For example, when asked by her mother, "What did you do in school today?", Maisie habitually said, "I forgot," and walked away. "Forget-ting" like "no-ing" became Maisie's chosen escape from kindergarten because she knew her teacher and her parents were monitoring her progress during the nursery school's summer program—one purpose of which was to decide which youngsters were "ready" for kindergarten and which of them were potentially "learning disabled." As Maisie became increasingly convinced she had no memory and her dread of autumn's approach and the beginning of school increased, her nursery school teacher noticed a sudden and marked regressive trend in her behavior and concluded that Maisie was too immature for kindergarten. Thus, Maisie's symptoms can be thought of as a school phobia in the making.

Maisie's parents, who had separated but were not yet divorced, disagreed with each other about their daughter's readiness for school learning. Her father, a high-achieving professional, believed she was as intelligent and ready for learning as her brilliant older brother, but her mother, also a professional, felt that Maisie needed "time to grow up" before school learning began. As a compromise to differing adult opinions, Maisie settled on the solution of having "no memory," which in her thinking was identical to having no mind. Thus, she avoided making up her mind with whom she agreed.

What Maisie actually tried to accomplish was to please both parents. In her assertion that she had no memory (mind), she only seemed to satisfy her mother's wish to delay her admission to kindergarten. The notion that she had no memory or mind with which to learn meant she was not really defying her father's ambitious push for academic learning. As the summer wore on and her dread of kindergarten reached a high pitch, Maisie took on a "hypochondriacal" attitude toward every small scratch or stomachache.

Early Treatment Progress

During her first hour with me, Maisie revealed promising cognitive functioning. At the age of 4 years, 9 months, she understood two out of four tasks of concrete operations (tasks typically understood by children who were two or more years older). Maisie also revealed a receptivity to a different way of thinking when, during her second appointment, she immediately understood an interpretive statement and applied to to everyday life. She told me how scared she was about every little scratch or stomachache and revealed that when she got sick she was taken care of by her father, who was a doctor. I then told her that all the aches and pains just meant she wanted her Dad. After this appointment, both parents soon reported a dramatic cessation of hypochondriacal complaints.

Although a decision had not yet been made about the school matter, the very next session Maisie announced with confidence, "I'm going to kindergarten in the fall." It thus seemed that the two symptoms of hypochondriasis and infantilism were related. She felt she had to be sick to keep her father's attention and had to be a baby to assure her mother's continued caring. To Maisie, growing up meant losing her parents. It meant her mother, who favored her remaining in nursery school for one more year, would no longer take care of her (and in order to remain in nursery school, Maisie knew she had to remain a baby). It also meant her father would no longer attend to her because growing up was synonymous with either never getting sick (and never having her father take care of her), or having to stoically suffer illness in uncared-for silence. I felt that a recommendation of another year in nursery school would escalate the intensity of the family myth, which to Maisie meant that kindergarten attendance implied instant maturity and that avoidance of kindergarten implied retaining babyhood. Since Maisie's teacher had felt that Maisie was ready for kindergarten before the sudden regression in her behavior, I recommended that Maisie enter the kindergarten of a school where academic expectations were geared to the child's individual socioemotional needs as well as to their cognitive capabilities. Fortunately, there was such a school in the region where Maisie lived.

Knowing and Remembering

As Maisie entered kindergarten, issues of knowing permeated our therapeutic work. Her complaints that she had "no memory" increased as she was
taken by her mother to school. When asked about this statement during her
appointment with me, she replied, "I can't think." She was told it was interesting that she said she could not think just as she entered kindergarten. Playing
with a battery operated toy ("Draw Poker"), which flips various numbered
cards on a display, she then named each number correctly. I told her she was
showing me that when she wanted to she could think and remember. Maisie
continued playing and behaved as if she had not heard.

Soon after, she began to play with Playdoh, and made a "pretend" hamburger, which led to the elaborate drama of a restaurant where I was the cus-
tomer and she the waitress. She seemed to be saying by her play that she would
like to serve me because I had served her in remarking she had a functional
brain which could remember and think. As though to signal that she still
needed me to serve her, especially in those situations at home in which she
often felt she could not remember or think, she asked if she could take the
Playdoh hamburger home with her, to which I assented, and requested that she
remember to do so by herself. As the time with me drew to a close, Maisie left
the restaurant play and went on to make supper for the dollhouse babies. When
her mother came to get her, she forgot to take the hamburger with her, thus once
more expressing her conviction—and wish—that she had no memory (mind).

As I was cleaning up from her play, Maisie and her mother returned for the
forgotten hamburger. When she saw I had stuffed it back into the Playdoh
container, she started to cry, feeling betrayed since I had made a big point
during her session that she could well remember when she wanted to. As I
remade the hamburger for her, she stopped crying, grabbed it out of my hands,
and left hurriedly.

What was doubtless an error in judgment, my not preserving the Playdoh
hamburger in anticipation that Maisie would return to my office for it, actually
created a second occasion for me to help her. As I remade the hamburger, I
hoped she understood a serious effort was underway to show that her memory
was functional when she wanted it to be. Whether she realized it or not, certainly it was significant that she had remembered the forgotten hamburger
while returning home in the car. My reforming the hamburger as well as her
mother's cooperation in returning Maisie to my office, perhaps proved to her
that we both appreciated her when she chose to remember, which implied that
we approved of her using her mind. Moreover, I may have seemed able and
willing to undo a piece of "forgetting" since I remade the Playdoh hamburger
which in Maisie's view I had seemed to forget to keep for her. Because the past
was brought into the present with relative ease by making a Playdoh hamburger, Maisie may have felt she could undo memory lapses just as easily
should they occur.

Five days later, Maisie asked me with a puzzled but curious look: "Is one
hundred the last number?" I told her: "For every number you can always think

of the next one." Smiling with interest, she said, "You mean one hundred and one?" Then she asked, "What about one hundred and ten?" When I waited for some seconds, she answered herself: "Oh yeah, there's always one hundred and eleven." As she left the office, I told her that there was a name for what we had been talking about. When she asked what I meant, I told her that the word was *infinity*, which means setting no limits on anything, such as numbers. I meant to suggest that she need not set limits on learning and knowing about numbers, or any other subject. Prancing out to greet her mother, she said, "I just learned a hard word, infinity, that's when there's always another number."

A conversation I had with Maisie's teacher after 4 months of therapy, and 2 months of kindergarten, revealed that Maisie had made an excellent social adjustment and an adequate academic adjustment to school. At about the same time, Maisie told me in more detail what she meant by having no memory, making another direct connection between having no memory and having no mind. She came to her session pretending not to know something which she had known the last appointment, namely, how to write the numbers from 1 to 10 correctly, and in a correct left-to-right sequence. When I began to playact stupidity as we played a game (I said, "Maybe I don't know this game"), she was delighted, laughed, and jumped up to erase the numbers she had written backward on the blackboard. Then she rewrote the numbers from 1 through 10 frontward and in correct left-to-right sequence.

As Maisie returned to play the game, she told me: "Shake your head all up." To this I wondered aloud if she fixed it so that she had no memory by confusing herself with a shook-up head? She nodded yes, and demanded again that I shake my head all up, which I did, and indeed it produced a sense of confusion in me. I said that must mean there was something I did not want myself to know. She smiled and told how shaking her head all up "made" her write the numbers backward. She said that writing numbers backward made her not want to go to school. When she said that her own behavior made her feel a certain way (i.e., it created an effect) she appeared to be giving magical significance to her writing backward behavior which gave her a reason for not wanting to go to school. It seemed to me she was saying her incompetent performance made her decide not to want to go to school. Deliberately writing backward, therefore, proved to Maisie that she did not want to attend kindergarten because she could not do the work properly.

She then showed me how shaking her head all up worked for her. As she shook her head, it became clear she combined a shaking of the head for yes with a shaking of the head for no, an acted-out ambivalence about knowing which had confused her. As she continued to shake her head all up before me as her audience, the head-shake of no stood out more clearly. It then became apparent that she was saying no to "know" by an increasingly vehement body-statement—that is, she was responding to the auditory identity of these two words—a reasonable association since she could at the age of 5 only hear and not spell the words *no* and *know*. But as she became more sure of the no in her ambivalent head-shake, the yes to know became ever more possible. Even though her head-shakes had been statements of no because they were those events which "made" her write backward, or by which she expressed her wish to avoid school, a yes could be seen in the events which followed. The subtle changes in her head-shakes which represented a move from no to yes once more reveals why behavioral observation is so critical in work with children.

When I asked Maisie if she was saying no to knowing the numbers, she nodded yes, said "*and* the ABC's," and again jumped up to use the blackboard. She wrote the numbers 1 through 10, but this time the numbers were all written backward and in an incorrect right-to-left sequence with an added illegibility which suggested a small child's scribbling. As I waited to see what she would do next, she said, "That's what I used to do in nursery school, but now I don't anymore." To this I said that now she knows how to write the numbers but knowing the numbers is different from saying no to them. Then, she erased the illegible and backward numbers and proceeded to write them correctly, but still in a right-to-left sequence. Again I waited and she explained, "I do it this way because backward is easier than forward." In saying so, she revealed that she knew precisely what she was doing; that she wrote numbers in a backward right-to-left sequence for some as yet unstated purpose. It also revealed an awareness that writing backward can be accomplished in two ways: in regard to the direction of the numerical sequence, or in regard to the individual number. I congratulated her on the good use of her mind in being able to accurately describe her behavior of which she was conspicuously aware, and asked what reason she had for thinking that going backward was simpler. She replied, "Easy! That way I can see the number I just wrote." And she was quite right. Since she was lefthanded, writing from right to left permitted her to check what she had just written. Writing this way ensured that she did not shield what she wrote with her left hand as one often does if lefthanded and writing in the typical order. She smiled proudly as I praised her ability to articulate her entirely valid observation—a cognitive success since behavior and language were accurate and in tune.

Cognitive Monitoring

Maisie's second experience with interviewing 3 months after her first cognitive interview showed by her choice of language that she literally did not want adults to see how intelligent she was. For example, when asked the classification question "More boys or more people?", she told me to close my eyes before she would answer. As I did so, she answered correctly, silently counting the number of people, and then said, "There are seven people, more people than boys." Her specification that I close my eyes expressed remaining ambivalence about others knowing how intelligent she was, perhaps the core reason for her dreading kindergarten. The request that I close my eyes might also have represented some fleeting intuition that one need only imagine the boy and girl dolls to answer the "more boys or more people" question; that is, as an adult I would not have to see the dolls to be able to answer or to check her answer, whereas as a child she might need these visual or tactile props. If so, her request that I shut my eyes was concealing but also revealing of her intelligence. In this way, I could only hear and not see how smart she was at the same time she showed she approached understanding that thinking logically suffices to answer a classification problem.

When later she explained she felt she "must" give some of the cookies I had given her to her "smart" older brother, it appeared she might have felt not only must she suppress awareness of her intelligence, but she must as well keep her intelligence a secret from her brother, lest he become jealous and retaliate. When asked, "Why can't there be two smart kids in your family?", Maisie decided against relinquishing any of her cookies. Thus, it seemed that presenting a cookie to her brother was appeasement for her challenge to his role in the family as the only smart child.

Conclusion of Therapy

After 6 months of therapy, Maisie had progressed so well in school and at home that her parents and I felt therapy was no longer necessary. She had shed both the infantile behavior and the hypochondriacal complaints. What helped Maisie learn to attend and to *enjoy* kindergarten was knowing that her behavior, even if "backward" reflected ingenuity and intelligent purpose. Since she suffered no negative consequences from using her mind in growing up (both parents continued to take care of her and were proud of her achievements) she could more deliberately and "willfully" exercise her intelligence in the age-appropriate task of mastering the kindergarten curriculum. Some years later, I learned that Maisie had won a music scholarship to a performing arts school.

SCHOOL ESCAPE ATTEMPTS AND DEVELOPMENTAL LEVELS

At the beginning of this chapter, I stated that what characterizes the school phobic youngsters whom I treat is their awareness of thought contradictions. But this awareness varies with developmental level and the self-reflexive sense. In my opinion, the self-reflective function possessed by children younger than approximately 7 or 8 is first intuitive and only gradually conceptual when it is then subject to the inner cognitive coordinations which correspond to those typical of concrete operations and later of formal operations. The early self-reflexive sense is often blurred with the perceived selves of other people or even with objects (things), symbols, and animals (pets). The differences in the ways school phobic young people perceive their thought contradictions and try to resolve them can be most clearly illustrated by comparing the symptoms and treatment progress of 17-year-old Caroline and almost 5-year-old Maisie. Their different abilities to understand and resolve thought contradictions resulted from their dissimilar abilities to reflect on the self's qualities (i.e., the intentions and motives which through action modify the environment). Thus, the differences in the school phobic youngsters I have known reside in varying levels of self-reflexive awareness, whereas the similarities among them reside in their tendency to confront ambiguity and to use the therapeutic encounter to get behind and move beyond thought contradictions.

It is important for the clinician to consider that the "taking of consciousness" (Bringuier, 1980, p. 45; Piaget, 1985) strengthens the child's identity. Events that hold potential for expanding selfhood are likely to occur during transitional phases, particularly those transitional moments which occur during adolescence. Seventeen-year-old Caroline, for example, became finely attuned to her motives as she contrasted what *she* did to make therapy work for her with what *she* did to make college unworkable for her. Her spontaneous activity in testing my intelligence made therapy work for her because, unlike her teachers, I invited her to share with me her logical puzzles at the same time that I admitted to not knowing all the answers. Essentially, Caroline and I were working on the two facts that she knew something I did not know (many of the answers to her conundrums) whereas I knew something she did not know (that she needed to feel both intelligent and protected). Her self-reflexive understanding which became more acute as we conversed helped her understand better what we both knew and that our differing perspectives did not mean we were working at cross purposes. Because she perceived that we had different areas of expertise, she could feel intelligent and deserving of protection. When she accepted my statement that she deserved protection from me, she no longer felt compelled to protect herself by doing the "stupid thing of cutting classes" to avoid undergraduate scholarship.

In the account of Maisie, I speculate that she initially thought the causes of her behavior were determined solely by her environment. By "environment" I include, in Maisie's case, specifics of her own behavior which she often saw as outside herself and as "making" her avoid school. I am referring to her statement that writing the numbers backward made her not want to go to school. In reality, writing the numbers backward *did* make her teacher think she was not ready for kindergarten. Thereupon Maisie became even more confused and convinced that her motives coincided with her teacher's opinions and actions. Furthermore, she probably thought words like *no* or *know* just existed, similar to Timothy who originally thought that words were given by an outside force or simply inhered in the world or society. To Tim it was only numbers that were "made up" by people. Because Maisie could not spell, she did not perceive that it was *she* who "heard" the *no* in *know* or in *knowing* or, therefore, that it was *she* who identified apprehension with negation. Even if she could spell, she probably would not have realized that it was *she* who perceived the *no* in *knowing*—although she might have eventually questioned her assumption that *no* is the same as *know* if she perceived that the word *no* has fewer and different letters than the word *know*. Caroline, on the other hand, knew that it was *she* who was attributing psychological meaning to her arguing with me. Her sense of self had developed sufficiently for her to catalog of what it consisted and to permit her to experience and understand at a moment's notice what she was contributing to an interaction and what I was contributing—or, more importantly—to understand that human interactions consist of communications between two distinct people even if she did not experience shared, respectful communications in some instances. It might be said, then, that in the experience of older children and adolescents in therapy, transitional phases in thinking are to cognitive psychology what preconscious affectivity is to psychoanalysis. When they become certain and insightful instead of doubtful and forgetful, they experience a heightened sense of their individuality.

However, Maisie could gain insight within an interpersonal interaction. She could intuit as she watched me "shake my head all up" that her perception of the *no* in *knowing* was not given by the environment or by some outside force but arose from an individual's behavior. She could intuit this because, for once, she was *not* confusing herself by this behavior but only watching me. Probably because individuals cannot fully observe themselves behaving unless they observe themselves in a mirror or in a film, Maisie concluded that the confusion she experienced came from the outside when she shook her head all up. Being not quite 5, she could not yet *conceptualize* what her behavior was and meant. Watching me suggested to her that the no she attributed to knowing originates in a person, in this case, me. She might have been open to the suggestion that a yes could be said to knowing because after I shook my head, I continued to behave intelligently and did not, as she had done in the past, use my momentary confusion to avoid learning, thinking, and "knowing" about her: I understood her motive for writing numbers backward. This might have meant that when *she* shook her head all up a different decision regarding knowing could emanate from her. Piaget and Inhelder's (1969) observation that egocentrism is most fully and finally relinquished around social interactions (p. 129) is once more pertinent to explain the startling progress Maisie made in one session. Certainly, Maisie did not fully surrender her egocentric attitude at barely 5 years. But she made significant progress in understanding herself as the result of observing me. Since therapeutic dialogues are often intense and highly focused, the effects of social interaction on the thought processes of children as young as Maisie can be observed.

Robin at ages 6 and 7 was somewhere in between Maisie and Caroline in self-development. Even though Maisie made amazingly rapidly progress in therapy, her thinking did not span two developmental levels as Robin's did (he was transitional when he began therapy and concrete operational 6 months later). Because of significant shifts in his ability to conceptualize problems, his progress highlights both his developing self-reflexive sense and his increasing ingenuity to resolve his thought contradictions. I am referring to the progress Robin made in self-reflexive awareness from the occasion he confused the numbers 5 and 11 to two subsequent occasions: (1) when he understood the symbolic significance of the Sorry card 4, and (2) when he differentiated a game piece (a symbol or "signifier") from that to which it referred (the "significate") at the *same* time he may have expressed his feelings about me by directing them at my game piece ("I'm not angry at *you*, I'm angry at your [game] piece"). As noted before, when he transposed 5 and 11, he did so matter-of-factly as though it was a most reasonable manipulation of these numbers. From his perspective it was indeed! Repeated use of symbols and conversing with me about them had a gradual impact on his thought processes and on his sense of self. Then, while making fun simultaneously he could deliberately express ambivalence about his mother by saying he "hated" and "loved" the same symbol (the 4 card). The final step in his symbol development was his talking directly about symbolization which he did when he said he was not mad at me but only at my game piece and implied that a thing could stand for (signify) a person.

As impressive as these developments were, Robin still displayed a fluctuating self-reflexive awareness and it was unclear the degree to which he perceived other people as being self-reflexive. He probably did not fully or comfortably understand that he was a "subject" among many who possessed self-consciousness. His fluctuating understanding that it was he who created symbols can be seen in his switch in the same sentence from articulating that he was not mad at me, only my game piece, to slipping into a confusion about our use of the word *sorry* ("You're going to 'sorry' me and I don't want to say goodbye to you"). When he said he thought I was going to "sorry" him he used the word *sorry* as a threatening verb and blended it with his statement that he did not want to say goodbye to me. Since his mother threatened him by moving him away from his father and by terminating his therapy with me, he thought I, too, would threaten him which would make him feel "sorry." He thus went from a clear separation of "signifier" and "significate" to a blurring of the uses of *sorry* as a verb in the game with feeling sorry in reality to, finally, a genuine confusion of a game's event with an anticipation of a separation in reality. He thought I might put him at a disadvantage in the game while I said goodbye to him in reality. He did not know he was the originator of these complex free associations.

But 8 months later, he thoughtfully considered his own behavior as he asked himself, "What did I have to be sorry about"—a self-questioning which suggested he understood his transformation of the word *sorry* into a verb represented his feeling that he had been made to feel sorry (he was "sorried") by other people. And, his question, "What did *you* have to be 'sorry' about?" implied he understood another person, like him, experiences both affect and awareness of affect. It can be said, then, that latency-aged children in therapy can better conceptualize and articulate a self-reflexive sense but their ability to do so is not as stable as that of preadolescents or adolescents. Furthermore, the self-reflexive sense vacillates especially when they try to coordinate their sense of themselves with the idea that significant other people are also unique. Because he was not always able to conceptualize and articulate the difference between the way his mother made him feel and the way he expected me to behave toward him (i.e., his mother transference), Robin confused his mother's intentions in withdrawing him from therapy with mine in playing the Sorry game. Differentiating his mother from me, thinking about his own feelings, and tracking down their origins was a difficult task for him which he nonetheless undertook with varying degrees of success.

Maisie did not attempt the complex task in therapy that Robin did. When she could not understand what originated in herself, or that both she and the other person had distinct selves, she simply denied or ignored that it was she who had originated something (e.g., the confusion resulting from her head-shakes) or she blurred her identity with others (she confused her teacher's opinions and actions with her own behavior). Contrarily, Robin was more likely to struggle openly and repeatedly with his self-concept. He did not blur his identity with mine or with his mother's (although he did blur his identity with his father's). Later, in therapy, in order to resolve problems, he took account of rather than denied or ignored many more "easily observable features" of them than Maisie did. Caroline did not blur, deny, or ignore. She only argued for her case against mine, and by proxy, her mother's. She did not confuse me with her mother or my opinions with her mother's; rather, she believed that if she could argue a point convincingly with me, she could do so with her mother. Although her arguing may originally have been set in motion to differentiate herself more thoroughly from me (as she might have wanted to differentiate herself more clearly from her mother), her working toward this goal could only have oc-curred had she felt a basic, unquestioned interpersonal distinction from me. She most wanted to assert that in addition to her identity her *views* were differ-ent from mine in an attempt to define two important aspects of herself: her intelligence and her right to be protected. Older children and adolescents seek to strengthen particular aspects of a well-conceptualized self by opposing others which, in a sense, is a form of self-practice.

Although the school phobic youngster tries to escape school in order to escape anxiety associated with thought contradictions, he or she embraces psychotherapy because it provides a safe arena to resolve them, including those inherent in defining the self. If school appeared safe to these youngsters and the curriculum permitted it, they would probably behave similarly in school: the young person's spontaneous associations between his own life experiences and the learning process are potentially educative. Undoubtedly for this reason Dewey (1956, 1963) believed that the curriculum ought to enhance the natural relationship between life-outside-school and life-in-school—the link between "experience" and "education." But today's children often remain confused because the curriculum does not bridge academic subjects and other life experi-ences. Because educators rarely notice that youngsters tend to switch indis-criminately from one comprehending process to another, they do not prescribe a curriculum which attempts to disentangle the young person's often distorted, but reasonable, associations between his unique experiences and those experi-ences which are shared by others. The potential of shared experiences, which Dewey envisioned for education, lie in those particular social exchanges that constitute scientific inquiry.

Thus, it is important to note that, when they began to feel comfortable in school, Maisie, Robin, and Caroline all delighted in searching for problems to solve and eagerly communicated the results of their inquiries to their parents and teachers. Maisie made words out of letters (be for *b* and why for *y*) and pondered aloud, her mother reported, whether "people make up some letters to sound like words on purpose." Robin became fascinated by synonyms, homo-nyms, and antonyms and spent hours working riddles or puzzles which re-quire the child to compare and contrast semantically similar words, aurally similar words, and "opposite" words. Caroline was deeply absorbed in Dewey's works before she graduated from college, especially his critique of "either-or" educational philosophies. I interpreted their "problem-finding" (Arlin's, 1975, term) as an extension of their thought contradictions, one of which first puzzled and then amused all three youngsters when they realized that "learning" in therapy refuted their conviction that they could not learn in school. Getting behind and moving beyond this central thought contradiction enabled these three young people, to the delight of many of their teachers, to invent and solve problems in school with enthusiasm.

Cognition and Inhibition

Throughout previous chapters of this book my aim has been to highlight the connections the youngster makes between academic learning and other phenomena. I have attempted to show how the child often confuses learning school subjects with understanding other people. Especially important is that children often "learn" how their parents react to their academic advances. I have only just begun to propose that to a child remembering past events resembles making new discoveries. To a child it is often surprising when he understands he has forgotten something he once knew rather well. The reapprehension of the once-known fact or affective experience seems similar to the original apprehension. Then he tends to confound remembering in therapy with remembering in school. A success in therapeutic remembering often excites the child, and he hopes to replicate the success by remembering in school. Similarly, a failed attempt to remember in therapy sometimes convinces the child that he is incapable of remembering in school. Although they are different, both remembering in therapy and remembering in school are altered by his progress in the use of concepts. Thus, one important purpose of this chapter is to clarify how conceptual development might affect a young person's use in therapy of suppression and repression.

My interest in the immature and mature modes of repression is both similar and different from the psychoanalytic view. Psychoanalytic theory postulates that early repression, "passive primal repression," is different from "active primal repression" or "secondary repression" (Frank, 1969). If a young child unconsciously or preconciously screens out noxious inner and external stimuli before he has achieved a solid self-reflexive sense, the results of this repressing are different for him compared to the results of the type of repressing the more mature child experiences. In discussing Sigmund Freud's theory of the unconscious, in which he attempts to reconcile facets of Freud's theory with Piaget's, Furth (1987) identifies the Oedipal child's age of 6 as the developmental divide between the self-centered child who has yet to turn decisively toward the social group and away from his egocentric perspective and the more mature child who, having suffered a "most painful and humiliating personal [Oedipal] experience" (p. 58) has reason to repress. Consistent with Freud, Furth views the repression arising from the Oedipal resolution as "primal repression in relation to which all later repressions are mere secondary symptoms, a follow-up to the original repression" (p. 58). Most useful for my purposes, Furth stresses the *activity* of repression when he asks and answers a central question after noting that the ego and the id are not clearly separate in young children:

> Remember, this [repression] takes place at a period in children's lives when the ego and the id are not yet clearly separated, nor is the separation of unconscious and conscious activity well established. So what shall we say to the legitimate question: who is doing the repressing and who is doing the construction of the fantasies that are being repressed? The answer is obvious: *the children are doing it* [italics added]. This is not something that simply happens to the children the way the first teeth grow and subsequently fall out when the second push up. (p. 60)

Similarly, I consider even the infant's or toddler's attempts to ward off unpleasant or unfamiliar aspects of his experience active and not passive. Furthermore, my view of repression differs from the psychoanalytic view in that I differentiate the absence of a cognitive structure from a suppressed or denied cognitive structure. Fantasies, often repressed, are in part built around concepts, which implies that repression contains a cognitive component. A child conceptualizes to fantasize and she also conceptualizes to suppress and repress. Lastly, I track intellectual development as it relates to changes in modes of inhibition and to the undoing of inhibition. My view is that self-consciousness develops over the life span and so do modes of fighting self-consciousness.

TRANSITIONAL AWARENESS AND PRECONSCIOUS AWARENESS

The youngster's receptivity to interacting with his environment certainly influences his ability to learn. Happily engaged in learning, he becomes increasingly aware of what *he* knows and thus more self-aware. Self-awareness, in turn, reinforces learning attempts because when he recognizes the connection between his intent and the results he produces, his investigations can be replicated and elaborated. But these investigations do not always proceed smoothly. The individual is at risk because comprehension is often partial or because events critical to a full understanding have been submerged. Nonetheless, self-awareness helps the individual understand why and how a reach for knowledge can go wrong. As I noted in Chapter 7, inhibition of awareness can come about as the result of unequilibrated assimilations (Piaget) or as the result of the lid on instinctual drives (Freud). Thus, the reach for knowledge can go wrong because of immature and unself-conscious learning attempts (e.g., transductive reasoning) or it can go wrong because of warding off all or part of what was once intensely experienced or fully apprehended. The child's or adolescent's use of concepts invades all these "not knowing" experiences.

The problem of awareness and repression in children as contrasted with that in adults is often alluded to by Sigmund Freud. For example, Freud (1959b) writes in his account of "Little Hans" that to talk of the unconscious and repression as distinct from other presumably conscious processes is "attributing a great deal to the mental activity of a child between four and five years of age" (p. 276). However, the theory he outlines on the unconscious in adults is presumed by and large to apply to young people. So later in his account of "Hans," Freud writes that he believed little Hans knew only unconsciously, not consciously, where his newly born sister had come from (not from the stork, as Hans's father had attested). The question then becomes in which instances does Freud's theory hold true and in which it does not. In other words, in what situations and at which particular childhood age does the theory of the unconscious apply?

In Anna Freud (1974), who wrote much later, we read that compared to the unconscious in adults the unconscious in children is not entirely separate from consciousness (for instance, perhaps little Hans and other child patients like him might have had some unrepressed awareness of the origin of babies); or that it is often difficult to form a therapeutic alliance with the child because in his mind there is no division between the "split-off" pathological parts of his personality and a healthy and conscious part which might help the therapist help him (p. 11). Although these points illuminate a problem in understanding and assisting children, they do not address how a function which inhibits mental activity can be part of the child's psychological repertoire before he has yet to fully develop it. Perhaps for this reason Schafer (1983) calls child psychoanalysis "applied" (p. 129)—so many aims and procedures of the analyst must be compromised in work with the undeveloped child that it often appears to be unanalytic.

Piaget has presented his view of "the unconscious" in many of his writings (*Play, Dreams and Imitation in Childhood*, 1962; *The Child and Reality*, 1973b; "The Affective Unconscious and the Cognitive Unconscious," *Journal of the American Psychoanalytic Association*, 1973a). For him, instances of pure assimilations, many of which he has described in detail in *Play, Dreams and Imitation in Childhood*, are "the unconscious" because the egocentric young child is unaware of his behavior and motives as he explores reality. Piaget's contribution to a theory of unawareness consists, in part, of describing the unself-consciousness which stems from the child's failure to accommodate to reality and to decenter. Sometimes there are powerful, intrapsychic blocks to accommodating and to decentering. In my view, events that surround the important people or objects (things) of the child's world with which he is absorbed sometimes arouse conflict and are warded off by a partially unself-conscious and undecentered self. By way of contrast, the mature, cognizing individual acknowledges the distinction between his intense encounters with reality, where some reality details remain unapprehended or unintegrated internally, and his equally intense and motivated attempts not to participate in or recognize reality.

Consider in this context an interesting statement Sigmund Freud (1960) makes about the complexity of unawareness:

> We recognize that the Ucs. [unconscious] does not coincide with the repressed; it is still true that all that is repressed is Ucs.; but not all that is Ucs. is repressed. A part of the ego, too—and Heaven knows how important a part—may be Ucs., undoubtedly is Ucs. (p. 8)

He refers to the fact that the analysand (adult) can at times resist a certain line of thought but remain unaware of it, an unawareness Freud attributes to the ego and describes as follows:

> We have come upon something in the ego itself which is also unconscious, which behaves exactly like the repressed—that is, which produces powerful effects without itself being conscious and which requires special work before it can be made conscious. (p. 7)

Freud's intuition that "Heaven knows how important a part" of the ego remains unconscious, or out of the field of awareness, seems remarkably similar to Piaget's view that as we are absorbed with and decline to integrate readily observable reality features, parts of our experience are out of our field of awareness. Even adults experience a near-total preoccupation with work projects so that they "forget themselves" or "lose themselves." Adults also sometimes fail to integrate details (even conspicuous ones) when these seem to challenge a strongly held or favored viewpoint. This occurs not just in everyday life experiences but also (and perhaps especially) in the psychotherapeutic treatment situation when the patient, working diligently to understand himself, is unaware of his resistances to understanding. Certainly the child's mentality often consists of just those reality features and intrapsychic processes with which he is absorbed both in everyday life and in psychotherapy but often unable to thoroughly organize. Thus, the exploring child produces "powerful effects" without being aware of the process by which he does so.

It is puzzling that Piaget (1962) does not address Freud's concept of the preconscious which would provide fertile ground for his discussion of "repression" from a cognitive-developmental perspective as distinct from repression from a psychoanalytic perspective. When Sigmund Freud (1960) wrote of the preconscious that it is "capable of becoming conscious" unlike the unconscious "which is repressed and which is not, in itself and without further ado, capable of becoming conscious" (p. 5), he seems to have made the distinction between awareness and unawareness more tenuous, especially when he said the preconscious is "unconscious only descriptively, not in the dynamic sense" (p. 5). Freud stated that the preconscious unlike the unconscious is accessible just as Piaget stated that symbolic meaning is accessible to the adapted child. But again, the major question in any given therapeutic situation is: Does the child's unawareness stem from his absorption with reality (his assimilations) or does it stem from his attempts to ward off aspects of his experience in which case his symbolization may conceal as well as reveal?

Piaget's cognitive psychology and Freud's psychoanalysis appear to come together in the questions individuals ask themselves about their own behavior. When a child asks herself about her behavior and her statements regarding a complex cognitive task, "Why do I do one thing and say another?" isn't she then engaging in what is generally meant by conscious introspection? The individual appears to be aware of self-inconsistency both when she questions the discrepancy between what she *says* she does and what she *actually* does and when she questions the discrepancy between what she says she *feels* and what she *does*. The ambivalence and the apparent contradiction the child feels in regard to another person can result in a suddenly or gradually unrepressed child wondering, "How can I hit my mother when I love her?" And these statements are quite similar to "How can I mean to say or do one thing but actually say or do another?" —self-questioning which might occur as the result of slips of the tongue, apraxia, and others "errors" (S. Freud, 1938). Do these discrepancies reflect that we do not want to know what we really mean, or do they suggest that we strive for self-consistency because consistency seems to tell us what we really mean and intend?

THE PROBLEM OF UNAWARENESS: DEVELOPMENTAL LEVELS

What, then, in infancy and early childhood could form the basis for the defensive and inhibiting maneuvers we call suppression, repression, and denial? Feffer (1982) wrote about the "logical paradox" in Freud's "anxiety-defense paradigm": "In short the ego has to know in order not to know" (p. 165). My question is exactly what the ego "knows" in order to suppress, repress, or deny. The infant does not yet possess the cognitive structures that would permit inhibition to operate in a way comparable to that in an older child or an adult. Nonetheless, in infants we can often observe behavior which suggests a rejection or warding off of experience, or of certain aspects of it. Moreover, if the term *repression* is evaluated in light of its probable mistranslation into English (Bettelheim, 1983), it is easier to understand that in infants and young children the forerunner of secondary repression consists of a "repulsion" of some aspects of experience (this word more nearly captures the meaning of Freud's concept). Relevant in this context is Furth's (1987) suggestion that the word *unconscious* should be hyphenated (un-conscious) which would imply an active *un*doing of something. He forcefully concludes, "I hold that whatever in a person is now unconscious was at some earlier time *made* to be unconscious" (p. 56). For example, an infant or very young child *makes* his experience unconscious by turning his head away when a strange adult approaches or as the result of excess stimulation, both rather commonplace events. This behavior is very different in intent from the infant's declining to search for the missing object: the infant wishes to ward off the approach of the stranger or excess stimulation and does so in the only way he can, while in the case of the missing object he can no longer visualize (conceptualize), he simply stops his behavior—he does not repell the missing object. An older infant or toddler can be observed actively repelling (pushing away) an unfamiliar or unpleasant object (thing) or person while the younger infant can only avert his face. This is a very early ontogenetic statement that what cannot be seen or what is pushed away does not exist. Again, such warding off is very different from the infant's unself-conscious absorption with a reality to which he avidly turns in contrast to that reality which he pushes away. All of this suggests that the child's first warding off efforts take the form of overt activity, a view not incompatible with Piaget's emphasis on action as the basis for the child's emerging thought constructions (internalized actions).

On a slightly more advanced plane, an effort to inhibit might take the form of a rejection of images associated with intense affective states. Concrete operational—and even preoperational—children can be observed changing their facial expressions and body gestures from interest in the other person or their environment to a blank look or immobile body postures. I have found it difficult, often impossible, to get direct confirmation from the child about what preceded the blank look and immobile body posture, but it can nonetheless be suggested that both the look and the body posture with which they face the world might reflect what they experience internally; namely, that their minds have become temporarily blank and that their bodies have therefore become inert. (Such a child might immediately or later attempt to express what caused the blank look or the inert body posture by "acting out" behavior—where actions without self-reflexive awareness substitute for articulate statements about feelings and thoughts.) Young children cannot confirm my hunch not just because a repressive process might have occurred, but because they cannot tell us all the complex reasons why their behavior takes certain forms. Rather, they remain unaware of the many reasons for their behavior—aware only of the results of their behavior—or they cannot coordinate simultaneously the multiple determinants of their behavior.

On the other hand, an older child who is self-reflexively aware might comprehend that what he once knew has now escaped him. Or, he is aware that he has deliberately pushed aside an image, a thought, or a feeling. He is more capable than the younger child of knowing in the abstract that psychological processes, such as repression, are possible because he is capable of thinking that there are functions of the human mind which apply to everyone, including himself. This realization enables him to explain to another person (his therapist, for example) that he did not want to think about an event, or that he pushed a certain thought along with its associated feelings out of his mind with the expectation that this other person will understand because such behavior is part of the human repertoire. For example, two children, both 11 years old, told me why they had assumed a vacuous stare and an immobile stance. One youngster said, "I always know that I'm thinking and feeling except when I do *this*! [she dramatized a vacant stare]. Then I'm blank!" Continuing with the discussion, she said, "You're always thinking. You *have* to think not to think!" The other youngster said about his "blank" look: "I'm stonewalling you. Now you can't read my mind because there's nothing to read. I'm not thinking!"

From my observations, it appears that the various defenses (i.e., repression, suppression, denial) are experienced as distinct only in late childhood or adolescence. Then these defenses can be conceptualized as distinct because the young person is capable of understanding the differences between refusing to recognize reality (denial) and thrusting aside his intrapsychic actuality (repression). It should be said once more that "denying" reality (refusing to recognize it) is different from being temporarily unable to cognitively integrate many complex reality features or to make knowledge schemes hang together coherently. The problem of conceptual development in relation to unawareness (or to "the unconscious") is conspicuous in this statement by Piaget (1973a):

So we find ourselves in a situation very comparable to that of affective repression: when a feeling or an impulse finds itself in contradiction with feelings or tendencies of a higher rank (emanating from the superego, etc.) they are then eliminated, through one of two processes, a conscious suppression or an unconscious repression. In the cognitive field we now observe an analogous mechanism, and it is indeed unconscious repression that we are dealing with. In effect, the child has not first constructed a conscious hypothesis and then set it aside. He has, on the contrary, avoided a conscious awareness of the schema. That is, he had repressed it from conscious territory before it penetrated there in any conceptualized form. (p. 255)

Similar to psychoanalytic theory, Piaget has described an unconsciousness (the "cognitive" unconscious) as that which is avoided without being fully conceptualized. But it is Piaget's own system which generates the concept of transition or partial understanding. It is not the question of *un*parallel cognitive development and emotional development which causes the difficulty in integrating Piaget's cognitive psychology and psychoanalysis; it is rather the difficulty in understanding the impact of conceptual development on unawareness—a difficulty which plagues both theories and which impedes the creation of a more cohesive theoretical unity.[1] In my view, a child inhibits most efficiently if he possesses the structures which permit self-reflexive awareness and a considered thrust from the mind. If the self-reflective function ("consciousness" or "cognizance") develops progressively, so must its handmaiden, inhibition. The child's cognizance of his individual experience, including his own conceptual repertoire, leads to its most efficient rejection. The correct intervention, then, is one that considers whether the child retreats from his attempt to understand a concept or whether he pushes away a fully or partially formed concept. In the case of an unformed or immature concept, the therapist ought to encourage thought development, but in the case of the warded off fully formed concept, the therapist need not aid the development of that concept.

Nine-year-old Lara, whose case narrative follows, gave evidence of both preconscious and transitional awareness as she struggled to find out why she

---

[1]Anthony (1957) and Greenspan (1979) write that the difficulty in synthesizing aspects of Piaget's cognitive psychology and Freud's psychoanalysis is Piaget's apparent rejection of the dynamic unconscious. Perhaps Piaget's (1962) statement that the "unconscious is everywhere" (p. 172) makes it seem to Freudians that Piaget denies the psychodynamics of a repressed unconscious since, according to psychoanalytic theory, the unconscious is not everywhere but is distinct structurally and functionally from consciousness. But preconscious content is often partially known to us or expressed by us (e.g., in acting out); and slippage often can be seen in everyday behavior, as Sigmund Freud (1938) describes, which can give the impression to the reader of *The Psychopathology of Everyday Life* that the unconscious is indeed everywhere; that there is continuity as well as discontinuity in the psyche. It was perhaps an acceptance of the dynamic unconscious which led Piaget (1976) to make the claim that "no one has contributed more than Freud to make us consider the 'unconscious' a continually active dynamic system. The findings in this book [*The Grasp of Consciousness*] lead us to claim analogous powers for consciousness itself. In fact, and precisely insofar as it is desired to mark and conserve the differences between the unconscious and the conscious, the passage from one to the other must require reconstructions and cannot be reduced simply to a process of illumination" (p. 332).

was afraid to go to school, and why she was inattentive to the learning task on those rare occasions when she attended school. Because Lara was in therapy from the ages of 9 to 11½, her progress spanned an important developmental divide which permitted me to observe how a child avoids understanding by repressing what has been apprehended as distinct from avoiding mature thinking. Similar to many other nonlearning youngsters, Lara had made many personal associations between events which justified her feeling that school was dangerous. These cause–effect connections were largely outside her 9-year-old awareness in the two senses which Piaget terms "unconscious." First, the meanings Lara attributed to school were not thrust from awareness but were rather so coalesced with her everyday experience that she was unaware of them as a fish is said to be unaware of water. Like Piaget's description of much younger children, she was unaware that *she* attributed symbolic significance to school attendance. Second, Lara did not first construct "a conscious hypothesis and then set it aside" in that she did not test whether learning in school would threaten her mother. Much like Betsy (see Chapter 5), she held onto immature thought and avoided stable mature concepts because of the threat knowing held for her: she had understood enough about the association she made between school learning and her mother's personality to conclude the less she knew, the better. Betsy felt that "the less I know, the better" regarding her deceased father, whereas Lara felt "the less I know, the better" regarding her mother who appeared to stifle Lara's attempts to learn in school and to make friends. Instead, Lara originated fractional explanations which she did not thoroughly consider and test and which, therefore, only partially penetrated her awareness. These incomplete explanations she treated either (1) as unquestionably true and/or (2) as so dangerous that further thought was inhibited.

During therapy as Lara became both preadolescent and transitional for formal operations, she began to reject fully formed concepts and their associated affects, and thus became unaware in a very different way ("unconscious") of parts of her experience. She became adept at screening out and warding off those very aspects of her experience which she had before not questioned or which she had taken account of only by way of immature reasoning.

LARA'S REJECTION OF SCHOOL

The case narratives presented in previous chapters of this book deal with youngsters who had to a significant degree *defined* themselves as incapable of or afraid of school learning. Lara, too, believed that she was incapable of learning and certainly she was afraid of school, so much so that she dropped out for a prolonged period during her psychotherapy with me. What differentiates Lara from the other children and adolescents discussed thus far was her *uncertain definition of self*. For her, school learning was entangled with the individuation process—a fact she explicitly articulated after 9 months of therapy. School learning, or any learning for that matter, meant she was distinct from her mother. Since being an individual separate from her mother appeared life-threatening to Lara, she avoided general learning, especially acquiring knowledge from an important person other than her mother, such as a teacher. Her enmeshed, most probably a "symbiotic" attachment to her mother meant that she could not afford to learn in school lest she fully "learn" she was a person dissimilar from her mother and, if so, in which ways distinct from and possibly more competent than her mother.

Lara's Family History

Lara was attractive and would have been beautiful but for her many exaggerated and contrived facial expressions. She often displayed nervous, jerky, clumsy gestures and appeared inhibited in using her body. When she sometimes relaxed into a charming, dimpled smile, it would soon become rigidly fixed. Just as her facial expressions were often masked and immobile, so was her sitting position since she rarely switched her posture or moved from the chair in which she usually sat. She was physically well-developed and paid scrupulous attention to her grooming and to current fashion.

Lara's mother was an identical twin which may be the primary reason she fostered an enmeshed attachment between her and Lara. Mahler *et al.* (1975) describe "symbiosis" as a

> feature of primitive cognitive-affective life wherein the differentiation of self and mother has not taken place, or where regression to that self-object undifferentiated state (which characterized the symbiotic phase) has occurred. (p. 8)

I thought Lara's mother had become accustomed in her own growing up years to the idea that "being close" was the same as being "identical" to another person. She expressed her need to be identical to others in a most interesting fashion during a parent conference while we were working together on developing better parenting strategies to help with Lara's problems. As Lara's mother explained that she had tried to replicate what she thought I recommended but found herself unable to implement what she imagined I would do, she said, exasperatedly, "I guess I'm not you!" Yet this statement that she was not me helped her get in touch with interpersonal differences which, in turn, helped Lara do the same.

Before Lara was born, her mother had taken her first job as an airline stewardess and had worked during part of her pregnancy. After Lara was born, she stayed home until Lara was 3 years. Lara's father was a traveling salesman for most of his adult life. Lara had an older sister who left home when she was as adolescent. Lara's family history the two years before Kindergarten and during the early grades of school thus revealed a curious pattern. She and her mother were rarely home together. This pattern continued until Lara, at the age of 9½, refused to leave home to attend school. At the initial parent conference, Lara's parents told me that after Lara's mother returned to work, both she and her husband noticed that 3-year-old Lara became unusually fearful when her mother left for work, a reaction they nonetheless attributed to "normal" separation anxieties. Persuaded as well by Lara's pediatrician that she would outgrow her symptoms, they did nothing about them until much later when Lara not only refused to attend school but also refused to leave home for any reason. Then, Lara's pediatrician noticed that her behavior appeared "odd." He focused primarily on the fact that when Lara and her mother came for the regular pediatric checkups, "They both had the same fatuous smile. In fact they would look like twins except that Lara's much younger and smaller than her mother." In addition to the fixed smiles the pediatrician described, I noticed that particularly Lara's mother avoided directing her gaze on the other person's face. To me her fixed smile and ceaseless back-and-forth eye movements which appeared to target the periphery of my face suggested she was avoiding recognizing another person. I wondered if these eye movements made Lara feel similarly avoided and unrecognized.

Despite the fact that other family members took care of her and tried to reassure her about her mother's return, Lara became panicky whenever her mother went off to work. Although she undoubtedly welcomed her father's presence (he often worked at home) and that of her preadolescent sister and her grandmother, who often stayed with her, she took comfort especially in her mother's long disance telephone calls which assured her that her mother loved her, informed her where the airline flight had taken her, and reassured her that she would return. As Lara's parents described her early history, I thought she was unusually anxious about her mother's repeated absences because she had not developed a sense of self distinct from her mother so that when her mother was away she could not imagine her mother returning to *her* because she could not predictably imagine herself as unique. When her mother was away, it might have seemed to Lara that an important aspect of herself was absent. So reassurances about her mother's return from people other than her mother only meant to Lara that her personality would return, an idea which would doubtless either create or intensify Lara's panic. What her mother's telephone calls accomplished, then, was to reassure Lara that *she*, or qualities of herself, still existed.

Ideas such as those I just attributed to Lara are probably not that uncommon in very young children. For example, many young children while bathing and watching the bath water run out are afraid of "going down the drain." One 2-year-old girl told me she thought she would "go down the drain" by "turning into liquid." Another very young child screamed when walking on a dock because he could see the ocean water through the slats. He exclaimed, "I could fit through there!" Very young children thus have an uncertain grasp of what their mutability consists of. Since they know or sense their bodies change as they "grow up," it seems possible to them that they could change into liquid or grow so thin as to fit through slats. What rescues many young children from pathology is the response of their parents to such prelogical ideas.

A normal parent will quite likely respond with rational statements explaining why a little girl cannot change into liquid or a little boy cannot fit through slats. The child will ascertain from the parent's explanation that the parent is not frightened which reassures the child, even if he or she cannot fully understand all the details of the rational explanation. Furthermore, a normal child is more likely than a seriously disturbed child to articulate the reason for her panic. Trusting her parents with the information that she might go down the drain because of a body's changeability into liquid, she assumes that if and when this did happen, her parents would protect her. When I asked the girl many years later if she would tell how she overcame her fear of the bathtub drain, she said: "I thought if I told you about it, you would rescue me if it happened. That made me feel better."

By way of contrast the enmeshed attachment between parent and child impedes the overcoming of normally childish fears in at least two ways. First, such children are less likely to be able to articulate to their parents why they are panicky. This is because an uncertain sense of self inhibits the young child from developing many skills, such as the ability to communicate during panic states. Lara's parents knew she was anxious "because she screamed all the time" but reported that she seemed unable to articulate the reasons for her panic in ways they could understand. Second, Lara's mother told me that she would become panicky when Lara did: "It's hard sometimes to know who is more hysterical — Lara or me!" This tended to reinforce the enmeshment because her mother's hysterical behavior did not support Lara's view of herself as unique. On the contrary, her mother's hysterical behavior reinforced the enmeshed quality of the mother–daughter relationship. From Lara's perspective, since she and her mother felt the same way, she and her mother must be indistinct. Unlike the 2-year-old described before, she could not say to herself: "My mother isn't scared so maybe I have no reason to be." Or, "My mother isn't scared so she will be able to rescue me or comfort me when I am scared." Because she would have realized she and her mother had dissimilar affective reactions, such inner statements would have reduced her anxiety and helped her understand she was distinct from her mother.

The numerous telephone conversations Lara had with her mother when she was in airports rendered Lara's phobic symptoms just barely manageable, a fact which changed instantly when in her kindergarten year, her mother stopped working. Now the situation was reversed: before Lara had been at home and her mother away; now *she* was away and her mother was at home. Lara could no longer make or receive the phone calls which kept her together with her mother because school policy did not permit children to call home or to receive calls. For Lara, this reversal took on magical significance. Because her mother stayed home, Lara perceived her mother as wishing to remain indistinct from her. This situation was exacerbated during Lara's first-grade year when her parents separated for 6 months. Lara's father moved out of the home and visited her infrequently during this period.

As if Lara did not already have enough reasons to recoil from school, knowledge acquisition threatened her attachment to her mother more than did the meaning of physical separation. Lara's school phobia became inflamed and out of control at precisely the developmental milestone when the propensity and opportunity to acquire knowledge is on the increase. For reasons which will be detailed throughout this chapter, knowledge to Lara meant disruption of her fragile sense of self. The fact that her father left home during her first-grade year added to the magical meaning she attributed to school attendance. She fantasied that her being elsewhere (school) meant to her father that he was free to leave her.

For Lara to understand her rejection of school I had to show her that knowledge of academic subject matter need not fatally disrupt her relationship to important other people nor her sense of who she was. I accomplished this by supporting her reemerging sense of herself and by showing her ways in which she might relate differently to her mother by relating differently to me. In effect, I helped her "know" herself at the same time that we talked about the risks of knowing in school. It might be said, then, that Lara's school phobia had developed into a "self phobia" which became apparent as she rightly focused on self-development in therapy. Developing aspects of herself later led her to resolve to return to school.

FIRST IMPRESSIONS OF LARA AND CLINICAL HYPOTHESES

Lara revealed her tendency to blend into the identity of the other person during her first visit with me. As I greeted her at the door and ushered her into my office, in an attempt to behave "appropriately" she began to copy every move I made and every facial expression. I felt she believed the only way to behave appropriately was to blend her behavior with that of the adult. When I turned to observe her incredibly accurate mimicry, she imitated that as well. This created the eerie feeling in me that there were two of me rather than me interacting with Lara. At this and other moments, she appeared to be only my shadow.

Mahler and co-workers (1975) identified the "shadowing" of the mother and the "darting away from her" as behavioral manifestations of the "rapprochement" phase of early child development. This phase follows one in which the child develops cognitive and locomotor skills, appearing to have a "love affair with the world" (p. 70). According to Mahler, the child's experience is a "love affair" because he does not yet recognize the consequences of more mature cognition and locomotion; his ecstatic enjoyment of the world is not yet encumbered by the realization that he is separate from mother. When he begins to recognize more fully that his autonomy has precisely the implication that he is separate and distinct from other people, he experiences a particular vulnerability associated with heightened ambivalence surrounding separations from his mother.

In some important respects, Lara was stuck in the "rapprochement" phase of development in that she rarely, when I first met her, projected herself as a unique individual. She certainly did not welcome those moments when she was faced by certain life circumstances with the fact of her individuality. But while Lara often shadowed my behavior or in some other ways expressed her perception that she and I were indistinct, initially she did not dare to "dart away" from me in therapy—either behaviorally or conversationally. She presented as serious, even morose, almost depressed, except during those times when she appeared to be recreating her mother's behavior. Then she became more animated but hardly daring. Even though she may have retained only the "shadowing" manifestation of the "rapprochement" phase of development when she was brought for therapy at age 9, the fact that she elaborated other aspects of this phase later in therapy suggests that she had developed typically until she was about 2 years. Given how Lara behaved when she presented for psychotherapy, I hypothesized that she had developed at least a tenuous ("core") sense of self in early childhood (before her mother resumed working) in which case she may not have known completely *who* she was but certainly *that* she was (Mahler *et al.*, 1975, p. 8). She knew especially that she was when she was physically with her mother or felt she was behaving in ways identical to her. Equally clear to me was her tenuous grasp of and her downright resistance to knowing *who* she was—what her special, individual attributes consisted of. Or, it could be said that she had developed a "domain" of relatedness (Stern, 1985, p. 27), which was focused primarily on an awareness of her mother in conjunction with herself. Put differently, Lara's "core" sense of self was often swamped by the influence of the motives, feelings, intentions, and behavior of the other person—her mother or individuals who reminded her of her mother. According to Stern's scheme, she must have sufficiently developed a "core" self to elaborate a "subjective" self. The corollaries of a "subjective" self—intersubjective relatedness and affect attunement—were greatly rewarded by Lara's mother.

Lara's psychological agenda, then, was *selected* for Lara by her mother's attention to Lara's attempts to mimic her. That is, the mother's "twin" fantasy dominated Lara's sense of self. She was most captivated by that sense of self in relation to others in which children discover that there are "other minds out there as well as their own" (Stern, 1985, p. 27). Thus, she was unable to develop further because she was more concentrated on that "other mind" of her mother than she was on her own mind. This probable aspect of Lara's development is important to note because, as children mature, they are increasingly prone to conceptualize what is on their own minds. If, in early childhood, their intuitive attempts to represent their minds as distinct from that of the other person is inhibited, then later their attempts to conceptualize mental contents and interpsychic differences are likewise inhibited. Prior to therapy, Lara had not fully developed that later "verbal" sense of self which expands "almost limitless possibilities for interpersonal happenings" (p. 28).

The child whose development appears to have gone awry commonly recapitulates developmental phases in therapy, perhaps because she senses that a reaction different from that of her parents will emanate from the therapist. Thinking retrospectively about Lara, it appeared to me that while she developed within normal limits until she was about 2 years, her "core" self was continuously threatened by her "subjective" self which, in turn, was continuously threatened by her "verbal" self. Throughout her therapy Lara appeared to approach and subsequently withdraw from acquiring new skills or information. She may have felt unable to share what she had learned with her mother because learning would indicate to her mother that Lara had developed differently than she had. It is thus interesting that Lara began to share with me in her therapy appointments what she had learned and to demonstrate her newly won skills. Perhaps I functioned as a "mother" to Lara when she, for example, decided to show me her new dancing skills but confined her ballet practice at home to the solitude of her room. Her decision to differentiate from me by "practicing" a skill she knew I did not possess seemed to reinstate the normal developmental trend which eventually resulted in her feeling more solidly distinct from me in general, and later, in feeling distinct from her mother. As we shared conversations about her dancing lessons, she did not seem as threatened by my participation in interpersonal exchanges as she had before. For once, mutuality seemed to enhance her "core" self.

Thus, what I stress here is Lara's self-crisis—not just the crisis in her attachment to her mother—as she approached and then shunned the realization that she was a distinct individual. Because she had for quite a long time believed in her identity-merged-with-mother, every time she dimly understood this need not be so, she experienced what Stern (1985) characterized as "a crisis of self-comprehension. The self becomes a mystery" (p. 272). And Lara's self-crisis was inextricably bound up with her school-crisis since the activity of academic learning, which occurs precisely at a time when a mother is absent, suggested to her that she was distinct from her mother. To use Mahler's (1975) scheme, Lara was unable to approach her mother for comfort after learning she was distinct from her mother.

About the difference between Mahler's view of infant development and Stern's view, it seems to center on the degree to which they perceive the normal infant achieving a sense of individuality out of a prior undifferentiated self–other experience (Mahler) or possessing an early sense of individuality which nonetheless changes dramatically throughout infancy and early childhood (Stern). Whichever way the individuation process originates, it surely includes the young child's desire to share with her parents her newly developed skills and acquired insights. However, it does seem to me that Stern more than Mahler stresses the intelligence the infant applies to self-development:

> This crisis in self-*comprehension* occurs because for the first time the infant experiences the self as divided, and rightly senses that *no one else* can rebind the division. The infant has not lost omnipotence but rather has lost experiential wholeness. (pp. 272–273, italics added)

So when Lara shared her newly won skill of dancing with me, she tried to solve a new "mystery." She tried to understand why she behaved as a unique individual with me but not with her mother. Furthermore, by sharing her dancing skills in conversation with me, she tried to align me as an important person on the positive side of competence ambivalence. Being more competent than other people (i.e., "better" at dancing than her mother or me) surely proved she was a distinct individual—a reality she was not sure was safe. In particular, she was not sure it was safe to be distinct from her mother in relationship to her father. Because of her mother's "twin" fantasy and her subsequent prohibition of Lara's personal and unique reaching out to others, her mother's return to work at just the moment Lara may have sought out her father in a manner typical of Oedipal children was an unfortunate coincidence. Lara may have concluded: "Because I was interested in my father, my mother left." She even might have concluded: "Whenever I am interested in other people, my mother threatens to leave."

EARLY TREATMENT PROGRESS

Lara's therapy first revolved around her attempts to free herself from the psychological hold her mother had on her. She soon began to see me as possessive of her as her mother had been and then tried to merge her personality with mine. Coincidentally, she began once again to ask her mother if she could play with neighborhood friends and if she could invite school friends home. When Lara tried once more to make friends as she got to work in therapy, I was able to support her age-appropriate developmental trend by both offering a "friendship" to her as well as to provide an opportunity for her to talk about her friends. Feeling friendly toward me but not always merged with me in therapy made continuing attempts to reach out to friends safe. Moreover, Lara's frequent, but not automatic, equivalence of me with her mother anchored Lara in familiar ground, especially as she felt her mother would approve of her behavior in therapy.

But Lara's beginning attempts to relate to me had other, more ominous, implications for her. Much like Robin, Lara behaved as though she experienced the feelings on coming to therapy as she did on going to school. Just as Robin was afraid his mother would leave him forever when he came to see me, and therefore would sit on her lap as I talked with him, Lara, too, was afraid that I would interrupt her relationship with her mother. She feared her mother would retaliate by not taking care of her which had worse consequences for her because, unlike Robin, she often could not imagine anyone but her mother taking care of her, not just because she felt indistinct from this parent, but also because by now her sister had left home and her father's work as a salesman frequently took him out of town. Since she depended so much on her mother and was anxious about her mother's capability to retaliate if Lara sought a "friendship" with me, she often resisted coming to therapy because once again it reassured her mother that she continued to be the most important person in Lara's life. Unlike Robin's mother, Lara's mother needed this reassurance before she could give Lara permission to attend therapy. Lara's mother told me: "I don't want therapy to make me and Lara grow apart but to come closer together. I brought her to therapy so she would go shopping with me again." Lara's mother referred to Lara's agoraphobia which prevented her from going anywhere including a shopping trip with her mother, a refusal which deprived her mother of togetherness when she most wanted it. Only when she saw that therapy did not distance her from Lara did she permit her daughter to keep the appointments.

I thought of the first phase in Lara's recovery as a loosening but not undoing of the psychological tie to her mother. An abrupt challenge to the mother–daughter attachment as a therapeutic goal would have threatened both of them and might have resulted in Lara's feeling completely unrelated to anyone. After I went to great lengths for 3 months to adapt her therapy appointments to her mother's plans for her, Lara finally began to feel comfortable about coming to therapy, which meant to both mother and daughter that I had no conspicuous intent to change what they did together—nor that they could do things together. Nevertheless, to feel related to me, Lara had continually to test her connection to her mother. Although Robin, who was much younger, could test his relationship to his mother by insisting that he sit on her lap as he talked with me, Lara who was both older and more symptomatic had to test it in a repetitive series of abstractly imagined events: if her mother threatened her appointments with me, would her mother be threatened by Lara's request to come to therapy? And, just as important, if her mother threatened her psychotherapy appointments, would I threaten not to reschedule these?

When Lara began to attend her therapy appointments regularly, she found a new strategy which she hoped would resolve her dilemma. As she now tried to accomplish two goals simultaneously—preserve her relationship with her mother and increase her attempts to interact normally with me and with her peers—she began to talk about copying every aspect of her mother's appearance and behavior. She did not merely enact the personality characteristics of the other person; now she conversed directly about this mimicking process. If she could "be" or "be like" her mother—and in this way give her mother that desired closeness (which her mother perceived as the result of being "identical" to the other)—then maybe her mother would allow friendships. Her interchange of "be" and "be like" in her statements revealed her ambivalence in leaving a nondifferentiated self-other state for a differentiation of self and other. On the one hand, her phrase "be *like*" showed she understood similes—an understanding which requires the differentiation of the symbol (Lara) from its referent (her mother). On the other hand, her repeated retreat in conversation to "*be* my mother" represented her resistance to what she, herself, now understood. It represented still another "self-crisis."

Lara soon told me of "reading my mother's mind"—of being able to anticipate what her mother would do—and her mother verified these mind readings by describing Lara's apparent omniscience, bragging, "Lara knows what I'm going to do before I do!" Lara further told how she had begun to imitate her mother's every facial expression and gesture. Furthermore, she soon announced she would "pretend" to be me by copying everything I did or said in what appeared to me to be an attempt to read my mind.[2]

Even when I did or said nothing, Lara mimicked me and seemed determined either to defy normal conversation with me or to make a joke of it. In an attempt to support her sense of herself as distinct from me (although she seemed to be making fun of my attempts to remain distinct from her), I said: "Well, then, I guess I'll have to be you, because someone *has* to be Lara!" She

[2]Lara may have felt that as a therapist I could read her mind. Thus, she may have been trying to create an intersubjective omniscience between us. Or she may have been trying to show that she was better at reading minds than I was, since she was better at reading her mother's mind than her mother was at reading Lara's—especially as Lara began to change in therapy and her mother could not so easily anticipate what was on Lara's mind.

answered with an animated giggle: "You can't be me! *I* want to!" When I pretended to sigh in relief, she laughed even more and clapped her hands.

What Lara meant to say in response to my statement probably reveals her understanding of a sort of logical necessity contained in "someone has to be Lara." She had first tried to be the same as me by copying everything I did or said. When I objected that this behavior meant that Lara was a missing personality, and suggested that to restore her presence, I ought to try to be like her, she understood the logic inherent in the following: (1) there are two distinct people in my therapist's office; (2) one of these persons is me, and the other is my therapist; (3) therefore, if I am my therapist, the other one has to be me. But this led her to the thought that personalities are not interchangeable for she said the equivalent of: You cannot possibly be me because I am me. Because this was so, she added: I *want* to be me. In a peculiar way a "necessity" (which was as psychological as it was logical) added to her courage to say that she *wanted* to be herself. My mock sigh of relief meant to her that because she was she, I *had* to be me (not her)—and I (like she) appeared to experience appropriate feelings of relief which she applauded.

A week later, when the subject of Lara's next appointment came up—since I was asked to reschedule it because of her mother's plans for her—I asked if her mother might bring her another day. To this she indignantly replied, "If you want to know what she's going to do, ask *her!*" Her reply made it obvious that she felt strong enough as a person to challenge the enmeshed attachment wherein she had earlier believed (or wished) that she could predict everything her mother would do. Our conversations helped Lara differentiate first from me and just a week later from her mother. In saying, "You can't be me...*I* want to!", she used both language and logic to transcend what until then had been the actuality of enmeshment with her mother. Stern (1985) has expressed well the potential benefits and hazards which accrue to the developed "verbal" self:

> Finally, with the advent of language and symbolic thinking, children now have the tools to distort and transcend reality. They can create expectations contrary to past experience. They can elaborate a wish contrary to present facts....Prior to this linguistic ability, infants are confined to reflect the impress of reality. They can now transcend that, for good or ill. (p. 182)

When Lara indignantly declined to read her mother's intent, she created both a new expectation and elaborated a new wish when she said she was *herself* and *not* her mother. But, as we shall shortly see, being *herself* and *not* her mother often led her to conclude she was "bad" or "incompetent me," self conceptions which jeopardized further self-development.

Death and Knowing

When Lara had been in therapy for 6 months, her older sister, who had left home a few months before, died in an automobile accident. This unexpected event precipitated a family crisis because of the close attachment Lara's mother had fostered in her older daughter and her ensuing rejection of her mother. At the age of 16, she had prematurely left home and avoided visiting her mother. Lara saw her sister's death as retribution for having grown up and leaving home, an idea she revealed when she said about her sister's departure, "She should have known better." Lara's mother needed to draw Lara even closer to her because of the agony and remorse she felt about the loss of her older daughter. The death of this "grown up" sibling, who had successfully left home but who soon after met a tragic death, aroused the affective core which had led to Lara's school phobia. Her sister's death occurred during the last month of Lara's fourth-grade year. During the following summer, Lara decided to drop out of school. But she continued to come to therapy and tried to understand why she was both afraid of school and school learning, and why she had dropped out just at that point in her life.

While analyzing her school dropout, she began by describing to me how every autumn since she had begun school, she would experience intense anxiety upon entering a new grade. This was not just the normal childhood anxiety that schoolwork will get more difficult with each grade. This unusually frightened child experienced an anniversary reaction every autumn to returning to school, as though she were returning to her kindergarten year when she first felt traumatically separated from her mother. Physical separation had always been traumatic in Lara's experience because it appeared life-threatening. To her it appeared shocking because she had always found it difficult imagining herself distinct from her mother so that a separation from mother called to Lara's mind the question of where *she* was—not just where her mother was. Her anxiety was fed by the particular understandings (1) that school indeed separated her physically from her mother and (2) that from her mother's viewpoint, physical separation held certain risks for their relationship at the very moment Lara learned in school how to become more independent. So when Lara separated physically from her mother, especially to attend school, she quite literally worried about the "death" of herself since her experience of self had invariably included her mother's personality. And one characteristic of her mother's personality which Lara understood all too well was the wish to be identical to the other.

As Lara told me about how she felt in the first few weeks of each new grade, she suddenly remembered (unrepressed) a dream she had had in kindergarten which she described breathlessly as a "nightmare." She became anxious and threatened not to tell me the dream because "I'd get even more scared thinking about it." To this I said that she could always stop talking about the dream if she got scared, intending to assure her that I was, at that moment, primarily interested in her feelings about the dream and only secondarily interested in what she remembered. I could make this statement with conviction because I did not suspect what would follow in the conversation—I was not aware how important the dream was she had almost confided. She resumed by saying that when the dream she had had in kindergarten recurred recently, she had awakened in the middle of the night. In the dream she had gone to school where her classmates had teased her. When I asked what the children had teased her about, she exclaimed, "They jumped up and down and screamed, 'school shows you how to be different from your mother!' I thought in my dream if I ever looked or acted different, if I ever *were* different from my mother, she would leave me and I would *die*!" She continued by saying that when she had returned in the fall to first and second grades, she would always remember the dream; and she also would experience the panic associated with it, although she tried pretending to be sick to stay away from school until the memory would dissipate. She further added: "When you pretend to be sick all the time, you eventually begin to believe it—I actually felt sick sometimes when I knew I really wasn't." She then told me how being away from school made her "forget" the dream, and so implied that her symptoms of illness were designed to keep her away from the school environment which reminded her of the nightmare.

At the age of 9 years and 9 months, Lara was capable of some first attempts at reflection about her immature cause–effect associations which were contained in and formed the basis for her dream. In telling the dream in therapy, she appeared to understand that she thought it was school which would make her different from her mother, and not her own natural tendencies toward self-development. School would thereby lead to her mother's rejection and desertion of her and this would cause Lara to die, since her mother would no longer take care of her. In a moment of incisive insight, Lara realized why she could never learn from her teacher but only from her mother: Being taught by her mother meant she would remain the same as her mother because she would only know what her mother knew. In Lara's words: "I only wanted Mom to teach me because that dream said I would be different in school." Coincident with Lara's greater understanding as she talked with me about her dream and her school dropout was her mother's statement to me: "School doesn't matter. So what if Lara dropped out! She can learn all she needs to know from me."

As so often happens, one insight led to another as Lara understood why she could ill afford to be taught in school and could risk only that learning which came from her mother's teaching. She admitted that since kindergarten she had been afraid she would "die *in* school." She further said it was this anxiety which made her pretend to be sick. Knowing seemed like dying because to Lara learning what her mother did not know "*in* school" signified Lara had become selfless. It did not occur to her that knowing what her mother did not know meant she *had* a self distinct from her mother which had *not* expired as it evolved.

Lara's self-reflexive awareness had become richer as she became more sensitive to her own motives. She had become aware of those erroneous thought constructions which fed her anxiety about school attendance and which she had earlier taken for granted as an unquestionable aspect of reality. She came to understand and to question these thoughts: When I was at home without Mom, I wanted her to be at home with me; Mom is now at home and, similar to how I used to feel, she wants me at home with her; school is what takes me away from Mom and home; therefore, I will not go to school. When she became aware of her thoughts (such as those just described) she became aware that it was *she* who made thought connections and who often rejected many of them so forcefully that she made them preconscious. "What makes ideas and dreams disappear?" Lara asked. When she realized she was capable of understanding and then rejecting the objectionable, she became aware of the mental function of repression.

Lara's dream which she had in kindergarten and, if her account was accurate, which she had repeatedly experienced thereafter, had not been consistently thrust from awareness until she was 8 years old. At the ages of 6 and 7 years, she had been reminded of the dream at the beginning of each school year, but had forgotten it at ages 8 and 9, until at age 9 years and 9 months, she remembered it in therapy once more.[3] She was probably once more reminded of the dream when her sister died because of the thematic similarity of the death threat to herself in the dream ("I thought in my dream. . . if I *were* different from my mother, she would leave me and I would *die*") and her sister's death in reality. When she remembered the dream in therapy, she realized that she had *not* thought of it lately (when she was 8 and 9 years), and then became aware that she had repressed it. She also realized that being away from school helped her repress thoughts and feelings because she understood that school attendance meant "being different from your mother"—a thought which she now readily understood she had wished to avoid. And just as important, repression and not learning became entangled in Lara's web of thoughts when she explained that she tried to avoid "learning" what would make her different from her mother and "learning" that she had unrepressed her nightmare. She stressed the verbs "to know" and "to forget" as she said: "I *know* I have been having that dream again. . . the one I *forgot!*" As she tried to express to me that she avoided school as much to avoid being reminded of the dream as to avoid academics, knowing and remembering became confusingly intertwined. Both the dream and academic learning told her she would be different from her mother in school. Remembering the dream *in* school provided the link in Lara's case between remembering (undoing the repressed) and original school learning. To Lara both "learnings" meant recognizing the self.

The insight that her school phobia rested on the quality of her enmeshed relationship to her mother helped Lara make distinctions where before she had made identities. She understood that while learning does depend in large part

[3]Clinical evidence, such as the patient's report of a dream, has been used in two very different ways: to build theory and to explain therapeutic progress. Although I had no reason to disbelieve Lara's story that her dream had recurred intermittently for some years, it should be said that the veracity of her report is both relevant and irrelevant. Two recent works of Spence (1982) and Eagle (1984) suggest that observations culled from the therapeutic hour are suspect as evidence for theory building because we tend to see what we wish to see which reifies certain concepts and theories. Similarly, Erikson (1964) writes that a clinician ought to be aware of the ways his research interests may affect the ways he understands his patients. Thus, the veracity of Lara's story of the dream and its recurrence is relevant to theoretical formulations since I use her account to illustrate some hypothesis I advance to explain differences in the child's experience of repression (and its undoing) as compared to the adult's. But, whether her dream had actually occurred, recurred, or had been forgotten as she stated was irrelevant to Lara's therapeutic progress because when she chose at a critical point in therapy to tell me about her dream, she experienced relief and understood herself better.

on memory, learning in school does not necessarily lead to the uncovering of the repressed. Then she was able to separate what happened in school from what happened in therapy. She was also helped to separate home from school and mother from teacher as she separated the blame she placed on her mother for her anxieties from the blame she placed on school. As she better understood her attachment to her mother and its relationship to her school phobia, she was momentarily able to put this connection aside and could begin to study what it might have been about school itself which had inhibited her reach for knowledge.

Because she wanted to show me how the teaching at her school could be improved, she began to playact being a teacher by instructing me how to draw and sew, both skills she had developed and refined which she knew I did not possess. She tried to preserve some positive aspects of her attachment to her mother by emulating her mother's teaching. But she was able to go beyond this by imagining better ways of tutoring me, a perceived recalcitrant student, who needed as much kindness within the teaching-learning interaction as she had earlier needed when she was afraid to go to school. As she gently encouraged me to get over my clumsiness at drawing and sewing, simultaneously she confided how she felt about school. She explained that in subjects at which she had no natural skill, such as math, she became frightened and nervous when she was told to add and subtract "faster, faster," when she felt she could not do it at all, much less be quick at it. As in the case of Timothy (see Chapter 4) school then became distinct from home, as she imagined herself to be a better teacher than her teachers which focused her on what it was about school itself which had added to her phobia.

When Lara accomplished the momentous feat of separating school from home and a teacher's role from a parent's, she began to project her conflicts into the therapeutic situation and to analyze them within the therapeutic relationship. This event implied a new or renewed ability to see herself as solid and distinct from me. Normal developmental trends began to assert themselves as she recreated or created for the first time those interpersonal situations which every child experiences in growing up. Most important to Lara in this phase of her therapy was her experimenting with multiple relating as she tried to meet and resolve her belated Oedipal crisis. As we will see in later pages, she first tested her ability to meet this crisis in her relationship to me, and then became bold enough to apply what she had understood in therapy to family life.

Knowing the Self and Defense

Recognizing herself as distinct from me as she taught me how to sew and to draw was critical in Lara's search for her motives for not learning or for refusing to attend school. Watching me learn something I had not known before meant she, too, was capable of learning what she had not known. This, in turn, suggested to her that she might learn subjects her mother had not studied or facts her mother did not know. Furthermore, the idea that she could learn about herself seemed to develop together with a desire not to learn about certain aspects of herself. But the desire to avoid recognizing certain of her personality characteristics was decisively different from Lara's assumption that she had no self. A sense of self told Lara it was she who chose when to be unaware of certain aspects of her experience, which she accomplished at first not by repressing but by suppressing some thoughts and feelings which occurred to her as she talked with me. In effect, Lara's differentiation from me in therapy brought her to the psychological moment wherein self-analysis is possible.

After 14 months of therapy, when she was 10 years and 2 months, Lara's conversations depicted a genuine curiosity about me. A heightened personal individuality led to interpersonal curiosity as she told me some of her "favorite" memories and then inquired about mine. She described as favorite memories winning an art contest and getting a pet for her birthday, memories which stood in sharp contrast to those which threatened her with extinction. Soon she asked what my favorite memories were by saying, "I bet your favorite memory is when you got married." When I assented truthfully that it was one favorite memory, Lara became instantly embarrassed, as though she had transgressed some Oedipal turf, and fell silent. As though to put safe limits on what she might know about me which would obviate the need for inhibition during the therapy hour, some minutes later she asked, "What is that barrier to your other room?" pointing to a door which had been boarded up and repainted to separate my office from other rooms in my house. The barrier, a physical obstruction between our exchanges in my office and what she could observe about my private life, permitted her to imagine what might be beyond it as she seemed to guess that the barrier indeed separated my office from my bedroom and other rooms. She continued the conversation by asking: "What is on the other side of that barrier? I bet it's your bedroom." When I answered among other rooms it was my bedroom, she began to laugh, and said she just had a funny thought which she would never dare say. I told her that the barrier indeed separated different aspects of my life, those with my husband, and those with my patients. At this she admitted her wish to know about the sexual activities of adults by making a joke that if the barrier were not there (if the door had not been boarded up), the people who came to see me would say, "Well, howdy!" I then replied that I could not be in two rooms at the same time, to which she again laughed and said, "I guess you never come in here unless you're talking with the kids you see."

Lara's phobia in regard to school and knowing had developed from the panic associated with forming a relationship with someone other than her mother to anxiety associated with an Oedipal figure in her life—her married female therapist. As she became Oedipal in relationship to me (she had fantasies about my husband), she no longer avoided knowing, but became wary of the results of understanding and sought to suppress them in an effort to keep them from either her own or my awareness. When she felt I had given her permission to know—I had said she was correct in her guess about what was on the other side of the barrier—she made clear that she was aware of her suppression as a mental function by saying she "didn't dare" talk about something which had occurred to her. Then, she was able to hear an interpretation (that the barrier separated different aspects of my life) which freed her to share the suppressed thought (her imagined greeting of "Well, howdy" as she spun the fantasy of being a part of my relationship with my husband).

Lara's deliberate suppression (what she dared not say) was related to other suppressions and to various repressions which became evident later in therapy. Six weeks after she had inquired about the "barrier," when she had been in therapy for 15 months, she made a first direct reference to her father. She described how when her parents had separated (some 4 years earlier), she had packed up all the toys he had given her, but had found herself unable to give them away. So she kept them hidden in her closet. She then described how curious she had been when she was little about her parents' activities, adding that she could not "find out what they did in the bedroom because my mother figured out what I was curious about and began to sleep with me." It is quite likely that Lara's mother slept with Lara to avoid her father, yet the sleeping arrangements had other meanings for her. She alluded to another source of her problems with her mother—her mother's relentless attempts to keep Lara away from her father or from knowing about his marital relationship. Also with this statement, Lara paired knowing with preventing knowing. She said her mother "figured" Lara out only to prevent her from "finding out." As soon as her mother understood Lara's motives, Lara seemed to say, she then set about preventing Lara from knowing anything more by preventing sexual events from occurring.

During this same session, she also related how her mother frequently told her not to reveal some goings-on in the family. I asked what things her mother wished her to keep secret from me to which Lara answered, "Everything about her...all the things she does or doesn't do...that's why I talk mostly about myself." Lara thus showed she was aware of her mother's secrecy and implied that either she did not know what her mother's secrets were or that she felt compelled to keep quiet about them. In an unexpected way, her mother's secrets helped Lara "talk mostly about myself," which in some sense reinforced her sense of self. This point illustrates that it is not the secrets of the adult which impede the child's development, but the unwelcome intrusion of the adult into the child's world and personality. On the contrary, the secrets of important adults probably motivate a child to find out if her attempts are not crushed by a massive effort to rearrange reality (such as a parent switching the bedrooms of family members or endlessly transferring a child from school to school). It was thus critical that at the moment Lara told me why she talked mostly about herself, I congratulated her on understanding what therapy is all about, and asked what else about herself she would like to share.

Nonetheless, Lara's deliberate suppressions increased in frequency, and they were the result primarily of the conflict she felt in relating to me as she became more involved with her therapy, which her mother correctly observed. At the close of her 15th month of therapy, Lara still had not returned to school, a fact which mother and daughter tried to hide from themselves by refusing to come to therapy appointments if they fell on school holidays. Lara's mother explained to me that "Lara's working very hard and *deserves* school holidays" when she would repeatedly cancel Lara's appointment if it was scheduled on those Monday holidays when school was not in session. It seemed to me that since school vacations imply school attendance, declining to come to therapy on school holidays permitted both Lara and her mother to play out the charade that Lara was attending school. By canceling Lara's appointment on school holidays, Lara's mother may have meant to say she was the teacher and home was school.

Another suppression when her mother canceled the previous week's appointment consisted of Lara's pretending she did not know why her mother had canceled it. Her suppression also pointed to the residue of Lara's symbiotic attachment to her mother. Since her mother decided to create the "reality" that Lara was attending school (she was working "very hard" at home), Lara felt she had no choice but to accept her mother's version by failing to remember the reason for her not coming to her appointment—her mother had planned to take Lara shopping.[4] When Lara came for her next appointment (she had missed one meeting after the one in which she talked for the first time about her father), I remarked that it had been a long time since she and I had met. Lara seemed to feign confusion and said, "I just can't remember why we weren't here last week," and in the use of "we" implied that the decision not to come had not been solely her own. It may have also implied by then she felt it would be appropriate for her mother to have entered treatment: if "we" (mother and daughter) were "here" (in my office), perhaps the underlying problem of their relationship would be the focus of my efforts. (I had suggested to Lara's mother when her first daughter died that she might consider psychotherapy, either in sessions with Lara or individually, but she rejected the suggestion, although she did express her appreciation of it by saying, "I'm grateful that you care that much about me." I continued to meet with both Lara's mother and father in parent conferences.)

Immediately after Lara said she could not remember why she had missed her last appointment, she launched into a discussion of her mother's "bad moods." She said her mother was always in a "bad mood" just before bringing Lara to therapy and, for that reason, she wished she did not have to come. Thus, Lara's new use of therapy was to avoid hurting her mother's feelings by wishing to stay home. Although she might have meant to voice her own resistance to therapy—that it was she, not her mother, who was in a "bad mood" about appointments—it would have been a therapeutic error to have said to Lara that she may have shared her mother's resistance. Such a statement would have

[4]Relevant in this context is Anthony's (1971) vivid description of the interaction of the mental systems of a disturbed ("deluded") mother and a young child, which can feed each other's disturbance in destructive ways. According to Anthony, "It is reasonable to suppose that when these two unusual systems, belonging to the deluded mother and to her preschool child, came into contact, they tend to create a common pool of paralogical ideas fed by unrealistic and irrational sources, and leading in time to the efflorescence of bizarre ideas and associations" (p. 268). Lara's mother was not manifestly psychotic, but she did confront Lara with her own version of reality as unquestionable and, furthermore, insisted that Lara accept that reality version without reservation. Lara might thus have felt she *had* to share her mother's fabrications in what Stern (1985) has termed an "intersubjective domain."

thrown Lara back to the symbiotic position. It would have implied to her that whatever she said about her mother was predictably true of her. Instead, I wanted to encourage the decentering process by clearly differentiating statements in reference to either Lara's mother or to Lara, but never including their dissimilar feelings (or other characteristics) in the same phrase. So I said I was sorry her mother was in a "bad mood" about bringing Lara to therapy. Then I added, "But I'm very glad to see *you*." To this Lara answered, "Once I get here, I like it. I wish I could stay longer than fifty minutes."

Thereafter, conversations between Lara and me focused increasingly on ways in which people are different, not similar. She seemed to have understood enough about her relationship to her mother and me to understand she could relate to two or more individuals. Understanding more than one important relationship prepared Lara to imagine relating simultaneously to her two parents and to those two important women in her life—her mother and me.

CLINICAL ISSUES

Triadic Relationships and Conceptual Development

The successful resolution of the Oedipal triad depends in part on the child's ability to decenter, and a successful resolution, in turn, most certainly matures the child's cognitive ability to see social situations from more than one perspective. The child comes to act as if she now knows: the fact that I am *like* my parent means I am *not* equivalent to her. The stable identification with the mother permits the daughter to comprehend that her mother's view of her father differs from her own. Because Lara had yet to progress beyond her atypical attachment to her mother, she had not fully developed a normal ability to be part of a triad. She could not identify with her mother because she had never separated from her comfortably. Equally problematic, before the age of almost 10½, she had not decentered sufficiently to understand consistently that her perspective was not the same as that of the parent to whom she had been overly attached. Because at times the symbiosis meant she *was* her mother, not just merely similar to her, she originally supposed that what was true for her mother was also true for herself. It thus seemed entirely reasonable to her that her mother would seek to keep her away from her father, or to prevent her from discovering details of her father's life, since in Lara's immature view, she-merged-with-mother was a realistic threat to the marital relationship. This might explain why she so off-handedly told me that her mother slept in her room in order to keep Lara from knowing what went on in the parental bedroom. She believed her mother had the practical aim to prohibit an identical other person from interacting with Lara's father. Lara had not thought of the obvious: If I am the same (person) as my mother, then why am I a threat to her?

As she became increasingly comfortable with me, Lara spoke prosaically about the past and present sleeping arrangements in her household. She was not anxious when she described both real and possible events in the family bedrooms. Although Lara was of a chronological age at which most children have become post-Oedipal, she was not yet post-Oedipal in the developmental sense. Oedipal themes did not surface from the preconscious in therapy but were instead *elicited* by her more normal attachment to me. This attachment had initially been modeled on her symbiotic attachment to her mother but more recently had become influenced by her approach to normality wherein, like a much younger child, she once again became curious about the sexual activity of adults. When she suppressed curiosity about me or my office by saying she dared not tell me about an Oedipal fantasy, I thought she had regenerated the normal development trend wherein suppression of sexual fantasies is followed by repression of them. I further thought that she had throughout her life span resisted leaving the developmental phase in which she differentiated herself from her mother because she was fearful of relating to both parents as a distinct individual. At each point in her subsequent development, she seemed to retreat to the safety of a blurred identity because the longer she postponed an eager differentiation from her mother and a normal attraction to and curiosity about her father, the more dangerous self-differentiation became. In other words, it was the threat of the Oedipal crisis at each point in her life experience that enticed her to retreat to the immediately preceding phase of reuniting.

Egocentrism versus Repression

It is important not to mistake the effects of egocentrism for those of repression. Initially, Lara's symptoms did not result from having repressed but rather from an underdeveloped—and thus an undecentered—sense of self. So my initial aim as Lara's therapist was not to undo repression but to wean her from the enmeshed mother–daughter attachment by encouraging interpersonal decentering. The first step was for Lara and me to understand her recreation of the mother–daughter attachment in therapy so that she might question whether she was the same as me—and by implication, whether she was the same as her mother. The second step was Lara's question: How can it be that my therapist does not have the same reactions (to what she talked about) as my mother? With this question, she could ask herself again if it was true that she shared every thought and feeling with her mother, as she had originally stated in early appointments. She became aware of some important differences between me and her mother: I did not seek to keep the fact of sexual life from her, nor did I indicate that the only aspect of my life was in the office and never the bedroom, nor did I divulge the specifics of my life in the bedroom. And most important, the existence of erotic life impressed itself upon her in contrast to the details of this life which remained unknown to her. All these elements of our interaction helped Lara become aware that I was different from her mother, that *she* was different from her mother and from me, and that people are different from one another. Although she understood that her time with me was special, as symbolized by my office, she knew I also had a special time with someone else (my husband). Perhaps because Lara did not have a relationship with this "someone else," it meant to her that she was not reacted to as though she were the same as me. This awareness combined with the fact that she knew I did have a relationship with another adult might have freed her from the symbiotic character of the transference and might have paved the way for her to question the value of her attachment to her mother. If so, this therapeutic development partially arose from real-life events rather than merely the analyzed past. Lara effectively practiced her separation from and identification with me by taking advantage of the fact that my office was in my residence.

Her more normal relationship to me gave her a reason to repress. Contrarily, by sleeping with Lara, her mother refused to give her the opportunity to guess about or to observe her parents in their bedroom. Without this sexual "knowledge" and a proper identification with the same gender parent, repression is improbable because the child is prevented from having a reason to repress; she neither "knows" about her parents' sexual behavior nor attempts to consolidate her alliance with her mother by expecting to relate differently to her father than her mother does. Although Lara may have fantasized about her parents' behavior when they shared the same bed, she could not be expected to repress her reactions to sexual events if they did not occur. Now, Lara had reason to repress but did not do so solely as the result of sexual impulses and fantasies. Many of the first repressions I witnessed during our conversations occurred as she stabilized her identification with me and tried to change the character of her attachments from enmeshed to reciprocal.

Recreating the Triad

Lara's forgetting during the therapeutic hour, and later her repressing what happened in therapy, revealed that she felt she had to suppress or repress the meaning of the therapeutic bond as well as her mother's attempted interference with it. She "forgot" why she had not come to her therapy appointment. Suppressing or repressing in my presence what she did with her mother and in her mother's presence what she did with me served two purposes: It left open the possibility that at any time she might return to her attachment to her mother, and it also created the opportunity to form a normal relationship with me. In permitting her these two possibilities, repression thus acted in an adaptive way for Lara. "Forgetting" was adaptive because it enabled her to form and to develop a fully triadic interactional nexus. Even though this was not erotic, her attempts to interact with two important people were in process very like the young child's first attempts to achieve a triadic equilibrium when struggling with relationships with her two parents.

As she perceived she was capable of relating both to me and her mother and that I did not retaliate when she revealed by protecting her mother that she was an important person in her life, Lara began to fantasize about her father and to reveal she wished to spend more time with him. Then, she found it difficult to imagine being *herself* with her father. Her feeling that it was unsafe to be herself with her father again reflected partial understanding as well as her impending adolescence. When she ventured toward the thought that she was herself (and an increasingly attractive self) her relationship with her father seemed unsafe because she had always assumed he would behave toward her as he had toward her mother-merged-with-Lara.[5]

Hence, it is significant that what Lara did repress, the dream she had in kindergarten which told her that school would make her different from her mother, was asexual and pre-Oedipal. Lara remembered this dream every autumn until she was 8 years when she repressed it. My view is that she repressed the dream at 8 years as the result of more developed cognitive processes. Lara had recognized that the dream "returned" to her consciousness as she returned to school after summer vacation and, with this recognition, she could push the dream from consciousness at age 8 on entering a new grade, whereas she was unable to do so at ages 5, 6, and 7.

But when she reported the dream in therapy at age 9½, she did not initially evaluate the dream as she told it: it was as if the dream told her what reality told her or as if the dream "explained" why she had become school phobic. The remembering and retelling of the dream (in this case, to me) became a "rational" explanation of her behavior in regard to school. She did not at first try to understand dreams as different from reality or to cogitate how she could change reality. She used dreams as justifications ("reasons") for behaving rather than recognizing that both dreams and justifications originate from motives. Furthermore, she could not imagine changing either her rationalizations or her behavior based on them. The dream and her memories of it merely revealed to her what her core problem was when she was a very young child, a problem which continued to the present. It had created a flood of unmanageable affect and had exerted an influence on her every autumn as she sought to keep both the dream and the affect associated with it from consciousness by refusing to go to school. Cognition had moved Lara ahead unevenly. She had become aware of the association between her return to school and the return of the dream about school, but at age 8 she still had not become consistently aware of herself as unique.

[5]While Lara's Oedipal experience was atypical, there was little evidence in her behavior to suggest an actual seduction by either her father or her mother—which, of course, does not rule out the possibility. It is probably most accurate to say that Lara's behavior spanned more than one level of psychosexual development as she tried to make her interactions with her mother both safe and more reciprocal and, at the same time, to make her interactions with her father safe as she recognized she could interact with him as an individual distinct from her mother. Yet she might have been at risk for homosexuality in adolescence and heterosexual acting out, since the young person typically experiences intensified same-gender attachments and homosexual fantasies in early adolescence which can outlive later developmental phases and become consolidated in late adolescence or early adulthood (Blos, 1962, 1979). However, preadolescent Lara's normal sexual curiosity and affective reactions to this as she became embarrassed and silent when she got an answer to her question about my bedroom on the other side of the barrier suggests that normal developmental trends had been at least partially reinstated.

Repression and Cognition

Repression in the normal child appears tied primarily to sexuality because we tend to ignore that most youngsters systematize their thought processes while simultaneously struggling with Oedipal fantasy. The speculation here is that repression is quite likely to be more efficient when it arises from those more mature thought processes which inform children of the difference between the trustworthy and the threatening. When children can reason about the difference between "good" and "bad" and apply or invent names for these personal or interpersonal experiences, they can be more systematic about what they avoid. In making the statement that cognitive progression accelerates during the Oedipal phase, I am not denying the child's Oedipal impulsivity nor the sexual quality of her fantasy life. I am saying that maturing thought enables children to deal with impulse and fantasy differently than they did in the past. I am also saying that repression can be seen in regard to various psychological themes.

In Lara's case, repression first occurred (in therapy) as she became able to conceptualize three different perspectives: her mother's, mine, and her own. If we view repression as partly arising from cognitive maturity, it is easier to explain Lara's experience of repression as often asexual. Cognitive maturity enables children to imagine many potentially threatening events, not just those that are sexual. Because she wished to protect two relationships (the one with her mother and the one with me) and because she had a firmer sense of her motives regarding the protection of these two relationships, in therapy Lara adaptively repressed the quality of her relationship to her mother and at home she adaptively repressed the quality of her relationship to me. In other words, during the therapy hour, her attachment to her mother seemed threatening and at home her relationship to me seemed threatening. Yet her cognitive advances permitted her to differentiate these two important relationships, and later to differentiate her two parental relationships. Children like Lara who develop atypically often repress what a *relationship* means—not just what a *sexual* relationship means. In Lara's case, repression was related to the conflicts she felt as she acknowledged a growing sense of self and formed reciprocal relationships, which often seemed riskier than fading into enmeshed attachments.

LATER DEVELOPMENTS IN THERAPY

Individuation and Increased Repression

During Lara's 16th month of therapy, she sought to test the safety of individuation in a most dramatic fashion by enacting and freeing herself from the symbiotic stance. Her primary motive was to find out if interpersonal understanding threatened her newly begun attempts at intrapsychic understanding. Would her past and present attempts to understand her therapist lead to a breakdown in knowing about and strengthening herself? How safe was it to discover the unique qualities of other people? Would understanding the personalities of others tempt her to mimic them rather than develop and "prove" herself?

She launched into a tirade about how "terrible" she was at making friends. But she listened appreciatively for a moment when I said that her tirade reflected a deep need for people. Then suddenly she pointed to the door to the hall which was next to the "barrier" she had remarked about previously, and asked where the hall led. I replied that it led to the other rooms we had talked about before. She declared that before coming to her appointment she had invented a trick to carry out, and asked that I leave her in the office and go out into the hall. Amused, but wary, I asked what she had in mind. She said that if I refused to leave the office, that meant I did not "trust" her.

With dramatic flair and an unusual sense of purpose, she said I must prove that I trust her and comply with her request: "If you agree to my trick, you have to follow through by really going out of here into the hall." It thus appeared that she had constructed a test of our relationship and, probably because of the friendly deliberation in her behavior, I went along with her request and left the office. Thereupon Lara promptly shut the door, stood back up against it, and refused to let me back in.[6] She refused to budge and threatened not to move until I told her what I did not like about her. Since I was aware that she wished to be in control of the interaction between us, that is, the therapeutic space, I said I thought she wanted to control what happened between us, and added that the only aspect of her behavior I could think of at the moment was that I did not like being shut out. She answered, "Come on! That's just a joke. You're not being serious!" I told her that it was no joke being out in the hall when she was in the office. She continued to insist that I answer her question: "What's wrong with me?" She also told me that she had in mind either to "shut out" or "shut up" her mother by enticing her into a closet or shutting her out of her room—both for the same purpose: "I want to know what's *wrong* with me?" When I refused to enumerate her imagined negative qualities or personality flaws, she became disappointed and pleaded: "Well, do you think I don't talk enough, or talk about the right things...or *look* right...what don't you like about me, isn't there anything? How *can* you like *everything* about me?"

As I listened to her it became clear, first, that Lara wanted a diagnosis ("what's wrong with me?") because now she felt distinct from others; the ab-

---

[6]To answer the objection that Lara's request ought to have been discussed and not acted on, I would like to assert that discussion without action is appropriate for adults and many adolescents but not always for children. Especially young children trust action more than discussion when they wish to find out whether the adult cares about them or what the adult intends. The same is true on many occasions in work with older child patients and adolescents who have serious symptoms. This is not to advocate that the therapist should engage in action interventions in a careless, seductive, impulsive, whimsical, or self-serving fashion. Action interventions must be as carefully thought out as spoken interpretations—perhaps, if it were possible, *more* carefully thought out. Specifically, neither Lara nor I were ever in any physical danger as she stood back up against the door and refused to let me in the office. There were no locks on the door, so that if I had to reenter the office to protect Lara I could have done so easily.

sence of a sense of self had been replaced by a doubting self. Second, she seemed to want recognition for her progress in therapy as she asked whether she had talked enough or about the rights things. So I described her progress in talking with me about her motives for behaving: "Lately you have been asking a lot of questions about yourself in therapy and my reactions to you." I compared her first months in therapy with her recent progress, intending to pinpoint that she had become much more reciprocally attuned which, I supposed, was why she was so concerned about my opinion of her: "*Before* you thought you could read my mind but *now* I think you know we can talk to each other about what we don't know about each other." I finished my remarks by saying that I surmised she was not just concerned about *my* opinion of her, but her *own* opinion of herself. I wanted to focus the discussion once more on her view that she had felt indistinct in the past because of the "wrong" feeling inside her; that is, she had tried to merge with the personalities of other people because she felt she was deficient in some way ("what's *wrong* with me?"). In attempting to solve this problem, she created a second one in which her merging attempts made her feel indistinct. She thus felt either "wrong" or selfless which now she addressed by causing a physical separation from me by requiring me to leave the office and testing whether she felt "okay" as a separate individual. She answered my simplified statements to her, "But that's so positive, isn't there *anything* negative?" When I said then I thought she wished to see if I would still like her even though she shut me out she opened the door. As I reentered the office, she quipped abruptly, "Maybe I should have asked you to tell me what's *right* about me!"

Searles (1986) reported similar questions asked of him by adults in psychoanalysis. In a chapter detailing borderline ego functioning, he interprets such questions as, first, representative of unconscious Oedipal longings; that is, when the adult in psychoanalysis asks the analyst "what is wrong with me," he means to inquire why there cannot be a romantic relationship between the patient and the analyst. More important for my purposes is Searles's assertion that the deeper unconscious meaning of "what's wrong with me" consists of the patient's implicit request that the therapist surrender his individuality to enter a symbiotic identity with the patient: "Why have you still not accepted me fully...and entered fully into a symbiotic identity with me?" (p. 93). Since Lara often wished to create a symbiotic twosome between me and her where she, not I, was the active, originating partner to the symbiosis, in this particular case she inquired what was "wrong" with her *after* requesting that I leave my office. To me this signified she wished not to create a symbiosis between the two of us but rather to create a physical distance between us within which she tested whether she was a viable personality. And, on a conscious level, to Lara it seemed improbable that even a therapist could "like" every aspect of her personality. I tried to address this therapeutic dilemma honestly by answering that I did not like being shut out of my office. When Lara heard me say that I nonetheless still appreciated her as an individual, she responded appropriately by implicitly asking that I enumerate her good qualities ("Maybe I should have asked you to tell me what's *right* about me").

For many months Lara had sat in my office in such a way as to face the door to the hall and the barrier which were side by side. When she gazed at the side of the room where the barrier and the door to the hall were, these two doors might have seemed to her like a fork in a road: one stimulated normal Oedipal fantasy and the other actually led to my bedroom. Since she had relegated me to the hall, the barrier might have represented an opportunity now open to her to experience Oedipal fantasy about what was on the other side. As if to make Oedipal fantasy safe, she put me outside the office so that she might fantasize without my interfering presence at the same time that, in a sense, I stood guard on the other side of the door lest she be tempted in reality to explore the other rooms of my house.[7] Because her mother had always prevented her from interacting with or knowing about her father at the *same* time that she seemed to invite a seduction by sleeping in Lara's bed, Lara's request that she be alone while facing the barrier with me as sentry in the hall seemed to be her way of moving normally through the Oedipal phase.

But, during the therapy hour, it became much more complex. Lara's demand that I leave was a replay of her earlier experiences of her mother's absences except that now she imagined control over my comings and goings. Her activity of banishing me showed she was aware of having felt controlled by her mother's decisions regarding leaving and returning. My statements were geared to turning this negative experience into a positive one. As Lara tried to turn the passive experience of being left into the active one of forcing me to leave, I tried to change the experience from negative to positive by implying that I remained sufficiently positive about her to continue my attempts to understand her however anxious she might have thought I was being shut out of my own office. Most important, if I were in the hall and she was in my office, she and I must finally, completely, and undoubtedly be two *separate* people!

Ten days later, Lara gave the first evidence of having repressed as the result of what happened in therapy. Her next regular appointment after the week she had dismissed me from my office had been rescheduled by me because I had gone out of town. When she came to her rescheduled appointment, she echoed my words of three weeks before complaining it had "been so long" since she had been to see me. To make explicit some connections implicit in her (flawed) reasoning, I told her as one might tell an adolescent or an adult that perhaps she thought I had been absent because she had shut me out the last time we met. To

---

[7]Most therapists have a few ground rules about how psychotherapy with children should be conducted. For example, Anthony (1982) describes how he gently suggests that a child stay put on the couch where he can play, talk, or relax (p. 351). My guidelines include requesting that youngsters play or talk to me in my office, or on the way to and from it. When Lara asked to roam about my house, I explained that my office was the special room in which I talked to young people. Thereupon she began to spin fantasies about those rooms which most interested her—first, the bedroom, and later the living room and the kitchen. Her curiosity about me as distinct from her had helped her guess that while I was inept at sewing and art, I was interested in music and cooking which she surmised from noticing a piano on the way to the office and from appraising my pleased reaction to her mother's gift of dried herbs. Furthermore, she apologized for having asked me earlier about the office barrier to my bedroom, observing accurately, "That's not what most kids my age would ask about."

this she reacted with a disoriented "Huh?" I thought she had forgotten her request that I leave my office because she was afraid she had offended me. I reminded her that she had wanted me to tell her what is wrong with her and was about to say that I had not been offended when her face broke out into a dawning look of recognition as she said, "Oh yeah! I did the same thing to my friend down the street, and she fell and hurt herself." I told Lara that no one had been hurt in my office—not their bodies nor their feelings—to which she sighed in relief and regained her (by now) normal interactional style.

Then, as though to alert me that she no longer denied her school absences, she confided how important it would have been had she kept her regular appointment (during the time I had been out of town) by recalling that if she had come for her regular hour, "It would have been the first time I came on a holiday. I was thinking I don't have a friend, but I still had you. And then you went away." She may have concluded that since she had recently banished me to the hall, I had retaliated by going away and missing her regular appointment. If so, she might have been recapturing the many scenes much younger children enact as they investigate with objects the causes of disappearing and reappearing, wishing to control the reappearance of people. In this particular case, Lara was certain she could cause me to disappear by demanding that I leave my office. But since she was afraid she had hurt my feelings, she was not so sure she could make me reappear. Most important was Lara's concise statement to me that she no longer needed to deny her school refusal (she could now confront the fact that she did not attend school and so could come to see me on a school holiday), and that she had differentiated the roles of "friend" and "therapist" in her life. Now, I was only therapist and not the wished-for friend of her first months of therapy.

CONCLUSION OF LARA'S THERAPY

By the time Lara had been in therapy exactly 2 years, forgetting and repression had become part of her typical repertoire in the therapeutic hour. At 11 years and 1 month, her "forgetting" seemed to be the result of repression and thus dissimilar from the momentary forgetting of 7-year-old Robin, whose memory lapses, in the instances I observed, always resulted in his recapturing forgotten thoughts. Lara's "forgetting" often spanned weeks and seemed to reflect a more developed mental structure: it often took many minutes or even several therapy hours before she could reclaim what she had forgotten, attempts which were generally accompanied by anxiety. I saw Lara's development of a mental structure which would enable an ongoing defensive mechanism to operate as the result of progressive intellectual development, a sign of mental health. For instance, I perceived a heightened self-reflexive sense in her need to know what I thought of her, which led her to repress those opinions she feared I might hold. By relating reciprocally, she wished to know what an important person thought of her. Because she feared a negative opinion, she created a situation to test that imagined opinion. When she became aware of what I might think or feel about the test (being banished to the hall) she repressed this event for the same reason she had originally brought it about.

Along with "forgetting" numerous facts about her life (i.e., declining to remember) two years of therapy marked other new developments, notably new efforts to reach out to others. For the first time since I had known her, beginning at Christmas, perhaps because her first appointment occurred during the holidays, she began bringing me presents, paintings or other of her art works. She also began to voice her interest in boys, and as she approached adolescence, gave one more piece of evidence that she was progressing normally. She told how, in one of her forgetful moments, she had phoned her boyfriend instead of her girlfriend. When told that this was indeed a convenient "forgetting," she laughingly answered that she had had the same thought.

But in spite of her progress, Lara, like Annie (see Chapter 4) was brought up short by the results of understanding. To Annie, math knowledge meant that she could not use two-digit addition to separate her problems from her mother's at the very moment she most wanted to. Thereupon, she seemed to sacrifice her greater understanding of two-digit addition as she asserted that the two digits of the numerical twosome could be added separately regardless of the numbers in question. She felt compelled to say that the two "problems" (her own and her mother's) must be detached because she wished to assert that her father's relationship to her was different from his relationship to her mother. Through math manipulations, she tried to resolve her Oedipal crisis. Similarly, Lara was brought up short as she became more decentered in her thinking. A decentered cast of mind told her, like her dream of the children at school, that she was different from her mother—a fact Lara often could tolerate, but her mother often could not. Her mother's inability to adapt to her changing child meant that interpersonal decentering had certain risks for Lara. Often she appeared aware there were risks involved in changing and seemed to wish to retard the progressive trend which would reveal that she was different from her mother and therefore a unique individual. Describing Piaget's view, Flavell (1963) has stated about the decline of egocentrism:

> social interaction is the principal liberating factor, particularly social interaction with peers. In the course of his contacts (and especially, his conflicts and arguments) with other children, the child increasingly finds himself forced to reexamine his own percepts and concepts in the light of those of others, and by so doing, gradually rids himself of cognitive egocentrism. (p. 279)

Since Lara had not yet returned to school, she had little opportunity to interact with peers compared to a normal youngster, but in her interactions with me, she did try to rid herself of egocentrism. A self-reflexive sense quickened with her declining egocentrism and she often understood that her individuality was a threat to her mother. For this and other reasons, she wished to interrupt therapy, possibly as a magical maneuver to stop her progressive trend.

But Lara also wished to test her opinions about discontinuing therapy against mine. Like the normal child who argues with peers, perhaps she wished to "argue" with me about her therapy. From the 17th to the 24th month of her treatment, she discussed how she felt about her anticipated withdrawal from therapy. She would present "reasons for" stopping therapy and "reasons against" expecting me to respond empathically, but also systematically. I felt if I merely said, "You're not ready to stop coming," she would have been disappointed, hoping I could support my position with rational statements. Moreover, as she discussed the termination of therapy, it became evident that her decision to discontinue held a positive motive. It meant a clearcut separation from me which was the result of her decision, not mine.

Then, from the 25th month of therapy until her last session, she concentrated on her anticipated return to school. It seemed to me that once she worked through her separation from me she could resolutely approach what had brought her into therapy: her ambivalence about school attendance. She tried to understand once again how her perceptions of her mother figured in her school ambivalence. She said one day, "Mom says things she doesn't really mean." When asked to elaborate, she explained that her mother had always said she wanted Lara to return to school, or take art lessons, or have friends, but "whenever I do, she always gets in a bad mood. That's what made me want to stay home, I felt I had to take care of her because she was so unhappy, and I hated those moods." She then explained that her desire to stop therapy was the result of her need to "prevent those bad moods," adding that her mother was so tense while driving her to therapy that she was afraid she would "crash the car." The fantasy of "crashing the car" bore an obvious connection to a real event (her sister's automobile accident) which had thrown Lara back into a renewed symbiotic phase with her mother.

But she also told me how she had recently set up a "keep out" drawer and a "keep out" shelf in her closet in which she kept her secret treasures, hoping that the signs on her drawer and closet shelf would be respected by her mother. Where before Lara shunned writing and spelling because doing so correctly would reveal she was "different" from her mother, now she relished writing and spelling correctly precisely because these activities differentiated her from her mother. Her message "keep out" asserted which parts of her room—presumably representing which parts of her life—were private.

I felt that Lara's wish to discontinue therapy should be respected because she had decided to return to school and had come a long way in understanding the genesis of her school phobia in her enmeshed attachment to her mother, and its roots in her mother's wish to subvert Lara's relating to her father, or other adults, such as a teacher or her psychotherapist. In an effort to support Lara as a person in her own right, it seemed wise to respect her decision in regard to both school *and* therapy. Even though I worried about her readjustment to school and believed our continuing to converse about her school anxieties might ease this adjustment, I also recognized, first and foremost, that Lara had made these two decisions on her own: returning to school, however much her mother may have disapproved of it, and deciding to stop therapy, however much her mother may have welcomed it. Second, it appeared that had I refused to accept her exercise of will in therapy, I might have been perceived by Lara exactly as her mother was perceived—overbearing in asserting my wishes over hers. Moreover, Lara needed to separate emotionally from me as she had earlier separated physically by demanding that I go out into the hall. My attempts to help her understand her continuing agoraphobia were not as effective as the simple act of letting her go. Even if I perceptively and adroitly commented that she had ingeniously disarmed her mother's attempts to keep her at home by sacrificing her relationship to me, she might have felt I was trying to bind her to therapy, or at least maintain her dependence on me by my clever remarks. Precisely because Lara had listened to my interpretive statements in the past and knew they reflected an empathic understanding, she may have felt she had to separate from me by leaving therapy. Once more, therapeutic empathy seemed to recreate the symbiosis she had experienced with her mother.

After Lara made the decision to discontinue therapy, it took her over a year to actually terminate. Perhaps my willingness to repeatedly discuss her intention to stop therapy meant to her that I was not eager to let her go. But I did tell her I was pleased she had made a decision about therapy on her own and if she wished to tell me, I would like to hear how she was doing in the future. In an unexpected way, my letting Lara go might have contributed to her ongoing determination to return to school. The message she got said decisions about relationships were hers to make, and through this support she was enabled to make and stick by a decision to return to school and renew old friendships.

When Lara came for her final appointment, she announced that she had a secret plan. The secret turned out to be a tape recorder with which she hoped to tape our last conversation, and as such her plan probably stood for the secret of our relationship. She had already taped a conversation she had recently with her father, which she played for me and listened to avidly. Watching my reaction to hearing her talk with her father, she got a positive response to her implicit question: Would I tolerate her normal interactions with him? She was able to observe my amused reactions as I listened to her father's jokes. Then she played a sequence she had taped without my knowing of our initial exchange at the door when she hid the tape recorder and impishly announced she had a secret. As the hour progressed, she became withdrawn and sad, and told in a moment of despair how her mother had interrupted her art lessons at school because she did not like the teacher. Since she seemed to be merging her experience of taking art lessons with her experience of therapy which was to end that very day, I told her that it was too bad she had to give up art when she was so good at it, and moreover, that she was very good at therapy as well. To this she answered: "At my age, we kids have lots of secrets we keep from you adults. Sometimes I want you to guess what they are, but I'd really rather keep them to myself. Don't you think that's normal?"

Her question to me indeed revealed a startling approach to adolescent normality. As I acknowledged her skill at self-analysis, she immediately voiced the typical adolescent wish to keep secret many of her thoughts and feelings. In this particular case, she referred to her accurate perception that it was normal to keep secret her feelings about her boyfriend. But it was also true that as she approached adolescence, the temptation to view relationships as cast in the old symbiotic mold once again surfaced in the final hour. She feared that I would intrude into her adolescent secrets, projecting once more onto therapy her experience at home with her mother. On leaving, she erased what she had taped of our therapeutic exchanges (but left intact her talk with her father), saying our conversation was for her "to remember and no one else to hear." Then she invited me to say goodbye to her mother, who was waiting outside in the car.

By saying she would "remember" our conversation, she seemed to reverse her recent and repeated tendencies to "forget." She also seemed to say that she intended to remember me differently than she did her father. By remembering me without an artificial device she suggested that she meant to internalize the quality of our interactions as she left therapy. Her parting statement implied that my silences meant my rejection of her. "When you say nothing, it makes me feel like I talk too much." "Talking too much" referred to Lara's perception of her mother's conversational style and showed how much she cared how she appeared to others as well as revealed her continuing feelings of vulnerability. Lara remained ambivalent about her mother's garrulity and wished me to reverse her identification with her mother by "saying something." In early childhood, she had had so few experiences of reciprocal relating that, as she was about to enter adolescence, she began to experience intense, but increasingly focused anxieties which meant, when she looked backward with a self-analytic glance, she had felt she had not been worthy to be a person in her own right.

Lara Two Years Later

A follow-up conversation I had with Lara 2 years later showed that she had kept her promise to herself to return to and maintain herself in school. As she gave up her relationship to me and perhaps then felt she was a more independent person, she could continue with school because she became less phobic about knowing itself. Learning in school and knowing in general could no longer tell her she was different from her mother (or from me) because she already knew it. And most importantly, school learning and general knowledge did not create a "self-phobia" because the development of her self in therapy had revealed to Lara that it was safe to be an individual distinct from at least one important female—her therapist.

Our telephone conversation revealed that she was truly comfortable only in those subject areas in which she was gifted (art, modern dance, and literature) which therefore felt safe, but she remained uncomfortable and cut classes in those subject areas which continued to give her difficulty (math and science). Still, knowing was no longer the threat it once was. She had completed the 7th grade, and while she had renounced her art lessons, she had continued with lessons in dance. About art she said, "I can learn all I need about art from myself." While she continued to submit to being taught in school or in dance class, she felt she had to teach herself art, and so echoed her mother's earlier statement, "Lara can learn all she needs to know from me." Lara's renewed relationship with her father continued, and they often shared times together in long walks or exercise, such as jogging. Her father had left his work as a traveling salesman and took part-time jobs teaching courses in business. This change in her father's work life held a potential risk for Lara in that school attendance might have seemed a more imposing threat to her relationship with her mother since she now might "learn" from her father who was a teacher — she might come to know what her father knew. She was probably helped to survive the risks of knowing because the change in her father's work life meant he was a more frequent presence in her life and could more actively participate in and support Lara's efforts to learn in school.

As Lara approached middle adolescence (14 years) and wished not to comprehend aspects of her experience, she behaved in the fashion of many a normal adolescent or adult by using a well-developed repressive defense. During our telephone conversation, in which she brought me up to date about her life, she forgot my first name, and then began to guess that it was Carol, possibly because the name Karen suggests caring (i.e., the colloquial "carin"). I thought she did not want to remember that I had cared about her. When she wished to inhibit understanding her ambivalence about my caring reaction, she did so in a more mature and efficient way than she had earlier when she simply avoided the school environment to inhibit understanding. Although her previous school phobia and avoidance of the school's environment can be viewed as effective in that she believed she prevented herself from perceiving how she was different from her mother, it was such a blatant and provocative escape that it created more problems than it solved and eventually caused her need for psychotherapy. Contrarily, her adolescent repression of my name occurred only between her and me. In this sense, it worked efficiently since her warding off efforts did not create any crises for other people (such as her mother or her teachers) nor did they cause a school crisis.

It can be said, then, that inhibition in the child which pervades action before mentation fully develops is more destructive to her progress than inhibition which primarily targets the child's thought (i.e., "interiorized" activity). Inhibition in children does exist before cognitive structures stabilize but because it impacts activity, it can hardly be called "passive." A strenuous form of activity is required to block another, motivated activity. Inhibition is active even though the result is passivity. Repression, which was for Freud the basis of adult psychopathology, actually marks a developmental milestone in children. Forms of inhibition permit the child to select not just what to repress but also what to understand. Moreover, the ability to comprehend paves the way for the child's developing capability to confront his reasons for inhibiting his psychic functions. Paradoxically, the very cognitive structures that permit inhibition allow its undoing.

CHAPTER 9

Cognition and Overcoming Inhibition

Conceptual development assists the youngster to overcome inhibition just as it aids and abets inhibiting functions. During the last several months of her therapy and also during our telephone conversations, I was able to observe a few significant instances when Lara succeeded in remembering what she had forgotten or when she was able to undo repressions. For example, when I returned to my office from the hall, she recalled that another version of her "trick" to make people speak the truth is to ask the other person "What's right about me" — not just "what's wrong with me." Similarly, she was able to remember my first name by free associating to the name Carol. (She said, "I was trying to remember your first name... It's Carol... no... I thought of Carol because of Christmas carols... when I first came [to therapy] it was Christmas... Carol sounds like Karen.") Just as important in adolescent Lara's case, when she remembered my name in a telephone conversation, she once more affirmed her sense of self as distinct from me but now on a more mature level than she had at age 3 when her mother appeared to "remember" and thus affirm her by calling her on the telephone. Now, *she* was active in "remembering" me in our telephone conversation while before she was passive when her *mother* remembered to call her from the airport.

But free association is not the only route to the undoing of repression in young people. On the contrary, because they conceptualize the undoing of forgetting and repressing differently from their adult therapists, other avenues to remembering are opened up in work with them. To children of all ages and stages, the undoing of repression and/or momentary forgetting appears similar to discovering something new. At the very least, they discover why they have repressed or forgotten. For the first time, they may even discover that repression as a mental function *exists*. Frequently, they also rearrange mental contents to take account of the recently reapprehended fact or feeling to form a different, often novel, perspective. In perceiving themselves and their environment differently, they feel they have "learned" something new in a safe way and have therefore reduced the hazards entailed by remembering and thinking. It can be said, then, that the anxiety which led to forgetting or repressing and the anxiety which may accompany the undoing of forgetting and repressing is overcome as youngsters uncover their motives for warding off and affirm it is their own insight which enables them to understand the warding off process.

RECONSTRUCTION VERSUS CONSTRUCTION OF THE PAST

According to psychoanalytic theory, repression in the adult patient is undone by free association which eventually leads him or her to some repressed or forgotten event and its associated affects. In the therapy of both adults and children, the critical question is the degree to which free associations "reconstruct" or "construct" events of the past. Perhaps the therapeutic process does not so much lead to a precise "illumination" of the past event as it does to a new configuration of it. A fresh view of the past represents the individual's renewed attempts to grasp what happened and to understand it in presumably a healthier way. When Piaget (1976) wrote of the "passage" from the unconscious to the conscious and said that it requires *re*constructions rather than simple illuminations (p. 332), I believe he meant to stress a *con*structive process of the conscious mind which seeks to take hold of that which may have been unself-conscious or preconscious. But this constructive process changes what has been ignored, suppressed and/or repressed, most especially in line with a child's progressive intellectual development. When Piaget (1973a), in a modest attempt to understand psychoanalysis, wrote of the problem of repression and its undoing as catharsis, he succinctly put before clinicians the problem of conceptual *re*organization:

> This process of becoming conscious cognitively recalls what psychoanalysts have described under the name of *catharsis*—simultaneously a "becoming conscious" of affective conflicts and a reorganization which permits them to be overcome. I am not competent in psychoanalytic theory and do not wish to be imprudent, but it seems to me that *catharsis* is something quite different from a simple illumination, or else we could not account for its therapeutic effect. It is a reintegration, a removal of conflicts through a new organization. But where does this new organization come from? (p. 257)

Similarly, some psychoanalytic writers since Freud assert that it is the new and ongoing mnemonic organization rather than a recovery of an exact copy of the past which is healing (Kohut, 1984; Leavy, 1973; Schafer, 1983; Spence, 1982). Spence calls this reorganization a *construction* of the past in contrast to a reconstruction of it in that events of the present inevitably add quality to remembered events. (Ekstein, 1966, makes a similar point about the attempts of seriously disturbed youngsters to reorganize their memories of the past.) The patient's attempts to rethink the past is healing, in my opinion, because (1) he realizes that his earlier perspective impeded his conscious goals and, (2) his efforts to reconceptualize heighten his self-reflexive sense which, with therapeutic support, leads him to question his motives in advance of his behavior.

Anna Freud (1971) writes about young children in therapy that free association to undo repression is neither possible nor necessary. She recognizes that the young child has not repressed for as long nor in the same fashion as the older child or the adult. Rather, she suggests that a therapeutic procedure to undo inhibition suited especially to the child would be the encouragement of his natural development (1971, p. 214). In my view, it is important to search the developmental trends of young people for therapeutic strategies to undo inhibition because twice in their lives the functions of the intellect approach operativity (concrete and formal operational thought). An approach to operativity increases the options for self-contradiction and for inhibition. A young person's increased awareness of his thought contradictions nonetheless often results in the undoing of suppression or repression while the cognitively secure adult's free associations often bring about the same result. That is, the individual finds it difficult to free associate when he has an unstable cognitive base to free associate to and thus tries instead of expand his thinking capability. The school phobic child or adolescent who has often apprehended more than other non-learning youngsters readily confronts thought inconsistencies, which releases previous thought patterns and unites them in a more mature and liberating aggregate. Those nonlearning youngsters who tend to retreat from thought contradictions — "overachievers" and "underachievers" — nonetheless can be encouraged in therapy to contemplate them, which often lifts the suppressive or repressive inhibition.

Apart from his learning style, it is the young person's fluctuating capability to reflect on the self which determines his ability and eagerness to consider *whether* he ignores, denies, forgets, suppresses, or represses. If he approaches self-understanding, he will question if he is seeking the truth about himself or if he is engaging in self-protective activities. If he is not fully capable of self-reflection or has reasons to inhibit the self-reflective function, he might use the tactic of fooling other people into thinking he neither has learned anything nor now possesses general or self-knowledge. In addition to the classical defense mechanisms, young people who wish to avoid learning often employ fooling as a way to camouflage their blossoming self-reflective activities and to prevent a significant other person from knowing their intentions. Fooling others is not merely disavowing affect; it also disavows the youngster's capability to acquire knowledge at the same time that it reveals an acute interpersonal understanding which permits him to foresee the success of his clever manipulations.

CHILDHOOD INHIBITION AND THE MEANING OF FOOLERY

The child's use of foolery to disguise what he knows and what he might reveal to others is a replay on a higher intellectual plane of the younger child's belief that what he does not know is not. Foolery is a complex and social variation invented by the child on the same theme of his alleged ignorance. Denial does not always occur within a social interaction. Contrarily, if a child can convince other people that he knows nothing, especially adults who seem to him to know everything, then these knowing adults seem to validate the child's wished-for stupidity. Thus, the act of foolery serves much like a warding off process because the knowing adult has said the child does not know. In a curious but always social way, the adult who believes the child to be stupid supports the child's attempts to push away what he knows and the affects associated with it—most importantly understanding his own intentions.

Matt, the boy who spelled backward except when he was typing (see Chapter 3), came to therapy at age 7 announcing, "I don't think. I never think about anything." His foolery during the therapy session had a double function: it sometimes prevented Matt from knowing what he thought or intended, and at other times, it had the surprising effect of undoing his thought inhibitions. After four therapy appointments, he expressed anger at his father by trying to fool me into believing that his father (who had brought him to therapy that day) was really his uncle: he implied that he had no father, only an uncle. In his imagination, he tricked me into believing him and this helped make his wish a reality. The following week when I pointed out that he had tried to fool me the previous week, he suddenly remembered what he had done, and said, "Oh yeah, I called my Dad 'names'—I said he was my uncle!" I thought when he called his father the "name" of "uncle" he had come closer to recognizing his anger at his father which originated in his conversations with his father about his college dropout. Matt knew from these conversations that his uncle and his mother had college degrees. This made Matt feel he could ill afford to learn in school lest he overtake the parent of the same gender whom he wished to admire. Learning in school thus meant he was like his uncle or his mother and not like his father. Calling names in this case contained a wish as much as it represented an insult.

Matt remembered he called his Dad his uncle not by manifest free association (although he may have free-associated silently) but by recognizing and attempting to transform a contradiction into a conception which clarified rather than confused his thoughts. When he heard me say, "There's always a good reason to try to fool people," her perceived the contradiction in my taking his foolery seriously. He may have even noticed that I was both amused and in earnest when I attempted to unearth his reasons for fooling. This may have prompted him to think and talk further about what was on his mind (his anxiety about spelling tests) and to clarify for himself why he sought to protect himself.

Matt had a history of enuresis which typically occurred the night before a spelling test, and which seemed related to his conflicts about school success. As he admitted his attempt to fool me, he also admitted that his enuresis the night before spelling tests "was not just an accident." But for 2 years he had called his occasional enuresis an accident and had therefore grown accustomed to thinking of bedwetting as having no cause, but merely being an accident. When he realized and admitted his responsibility for these "accidents" and their relationship to spelling tests, he seemed to change his mind that the enuresis was related to spelling at all. In his next breath, he explained how he had been wrong to say he always had a spelling test the day after he had wet his bed. This renewed attempt to fool me into believing that there was no relationship between these two events was intended to prevent him and me from knowing what he now thought. His foolery acted in much the same way as denial or repression does in adults: It permitted him to avoid thinking about a motivated event to which anxiety was tied.

But, as his session came to an end, Matt wanted to show me a spelling test on which he had gotten a good grade. Evidently he had forgotten his earlier denial of the connection between spelling tests and enuresis. As he fished the test out of his pocket he saw it was dated the day after he experienced enuresis — clear evidence that indeed there had been a connection between the enuresis the night before and the spelling test, which his mother had reported in his presence before his appointment began. When he saw that I noticed the date although I said nothing, a sheepish grin came over his face as he explained quietly, "I just wanted you to think I was dumb."

Matt's intent to fool me consisted of one self-contradiction after another. While in school and at home he could succeed in fooling adults, he began to perceive he could not fool me in therapy. In an attempt to escape what he really knew about himself and what he surmised I knew about him, he produced consecutive incongruities not just to camouflage his and my thought processes but also, surprisingly, to test his and my intelligence. He first asserted a connection between enuresis and spelling tests which he then denied in his attempt to persuade me that there not only had been no recent connection between these events but also there never could be. Then he momentarily forgot his attempt to fool me as he fished the spelling test out of his pocket on which he got a good grade. When he recognized contradiction in his statements and behavior, he came up with still another contradictory explanation: he found it difficult to admit that he *had* gotten a good grade because before he *always* tried to make adults believe he was dumb. Being "dumb" to Matt also meant denying that he could think of reasons for his behavior. But convincing others that he was incapable of thinking of reasons, he now knew, was evidence of his intelligence. Then he realized that he wished to deny that anxiety had led to enuresis and to conflict about success as he quietly admitted he only wanted me to "think" (i.e., believe) he was dumb at the same time that he implied I knew otherwise.

Foolery acted similarly for Betsy (see Chapter 5) whose impersonations of stupidity before therapy were more pervasive than Matt's. If the important adults in her life thought she knew nothing, then in reality she did not; that is, what she did not know or feel did not exist or had not occurred. But, as she progressed both in school and in therapy, she put foolery to very different uses in a dramatic reversal from being an alleged stupidity indicator to an intelligence indicator. Betsy, too, became aware in therapy of her thought incongruities and became fluid in her use of defenses, which is a sign of mental health. Just as she had been expert in projecting the "dumb" act, she became equally expert in setting traps to prove that she was just as smart as other people, or even smarter.

One day she revealed this switch in what she projected about her intelligence while talking with me. Playing doctor with a toy stethoscope she put it to her heart saying, "You can really hear your heartbeat with this, even though it's a toy." She said this with the same innocent nonchalance which had earlier accompanied her pretense of ignorance, and thus I was momentarily fooled because I thought she was again pretending not to know the difference between reality and fantasy. As she probably observed my puzzled look, she said, "Here, you try it" and handed me the stethoscope. When I did try it I found that indeed it was possible to hear a rather loud heartbeat. Betsy's complacent smile as she continued to observe me indicated the deliberate shift in her beguiling attempts. Smiling like a Cheshire cat, she showed she was as conspicuously aware of her intent as one of Shakespeare's fools, who deliberately and intricately play at deceiving other characters. Before, Betsy had played the fool to trick the other "players" in her life (family members and teachers) and understood that I, as "audience," appreciated the irony of her skillful performance — as one would appreciate a Shakespearean actor. Now, Betsy turned on me, her "audience," and made me foolish in one last attempt to avenge the myth of her mental retardation. I, as adult doctor, had become "dumb" while she, as child doctor, was smart. In one dramatic stroke within the transference she once more created and reversed the very situation which brought her to therapy.

CHILDREN'S STATEMENTS ABOUT FORGETTING AND REMEMBERING

Children rarely make statements about "repressing" because it is a difficult concept for them to grasp, but often they are aware of and comment about their "forgetting." When aware of forgetting, they usually exclaim about "remembering." Often it is the linguistic quality of a sentence that reveals whether a child is suffering from the effects of a defense such as repression or whether his behavior stems from the absence of a cognitive structure. When a child lacks a concept, he often makes flat, untrue, or immature statements. Children talk differently when they forget or repress facts and feelings — especially when they become aware that momentary forgetting and repression are concepts which apply to human behavior. If the adult is able to catch most of what the child says, he or she can discern the child's awareness of forgetting and repression by the language he uses. That is, the self-reflexive child's language is different from that of the less developed child who, as likely as not, lacks certain concepts and therefore does not forget them or repress effect associated with them.

Seven-year-old Rudy (see Chapter 2) had come to therapy because his mother believed he was mentally retarded and wanted advice from me about how best to "educate" him. Initially, Rudy rarely revealed in therapy that he had suppressed, forgotten and/or repressed but was more likely to abruptly assert what he knew (that the words *six* and *nine* which stand for these visually similar numerals are written differently) or, when he trusted me, to request information he did not possess. But, during the ensuing 2 years of therapy, he developed both an effective use of suppression and repression as well as a way to signal to me that it was underway. One day when he was 8½ years old he noticed a small dirt spot on the dollhouse boy's head as he was pretending that this boy doll had messed up the dollhouse dishes which were neatly set up for supper. Then, Rudy made the boy doll throw his homework papers all around the dollhouse living room. He had carefully positioned the dollhouse father doll to stand by watching the boy doll's antics which suggested that his father disapproved of his mother's supper preparations and also disapproved of Rudy's rejection of unfinished homework papers. When Rudy noticed the small dirt spot on the boy doll's head, he called it a "wound" and asked that I put a Band-aid on it. By having me put Band-aids on the doll's head he communicated to me that he wished to change—to cure his alleged mental retardation. I thought Rudy had correctly understood that his family's myth meant he could do nothing about his school problems because his parents perceived them as irreversible. Putting Band-aids on the doll's head symbolized that Rudy not only wished to heal his "wounds" but also his conviction that he and I could cure them in therapy.

Rudy took the therapeutic work a step further when he remarked that the father doll had no "wounds" (no dirt spots). In turn, I said the father doll probably did not want to have anything wrong with his head. On hearing this Rudy abruptly stopped the doll play and began to look for something else to play with, saying without finishing, "I think I'll do..." It was my impression that Rudy left the play because he thought I meant indeed there was nothing wrong with the father doll's head but that there *was* something wrong with the boy doll's head. To Rudy this could have meant I validated his parents' belief that he was mentally retarded, which had created Rudy's anxiety about his brain's capability to function. As I was about to explain more thoroughly what I meant, he seemed to contemplate what he would do next as he said, "I think I'll do...", but again trailed off not completing his thought.

Notable was that twice he expressed that he now thought before he acted whereas before he had always acted before he thought. Moreover, he implied doing cannot exist without thinking when coexisting in the same sentence. When I realized that he had used the verb "think" before the verb "do," I started to comment again about his behavior, but again he interrupted me by saying, "I never know what I'll do." Rudy's statement that he never knew what he would do suggested to me that he had thought of doing something and then rejected—and possibly repressed—his intent. If Rudy had not gotten at least a brief glimpse at understanding his intent, he would not have felt a need to assert "I never know what I'll do."

Contrarily, a child Rudy's age would probably not say that he never *knows* what he's going to *do* about a difficult cognitive task—aspects of which he ignores. Such a child attempts to *do* the task and asserts wrongly what he thinks he knows about the connection between his intent and its results. Instead, Rudy expressed that he chose to reject his intent by an inner assertion that it is possible in the abstract to know what he was going to do before he did it. It seemed to me that because he *had* conceptualized in advance what he was going to do, he was in a position to reject his intent and his underlying motives. If so, he was approaching and avoiding self-reflexive awareness. In saying "I think I'll do" twice, he appeared to come in touch with his intent which he finally thrust aside by a denial that thinking and action can be related.

A similar instance occurred in the behavior of a brilliant schizophrenic girl (whose statement is included here because it vividly illustrates the prehension required by repression) who had acting out symptoms since the age of 18 months. As she developed greater control over her behavior, one day at the age of 8 I heard her say, "I don't *want* to think about what I'm going to do before I do it." This verbal outburst, which occurred as she pretended to talk to a teddy bear, illustrates the double awareness of the self and the possibility of thrusting from one's awareness that which one would rather act upon but not think about. As in Rudy's case, she had deduced that thinking in advance of action is possible. Furthermore, both children by virtue of their own insights were on the verge of undoing thought inhibitions. When I asked them such questions as, "What's so terrible about thinking?" or "Why stop thinking now?", both children continued conversing with me. The girl told me "thinking isn't as much fun as hitting." Rudy returned to the doll play, removed the Band-aid from the boy doll's head, and pretended the boy doll "invited a friend over to play baseball."

These children's statements are quite different from those made by the child who has not rejected what he or she has apprehended but instead only lacks more complete understanding. For example, Jamie's statement "Yes, but he's older" regarding her brother, or Lara's statement "My mother began to sleep with me" regarding the family's sleeping arrangements, do not reflect an intent to deny or suppress the known or an unconscious attempt to repress impulsivity. In Jamie's and Lara's word choice or word arrangement there is no implication of rejection; these statements are rather straightforward assertions representing a child's view of reality as best as it can be expressed.

Robin's Forgettings and Their Undoing

In Robin's case the undoing of momentary forgetting occurred in those few instances near the end of his treatment when it became obvious during his therapy sessions he had begun to forget and to repress. He did not try to ward off awareness in the same way as Matt or Rudy did; Robin tried hard to "know" reality and to alert me to what had happened or was going to happen. Matt tried to ward off certain aspects of his experience by fooling, Rudy tried to ward it off by denying it was possible to know his intent, but Robin became anxious when he understood he might have forgotten.

To Robin forgetting meant there was something wrong with his brain; knowing he had known something but had "forgotten" it represented the earlier anxiety that his brain was nonfunctional. At first, he was anxious about having forgotten the events that occurred in therapy ("What I learned here") meaning how to play games. His statement nonetheless contained the preconscious suggestion that learning about the self was related to knowing in general. Then he was uncertain about whether or not his father would accompany him on a trip to see his grandmother because he had forgotten his mother had told him about his father's plan to accompany him. The first interpretive statement I made to Robin about a specific instance of forgetting as I told him what he knew would come back to him was centered around his anxiety about having a nonfunctional brain. His sigh of relief when I stated this told me that he had been reassured about his brain's capability to think (remember). Later statements I made to Robin which were aimed at helping him undo forgetting or repressing assured him that the fact of forgetting or of repressing did not mean that his brain was not working. On the contrary, his forgetting, I told him, meant that his brain was working very hard. Such a statement can often lead a young child to recognize the forgotten or repressed material instantly. The child takes the interpretation further and confronts himself with the inherent contradiction in a brain's working very hard not to "work" (i.e., to think or remember). Thereupon the child asks himself how and why this occurs, and with this self-questioning is quite likely to uncover the emotions and/or motives responsible for the forgetting and/or repressing, as Robin did when he remembered that he had forgotten his father was to accompany him on a train trip because he had been angry at his father that day and wished to be independent of him. The youngster who confronts ambiguity, contradiction, and ambivalence and who asks himself the equivalent of "How can I wish for that which logically excludes this" or the equivalent of "How can I feel contradictory emotions about the same person" often locates the reason in a compelling emotional state underlaid by tenacious motives which *must* explain it: "I *must* have been *very* angry (or jealous or guilty) to have thought in such a contradictory (or illogical) fashion." The youngster's recognition of his thought inconsistencies in many cases leads him to the original motive and/or emotions as exemplified by Robin's reaction to my statement that his brain had to work very hard not to remember; this statement had the double function of uncovering forgotten material at the same time that it reassured him about his intelligence.

Lara's Inhibitions and Their Undoing

Lara's repressing and her undoing of repression both seemed to coincide with the development of abstract thought. Compared to the momentary forgetting, denial, suppression, and foolery of Robin, Rudy, and Matt, who were almost 5 years younger than Lara, her repressing seemed to be more efficient. In Lara's case it took a severe and obvious trauma to undo one of her repressions. It was the traumatic death of her sister that brought to Lara's consciousness the dream she had repressed approximately 2 years earlier. (Had she not been in therapy, her sister's death might have led to a redoubling of her warding off efforts.) Robin, Rudy, and Matt were often able to undo the warding off process fairly easily.

Lara's second experience with interviewing at the age of 9½ (which occurred 6 months after her first interviewing experience) revealed that she understood two tasks of formal operations. The capability for abstract reasoning preceded by 9 months her statement "*I* just can't remember why *we* didn't come last week" (emphasis added). This statement revealed that she was aware of suppression and/or repression and partially capable of undoing it. She seemed to be saying it was *she* who could not remember why the action of coming to therapy had been inhibited. The inhibition of actually coming to therapy was shared by her mother; but the remembering appeared to be Lara's responsibility because she said that *she* "just can't remember." With her revealing statement, she appeared to be aware that the inhibition of an action, the inhibition of remembering, and the reestablishing of both activity and remembering are typical human functions. She now knew she was a "subject among many." What remained unclear because of her attachment to her mother was whether *she* should reestablish *both* heretofore unused functions of acting and remembering — but she did not doubt or deny that they ought to or could be restored.

In her last months of therapy, Lara undid the suppression of her intelligence and self-reflexively restored its functions. She was then able to link her antiquated belief that she was "stupid" with her past attempts to inhibit intellectual functioning. For a long time, Lara had mistrusted and misappraised her intellectual potential because it was associated with going to and succeeding in school which would "tell" her that she "was different" from her mother. Because her performance in school was infused with ambivalence and was thus unpredictable, she wavered in her belief that she *was* intelligent. It was not so much that her native intelligence had atrophied but that her belief in her intelligence had atrophied as she failed to apply it. Similar to Matt she was worried that she may have aided adults in their opinion that she was stupid.

Nonetheless, she had often revealed early in therapy what she sought to conceal as she burst out with statements almost in spite of herself which showed how competent she was. When, at age 9, she was asked to put her finger on a mark on a rubber band before it was stretched, she immediately said, "I'm not good at math." In her reluctance to comply with my request (just as she had been reluctant to go to school) she understood that a mathematical principal was at issue — all the more impressive because math was the very subject which had made Lara feel insecure. When she was reinterviewed 6 months later, she had become eager to affirm her intellectual potential as part of her personality — at least within the safe confines of the therapy appointment. About what a mark on a rubber band does if the band is stretched, she said, "The mark stays there because the whole band moves and the mark moves along with it." She also went directly from comments about the interviewing task to comments about school. Inhibition had first subsided when she answered my "math" questions; it continued to be at bay when she recalled problems she had experienced with her teachers: "It's not that I'm dumb or they're dumb, it's just that we think differently about art." Like Betsy's undoing of foolery, she momentarily undid the "stupid act," and in so doing undid the self-imposed inhibition of the intellectual function and openly recognized the fact of her potential. Repeated affirmations of her intelligence helped her believe she could unravel reasons for suppressing and repressing; that is, she now behaved as if she was a symptomatic *but* intelligent, "treatable" patient who, by behaving sensitively and insightfully, convinces the therapist that psychotherapy is appropriate.

Lara's approach to abstract "as-if" thought could be seen most vividly in her last month of therapy when she struggled to understand her reasons for stopping therapy, for starting school, and how she felt about both. She gave her attention to a dream which she felt she *could* remember. In the dream she had found presents with her name written on them in a cabinet in my office. She readily connected the imagery of the dream with her actual safeguarding of her father's gifts and said that both dream and reality meant she "wanted to keep the good stuff safe." Her individuality emerged as she recognized the symbolic significance of "presents with my *name* on them" expressing that therapy had helped her become more herself. She contemplated the fact that the dream revealed she was behaving toward me as if I were her father. She further remarked that before she had behaved toward me as if I were her mother. "It seems like in the dream you were kind of like my father because you gave me presents with my *name* on them. . .but that's confusing because before I know I treated you like my mother." By this, I thought she meant to say that in the beginning of therapy she had behaved as if there existed a symbiotic bond between her and me, but by the end of therapy she had made me more like her father with whom she had always interacted more reciprocally. Although abstract thought and the development of firm concepts contributed to Lara's capability to suppress and repress, both also contributed to her capability to discuss intelligently why she might have made symbolic as-if connections between remembered events of dreams and remembered aspects of therapy.

Similarly, her erasures of our taped and last therapy conversation might have symbolized an attempt to ward off, but her *stated intent* to remember what we talked about surely represented the opposite. By choosing to erase our conversation but remember me and choosing to keep the recorded conversation with her father, Lara seemed to have settled for the moment her Oedipal situation. She reached toward a silent identification with a nurturing adult of the same gender at the same time she cherished an interaction with her father.

DECENTERING AND THE UNDOING OF FORGETTING AND REPRESSING: DEVELOPMENTAL LEVELS

The foolery of the latency-aged children described earlier requires some degree of decentering. The child must know that his perspective differs from that of the other person; otherwise he could not hope to gain an advantage by fooling—an act which requires understanding that the other person does not always appreciate what the child knows. But this decentering is nonetheless incomplete compared to that of an adolescent who not only understands he has a perspective different from others, but that one's self can be thought of as a member of a larger group of selves, and in that sense, one's self can be thought of objectively. It requires precisely this thought development for the individual to understand more completely the process of repression or, for that matter, any mental activity. To put it another way, the older child or adolescent acts as if he is not just subjectively himself but as if he can also objectify his personality within the larger context of human psychology and social relations.

An awareness of repression thus requires a decentering where the subject observes the self as an object. The "acting, then thinking subject" Piaget described is first an infant who energetically wards off unwelcome stimuli by averting his face and pushing people or things away. Even though the infant may be aware of turning away in the act of doing so, as soon as the unpleasant or unfamiliar stimulus is out of sight, he appears to be no longer aware of it or of having just turned away from it and instead appears to be only aware of what he is presently attending to. Minutes later, he may again turn toward the stimulus, thus warding off is less efficient because it is not an ongoing process, but is continuously reinstated in the infant's behavior. A school-aged child may be aware of "forgetting things," but he is not yet able to treat himself as an "object" in an abstract discussion about forgetting as a mental process which may apply to his own behavior. Nor is such a child able to articulate as well as a preadolescent or an adolescent what the suppressive or repressive process feels like.

For example, 7-year-old Robin often would exclaim to me, "See what I mean, I forgot again!" as he tried to understand why certain thoughts or feelings associated with these thoughts escaped him. He was able to comment about the fact that he knew he could not remember something which he used to know, but he could not contemplate his forgetting in the context of the abstract terms suppression or repression at the same time that he introspected about the specifics of the suppressed or repressed but now remembered thought. Many aspects of the warding off process had to be discussed *seriatum* with Robin because at age 7, his cognition had developed only to the degree that he could contemplate two or three aspects of a problem simultaneously—and even that was difficult for him when the problem was fraught with emotional meanings. Typically, he would exclaim about his forgetting, then explain what the forgotten thought was, and finally he would tell what feeling had caused the forgetting: "See what I mean, I forgot again! I forgot my father would take me on the train to see my grandmother." Twenty minutes later: "I was mad at my father today." These separate events in Robin's mental experience were never synopsized by him because that would have required a consideration of too many concepts at once.

By way of contrast consider the statements made by Valerie, a 13-year-old girl who had begun to disrupt classes in school and had refused to do her work because she sensed that her parents were about to separate. When her parents finally parted, this girl said she had known all along that her parents would get a divorce. She then remarked, "I noticed without noticing I was noticing that they were having problems getting along. When I got into trouble at school, I could forget about them." She, unlike Robin, was able to consider why she may have repressed (her anticipation of parental separation) at the same moment that she was able to articulate what the repressive process meant to her. She could notice without consciously introspecting but nonetheless recapturing what she had noticed. And finally, she linked her acting up in school with her intent to forget: "When I got into trouble in school, I *could* forget about them" (emphasis added). She implied that she got into trouble *in order* to forget about her parents' problems.

Another boy, Gerald, came to therapy because of his habitual use of the phrase "I don't know" which changed from meaning that he wished not to think about answers to questions asked by teachers or parents to meaning he wished not to know the details of much of his daily experience — what he understood he really knew. After 3 years of therapy, when he was 14, he was once more questioned by his mother about his math homework for the next day. He answered, "I don't know what it is...I mean, not that I know of!" His humorous statement indicated his abstract understanding of repression, signifying an individual can know something without knowing he knows it. Since what he referred to was a math assignment, which in his mind stood for the hardest-to-know aspects of reality, it occurred to me that not knowing and repressing were often connected in Gerald's thinking. In a kind of double entendre, he expressed his amusement at his systematic attempts to block understanding and to repress; he meant to say he was not presently rejecting mature thought (that he knew of) nor was he presently repressing (that he knew of). But since he had become increasingly aware in therapy of his tendencies to reject both knowledge and unpleasant affect associated with it, he was not quite sure the abstract term, repression, did not at that moment apply to him. These complex ruminations, which in condensed form lay behind his humor, revealed to me that Gerald had become capable of a more thorough analysis of himself which comes about only as the young person in therapy decenters.

A most interesting difference in the undoing of momentary forgetting and repression in the preadolescent or adolescent as compared to the younger child is the development in the older youngster of equilibrated cognitive structures which permit decentering to occur in regard to the therapist. The more mature young person becomes enabled to engage in "if-then" thinking about his conflicts which means he has become able to hypothesize in the fashion of a scientist about the reasons for his behavior (which does not mean that blind spots in his thinking do not occur). Thus, the sense of self is relatively stable in relationship to the other person in the older as compared to the younger individual. Especially a mentally healthy youngster knows comfortably that his self is distinct from the selves of others, whether this experience of "self" and "other" is internally assumed by the individual in a powerful, continuous, and intermittently blurred fashion (Kohut, 1977, 1984) or whether this experience of "self" and "other" is perceived within an actual, specific interpersonal exchange. Distinctions made between himself and others might lead to such "if-then" thoughts as "*if* I am likely to forget unpleasant experiences, *then* other people are likely to do so." Then I, as therapist, am more deliberately included in the therapeutic space because interpersonal decentering and interpersonal curiosity create the youngster's need to validate suppositions about other people. By this I mean that interpersonal "equilibrations" occur in therapy between patient and therapist, which permit the cognitively mature patient to balance more equitably his previously internalized self-other experiences. As young-sters become increasingly aware in therapy of themselves as intelligent, poten-tially knowing, and unique individuals, they become enabled to redress the balance of "self" and "other" to include a fuller, stronger, and more accurate representation of themselves in conjunction with a less threatening, overpower-ing, and unreasonable "other." If "equilibration" is "a continuously changing balance of active compensations" (Furth, 1969, p. 261), then interpersonal "equilibrations" consist of the previously symptomatic young person in therapy offsetting earlier personal weaknesses with present strengths and correcting real or imagined overpowering characteristics of the other person by perceiving him or her as more of an equal and, most importantly, as a kind, nurturing, and responsive other person.

Then, in the presence of an apparently kind, nurturing, and responsive therapist, the youngster reinforces the decentering process by repeatedly con-structing abstract principles by which individuals behave and by imagining standards by which each interpersonal event can be evaluated. The youngster can, for example, comfortably and sometimes humorously or indulgently re-mark that certain mental functions obtain for everyone and remind the thera-pist that he or she has "denied" or "forgotten" something. An awareness that important mental functions exist in the experiences of everyone makes it safe for the young person to examine forthrightly why he might have denied reality or repressed motives — especially when he hears from his therapist that he was often correct in observing an instance of "denial" or "forgetting" in the thera-pist's behavior *and* that a particular therapeutic exchange is perceived differ-ently by him and his therapist. Consequently, the decentering trend which helps the individual participate in the therapeutic process often leads directly to the undoing of inhibition as the mature youngster becomes sharply aware that his impressions of an event are at variance with his therapist's.

A child who displayed these tendencies was 14-year-old Jed, a brilliant boy who was engrossed in the appeal psychoanalysis had for him. He prided himself on his intelligence and often thought of himself as an intellectual, and was as interested in psychoanalysis because of the intellectual tradition of which it is part as much as to understand himself. Jed's parents were both scholars and had admired Jed's high intelligence since he was a small child. Jed's family life was stable but he had suffered many physical symptoms as an infant and, in second grade, had lost an equally brilliant older sibling who died of a congenital illness. Jed worked hard in therapy to understand why he was in conflict about that which he most cherished — reaching for and living out the goals and values of the scholar.

Jed became particularly fascinated by the concept of undoing repression which, at first, meant to him to gain control over the thoughts and feelings he wished to avoid. Next, he became absorbed in the apparent contradiction in the mind preventing and regaining understanding — a contradiction he assumed existed only in the minds of young people or in the experience of those who were uninformed. One day, he revealed this gap in understanding as he cor-rectly understood that I had forgotten something he had told me the week before. He exclaimed: "How can *you* be repressing? You can't *possibly* repress if you understand psychoanalysis and what repression means and how it works!"

Jed was aware that he often forgot relatively painless events of the recent past, such as a school test scheduled for the next day. Since he forgot routine events which held relatively little threat for him, he worried that he would forget all of his past, much of which had been traumatic. He resisted the idea that repression is often not in our control because he wished to control what he knew and when he knew it. He felt that I must have that control he wished for because he understood that I knew more about psychoanalytic psychotherapy than he did. He reasoned: Understanding psychoanalysis means one can control repression; my therapist understands psychoanalysis; therefore, she does not repress if she does not want to. He felt comforted by the thought that I could bring back my past at a moment's notice. He hoped that I would teach him how to bring back his past so he could feel more at ease with it. He also reasoned: If my therapist represses, she wants to repress; therefore, she does not want to remember me and what I said because she does not like me.

When he exclaimed, "How can *you* be *repressing*?" I explained there were always reasons for young people *and* adults not to remember. At this he said that since there were reasons for forgetting, there must be rules for remembering. Then, it seemed to me that he was confusing "reasons" and "rules" and furthermore, that he was confusing the psychoanalytic "rule" to free associate in order to uncover forgotten memories with society's rules (e.g., laws). Jed was well familiar with the psychoanalytic "rule" as the result of his interest in psychoanalysis and his reading of Freud's books. So I told him that the "rules" for remembering were not the same as the "reasons" for forgetting nor were they the same as the laws of society. My statement was followed by a long pause and then a deep sigh as he said, "You mean there's no *law* that says you *have* to remember what you've forgotten?" I thought my statement which differentiated reasons from rules and one type of "rule" from another relieved him because he now felt neither he nor I had transgressed by not remembering. Now he seemed to understand psychoanalysis better as he comprehended that remembering especially traumatic past events could be accomplished only by wanting to remember and not by fiat.

The inconsistency in Jed's view of repression as it applied to himself and as it applied to me reflects a cognitive immaturity as well as the residue of previous emotional conflicts. Jed's statement revealed that he remained egocentric in regard to one particular topic. His perspective regarding repression was egocentric because he had not fully understood that he was one subject among many to whom the concept of repression applied. He believed that my understanding of repression would preclude its occurrence in my experience but that he, as less knowledgeable about psychoanalysis, was subject to repression. He maintained a discontinuity between himself and me which did not apply in reality. He did not understand that it is not the mental functions themselves which differ in a mature adolescent compared to an adult, but the differing capabilities of the two age groups to recognize repression, to undo it, or to apply this concept to other people. In an amusing way, he revealed his egocentrism in not understanding that he and I were the same in some important respect. He had turned into its opposite the assumption of very young children who presume that the other person always shares their perspective, and never sees things differently.

The lapse in this brilliant boy's comprehension could be traced to his childhood feeling that he had to be more grownup than his agemates. Being grownup meant that he would be safe in being similar to his parents who had survived and dissimilar from his sibling who had died as a child. Therapy helped Jed perceive that he could safely postpone adulthood until, in his words, he had "survived adolescence." Then, he made more of the differences between adolescence and adulthood than was warranted. He as adolescent could submit to repression for reasons he easily saw as serving him, whereas I as an adult could not. My adult status meant that I understood everything so well (especially about him) that the typical defensive and often problematic mental functions would never occur. To Jed, adult understanding wipes out adult defenses. In this way, he protected himself as an adolescent and preserved the image of adulthood which he would have liked during his childhood to have seen in his parents' behavior—that their superior understanding would efface all of their problems and his, too.

Another most interesting example of interpersonal "equilibrating" occurred when 13-year-old Mario gave evidence of repeated forgettings during a single 50-minute hour. He became frantic because he could not recover his thoughts immediately and seemed to be afraid he would permanently lose what had occurred to him. He accurately observed that I was surprised he had forgotten the thoughts he had expressed just a few minutes earlier. Then, he took note of the fact that what was true of me was not true of him: I had remembered and he had forgotten. As he easily noticed how surprised I was at his behavior, he was once more caught off guard as he observed me in relation to himself. This is another example of a self-other experience which is measured against an equilibrated structure. The structure that Mario had attained consisted of (1) a firm and basically positive self-concept; (2) a clear understanding of my intention to understand him—including why he forgot in psychotherapy appointments; and (3) an understanding that as human beings we shared certain mental functions. Thus, when he saw the discrepancy between his behavior and mine, his correct observations motivated him to consider why he might have forgotten in the first place. To use Mario's words, "If *you* can remember, then so can *I*!" Embarrassed by his repeated forgettings, and by the threat of repression of which he was acutely aware, he first made jokes about his forgetting and said, "I always knew I couldn't think straight. . . my jokes always go off crooked." Then, whatever silent associations were stimulated by his jokes led him to a moment of insight when he told me how he felt about his absent-minded mother who habitually asked him to remember possessions which she typically forgot, such as the keys to the family car. As he suddenly recaptured some of his forgotten thoughts, which included his mother's "weird" request that he remember her forgotten keys, he exclaimed: "Why should I do *her* brainwork for *her*. You and my teachers give *me* enough as it is!" He tried to express that both his therapist and his teachers expected "brainwork." I expected him to remember what he had forgotten and his teachers expected him to learn what he had not learned. What Mario meant to say about brainwork represented two different uncoverings: that which had been repressed and that which had been unlearned. To Mario, these two tasks of uncovering were difficult enough. Consequently, his mother's asking him to remember for her was quite unfair.

To youngsters who fight learning, evading learning is to knowing as forgetting is to introspecting; that is, they often discover that just as knowing is disrupted by not learning, so is introspecting disrupted by forgetting. Their analogy requires the participation of the two spheres of the psyche thus coalescing affectivity and intelligence. Young people intuitively understand that we can, at times, be energized to comprehend and to inhibit. It is inappropriate to disavow the threat of knowing in the etiology of learning disorders because general knowledge of which self-knowledge is a special consequence holds for the child and adolescent the potential for unexpected, often welcome, changes in themselves and in their lives. The threat to the young person who rejects learning or who is afraid to attend school is his inability to anticipate or to control where either academic or self-knowledge will lead. The child or adolescent becomes fearful of knowledge precisely because of its power.

CHAPTER 10

The Determination to Learn

My main objective in writing this book is to claim that young people are capable of inquiring about the risks of knowing. The major impact of my psychotherapeutic efforts with those who have decided not to learn stems from my conviction that they can conjecture about learning differently from the past and thus change the course of their lives. Perhaps this view stimulated a similar conviction in them which renewed their learning and knowing attempts. If so, there can be no better rule in work with young people who refuse learning than for their psychotherapist or their teacher to demonstrate to them that they can overcome the impediments to learning they themselves create.

The deliberate nonlearner decides to learn as the result of the changes he makes in one or more realms of his experience. Usually he first changes his attitude toward learning in his psychotherapy sessions, which is often followed by attitude changes in school and at home. If he makes changes in school, it is because he perceives his teachers as helpful and trustworthy instead of skeptical or oppositional. Or he makes changes because his teachers perceive *him* as cooperative and trusting. At home, the youngster either produces a change in his family's "myth" by behaving differently in school or he is helped to learn in school because family members begin to perceive him differently. Whichever way change in attitude and learning style comes about for the young person, he becomes more sensitive to his learning successes and less preoccupied with himself as a "school failure."

Piaget's (1976, 1978) ingenious view is that often children's "failures" contain "successes." Success resides in the child's competent behavior; failure resides in his temporary inability to conceptualize and therefore to articulate which of his actions are competent and why. When Piaget calls the child's misrepresented but competent behavior "precocious," I understand him to mean that concentration on a child's successful actions tell us as much—or more—about his knowledge than concentrating on his inaccurate statements. For clinicians the view that a "failure" contains a "success" is a potent therapeutic tool just as for teachers it represents a potentially educative attitude. But, unlike Piaget's subjects, before therapeutic intervention the nonlearning child or adolescent often experiences failure in what he does. It is not just that he fails to explain what he does successfully, but also that he does not succeed in school.

SCHOOL FAILURE AND SCHOOL SUCCESS

Piaget's subjects presumably understood natural phenomena or interview questions without overwhelming intrapsychic, family, or educational impediments. In comparison, renewing and *legitimizing* the learning attempts of deliberate nonlearners is arduous because not only do they need help in changing their learning behavior and in developing those thought processes which could explain their achievements, but they also must combat the pessimistic attitudes toward their learning attempts emanating from their parents and teachers. For example, if a nonlearning child is given some Cuisenaire rods to help with his math learning, he often refuses to manipulate them. Or, if he consents to "experiment" with them, he does so in a way so as to prevent himself from understanding that the colors and lengths of the rods are deliberately coordinated. Instead, he would either play with the rods haphazardly so that this insight is impeded, or he would deliberately flout the color–length coordination when he understands intuitively that such a coordination might intentionally exist. Likewise, a child who refuses to answer the question "What is nine times eight" or the child who does not bother to memorize the multiplication tables is different from the child Piaget often describes who is both successful and a failure. These defiant or indifferent behaviors create the pessimistic attitude in the adult. This attitude, in turn, inhibits a child's successful school learning because he feels at odds with his teacher. Unlike an adult, a child does not always know that a school subject can be learned irrespective of his feelings about his teacher. If a child or even an adolescent feels animosity toward a particular teacher, he is often unaware that the school subject which this teacher disseminates could be learned elsewhere (e.g., by reading the encyclopedia, by being taught by another teacher). It is not simply that the youngster often cannot choose another teacher which impedes his learning from a mistrusted or disliked adult. It is also that he does not question whether a subject matter exists apart from the particular person who teaches it. And often when he *does* recognize he could learn the subject from a book rather than a mistrusted teacher, he often tries to "punish" the disliked teacher by rejecting the very subject he teaches.

Teachers who are confronted with nonlearning children and adolescents rarely examine the specific reasons they may have for failing because failure is perceived by teachers as irreversible; that is, teachers identify failure with irreversible physiological flaws and therefore discern neither a reason for explaining school failure further nor a remedy which targets the child's own decision. Even when teachers begin to understand that the child is not disabled they often do not search for specific reasons for his failure because they are frustrated by the fact that the youngster repeatedly refuses the teacher's attempts to help with learning. They become understandably fatigued by the young person's defensive efforts and sometimes return to the learning disability hypothesis. Then, as both teacher and youngster continue to expect failure, a self-fulfilling prophecy obtains in which a youngster who is labeled disabled behaves insecurely, indifferently, or stubbornly.

Although repeated failures are affectively troublesome, equally important is the fact that inept actions in school do not have the same integrating effect on the child's cognitive endeavors as successful actions do. Even a successful action without an accompanying articulate explanation does not necessarily have a confirming effect although, as Piaget (1976, 1978) has shown, the discrepancy between "precocious" activity and incorrect explanations often impels the child to reintegrate cognitive functions. Children who succeed in some respects pay attention to their achievements, whereas children who feel they have failed conclude they are "bad" or "no good." This is why it is important in any therapeutic endeavor to stress in a conversation with a youngster the ways in which he has succeeded.

Even though it is often difficult for teachers to escape the pitfalls of labeling, they can be persuaded to reconsider their opinions about nonlearning behavior. As the result of the youngster's renewed learning, teachers often try to apply labels more selectively, such as perceiving him as adequately qualified in all school subjects but the one in which he is still perceived as "disabled." For example, 10-year-old Tim's (see Chapter 4) brilliant math performance did not convince his teacher to discard the disability label she attached to him. If anything, his math ability strengthened her view of him as reading disabled. For months she vacillated in her opinion of Tim's learning capability but finally did change her attitude toward his alleged disability when she saw that his reading performance had improved 3½ grade levels in 10 months. Contrarily, 11-year-old Dillon's (see Chapters 1 and 6) teacher reacted to both learning failures *and* successes by attending to his areas of strength before he corrected his areas of weakness. She began to doubt that he had "spelling dyslexia" on the soundness of his other language skills (reading and the ideas he used in creative writing) which helped Dillon in two ways: he found validation in some language areas which led him to try harder in spelling, and he sought to understand his successes in reading and creative writing which helped him evaluate his behavior in general. Dillon's successes were frequent enough and occurred early enough in his development that they helped overcome the label "disabled" which had been applied to him the year before he began psychotherapy. Similar to many other more mature nonlearning children, he brought a self-reflexive sense to his therapy appointments. He often contrasted a "victorious" self with a past "overpowered" self.

In younger children, a sense of school success can be inhibited because they are overwhelmed by their school failures and therefore do not reflect on their successful activity. One 7½ year old, Mark, told of his memories of "always making mistakes" in school which he compared to his good grades of the present. But before the age of 7½ and before he became willing to try to achieve in school, this boy had probably been the victim of a tendency to overgeneralize: One mistake meant "always making mistakes." Rosen (1985) examined this tendency in some individuals:

> On the basis of one or a few failed attempts at reaching a goal, the patient labels
> himself as a failure...The patient does not reason that although he failed today
> he may succeed tomorrow and that the very failure itself could become a source
> of learning to help transform it into later successes. (p. 255)

Just as important as Mark's tendency to overgeneralize was his teacher's tendency to concentrate on his failures and assume they would occur in the future.

In my work with Mark, I set about to transform his experience of failure into an experience of success by asking him why he thought he always made mistakes when he was succeeding in therapy. To this he tried to understand why I seemed to react differently from some other adults, and responded, "You must like children a lot?" Mark nodded affirmatively when I answered his implicit question by saying, "Yes, I do, even if they make mistakes." My concentration on his successes in therapy—his sincere attempts to understand himself—helped him think about his behavior elsewhere. Then, in subsequent weeks, he was able to talk about an emerging view of himself as someone who "*sometimes* makes mistakes." When he began to identify those occasions when he was successful, he was motivated to examine precisely which of his actions had been successful.

Like Mark, 14-year-old Gerald perfected the idea that he always misunderstood school assignments. Thus, he was surprised when he began to achieve in science class. About subjects other than science, he said, "School isn't supposed to show us anything important—it's only memorizing." On another occasion, he exclaimed, "Schoolwork isn't *supposed* to mean anything! I just have to get by!" In response, I commented that his reaction to science was different from his complaints about other school subjects and inquired why he was not just memorizing or merely "getting by" in science. To this he grinned and said, "I thought if I didn't let myself find out, I wouldn't have to pretend I was stupid. But my science teacher found out about me not finding out!" His joke revealed to me that his teacher's discovery of his motives in regard to learning initiated his own attempts at scientific investigation. And, since he was successful in science class, he felt compelled to explain to me why he had shunned academic understanding in the past: to avoid the work required of a knowledgeable individual to masquerade stupidity. Many years later, I learned that, as a young man in his twenties, Gerald was gainfully employed as a medical technician.

Gerald's statements imply that as youngsters repeatedly forfeit the opportunity to learn, they become entrenched in a position which obliges them to deny they are intelligent persons. Nonlearning and inhibition of self-awareness thus become a double hazard in the youngster's development. A therapeutic endeavor which aims to sensitize the young person to the self-knowing required by understanding one's motives for deliberately evading school or for methodically failing when in school lifts the two inhibitions regarding self-understanding and academic understanding. To say it another way, an increased determination to learn derives from success in understanding the self in therapy and in understanding conflict-free subject matter in school.

FAMILY MYTHS AND ACTUALITIES

Before therapy, a family "myth" is an actuality to the nonlearning young person. The most common and compelling myth held by the families of the nonlearning child and adolescent was that he or she was incompetent or disabled. Another common myth, related to alleged incompetence, was some parents' claim that "children do things for no reason." Imagined incompetence and/or disabilities suggested to these parents that there was no *other* reason for their child's behavior and, therefore, no reason to look beyond the imagined incompetence or disability. There is no message more devastating to the youngster who tries to think, or no message more convincing to the child who believes he has every reason not to think, than to hear his parent (or other adults) say he does something without reason. This implies to the child that his brain contains no reasons or is incapable of reasoning.

By the time the young people discussed in this book were brought to me for psychotherapy, both they and their families had lived out for many months or even years the myth that there was something wrong with them—"something" that would take a great deal of effort to correct. A great deal of effort by all involved *was* required to unravel the complex reasons for one allegedly incompetent family member to reject learning in a family otherwise consisting of intelligent individuals. But, as therapy progresses for these intelligent young people and their families, and the youngster begins to renew his learning attempts and experiences some learning successes, the family "myth" that he cannot learn evolves into the family "actuality" that he can learn. Yet this is a complex process with many fluctuations in which the young person or other family members often doubt their discovery that he can learn and often return to the antiquated view that he cannot. If his parents return to the myth that he cannot learn because of some temporary failures, the youngster often experiences an intense discontinuity between his renovated view and the earlier myth apparently revived by family members which, once more, dictates that he is incapable of learning. He then reacts by saying that what his parents or siblings believe or declare about his awkward learning attempts are "lies," "misleading" or "distorting" statements, depending on the perspicacity of the youngster who now actively compares his perspective with those of family members. Consequently, what makes psychotherapeutic intervention risky for these youngsters is their inveterate conviction before therapy that they cannot be helped and their parents' wavering conviction during therapy that their learning attempts can be restored. Sometimes they feel they cannot be helped because their nonlearning is tied to an actual irreversible event, such as the death of a parent in Betsy's case (see Chapter 5), or the onset of a parent's deep-seated symptomatic behavior as in the case of Tim's father (see Chapter 4), or to the child's gender or his adoption as in the cases, respectively, of Jamie (Chapter 6) and Dillon (Chapters 1 and 6). These irreversible life events had become linked to an imagined irreversible "disability." The children thought something like this: Because I cannot change the fact that my father died, that my father had a "nervous breakdown," that I am a girl, or that I am adopted, I cannot change the fact that I am failing in school.

Even in cases where there is no actual irreversible life circumstance to which the young person's nonlearning is connected, a strongly held family conviction often justifies his nonlearning. In the case of Rudy (Chapters 2 and 9), the suspicion that he was mentally retarded was so strongly held by family members that for years he perceived as "real" his alleged genetically determined incompetence. Other children often understand that a change in their learning behavior will be met with surprise by their parents. For example, Katherine (see Chapter 6) understood that her improved academic performance after 6 months of therapy did not create a different parental expectation. She sensed that her parents assumed her "perfectionistic" attitude was an irreversible aspect of her personality. They believed they had adapted (i.e., resigned themselves) to Katherine's core problem which they assumed facilitated her recovery. They did not perceive that she had by her own efforts surmounted her conflict wherein she wished to know in advance of being taught which contradicted her increasing fancy for learning new subjects and a variety of skills. I was able to change the myth of Katherine's irreversible personality trait of "perfectionism" by showing her parents how reasonable it was for her to share literature with her father while her mother took care of her two small brothers. Then they could appreciate Katherine's intelligence in deliberately letting other school subjects slide while she chose to excell *especially* in literature so that, while her much-admired mother tended to her brothers' needs, she could converse knowledgeably with her father.

CORRECTING FAMILY MYTHS

My task as psychotherapist is to create an actuality for both parent and child which is more productive than the family myths. My intent is to sensitize the parents of nonlearning young people to the changes in their behavior which their parents might not notice because the changes are either subtle or appear transitory before they become firmly established in the young person's repertoire. Sometimes the parents do notice a change but they do not know how to respond. As part of the therapeutic endeavor, I attempt to heighten the meaning for his parents that a youngster's discernible, spontaneous behavior has for potential development. My discussions with parents are focused on what they tell me directly about a young person's changed behavior as well as on what improvements his teachers notice. Still more evidence about his altered behavior is drawn from the therapeutic hour which, with the youngster's permission, I use to illuminate the discrepancy between what he attempts in my office and what he might reject in school or at home because of ongoing antipathy to learning.

A healthier actuality evolved for Annie (see Chapter 4) and her mother when I talked with her about Annie's handwriting papers brought from school. Annie's mother showed them to me because Annie often tried to tell her mother what her handwriting mistakes meant. On one significant occasion, there was the single error of a small "i" for a capital "I" on a particular worksheet. Annie's mother had not noticed that Annie had capitalized correctly the first letters of all other words which began a sentence, or that she had capitalized correctly those other first letters of words, such as the names of people or of geographical locations. What Annie's mother did focus on was the minus 1 (-1) the teacher had written on Annie's paper, which referred to her single mistake in this sentence: "i had a good time on my trip to Vermont." This sentence was followed by one which included "mommy" capitalized correctly: "Mommy took us all swimming." My task here was to alert Annie's mother to Annie's selective use of capitalization when it served her purpose. In this case her purpose was to express that she respected her mother as a person, so she capitalized the word "Mommy," but she was not so sure she respected herself, so she referred to herself as an "i," and not an "I."

At first, Annie's mother did not believe that Annie's mistake reflected a selective use of a writing rule she thoroughly understood. The myth that Annie was not very intelligent which her mother had initially supported by pointing to math mistakes had carried over to other school subjects so that every mistake Annie made was seen by her mother as evidence of a spreading disability. When Annie began to capitalize "I" when she referred to herself as the result of my telling her "You can still always call yourself 'I' even though you make mistakes in math," her mother adopted a new myth to replace the earlier one. Frustratedly, she told me, "Then Annie's mistakes must mean she's just careless!" The next step in replacing the disabling myth with the selectively used intelligence actuality was to show her mother how *carefully* Annie had refused to capitalize one letter out of twenty-six which referred to herself.

The evidence that was most convincing to Annie's mother that Annie had fought some aspects of learning for her own purposes came from Annie's improved math performance. But again, this required several phases of sensitization because, as Annie's mother saw that Annie understood multiplication in her session with me, she rapidly came to two conclusions: that Annie could only learn in a one-to-one situation, which meant she could never learn in a classroom, and that Annie's purposes included thwarting her mother in deliberately not learning math which her mother most wanted her to learn. However fictional these two conclusions remained, they were nonetheless closer to Annie's actuality than the initial hypothesis Annie's parents put forth which was that she was math disabled.

What finally convinced Annie's mother that Annie was not disabled in any subject was her sudden decision at home to imitate her teacher with great dramatic flourish by correctly writing and solving math problems in the manner of a pedagogue. Only then did Annie's mother feel that Annie could learn in an ordinary classroom setting, and that Annie's attempts to thwart her were a reflection of a psychological conflict which could be resolved. Earlier Annie's mother had come to trust me as Annie's therapist, and often thought I worked magic with Annie which could not be reproduced elsewhere in her life, but her trust in me was not sufficient to bring a full resolution to Annie's math problems. What was needed and what Annie intuitively knew was her increased willingness to display her math prowess when she was not with me but instead with her mother.

Generally, the closer the family myth is to the child's personal actuality, the easier it is to bring about a change in family attitudes. Initially, Annie's mother thought Annie was deficient only in math. Although she worried that Annie's deficiency would spread to other subject areas, with counseling she could perceive that Annie was intelligent in some or most subjects. Compare the myth Annie's mother held for her nonlearning—that she was math-disabled—with the myth Rudy's parents held for his school failure. Helping Rudy's parents was an arduous process because they had to overcome their entrenched belief that he was deficient in all subject areas. This required a massive attitude shift and an admission of an egregious error in judgment. Even more important, the myth of Rudy's mental retardation protected both Rudy and his parents from their accumulated anger at him; that is, to protect themselves and Rudy from their anger at his colossal school failure, his parents concocted the myth that his failing school, which had begun in kindergarten when he flatly refused to learn the alphabet or to count, must mean he was mentally retarded. The sham of mental retardation served to mitigate his parents' anger and enabled them to behave protectively toward Rudy. As his parents brought him to see me for psychological evaluation, they were and remained wary of what they might find out from me.

As Rudy heard me say time and again that his behavior reflected intelligent purpose, he gradually began to learn in school. A turning point came when one day I praised him for showing me his homework papers which he had correctly completed. To my praise he said, "I think when I do good, I do bad." On a subsequent occasion he said, "When I do good, I feel bad" (his second experience with interviewing when he understood one advanced Piagetian task at 8 years, about 2 years earlier than expected). I thought he meant to express that his achieving in school deflated the fiction that he was mentally retarded, which meant that his parents had every reason to become angry at him for his earlier rejection of learning. The activity of "good" learning was "bad" because it brought to his parents' attention that they were wrong in their opinion of him as mentally retarded. "Doing good" faced them with the awesome task of dealing with their longstanding anger at Rudy's early school failures.

Yet there was a risk in talking with Rudy's parents about his competence ambivalence. A release of their pent-up anger would be the certain result of my statement that Rudy was deliberate, not stupid. Faced with angry parents, Rudy might have concluded indeed he was right that he "does bad" when he "does good." On the other hand, the myth of mental retardation only perpetuated the very situation both Rudy and his parents sought to change: his poor academic performance. I decided the benefits outweighed the potential risks and asked Rudy if I might talk with his parents about his idea that "being good" at schoolwork could have dangerous consequences. Because that day his teacher had praised his completed work Rudy easily gave his permission. His attachment to his teacher and the pleasure he had gained from her praise (she did not think he "did bad" when he completed his homework) gave him the courage to imagine, together with her help and mine, that he would either survive his parents' anger or they might actually react to him differently.

As expected, Rudy's parents became exasperated when they heard it was my opinion that he was normally intelligent and had reasons for not learning which he was beginning to express in therapy. Although I did not quote Rudy, I did intend to get across the distinction between a deliberate act and an unintelligent one. Rudy's parents became angry at me for delivering this message, and it seemed their anger at me deflected some of their anger at Rudy. As his therapy continued, Rudy's parents underwent dramatic changes in their attitudes toward Rudy and toward receiving counsel from me about him. Rudy's father withdrew from parent meetings because he felt there was no longer any need for counsel since I had discovered the root of Rudy's problems. Rudy's mother became increasingly invested in conferring with me and eventually understood how her mental retardation myth shielded her from her own angry feelings. She concluded one conference by exclaiming: "Now that I see he *can* learn, but stubbornly refuses, I get angrier at him than I used to!"

The notion that a child has reasons for his behavior also threatened Dillon's parents. At first they steadfastly clung to the myth that Dillon had no reasons for his destructive behavior toward toys or neighborhood friends. But they soon became aware of the threat his reasons posed for them and, as he, too, began to understand his reasons for rejecting learning, their increased understanding magnified Dillon's progress in therapy. After I repeatedly asked Dillon's parents about the possibility of his having a reason for refusing to do his homework, for breaking a toy, or for having fights with other children, their attitude reversed dramatically one day when his mother reported that Dillon had broken his favorite toy "for no apparent reason." In the next breath she described how Dillon had played with it just the previous day when a neighborhood boy, who was believed to be retarded, had come over to play. In a moment of sudden insight, Dillon's mother exclaimed: "If what you say is right—that Dillon is afraid he's stupid—that must be why he broke the toy." She continued by describing how he had repeatedly manufactured reasons to avoid playing with this particular child, which she viewed as unkind and summed up humorously: "I guess he broke the toy so he wouldn't have to play with that kid; I guess he thought if he played with him, he'd get to be retarded too, as though it's catching like a *cold!*"

If I am able to get across the fact that the youngster often thinks reasonably, it helps liberate both him and his family from confining fictions which, in turn, creates opportunities for both child and parent to originate healthier perspectives. This is yet another example of the increased efficacy psychotherapy with young people has when it brings about an attitude change in the parent. But, this is by no means an easy task because the parents usually have very potent reasons for disbelieving their child's motives or reasoning ability. Most frequently, their disbelief represents a self-protective attempt to avoid their angry feelings on realizing that the youngster's reasons for rejecting learning transcend their cherished conscious reasons for him to learn.

THE DECISIONS OF CHILDREN AND ADOLESCENTS

A decision to learn or not is a willed act; that is, behind the "red herrings" young people put forth to explain their school troubles lie decisions that represent especially in the older youngster a developing volitional faculty. For Piaget (1981) *will* is the affective analogue of intellectual operativity, and like it, the result of an increasing tendency in the youngster toward decentration. The activity of willing results from the conflict between two compelling impulses or tendencies wherein the impulse that is initially weaker must become strong for an action to reflect a true sense of will and the cognitive coordinations which support it. It is not until they become concrete operational in their thinking, then, that youngsters become able to put one impulse or tendency aside and favor the weaker one—for example, by occasionally refraining from retaliation when a friend has hurt their feelings because of enduring positive affect toward friends.

At first glance, it might seem that Piaget's use of the term will resembles Freud's concept of superego, as in the case of a child's believing he should not hurt a friend because hurtful actions toward friends are not "right" and therefore may make the child feel guilty. A careful reading of Piaget suggests that what he means by will is rather more pragmatic compared to what Freud means by superego and its functions which are often unconscious and irrational. Thus, will in Piaget's sense seems to be more a function of the ego than of the superego. Consider one of Piaget's examples. He decided to forego a walk in order to finish his work. By doing so he put aside his impulse to enjoy the outdoors for the more pragmatic aim of meeting his work demands. This example signifies that the exercise of will might be most usefully likened in psychoanalytic theory to a success of the reality over the pleasure principle: the imagined gratification gained from a successfully completed work won out over the immediate pleasure of a walk in the sunshine. While as clinicians we might easily expect patients to express affective reactions more diversified than just willed resolve which tends to reflect and promote normative cultural values, the concept of will does serve to explain one reason for rejecting learning. It points to that complex of affective reactions which represents the decentering process in the concrete operational child who, despite the value society places on education, decides on school failure as a course of action.

The importance Piaget gives to the childhood act of willing comes close to what Erikson (1950) described in his discourse on the "eight stages of man." A schoolchild's idea that he can affect the direction his life takes derives, in part, from his earlier struggles in preschool or at home practicing his autonomy, for example, as he decides how and when to use the toilet. A child in such a situation either feels basically autonomous or doubtful. If he feels more autonomous than doubtful, this sense of self nourishes his later ability to exercise his initiative in embracing school learning. He willingly gives up one impulse—the one to play—in favor of another—the one to learn—because the thought "this is *my* decision" aids him to favor one initially weaker impulse over a presumably captivating alternative. He then becomes industrious in applying himself to learning, including clever discoveries of the ways in which play and learning are related by thinking about what can be learned through playing. But a child who rejects learning or who refuses to attend school appears to be under-developed in autonomy, initiative, industry, and even will—although his "will-fulness" is often conspicuous. Neither adult nor child perceive initiative or industry in the rejection of schoolwork because adult and child alike believe he has submitted to the apparently easier decision to reject learning for play when in school or to stay home in order to play.

I have stressed throughout this book that children and adolescents who refuse learning fall into the two groups of transitional and operational: they are either transitional for concrete or formal operativity, or they have solidified cognition sufficiently to be either concrete or formal operational. Because of their anxious reactions to ambiguity and the unpleasant connotations attached to maturity, transitional youngsters before therapy or during it often give up the struggle and hold fast to the easy path of play and recreation. When these young people become either concrete or formal operational as the result of spontaneous development or of successful psychotherapy, their deliberation can be seen in voluntary cognitive improvisations. Then they lack neither autonomy nor will but are at risk as scholars because they turn on its head the cultural dictate which offers learning as the moral good. As long as academic learning contains meanings that threaten these operational young people, the impulse they seek to negate is the will to learn. The chronically phobic young-ster in particular energetically reverses the stronger impulse to learn when he rejects the school environment and either pretends to play or spends hours languishing in vapid activity. The fact that they have to inhibit the ontogeneti-cally earlier impulse to learn explains why in many instances it appears to be an ongoing struggle for nonlearning youngsters to turn away from learning. Then the individual's identity begins to revolve around the rejection of under-standing whether it involves one particular subject, most learning, or the school itself.

Thus, it appears that the transitional young person who retreats from knowledge and returns to earlier thought patterns is acting in line with the pleasure principle, whereas the concrete or formal operational youngster who has developed a firmer resolve regarding learning shoves it aside for some imagined future gain and behaves more in line with the reality principle. That is, aspects of his "reality"—in truth, his actuality—have pressured him to conform in ways which include resisting school learning. The reality principle does not take hold of a retreating transitional child in the same way as it does a child or adolescent with a stable conceptual system because the uncertain youngster shies away from reliable concepts. One of these concepts, a sense of time or especially of the future, is essential to the choice of a future gain over a present gain. Before the child can conceptualize what a future gain might have in store for him, or that there is such a thing as a future, the rewards inherent in a future "reality" are lost because the rewards or punishments inherent in the reality of the present overwhelm him. He most certainly has an accurate sense of the rewards and punishments immanent in his present situation which is why he focuses on them rather than to attend to the promise a dimly perceived future holds. Eugene, the 4-year-old brother of Jeremy (see Chapter 5), expressed his transitional stance in regard to learning when he said, "When they teach me numbers in school, I just walk away." He walked away from learning because he was flooded by ongoing anxiety about learning. He could not imagine a future reward attached to learning because he could not imagine a future. Conceptual fluency might have posed a challenge to Eugene's easy rejection of numbers.

Timothy, on the other hand, kept it to himself that he knew and what he knew, and in so doing exercised his resolve in the service of what to him was the long-term gain of protecting his nonlearning father. Like Tim, Robin showed by his emphasis on the verb "to know" that knowing served him in some instances, especially those in which another person helped him clarify what he understood and validated his many attempts at discovery. Then he became convinced that he could learn when he wanted to: his will regarding learning was in place when he wanted to apply it. Some children, such as Betsy and Maisie, became transitional for concrete operations soon after they entered treatment. Betsy's earlier habit of clinging to transductive thought because it was safer than logical thought represented the choice of the easy. As she spun reasons on a more advanced thought level to explain her nonlearning, namely, her fear that in growing up she would suffer the same fate as one of her parents, she began to struggle against her chronic tendency to avoid learning. In developing deductive schemes which appeared to explain her ambivalence about learning, she also revealed that she was no longer fighting thinking. Rather, she was explaining why in her ongoing attempts to learn, she might occasionally resist it. Her will regarding learning had been transformed once more as she reversed her rejection of understanding into an acceptance of mature thought which included identifying reasons why she might, on occasion, still feel tempted to embrace the obsolete nonlearning stance.

Maisie, who was much younger than Betsy, was caught just as she attempted to mount a strategy which would have kept her more than adequate intelligence on hold as she tried to please both parents and to appease her brilliant brother. When I first knew her, she was quite happy to take the easy way out in her assertion that she had no memory or mind, and was quite ready to find her identity in her childish charm and graceful beauty. Therapy, which was aimed at showing her what she knew, helped her reactivate progressive intellectual development so that, in a short time, she was able to develop those concepts which helped her tell me how writing backward was an intelligent act which served her. Writing backward because she was lefthanded stood as one intelligent act in a whole series of intelligent behaviors, and did not represent stupidity nor did it any longer symbolize that Maisie could not learn.

The young child does not have the operational structures which would permit a deliberate and self-reflexive decision to fail. Although not more pathological, before therapeutic intervention, the stance of the preoperational child or the child transitional for formal operations is more one of retreat than a forceful, considered rejection of school learning. The operational youngster has positively identified with some aspects of his family's myths about him, and exercises his will by deciding not to learn. The complement to a decision like this is the child's growing ability to keep secrets. Since he has a pretty good sense what his parents actually know about him, he can decide what to keep private. Such a child straddles the conflict in his perspective as opposed to his family's and exercises his will in playing out both aspects of the implicit dispute. He learns spontaneously but appears to reject learning by keeping what he knows shut off from family members and from teachers. These concrete or formal operational youngsters continue to learn through their own "perturbations" (Langer's, 1969, term), but with the persistent intrusion of their family myth or the apparent intrusion of the teacher who is seen in much the same way as the parent, they wall off their developing logic from many aspects of life. Most formal operational and many concrete operational young people are able to accomplish this complex, deliberate bifurcation of their developing intellects, still more evidence of their native intelligence. The young people who achieve this do so in different family constellations, where the invariant is the parents' disbelief that the child or adolescent is competent. This may be why it has been difficult to pinpoint *the* antecedent of the child's or adolescent's nonlearning. The antecedent is not an easily identifiable variable or combination of these, such as social class, parental separation or divorce, birth order, level of intelligence, a specific disability, the quality of teaching (e.g., whether progressive or traditional), or individual teachers. It is rather a psychodynamic process between parent and child, which is often projected by family members onto teacher and child, and which leads him in some situations to shut off his mind but in others to continue to develop it. In that they shape psychological processes between parent and youngster *within* the three nonlearning categories (overachievers, underachievers, and school phobics), the incidence of parental separation and divorce as well as the incidence of birth order may be antecedents of a particular *style* of nonlearning selected by the young people in my group.

Piaget (1981) speculated that affectivity can accelerate or retard cognitive development. To illustrate this point, he cited Spitz (1945) who described the deleterious effects of an impoverished environment on hospitalized infants. Similarly, Cowan wrote in the preface to Piaget's (1981) *Intelligence and Affectivity* that

> affect influences our tendency to approach or avoid situations; in turn, this influences the rate at which we develop knowledge, accelerating it in some areas, slowing it down or preventing it in others. (p. xi)

The young people described in this book were not subjected to impoverished environments in the usual sense, but the adults' belief that they were disabled prevented that normal stimulation to their minds which springs from a parents' or a teacher's conviction that they are potentially knowledgeable. Sometimes the family myth permitted the learning of certain facts or the exercise of particular expertise, so the child became accelerated, even gifted in some respects as Tim did in math and Lara did in art and dance. It is common for the child or adolescent in psychotherapy to reveal with regard to unlearned subject matter that he has developed just those logical structures or has understood just those concepts that are inherent in the assigned inquiry at school, but has deliberately failed to concentrate in school or to attend school when he knows he will be expected to apply what he has been learning spontaneously.

When they are given the benefit of our conviction that they can learn, children and adolescents respond as though they are astute and potentially erudite persons. Youngsters who have become aware of their complicity in their learning failures often rethink their academic struggles in terms of ability versus attitude. One 16-year-old boy concurred with the major thesis of this book when he was told that children are capable of making decisions about learning. He said: "You're right. That's because studying is a matter of attitude, not ability." Young people often make ability irrelevant as they begin to concentrate on their attitudes toward learning and studying. A renewed positive attitude toward investigation makes ability irrelevant because their earlier decision not to learn suggests to them that a change of mind can lead to a positive outcome. Both decisions are theirs.

Appendixes

APPENDIX A

TABLE A-1
Mean IQ Score by Grade among Children Tested[a]

Grade	Number of childen tested	Wechsler Preschool and Primary Scale of Intelligence	Stanford Binet —Revised	Wechsler Intelligence Scale for Children —Revised
K	4	119	120	125
1	4	—	—	122
2	4	—	—	118
3	6	—	—	110
4	7	—	—	124
5	3	—	—	136
6	2	—	—	120
7	2	—	—	113
8	1	—	—	150
Total	33			

[a]Among the 33 children tested, the range of IQ scores is 90–150 where a score of 100 is average.

APPENDIX B

Screening Tests

Listed below in alphabetical order are the screening tests given to 41 of the 60 children.

Audiological Evaluation
Auditory Association Test
Auditory Memory Test
Beery Test of Visual-Motor Integration
Bender Visual-Motor Gestalt Test
Detroit Tests Of Learning Aptitude
Developmental Test of Visual-Motor Integration
Frostig Movement Skills Battery
Full Range Action-Agent Test
Graham Kendall Memory for Design Test
Gray's Oral Reading Test
Harris Tests of Lateral Dominance
Henja Developmental Articulation Test
Human Figure Drawing Test
Illinois Test of Psycholinguistic Abilities
Jordan Left-Right Reversal Test
Keystone School Vision Survey
Lincoln Intermediate Spelling Test
Lincoln-Oseretsky Motor Development Scale

Neurological Examination for "Soft Signs"
Northwestern Syntax Screening Test
Peabody Individual Achievement Test
Peabody Picture Vocabulary Test
Preschool Language Scale
Purdue Perceptual-Motor Survey
Reynell Development Language Scales
Rorschach Test
Santostefano Cognitive Control Battery
Slingerland Screening Test
Slossin Oral Reading Test
Spache Binocular Reading Test
Test of Emotional Development
Thematic Apperception Test
Wepman Spatial Orientation Memory Test
Wepman Visual Discrimination Test
Wide Range Achievement Test
Woodcock Reading Mastery Test

APPENDIX C

TABLE C-1
Number of Screening Tests by Grade among Children Tested

Grade	Age	Number of children tested	Number given one test	Number given 2–3 tests	Number given 4–5 tests	Number given 6–14 tests
K	4;5–6;4	6	0	4	2	0
1	5;9–7;6	7	1	4	2	0
2	6;11–8;5	6	3	3	0	0
3	7;6–9;1	6	4	1	0	1
4	9;1–9;8	6	3	1	0	2
5	10;2–11;11	4	3	1	0	0
6	12;2–13;0	4	1	3	0	0
7	12;0–12;10	2	0	2	0	0
Total		41	15	19	4	3

Piagetian Interview Tasks

A total of eight interview tasks were used in this study. Younger children were given four of these, while children aged 9 or 10 were given 6 or 7 (I often excluded the easiest tasks for older children to avoid appearing to insult their intelligence). Preadolescents and adolescents were presented with the three tasks of formal operations and one or two of the other tasks—usually classification without objects and conservation of length (to be described below).

The eight interview tasks are: conservation of number, conservation of length, classification with objects, seriation, classification without objects, two tests of the mathematical concept of distributivity, and an angle of incidence task. In choosing the particular tasks, I tried to estimate what would naturally appeal to the child, hoping to engage his interest in the interviewing. Especially in the beginning of interviewing his interest in answering questions was minimal due to disagreeable school experiences. Also, these particular tasks are easily administered requiring a minimum of equipment and complex procedures.

Consistent with Piagetian interviewing technique, the child's responses, his "judgments," are succeeded by my request for his "justification" of his answer. Since the request for justification differs according to the task's content, this is given as well. If the child is unclear about his answer, or it appears to me he is on the verge of understanding something new, I engage him in conversation by "counter-suggestion." Counter-suggestion statements are included in the task descriptions.

The children's answers were written down verbatim. So were other relevant observations, such as the child's facial expressions, gestures, posture, his spontaneous play with the materials, spontaneous questions and comments, and so forth. A description of each task follows.

TASKS FOR CONCRETE OPERATIONS

Conservation of Number

This task is adapted from Piaget, *The Child's Conception of Number*, 1965b. Two identical glasses are presented to the child, who is told one glass is his and one is the interviewer's. They are filled with 10 marbles each by the interviewer and the child dropping the marbles 1 or 2 at a time into the glasses. Then the child is asked, "Do we have the same number of marbles in our glasses?" If the child says no, the interviewer recounts the marbles in each glass. If the child answers yes, the interviewer empties his glass of marbles into a narrower, taller glass and the child is asked "What (or how) about now? Do we have the same number of marbles?" (Almy, 1966). If the child appears not to understand the question, he is asked, "Do we have the same or different number of marbles now?" The child is asked "How do you know" to elicit a justification.

Counter-suggestion

If he vacillates in judgments or justifications, the child is asked to consider a statement about "children" in general so as not to suggest I am disclosing confidences. As I point out the rise in marble level, I say, "Some children say there will be more marbles in this thin glass because now they come up to here on the glass."

Conservation of Length

This task is adapted from Piaget, Inhelder, and Szeminska, *The Child's Conception of Geometry*, 1960. The child is presented with two strings of different lengths wherein the longer is placed so that endpoints to the shorter are contiguous. He is asked, "Are these strings the same or different lengths?" After the child answers, the longer string is curled so the endpoints of the shorter string extend beyond the curled, longer string. The child is asked again whether the two strings are the same or different lengths. He is required to justify his answers by being asked about both comparisons, "How did you know?"

Counter-suggestion

"Some children tell me that this [longer] string is shorter because it doesn't extend to here (or come out as far as this [shorter] one)."

Classification with Objects

This task is adapted from Piaget's classification task with brown beads and wooden beads (*The Child's Conception of Number*) 1965b. The child is presented with an array of wooden Fisher-Price dolls. The child and interviewer count the number of boys and girls. Depending on the sex of the child, in the array there is either one more boy than girl or the reverse. The child is asked: "Are there more girls/boys or more people?" Since most children want the greater number to favor their sex, boys are asked "Are there more girls or more people?" and girls are asked "Are there more boys or more people?" A justification is elicited by asking the child, "How did you know?"

"Some children tell me that because there are more girls than boys (or more boys than girls), that means there are more girls than people (or more boys than people)."

Seriation

This task is adapted from Piaget's correspondence between flowers and vases, *The Child's Conception of Number*, 1965b. The child is presented with a series of five houses and five dolls in graduated sizes. The dolls can be taken apart at the waist and the roofs come off the houses. The child is shown each assembled doll and house and told that each doll has a house. Then he is asked to show which doll goes with which house. He is asked, "How did you decide to do it that way?"

Counter-suggestion

"Some children say you can't answer this question because the dolls don't fit in the houses."

Classification without Objects

The child is asked, "If I were to ask you are there more Americans or people, what would you say?" He is asked how he knows.

Counter-suggestion

"Some children tell me that since there are more Chinese than Americans, there are more Chinese than people."

TASKS FOR FORMAL OPERATIONS

First Task of Distributivity

This task is adapted from Piaget, "Some Aspects of Operations," in *Play and Development*, 1972a. The youngster is presented with a thick rubber band with a mark penned on it slightly off center. He is told that I will stretch the band. Prior to stretching, the child is asked to put his finger where he thinks the mark will be after the band is stretched. Then he is asked, "How did you know?" or "How did you decide to do it that way?"

Counter-suggestion

"Some children say the mark will be a little bit over here [to the right or left of the mark]."

Second Task of Distributivity

This task is adapted from Piaget, 1972a. The youngster is presented with two identical glasses filled half full with an equal amount of water. The interviewer has another container of water and a measuring pitcher with lines indicating a half cup and a full cup. The youngster is first asked whether he thinks the amount of water in the identical glasses is equal (or if the water amount is the same or different in the two glasses). Then the water from both glasses is poured into the measuring pitcher. After that, I tell the young person the water will be doubled by pouring water from the extra container into the pitcher. Then the interviewer returns the doubled water to the two identical glasses wherein each glass has an equal amount of water. The interviewer asks the youngster whether he thinks the amount of water in the two glasses is equal. Then the child is asked, "How much more water do we have in this glass and in this glass (or in these two glasses) compared to when we started?" He is asked to tell how he knows.

Counter-suggestion

"Other children say it will be half again as much."

Angle of Incidence Task

The interviewer tells the youngster she is going to draw a picture of a boy (or girl) throwing a ball against a wall. Then I draw a line representing the ball approaching the wall at an angle. Then the youngster is told, "Show me the way the ball bounces off the wall by drawing the path the ball will take as it bounces." Again, the young person is asked how he knew the answer.

Counter-suggestion

"Some children say that the ball will return to the boy (or girl) exactly the same way he (she) threw it."

DEFINITION OF PREOPERATIONAL, CONCRETE OPERATIONAL, AND FORMAL OPERATIONAL THINKING

When I characterize a child in the text as preoperational, I mean he has understood no tasks of concrete operations. When I characterize a youngster as either concrete or formal operational, I mean the youngster has understood all tasks of either concrete or formal operations, including giving adequate justifications for his responses. When I call a child or adolescent "transitional," I mean he or she had understood some but not all tasks of concrete or formal operations.

SAMPLE OF ADEQUATE JUSTIFICATIONS FOR TASK JUDGMENTS

Conservation of Number

"All you did was pour them into a different glass; you didn't take any away or add any." "It doesn't matter what shape that glass is; so what if it's thinner! If you pour them all, it's the same number."

Conservation of Length

"You can always do this to it to show it's longer [child straightens out the longer string]." "It was longer to begin with so it will always be longer." "You just changed the shape of the longer string." "No matter what you do to it, it will always be longer than the other one." "You'd have to cut it for it to be shorter."

Classification with Objects

"If you group the boys and the girls together, there are more people than the boys/girls." "All together there are nine people which is more than the five girls/boys." "There are more boys than girls (or girls than boys), but there are more people altogether."

Seriation

"You pair according to size; this is the biggest pair, this is the next biggest, this is the middle pair, this is the next to smallest, and this is the smallest." "They go together according to which is the biggest, the second biggest, the third biggest, the next to smallest (or the fourth biggest), and the smallest (or the fifth biggest)."

Classification without Objects

"First of all, there are more Chinese than Americans, and second of all, there are many different varieties of people which add up to more than just the

Americans." "Americans are only one kind of people; there are Spanish, French, Indian, which makes up more people than just the Americans." "Americans are only one of the many groups of people." "I thought it was common knowledge that there are more people than Americans; Americans are one national group among many groups."

First Test of Distributivity

"The mark doesn't have feet and can't walk around, it stays where you drew it and stretches with the rubber band." "If you stretch the rubber band, you'll stretch the mark too, but it stays where you drew it." "If you stretch the whole band, you'll *have* to stretch the mark, but it still stays where it is."

Second Test of Distributivity

"You had one-half cup before and now you have one cup; that's double (or twice as much) because you doubled all the water." "You have double because you doubled all the water."

Angle of Incidence

"I've watched balls hitting a wall and the angle is always the same if you're comparing how it hits and how it bounces off." "It depends on how it hits the wall; if it hits at this angle, it will bounce off at that same angle." "You can tell the angle the ball will bounce off at by looking at the angle it hits the wall." "The angle is the same at which the ball hits the wall and bounces off."

APPENDIX E

Follow-Up Data

When the children's therapy was discontinued, I asked them whether they would like to keep me informed of their progress. If a child was reluctant to keep in touch, I respected this decision. Seven of the 60 childen gave noncommittal or unenthusiastic responses when I inquired about future contact. I lost track of 17 youngsters and their families as the result of either their geographical relocations or my own.

If the youngster was eager to inform me of his progress, I inquired whether he or I should initiate the contact and proceeded accordingly. The parents usually volunteered to keep me informed. The data given in the table which follows qualified as "follow-up" when I had contact with the young person and his parents a full year or longer after therapy was terminated. Sometimes I had telephone conversations with the youngster and/or his parents. Other times, the youngster and/or his parent kept in touch by letters. Occasionally, a child or adolescent and his parents would drop by for a visit.

Our communications, reflected in the table, usually centered on the two topics which had been the focus of our therapeutic exchanges, namely, family life and school experiences. The follow-up data revealed that all 36 children had moved normally through the grades subsequent to therapy discontinuation.

TABLE E-1
Follow-Up Data N = 60

| | | Number reporting improvement 12–23 months after therapy | | | | Number reporting improvement 24–60 months after therapy | | | |
| | Number of children | School adjustment | | Family adjustment | | School adjustment | | Family adjustment | |
Grade[a]	followed	Child[b]	Parent[c]	Child	Parent	Child	Parent	Child	Parent
K	5	3	3	3	3	2	1	2	2
1	6	3	3	3	3	3	2	3	3
2	4	2	2	2	2	2	2	1	2
3	5	4	4	3	3	1	1	1	1
4	4	4	4	4	4	—	—	—	—
5	3	2	2	2	2	1	1	1	1
6	3	3	3	3	2	—	—	—	—
7	2	1	1	1	1	1	1	1	1
8	1	—	—	—	—	1	0	1	1
9–13	3	—	—	—	—	3	3	3	3
Total	36								

[a]This is the school grade the child was in when he or she began therapy.
[b]Improvement reported by the patient.
[c]Improvement reported by the parent. In many cases I had follow-up data from only one parent. When I had follow-up information from both parents, I reported "improvement in adjustment" from parents only when they agreed.

TABLE E-2
Follow-Up of Youngsters Treated since 1985 (N = 41)

| | | Number reporting improvement 12–23 months after therapy | | | | Number reporting improvement 24–48 months after therapy | | | |
| | Number of children | School adjustment | | Family adjustment | | School adjustment | | Family adjustment | |
Grade[a]	followed	Child[b]	Parent[c]	Child	Parent	Child	Parent	Child	Parent
K	9	2	2	2	2	6	6	7	7
1	3	2	2	2	2	1	1	0	1
2	4	—	—	—	—	3	3	3	4
3	4	2	2	2	2	2	1	2	2
4	3	1	1	1	1	1	1	2	2
5	2	—	—	—	—	2	2	2	2
6	4	2	2	2	2	2	2	2	1
7	4	3	3	2	2	1	1	1	1
8	2	2	2	2	2	—	—	—	—
9–13	3	—	—	—	—	3	3	3	3
Total	38								

[a]This is the school grade the youngster was in when he or she began therapy.
[b]Improvement reported by the patient.
[c]Improvement reported by the parent. In many cases I had follow-up data from both parents. I reported "improvement in adjustment" from parents only when they agreed.

References

Almy, M. (1966). *Young children's thinking: Studies of some aspects of Piaget's theory*. New York: Teachers College Press, Columbia University.

American Psychiatric Association. (1987). *Diagnostic and statistical manual of mental disorders* (3rd ed., rev.). Washington, DC: Author.

Anthony, E. J. (1954). The significance of Jean Piaget for child psychiatry. *British Journal of Medical Psychology, 29*, 20–34.

Anthony, E. J. (1957). The system makers: Piaget and Freud. *British Journal of Medical Psychology, 30*, 255–269.

Anthony, E. J. (1971). Folie à deux: A developmental failure in the process of separation-individuation. In J. McDevitt & C. Settlage (Eds.), *Separation-individuation*. New York: International Universities Press.

Anthony, E. J. (1982). The comparable experience of a child and adult analyst. *Psychoanalytic Study of the Child, 37*, 339–366.

Arendt, H. (1978). *The life of the mind*. New York: Harcourt, Brace & Jovanovich.

Aries, P. (1965). *Centuries of childhood: A social history of family life*. New York: Knopf.

Arlin, P. (1975). Cognitive development in adulthood: A 5th stage. *Developmental Psychology, 11*, 602–606.

Berger, E., Prentice, N., Hollenberg, C., Korstvedt, A., & Sperry, B. (1969). The development of causal thinking in children with severe psychogenic learning inhibitions. *Child Development, 40*, 503–515.

Bettelheim, B. (1967). *The empty fortress*. New York: Free Press.

Bettelheim, B. (1980). *Surviving*. New York: Vintage Books.

Bettelheim, B. (1983). *Freud and man's soul*. New York: Knopf.

Bettelheim, B. (1987). *A good enough parent*. New York: Knopf.

Bettelheim, B., & Zelan, K. (1981). *On learning to read*. New York: Knopf.

Blos, P. (1962). *On adolescence*. New York: Free Press.

Blos, P. (1979). *The adolescent passage*. New York: International Universities Press.

Brazelton, T. Berry. (1976). Inception and resolution of early developmental pathology: A case history. In E. Rexford, L. Sander, & T. Shapiro (Eds.), *Infant psychiatry*. New Haven: Yale University Press.

Bringuier, J. (1980). *Conversations with Jean Piaget*. Chicago: University of Chicago Press.

Brodie, R., & Winterbottom, M. (1967). Failure in elementary school boys as a function of traumata, secrecy, and derogation. *Child Development, 38*, 701–711.

Bruner, J. (1966). *Toward a theory of instruction*. Cambridge: Harvard University Press.

Bruner, J., Olver, R., & Greenfield, P. (1966). *Studies in cognitive growth*. New York: John Wiley and Sons.

Case, R. (1985). *Intellectual Development: Birth to childhood*. Orlando, FL: Academic Press.

Chalfant, J. (1989). Learning disabilities: Policy issues and promising approaches. *American Psychologist, 44,* 392–398.

Coles, G. (1987). *The learning mystique.* New York: Pantheon.

Coolidge, J., & Brodie, R. (1974). Observations of mothers of 49 school phobic children. *American Academy of Child Psychiatry, 13,* 275–285.

Coolidge, J. (1979). School phobia. In J. Noshpitz (Ed.), *Basic handbook of child psychiatry.* New York: Basic Books.

Cowan, P. (1970). The nature of psychological-educational diagnosis. In D. Carter (Ed.), *Interdisciplinary approaches to learning disorders.* New York: Chilton.

Cowan, P. (1978). *Piaget with feeling: Cognitive, social and emotional dimensions.* New York: Holt, Rinehart & Winston.

Cowan, P. (1982). The relationship between emotional and cognitive development. In D. Cicchetti & P. Hesse (Eds.), *Emotional development.* San Francisco: Jossey-Bass.

Dewey, J. (1956). *The child and the curriculum. The school and society.* Chicago: University of Chicago Press.

Dewey, J. (1963). *Experience and education.* New York: Collier Books.

Eagle, M. (1984). *Recent developments in psychoanalysis: A critical evaluation.* New York: McGraw-Hill.

Ekstein, R. (1966). *Children of time and space, of action and impulse.* New York: Appleton-Century-Crofts.

Elkind, D. (1979a). *The child and society.* New York: Oxford University Press.

Elkind, D. (1979b). *Child development and education.* New York: Oxford University Press.

Elkind, D. (1981). *Children and adolescents: Interpretive essays on Jean Piaget.* New York: Oxford University Press.

Elkind, D. (1987). *Miseducation.* New York: Knopf.

Erikson, E. (1950). *Childhood and society.* New York: W. W. Norton.

Erikson, E. (1962). Reality and actuality. *Journal of the American Psychoanalytical Association, 10,* 451–473.

Erikson, E. (1964). *Insight and responsibility.* New York: W. W. Norton.

Feffer, M. (1982). *The structure of Freudian thought: The problem of immutability and discontinuity in developmental theory.* New York: International Universities Press.

Flavell, J. (1963). *The developmental psychology of Jean Piaget.* Princeton, NJ: D. Van Nostrand.

Frank, A. (1969). The unrememberable and the unforgettable: Passive primal repression. *Psychoanalytic Study of the Child, 24,* 48–77.

Freud, A. (1968). *The writings of Anna Freud: Indications for child analysis and other papers.* New York: International Universities Press.

Freud, A. (1971). *The writings of Anna Freud: Problems of psychoanalytic training, diagnosis, and the technique of therapy.* New York: International Universities Press.

Freud, A. (1974). *The writings of Anna Freud: Introduction to psychoanalysis.* New York: International Universities Press.

Freud, S. (1938). *The basic writings of Sigmund Freud: The psychopathology of everyday life.* New York: Modern Library.

Freud, S. (1959a). *The standard edition of the complete psychological works of Sigmund Freud: Inhibitions, symptoms and anxiety.* London: Hogarth Press.

Freud, S. (1959b). *Collected papers: Analysis of a phobia in a five-year-old boy.* New York: Basic Books.

Freud, S. (1960). *The ego and the id.* New York: W. W. Norton.

Freud, S. (1963). *An outline of psychoanalysis.* New York: W. W. Norton.

Furth, H. (1969). *Piaget and knowledge: Theoretical foundations.* Englewood Cliffs, NJ: Prentice-Hall.

Furth, H. (1987). *Knowledge as desire: An essay on Freud and Piaget.* New York: Columbia University Press.

Greenspan, S. (1979). *Intelligence and adaptation: An integration of psychoanalytic and Piagetian developmental psychology.* New York: International Universities Press.

Greenspan, S. (1981). *Psychopathology and adaptation in infancy and early childhood: Principles of clinical diagnosis and preventive intervention.* New York: International Universities Press.

Group for the Advancement of Psychiatry (1966). *Psychopathological disorders in childhood: Theoretical considerations and a proposed classification.* New York: Author.

Holt, J. (1964). *How children fail.* New York: Dell Publishing.

Holt, R. (1989). *Freud reappraised: A fresh look at psychoanalysis.* New York: The Guilford Press.

Inhelder, B. (1968). *The diagnosis of reasoning in the mentally retarded.* New York: John Day.

Inhelder, B., & Piaget, J. (1958). *The growth of logical thinking from childhood to adolescence: An essay on the construction of formal operational structures.* New York: Basic Books.

Inhelder, B., & Sinclair, H. (1969). Learning cognitive structures. In P. Mussen, J. Langer, & M. Covington (Eds.), *Trends and issues in developmental psychology.* New York: Holt, Rinehart and Winston.

Inhelder, B., Sinclair, H., & Bovet, M. (1974). *Learning and the development of cognition.* Cambridge: Harvard University Press.

Kagan, J. (1984). *The nature of the child.* New York: Basic Books.

Klein, M. (1964). *Contributions to psycho-analysis 1921-1945: Developments in child and adolescent psychology.* New York: McGraw-Hill.

Kohut, H. (1977). *The restoration of the self.* New York: International Universities Press.

Kohut, H. (1984). *How does analysis cure?* Chicago: University of Chicago Press.

Kris, E. (1951). Ego psychology and interpretation in psychoanalytic therapy. *Psychoanalytic Quarterly, 20,* 15–30.

Langer, J. (1969). Disequilibrium as a source of development. In P. Mussen, J. Langer, & M. Covington (Eds.), *Trends and issues in developmental psychology.* New York: Holt, Rinehart & Winston.

Leavy, S. (1973). Psychoanalytic interpretation. *Psychoanalytic Study of the Child, 28,* 305–330.

Levy, S. (1984). *Principles of interpretation.* Northvale, NJ: Jason Aronson.

Loewenstein, R. (1951). The problem of interpretation. *Psychoanalytic Quarterly, 20,* 1–14.

Luborsky, L. (1967). Momentary forgetting during psychotherapy and psychoanalysis: A theory and research method. In R. Holt (Ed.), *Motives and thought: Psychoanalytic essays in honor of David Rapaport.* New York: International Universities Press.

Luborsky, L. (1984). *Principles of psychoanalytic psychotherapy.* New York: Basic Books.

Mahler, M. (1942). Pseudoimbecility: A magic cap of invisibility. *Psychoanalytic Quarterly, 11,* 149–164.

Mahler, M., Pine, F., & Bergman, A. (1975). *The psychological birth of the infant.* New York: Basic Books.

McGuinness, D. (1985). *When children don't learn: Understanding the biology and psychology of learning disabilities.* New York: Basic Books.

Miller, A. (1981). *The drama of the gifted child: How narcissistic parents form and deform the emotional lives of their talented children.* New York: Basic Books.

Newman, C., Dember, C., & Krug, O. (1973). "He can but he won't": A psychodynamic study of so-called "gifted underachievers." *Psychoanalytic Study of the Child, 28,* 83–129.

Oxford English Dictionary. (1971). Glasgow: Oxford University Press.

Pearson, G. (1954). *Psychoanalysis and the education of the child.* New York: W. W. Norton.

Piaget, J. (1924). Les traits principaux de la logique de l'enfant. *Psychological Archives, 13,* 273–304.

Piaget, J. (1952). *The origins of intelligence in children.* New York: International Universities Press.

Piaget, J. (1954). *The construction of reality in the child.* New York: Basic Books.

Piaget, J. (1962). *Play, dreams and imitation in childhood.* New York: W. W. Norton.

Piaget, J. (1963). *The child's conception of the world.* Paterson, NJ: Littlefield, Adams.

Piaget, J. (1964). Development and learning. In R. Ripple & V. Rockcastle (Eds.), *Piaget rediscovered.* Ithaca, NY: School of Education, Cornell University.

Piaget, J. (1965a). *The moral judgment of the child.* New York: Free Press.

Piaget, J. (1965b). *The child's conception of number.* New York: W. W. Norton.

Piaget, J. (1967). *Six psychological studies.* New York: Random House.

Piaget, J. (1971). *Science of education and the psychology of the child.* New York: Viking Press.

Piaget, J. (1972a). Some aspects of operations. In M. Piers (Ed.), *Play and development.* New York: W. W. Norton.

Piaget, J. (1972b). *The principles of genetic epistemology.* London: Routledge & Kegan Paul.

Piaget, J. (1973a). The affective unconscious and the cognitive unconscious. *Journal of the American Psychoanalytic Association, 21,* 249–261.

Piaget, J. (1973b). *The child and reality: Problems of genetic psychology.* Harmondsworth, Middlesex, England: Penguin Books.

Piaget, J. (1976). *The grasp of consciousness: Action and concept in the young child.* Cambridge: Harvard University Press.

Piaget, J. (1978). *Success and understanding.* Cambridge: Harvard University Press.

Piaget, J. (1981) *Intelligence and affectivity: Their relationship during child development.* Palo Alto, CA: Annual Reviews.

Piaget, J. (1985). *The equilibration of cognitive structures: The central problem of intellectual development.* Chicago: University of Chicago Press.

Piaget, J., & Inhelder, B. (1969). *The psychology of the child.* New York: Basic Books.

Piaget, J., Inhelder, B., & Szeminska, A. (1960). *The child's conception of geometry.* New York: Basic Books.

Pine, F. (1985). *Developmental theory and clinical process.* New Haven: Yale University Press.

Rist, R., & Harrell, J. (1982). Labeling the learning disabled child: The social ecology of educational practice. *American Journal of Orthopsychiatry, 52,* 146–160.

Rosen, H. (1985). *Piagetian dimensions of clinical relevance.* New York: Columbia University Press.

Schafer, R. (1983). *The analytic attitude.* New York: Basic Books.

Searles, H. (1986). *My work with borderline patients.* Northvale, NJ: Jason Aronson.

Secord, P., & Peevers, B. (1974). The development and attribution of person concepts. In T. Mischel (Ed.), *Understanding Persons.* London: Blackwell.

Shapiro, T. (1979). *Clinical psycholinguistics.* New York: Plenum Press.

Spence, D. (1982). *Narrative truth and historical truth: Meaning and interpretation in psychoanalysis.* New York: W. W. Norton.

Spitz, R. (1945). Hospitalism. *Psychoanalytic Study of the Child, 1,* 53–74.

Stern, D. (1985). *The interpersonal world of the infant.* New York: Basic Books.

Tuma, J. (1989). Mental health services for children: The state of the art. *American Psychologist, 44,* 188–199.

Vail, P. (1987). *Smart kids with school problems: Things to know and ways to help.* New York: E. P. Dutton.

VandenBos, G., & Stapp, J. (1983). Service providers in psychology. *American Psychologist, 38,* 1330–1352.

Vereecken, P. (1965). Inhibition of ego functions and the psychoanalytic theory of acalculia. *Psychoanalytic Study of the Child, 20,* 535–566.

Viderman, S. (1979). The analytic space: Meaning and problems. *Psychoanalytic Quarterly, 48,* 257–291.

White, R. W. (1963). Ego and reality in psychoanalytic theory: A proposal regarding independent ego energies. *Psychological Issues, 3,* 1–210.

Wolff, P. H. (1976). Developmental and motivational concepts in Piaget's sensorimotor theory of intelligence. In E. Rexford, L. Sander, & T. Shapiro, *Infant psychiatry: A new synthesis.* New Haven: Yale University Press.

About the Author

Karen Zelan was trained as a psychotherapist by Bruno Bettelheim at the University of Chicago's Orthogenic School. With Dr. Bettelheim she coauthored the book *On Learning To Read* and an article, "Why Children Don't Want To Read," for *Atlantic* (1981) magazine. Formerly a senior supervising staff psychologist at Boston's Children's Hospital and an instructor at the Harvard Medical School, she now resides in Berkeley, California, where she has a private practice treating children, adolescents, adults, and families.

Index

331